AMERICAN MATHEMATICAL SOCIETY
SEMICENTENNIAL PUBLICATIONS

IN TWO VOLUMES

Volume Two

SEMICENTENNIAL
ADDRESSES of the AMERICAN
MATHEMATICAL SOCIETY

NEW YORK
AMERICAN MATHEMATICAL SOCIETY
1938

COMPOSED, PRINTED AND BOUND BY
THE COLLEGIATE PRESS, GEORGE BANTA PUBLISHING COMPANY
MENASHA, WISCONSIN

PREFACE

The second semicentennial volume contains brief treatises on eight representative subjects and a historical summary of American contributions to mathematics during the past fifty years. The treatises have no set form in common; the various subjects are dealt with as each author has thought best. Some are either chronological or contain many references to early contributors; others are concerned chiefly with recent developments. Not all subjects could be covered fully in either the treatises or the history. It is hoped, however, that this volume will serve both to reveal what has been accomplished in America since the founding of the Society, and also to acquaint mathematicians with current problems and research in many fields.

THE COMMITTEE ON PUBLICATIONS

CONTENTS

FIFTY YEARS OF ALGEBRA IN AMERICA, 1888-1938

BY

E. T. BELL

In spite of all the blandishments of self-love, the facts associated at first with the name of a particular man end by being anonymous, lost for ever in the ocean of Universal Science. The monograph impregnated with individual human quality becomes incorporated, stripped of sentiments, in the abstract doctrine of the general treatise. To the hot sum of actuality will succeed the cold beams of the history of learning.—Santiago Ramón y Cajal.

1. **The general trend.** In connection with the fiftieth anniversary of the American Mathematical Society, it was decided to present brief reports of the progress of mathematics in America during the fifty-year period, 1888–1938, of the Society's existence, and algebra was one of the topics selected for report. As the Latin-American countries appear to have preferred analysis to algebra, America in this report refers only to the United States and Canada.

The output of algebra in America during the past fifty years seems enormous, even disconcerting, to anyone attempting to survey it all in brief compass. A mere bibliography of the more than one thousand research papers on algebra published by American authors during the period under review, with only a line or two indicating the nature of each contribution, would exhaust the space available for this report. Consequently, only the broader aspects of the rapid growth from the age of relative algebraic innocence, when everything was special and detailed, to our present highly sophisticated abstraction, can be considered here. The influences that appear to have been mainly responsible for the evolution of abstract algebra in this country will be kept in view, although frequently they were obscured in a welter of particulars.

It may be said at once that American algebra, contrary to what some social theorists might anticipate, has not been distinctly different from algebra anywhere else during the fifty-year period. According to a popular theory, American algebraists should have shown a preference for the immediately practical, say refinements in the numerical solution of equations occurring in engineering, or perfections of vector analysis useful in physics. But they did not. The same topics—algebraic invariants, linear groups, substitution groups, postulational technique, linear algebra, and some others—were fashionable here when they were elsewhere, and no algebraist seems to have been greatly distressed because he could see no application of his work to science or engineering. If anything, algebra in America showed a tendency to abstractness considerably earlier than elsewhere.

Although algebra in America has not been radically different from any other, there is one respect in which its progress during the past half century differs from that in some other countries, and that is the sudden acceleration imparted to research by the creation of the American Mathematical Society fifty years ago. Two other events also were of the first importance for research in all mathematics, not merely in algebra, on this continent: the opening of the University of Chicago in 1892, and the foundation of the Transactions of the American Mathematical Society in 1900, with E. H. Moore, E. W. Brown, and T. S. Fiske as editors.

When the Society was organized, a small group of American mathematicians highly trained, for the most part in Germany, in what was then modern algebra were already beginning their task of civilizing America algebraically. It was the devoted work of these men, their first-rate competence, and their enthusiasm for modern ideas which started the renaissance of algebra in this country. "Renaissance" is hardly the right word; there was practically nothing to be reborn. This may seem a perverse position to take when it is remembered that in 1888 there were ten volumes of the American Journal of Mathematics, founded by J. J. Sylvester* in 1878, already on the shelf, and that many of those volumes were crammed with projective invariants. For an understanding of what developed after 1888, it is necessary to see the grounds for this position. Sylvester's enthusiasm for algebra during his professorship at the Johns Hopkins University in 1877–1883 was without doubt the first significant influence the United States had experienced in its attempt to lift itself out of the mathematical barbarism it appears to have enjoyed prior to 1878. Elementary instruction was good enough, perhaps better than it is today; research on the European level, with one or two conspicuous exceptions, was nonexistent. For all his enthusiasm, the singularly individual Sylvester could not breathe life into a corpse. His premature opportunity had to await a less inhibited generation. Under Sylvester's personal inspiration, several of his pupils did creditable and even brilliant work; but when they left the warmth of his enthusiastic personality, they either abandoned mathematical research, or rapidly chilled in a deadening round of pedagogical drudgery in colleges and universities administered by mediocrities for the perpetuation of mediocrity.

From this distance in time it appears that the greatest service which the Johns Hopkins University rendered mathematics in America was not the importation of a distinguished mathematician, nor even the subsidizing of the American Journal of Mathematics, but the impulse which its living example gave to some older American universities and colleges to raise themselves from the mathematically dead. Long before Sylvester came among us as a missionary for what was then the "modern higher algebra," the United States had one great algebraist; but Benjamin Peirce made only

---

* Unless there is possibility of confusion, initials will be given only the first time that a name appears. Papers cited may be easily located by noting dates and referring to the Jahrbuch über die Fortschritte der Mathematik.

a negligible impression on his American contemporaries in algebra, and his work was not appreciated by their immediate successors until it had received the nod of European condescension. American algebra did not stand on its own feet until long after its most original representative had abandoned the subject.

With the pioneers who began their work about the time the Society was organized, the case was entirely different. American-born and educated, they understood conditions in this country as not even the most intelligent alien could possibly understand them. Their postgraduate training, too, had been much broader and more vital than they could have received anywhere in the English-speaking world at the time. The debt of American algebra to the Germany of the late 1880's and early 1890's is very great, and is no less so because some of those German-trained pioneers were the first to attain independence from their teachers.

Among these first moderns, F. N. Cole was one of the most influential, both through his own work and through that of his many pupils to whom he imparted his quiet, effective passion for the theory of finite groups. Although Cole had studied with Felix Klein, and had an unbounded admiration for Klein's methods, his own rigorously exact work in substitution groups was not reminiscent of Klein. Cole advocated what has been called "pure group-theory" as the proper approach to the subject as it was in the 1880's and 1890's. Of Cole's pupils in groups still active, G. A. Miller is the most prolific, and has been for over forty years. Miller in his turn trained numerous specialists, each of whom made at least one contribution to some phase of substitution groups and, later, to abstract finite groups.

Progress after the first infusion of modern ideas was extraordinarily rapid. In the five years (1888–1893) from the founding of the Society to the Chicago Congress, algebra in this country reached maturity, and was able to hold its own with the average, or perhaps a little better, of what was being done elsewhere.

This is not the occasion for a history of mathematics in the United States; but when such a history is attempted, particularly for the past forty years, the historian will doubtless be impressed by the tremendous influence of one man, E. H. Moore. In the late 1890's and early 1900's, the history of mathematics in this country is largely an echo of Moore's successive enthusiasms at the University of Chicago. Directly through his own work, and indirectly through that of the men he trained, Moore put new life into the theory of groups, the foundations of geometry and of mathematics in general, finite algebra, and certain branches of analysis as they were cultivated in America. Moore's interests frequently changed, and with each change, mathematics in this country advanced. His policy (as he related shortly before his death) in those early years of his great career, was to start some thoroughly competent man well off in a particular field, and then, himself, get out of it. All his work, however, had one constant direction: he strove unceasingly toward the utmost abstractness and generality obtainable. It is to Moore's influence that much of the abstract development of the first two decades of this century in American algebra can be traced. Not the least of Moore's contributions to algebra was the encouragement he gave the University of Chicago's second Ph.D. in mathematics, L. E. Dickson, who took his degree at the age of 22 in 1896. After that, it was no longer necessary for young Americans to go abroad for their training in algebra, and very few have.

The basic training of both Moore and Dickson was received wholly in this country, and to a considerable extent each was self-taught. Not till both were mathematically mature did they visit Europe, Moore to profit by contact with Kronecker and Weierstrass at Berlin, and Dickson by the lectures of Lie at Leipzig. This may serve as a rough measuring stick of mathematical progress in America during the first decade of the Society's existence. But the measure is only rough, or possibly quite inapplicable, for it has not yet been demonstrated that first-rate capacity needs any teacher other than opportunity. Moore appears to have made his own opportunities and to have used the experience thus acquired to give others with the right stuff in them their due.

The early influence of the Chicago group has been emphasized because it gave the first strong impulse, so far as algebra in America is concerned, toward that increasing abstractness which characterizes algebra today, and which first became a universal fashion with the work of Emmy Noether and her pupils, beginning about 1922. This, the latest phase of algebra as it exists today, will be noted later. For the moment, it may be observed that this urge toward the utmost generality attainable has been consistently followed by one school of algebraists in this country for about forty years. In fact, if there is any clue through the tangled jungle of elaborate theories and special theorems for the past fifty years, it is perhaps only this steady progression from the particular to the less particular. Each of several fields of algebra—the theory of forms, groups, hypercomplex number systems—was cultivated intensively at first as a preserve of special problems sufficiently difficult to tax the skill of the solver, each investigated apparently for its own sake and without any deliberate attempt at the generality which frequently accompanies an abstract attack.

The great lesson which David Hilbert taught algebraists in 1888 with his finiteness proofs in algebraic invariants, that a general problem is often more vulnerable than any of its special cases, was received with a certain reluctance. Part, at least, of that fruitful lesson might have been learned even farther back, from Richard Dedekind. But, as it was, it took a full third of a century for the lesson to sink into the general algebraic consciousness. Our only comfort is that our energetic young contemporaries may be overlooking something in their devotion to the general as interesting as what our predecessors missed in their pursuit of the particular.

There are, of course, two sides to this whole question of abstractness, and both are amply illustrated in the past fifty years of American algebra. Valuable hints for an abstract attack were undoubtedly suggested by the vast accumulations of isolated facts; but in the earlier stages the very desirability of a general objective seems to have been doubted. "Abstract" was sometimes mistaken as a synonym for "vague," or "facile," and occasionally the mistake was not (and is not) a foolish one to make. Thus in the earlier evolution it was accounted a work of great merit to dissect out the minute anatomy of a narrow category of algebraic invariants, of linear algebras, or of substitution groups; and to label and classify the results like specimens in a museum of morbid pathology, without once glancing up to catch a glimpse of the whole organism or of its genus.

With sharper insight, the apprentices of the first masters saw that much of this detail painstakingly elaborated by their teachers could be ignored in favor of a simpler, more direct and more abstract formulation, until today, algebra is so excessively abstract that some who have not grown up with the subject are apt, occasionally, to imagine that a discovery of fundamental importance—whatever that may mean—has been made when old things have been merely simplified or rechristened in a more euphonious terminology.

In favor of the details cherished in the earlier period, this may be said: not even the most abstract of abstract algebra can take root and flourish in an absolute vacuum. From one point of view, the abstraction of a particular discipline is akin to the Alexandrian period of criticism and commentary, when Greek geometry kept some semblance of life in itself by feeding on its rich past. Much of that past richness was undoubtedly perfected. But the vigorous daring of invention, the fruitful curiosity about untried things, and the boldness to be unorthodox, were all but completely sterilized. Isolated facts in algebra may be as useless, even for algebra itself, as fragments of shattered rock on a desert. Many believe they are. But unless there are available a few suggestive algebraic phenomena in the beginning, what is to determine the direction of abstractness and generality? Possibly no determination is required; but if such is the fact, there exists no evidence in support of it. Why, in particular, should some algebraist prefer to elaborate one set of postulates rather than another? For at least half a century before the intensive study of groups began, it would have been easy for any logician to state the postulates for a group and to get what superficialities he could out of them; but it was only when a considerable body of detailed information about particular groups and their applications was available that rapid progress was made in the algebra of abstract groups.

In short, neither the special nor the general has been solely responsible for the progress of algebra, in either division, at any time in the past, and there is at present no evidence that one can be cultivated independently

of the other if algebra is to continue to grow. The interest here in this inter-
play between the particular and the general is that in the past third of a
century the trend has been increasingly away from the particular. Finally,
if the modern abstract algebra of the past two decades is still too close to
us for an impartial appraisal, it does appear that many aspects of the algebra of groups, rings, and fields which were hitherto obscured by a multi-
tude of special details, are now seen to be simple consequences of underlying general concepts.

2. **Statistical data.** Although there is no sharp boundary between
algebra and other fields, some sort of line must be drawn for the purposes
of this survey, and it will be drawn at arithmetic. This seems reasonable
enough, as the theory of numbers has not been considered by arithmeticians as a province of algebra since at latest 1801, although parts of the
theory are frequently included in treatises on algebra. The reasons for
such inclusion are obvious, but they do not reduce the peculiar difficulties
of arithmetic to exercises in algebra.

During the past fifty years American algebraists have had eight major
interests:

(G) Theory of groups, 43.44; (M) Miscellaneous, 14.35; (L) Linear
algebra, 14.10; (P) Postulate systems, 8.46; (J) Modular invariants, 7.14;
(E) Theory of equations, 5.61; (I) Algebraic invariants, 5.23; (R) Recent
abstract algebra. 2.20.

The order of the topics is that of the number of research papers published by Americans from 1888 to 1938 in the respective topics, in
descending order from (G) to (R). Again no absolute separation of the
several fields is possible; but it seems probable that a reassignment of
certain borderline contributions from one section to another, such as from
(G) to (E) or vice versa, would not alter the order (G) to (R). The numbers
give the percentages for the respective topics in a total of slightly over one
thousand papers, published in research journals, whose character is un-
equivocally algebraic. Abstracts of papers subsequently published in full,
or not published at all, have been excluded, as have also all solutions of
problems and all but one or two of the expository articles. No claim for ex-
haustiveness is made; but again it is probable (from a detailed analysis not
reproduced here) that the percentages here given are not significantly in
error.

As continuous groups belong to analysis rather than to algebra, they
are not included in (G). Parts of Boolean algebra are assigned to (P),
which does not include papers of greater philosophical than mathematical
interest (such as would not usually be published in a mathematical journal); (M) will be described presently; (E) includes the Galois theory; (J)
is classified as arithmetic by Dickson, one of its creators, in his *History
of the Theory of Numbers*, but enough of its interest is algebraic to justify

its inclusion here; and (R), small in volume, is so prominent at the present time that it merits a separate although somewhat loose compartment. Several of the papers in (P), especially some in the period 1906–1917, could be assigned to (R).

Into (M) are put all contributions to algebra not otherwise classified, for example, the theories of determinants, matrices, quadratic and multi-linear forms, aspects of quaternions other than those naturally assigned to (L), linear dependence, reducibility of polynomials, and triad systems.

Another type of algebra (it is certainly neither arithmetic nor analysis) would be included in a detailed report but is omitted here: the numerous algorithms of the finite calculus, such as E. McClintock's calculus of en-largement, the various symbolic methods of the writer and others for use in arithmetic, adaptations of Grassmann's somewhat neglected techniques, and various other algebraic calculi devised for specific purposes which have claimed a considerable share of the attention of American workers during the past fifty years.

The distribution decade by decade of the thousand plus papers men-tioned reflects the influences noted in the first section. An indicated decade, as 08–17, in the following table includes both the first year and the last, as 1908, 1917; the third row gives the percentages of the total output ap-pearing in each decade (1)–(5).

(1)	(2)	(3)	(4)	(5)
88–97	98–07	08–17	18–27	28–37$\frac{1}{2}$
10.45	21.23	23.49	16.33	28.50

The sudden drop in (4) is due to a decline of 54 per cent in the con-tributions to the theory of groups in the decade 1918–1927 compared to 1908–1917. The equally sudden rise in (5) is accounted for by an increase of 333 per cent in the output of linear algebra in 1928–1937 over the preced-ing decade.

In tabular form, with (G), · · · , (R) and (1), · · · , (5) as before, the (smoothed) percentages of the several topics in each decade are the follow-ing.*

	(G)	(M)	(L)	(P)	(J)	(E)	(I)	(R)
(1)	9.0	19.2	1.4	0	0	13.6	52.8	4.3
(2)	33.0	7.9	19.7	23.3	4.1	13.6	2.0	0
(3)	27.8	19.8	10.9	11.1	60.7	6.8	25.2	0
(4)	13.0	19.4	12.2	23.5	34.3	20.4	12.8	12.9
(5)	17.2	33.7	55.8	41.1	1.0	45.6	7.2	81.8

From the decade (3) to (4) there was a sudden drop of about 30 per cent in the output of algebra in America; from (4) to (5), a sudden rise

* Thus, about 33 per cent of the total output *in groups* fell in (2); in (*P*), about 23.5 per cent of all contributions *to this division* fell in (4).

again of about 75 per cent. A social statistician might correlate the drop with the entry of the United States into the World War in 1917, and the depression during the post-war decade. An easy analysis, however, shows that on this reasonable hypothesis, only those algebraists who specialized in groups were heavily drafted or deeply depressed; and without further analysis this seems improbable. During the same disastrous decade, postulate systems and the theory of equations even enjoyed a marked boom. These awkward discrepancies between plausible theory and obstinate fact are typical of many in the evolution of modern mathematics.

3. **Groups.** The intense activity of American algebraists in the theory of groups during the past half century was due to a few active men who induced numerous proselytes to contribute at least one paper apiece relating to groups. A statistical analysis of the total output in groups assigns all but a small fraction to Miller, Dickson, and men or women who took their advanced degrees under one of these.

The analysis also shows that the number of contributors who published one paper on groups, usually on some narrowly specialized detail of the theory, "in partial fulfilment of the requirements for the degree of Doctor of Philosophy," and who published little or nothing thereafter, is disproportionately high compared with other fields of algebra. Again, the percentage of those who started in groups and subsequently abandoned the subject to take up others in which they are still active, from differential equations to statistics, is higher than for the rest of algebra. From this several conclusions are evident, only one of which is of immediate interest: the great output in groups was largely the work of about six men.

In any account such as the present, confined to the work of a single continent, it is difficult to avoid leaving the unintentional impression that the work in question sprang full-armed from the heads of the workers concerned. Of course it did nothing of the sort. Without the international background of mathematical knowledge and the constant commerce of ideas between the old world and the new, American mathematics, if it had existed at all, would have been something quite different from what it was during the past fifty years. This can be verified by consulting the frequent references to foreign work in American papers. In particular, without the inspiration of the work of C. Jordan in France, G. Frobenius and O. Hölder in Germany, and W. Burnside in England, to mention only four whose activity partly overlapped the fifty-year period, the history of the theory of groups in America would be much shorter than it is. Similar statements apply to the other fields of algebra cultivated in this country, with the exception of modular invariants.

The earliest American contributions to groups or their applications are almost coincident with the founding of the Society. In the American Journal of Mathematics for 1886 (vol. 8), Cole discusses a problem, suggested to him by Klein at Leipzig, on the general equation of the sixth degree, in which, naturally, groups enter. In 1887 (ibid., vol. 9), he observes in the course of his paper on *Klein's Ikosaeder*, "Of chief interest, however, for the present discussion are the remarkable systems of relations which exist between the theory of *groups of operations*, of which the theory of substitutions constitutes a part, and nearly all other mathematical branches." From this the great importance which Cole attached to exhaustively accurate enumerations of permutation groups of a given order or degree can be anticipated.

Correcting the oversights of his predecessors, Cole in 1893 gave the first accurate determination of the permutation groups of degree seven. This was the beginning of such enumerative work in this country. Cole's methods were those of pure group theory. He had a distaste for long algebraic computations, and frequently expressed his admiration for the skill with which H. Weber explicated intricate theories with a minimum of calculation. His own style reflects this ideal. In the words of G. A. Miller, "during the years 1893–1895, I lived in Ann Arbor, Michigan, at the home of F. N. Cole, who inspired much of this early work." The work referred to is the determination, by Miller, of all permutation groups of degrees eight, nine, and ten.

Although groups were thus well started by 1893 in this country, they were still somewhat beyond the general run of American algebraists. The lucid expository paper of 1891 by O. Bolza (American Journal of Mathematics, vol. 13) *On the theory of substitution groups and its applications to algebraic equations*, did much to popularize the subject and to acquaint young Americans with the outlines of the Galois theory of equations. This paper is a summary of Bolza's lectures at the Johns Hopkins University in January and February, 1889. An editorial footnote states: "This subject being one on which no separate work is found in the English language, Dr. Bolza's development of it here will prove extremely helpful to all students of the subject, especially by supplementing and illustrating the more extended works of Jordan and Netto." To the works mentioned, J. A. Serret's might have been added as a source of inspiration to early American students of groups. In 1892 Cole's translation of E. Netto's *Substitutionentheorie* appeared, including its occasionally unfortunate account of the Galois theory. Nevertheless, the translation did much to spread the gospel of groups, from Baltimore to Berkeley.

The advantages, and indeed the necessity, of abstraction were recognized early. In his paper at the Chicago Congress of 1893 announcing the discovery of the simple group of order 504, Cole remarks: "In an abstract theory like that of groups, too much must not be expected in the way of general development from the accumulation and study of individual examples. No amount of such experimentation could have led to our modern knowledge. Progress is from abstract to abstract." To the same Congress, Moore communicated a memorable instance of the art of abstraction, when he proved incidentally in his paper on a doubly-infinite set of simple groups that every existent finite field is the abstract form of a Galois field of prime-power order. This paper clearly marks the beginning of abstract algebra in America. That the direction of abstract algebra changed at least twice subsequently, once (in 1902) with the introduction of postulational methods, and again (after 1910) as a result of the work of E. Steinitz (*Algebraische Theorie der Körper*, 1910), does not affect the preceding statement. Moore knew exactly what he was doing, and why; and he missed no opportunity to insist to his colleagues and pupils that the existence of analogies, however superficial at first sight, between different theories, is strong presumptive evidence of an underlying, abstract identity that should be uncovered and followed out in all its implications.

In the spring of 1894, Moore lectured on groups at the University of Chicago. The lectures appear to have partly inspired Moore's paper on the group of isomorphisms of a given group (discovered simultaneously and independently by Hölder). They also partly inspired something of greater significance for the development of groups in America. In a footnote to his paper, Moore states: "In connection with the members of that course [Spring, 1894], Messrs. Brown, Dickson, Joffe, Slaught, and I worked up the linear fractional configuration [for certain cases]. I take this opportunity to thank them for their cooperation, and especially Mr. Dickson, who quite recently completed the tables as given above." Moore himself made the fruitful discovery in 1898 that every finite group of linear transformations on n variables has a Hermitian invariant.

Dickson's doctoral dissertation, *The analytic representation of substitutions on a power of a prime number of letters with a discussion of the linear group*, was published in 1896, and in 1901 appeared his treatise, *Linear Groups with an Exposition of the Galois Field Theory*, still the standard work and source in its province. In this, and in his numerous papers on linear groups in a finite field, Dickson emphasized the advantages of working ab initio with the general abstract case which, by Moore's theorem on finite fields, could be taken as the Galois field of prime-power order. He was thus enabled to unify and greatly extend the work of his predecessors, including Jordan, on certain categories of linear groups.

From such favorable beginnings, comparatively modest in volume, the river of American contributions to the theory of groups took its rise. During the second decade of the Society's existence, the stream was in full spate; and although the crest of the flood passed with the end of the decade, abnormally high water was recorded from several stations all through the following decade. Had the deluge continued to rise at its initial rate, editors of mathematical journals would have been drowned in their burrows before 1938 by an annual flood of 2,400 papers on groups. Nature came to the rescue, as it usually does in a dire emergency; the slow, difficult growth of younger ideas diverted tributaries to the main river of the

late 1890's and early 1900's, and disaster was averted. If past experience
is any criterion, it is not healthful for any science to canalize over forty
per cent of its energy in one narrow bed.

The digestion and codification of the vast mass of fairly general theories
and minutely detailed theorems in permutation groups, linear groups, and
abstract groups now scattered through the literature is a task for a corps
of encyclopaedists. In glancing over some of this old work, any reviewer
must be arrested by the numerous interesting results now in rapid process
of being completely forgotten. It is quite possible that some of these will
be rediscovered as by-products of more powerful methods of investigation;
but in the meantime it would seem that the theory is ripe for a harvesting.
Other fields of mathematics (determinants, arithmetic) have been gleaned
so that it is possible for those interested to locate immediately what has
been found and to imagine new things to be discovered. As groups appear
to be entering a new phase along with the rest of abstract algebra, it might
reward three or four competent men to undertake the drudgery of a comprehensive technical history of the subject. An exhaustive history—the
only kind likely to be of permanent value—is probably beyond the combined capacities of any two men.

In the decade 1898–1907, the enumeration of substitution groups, and
of particular kinds of such groups, was vigorously continued by Miller
and his pupils, some of whom quickly became foci of activity, while Dickson led in the field of linear groups. There was also an intensive search
for simple groups. This period was conspicuous for the minute examination
of special categories of groups, with what end in view, if any, is not now
clear. Frequently, an apparently adventitious feature common to a few
substitution groups of low order or degree was seized upon as the defining
characteristic of some species of groups and the species was duly trapped
and mounted. From such taxonomic work there presently developed a
tendency to greater abstractness, in the definition of certain well known
groups, such as the alternating and symmetric, by systems of independent
generators. Problems of a totally different and deeper nature, which might
be described as the asymptotic enumerative theory of groups, were attacked in researches still incomplete, notably by W. A. Manning and H. F.
Blichfeldt. In substitution groups, many investigations centered in transitivity and primitivity (or their opposites), a direct outgrowth of the earlier
enumerative work of the preceding decade. Prime-power groups and their
subgroups were intensively investigated. A notable result for its time in
this direction, presently overshadowed by the more general theorem of
Burnside, was Cole's proof of the simplicity of groups of order p^3q^3. Group
characters were not a frequently used tool in this period, although a paper
of Dickson's in 1903 reformulated the method for American algebraists.

Two significant straws in the general stream of this prolific decade attracted some notice at the time, but nothing comparable to what they

might have done had the present outlook on algebra been foreseen thirty years ago. One was E. V. Huntington's paper of 1902 on an independent set of postulates for a group; the other, Moore's of a few months later on the same topic. These were followed by many investigations of a broadly similar kind, including Dickson's postulates of 1905 for groups and fields. The four years from 1902 to 1905 saw the abstract outlook in American algebra clearly visualized.

A small sample of the topics most frequently treated in groups during this second decade of the Society's existence will be exhibited presently, to give some idea of the extraordinary richness, and perhaps also of the equally extraordinary confusion, of the general output. Direction and co-ordination, except in the work of the more productive men, appear to have been almost wholly lacking. It remains for our successors to sift this un-organized mass of material and reduce it to some semblance of order. It also remains for them to judge whether the following forecast from Klein's address to the Chicago Congress in 1893 has been borne out in the forty-five years from then to the present. "Proceeding from this idea of groups, we learn more and more to coordinate different mathematical sciences. So, for example, geometry and the theory of numbers, which for long seemed to represent antagonistic tendencies, no longer form an antithesis, but have come in many ways to appear as different aspects of one and the same theory."

Has this proved true in any creative sense? If it has, where are the sig-nificant contributions to the geometry of numbers, to take the specific in-stance cited, that have come into arithmetic through the theory of groups? If there are few or none such at present, this may be due only to the pre-occupation of specialists in groups with groups as an end in themselves. And if it is pointless to expect from specialists in a particular field applica-tions in which they are not interested, it seems equally pointless to attempt to justify activity in that field by an appeal to hypothetical applications which do not exist. Autonomy here, as elsewhere, is the safest rule.

To sample the output of this decade 1898–1907, a selection of topics pointing in the direction of abstractness, dealing with the general structure of finite groups, may be noted first. Miller's innovations in commutator subgroups (1896) were further exploited. J. W. Young investigated the group of isomorphisms of (certain special) prime-power groups, also group holomorphisms, while Miller discussed the holomorph of a cyclic group; H. C. Moreno and Miller investigated non-abelian groups all of whose sub-groups are abelian, and W. B. Fite introduced and analyzed the metabelian groups. Miller gave a notable extension of Sylow's theorem. Dickson in-vestigated the group defined by the multiplication table of a group, and in his prolific work on linear groups, attained the maximum of generality by considering such groups in Galois fields and in an arbitrary field. The postulational treatments of groups by Huntington, Moore, and Dickson have been mentioned previously, and will be considered more in detail in a later section. The characteristic subgroups of an abelian group were investigated by Miller.

In another direction, Manning attacked groups, not from the angle of order or degree as was customary at the time, but from that of class, beginning work which was continued through the following decades to the present together with a serial research on the order of primitive groups. Blichfeldt introduced new methods into the determination of the order of linear homogeneous groups.

Several writers, including Fite, Miller, and L. I. Neikirk, investigated prime-power groups, but usually not the general case. O. E. Glenn considered the groups of order p^2q^r (p, q prime). Abstract definitions for the general symmetric and alternating groups were given by Moore, while Dickson did the same for the simple groups of orders 504 and 660, and exhibited a triply infinite system of simple groups. Dickson also determined all the subgroups of the simple group of order 25,920. W. Findlay discussed the Sylow subgroups of the symmetric group; primitive and imprimitive substitution groups were investigated by H. W. Kuhn, H. L. Reitz, and Manning (with respect to class), among others, while Blichfeldt considered imprimitive linear homogeneous groups. Several categories of linear groups, including the ternary orthogonal, the hyperorthogonal, and new species, were exhaustively investigated by Dickson.

The foregoing small sample may serve to give some idea of the prevailing interests in the theory of groups during the second decade of the Society's existence. In the following decade, before the sharp recession set in, the work was of the same general character. As the third decade passed, the interest in linear groups steadily declined. So also, with the exception of a few persistent and indefatigable specialists, did that in substitution groups. In particular, Cole's program of exhaustively determining all the substitution groups of a given order or degree by the classical methods, seemed by the middle of the fourth decade to have been pushed to the limit of human endurance and even slightly beyond. Thus, in 1912, E. R. Bennett determined the primitive groups of degree twenty. A specimen of what can be done by more powerful current technique, originating partly in the work of P. Hall, is offered in the census of groups of orders 101–161 (omitting 128), by A. C. Lunn and A. K. Senior in 1934, and of orders 162–215 (omitting 192) in 1935.

A very small sample of the further production in groups will have to suffice to indicate the continued activity of men already in the field in 1907, the enlisting of new recruits, and the general nature of the problems considered. It does not follow, of course, that omissions are or were less meritorious than the few inclusions necessary for a random sample: questions of merit may be left to the tribunal of posterity—if posterity is to bother its head about such questions.

In 1908, Dickson represented the general symmetric group as a linear group. Fite in 1909 discussed the irreducible linear group in an arbitrary domain. A. Ranum in 1910 gave an unusual application of groups to the classes of congruent quadratic integers modulo a composite ideal. Manning (1911) found a limit for the degree of simply transitive primitive groups, and Miller, among many other things, wrote on cosets. At the suggestion of Cole, L. P. Siceloff in 1912 examined the orders 2,001–3,640 for simple groups. In 1913–1914, H. H. Mitchell, using in part geometrical methods, determined the finite quaternary linear groups and the primitive collineation groups in more than four variables containing homologies. Fite in 1914–1915 continued his work on prime-power groups. Miller, Blichfeldt, and Dickson in 1916 produced in collaboration a treatise, *Theory and Applications of Finite Groups*, each author covering the topics in which he had specialized. R. W. Mariott in 1916 investigated the group of isomorphisms of the prime-power groups of order p^4, and in 1919 Miller wrote on the number of subgroups of prime-power groups. Except for the unabated productivity of a few of the older specialists, the general output of group literature began to decline. There were, however, several minor relative maxima in the curve of production. What followed 1920 was for the most part much like the work of the decade preceding 1920. Thus, in 1923, H. A. Bender wrote on the Sylow subgroups of certain groups, M. M. Feldstein on the invariants of the linear homogeneous group modulo p^k, and Miller on fundamental theorems in substitution groups. In 1924 Bender wrote on special prime-power groups, and Cole made one of his last contributions to the theory with a determination of the simple groups up to order 6,232. In 1925, L. Weisner discussed the Sylow subgroups of the general symmetric and alternating groups. In 1927 Bender attacked the problem of determining the groups of order p^5 (p prime); in 1928 Brahana wrote on certain perfect groups, and M. J. Weiss on certain primitive groups. In 1929 (and 1933) Manning applied his methods to the degree and class of multiply transitive groups. In 1929 Manning discussed the primitive groups of class 14, and in 1933, C. F. Luther, those of class u. In 1934, Brahana investigated metabelian groups, and Lunn, in collaboration with Senior, gave a method for determining all solvable groups with examples of its application. Metabelian groups were discussed again in 1935 by C. Hopkins; and in 1936, P. Hall of England and G. Birkhoff investigated the order of the group of isomorphisms of a given group.

The last three specimens in this sample are from 1937 and illustrate the newer tendencies and, for once in the history of American contributions to finite groups, a mathematical response to a physical question: F. D. Murnaghan devised a practicable method for calculating the characters of the symmetric group, of use in the quantum theory. Finally, A. H. Clifford wrote on the representations induced in an invariant subgroup, and H. Weyl on the commutator algebra of finite group collineations.

As the fifty-year period closes, Miller is as active in groups as he was almost at its beginning; the other most prolific American leader in the general field of groups, Dickson, turned his major efforts in other directions several years ago. Of the earlier leaders, Cole died in 1926, Moore in 1932. If the foregoing outline, necessarily bare, has recalled to younger American workers in groups their indebtedness to the quaternion of leaders responsible for one of the most active periods in the history of algebra in this country, it will have served its purpose. And if some of the earlier work now seems a trifle old-fashioned, it appears probable that the same will be true of much that now is fresh and vivid when the Society celebrates its hundredth anniversary. However, this extremely mild prophecy may prove as unfortunate as a similar one to be quoted presently from H. Poincaré.

4. **Postulational methods.** The modern postulational technique is almost exactly the same age as the Society, although American mathematicians did not enter this particular field until about thirteen years after it was opened. It is customary to date the beginning of the formulation of postulate systems from the monographs of G. Peano, *Arithmetices Principia nova Methodo exposita*, and *I Principii di Geometria logicamente expositi*, published in 1889. The subtle logical analysis of the foundations of arithmetic by G. Frege is almost contemporaneous, but its later importance has been chiefly epistemological.

Peano's pioneering efforts initiated a great many other things in addition to the specific purpose for which they were undertaken. If modern abstract algebra, like the modern abstract form of other mathematical disciplines, grew from the precise formulation of sets of postulates for the various fields of classical algebra, as claimed by some familiar with the subject, then Peano's early work is indisputably its root. Lobatchewsky, apparently, was the first to establish the independence of any postulate, but this is hardly relevant here. Again, much of the present critical work on the foundations of mathematics, also a considerable part of symbolic logic, can be traced back to sure beginnings in Peano's first logical analyses in a symbolism especially designed for the purpose of precise logical analysis.

A few of Peano's contemporaries, particularly G. Loria, to be followed shortly by M. Pieri, A. Padoa, and M. Pasch, welcomed the innovation enthusiastically, in spite of the queer new symbols in which it was clothed, and prophesied a brilliant future for the newcomer. The costume of the new science no doubt struck conservative observers as slightly bizarre; but a mere eccentricity in dress seems a pretty feeble excuse for showering a timid stranger with empty bottles. The reaction of many on seeing something they had not seen before was that of the cockney navvy: "'Ere's a strainger, Bill. Let's 'eave 'arf a brick at 'im." Following Poincaré's bold lead, it became a mark of superior intelligence to refer scornfully to Peano's symbolic language as "Peanese," and to discount the serious efforts of those (including B. A. W. Russell) who, going far beyond Peano's primitive symbolism, sought to express mathematics in a language which would enable mathematicians to apprehend what it was they were always talking about.

"The symbolic language created by Peano," Poincaré wrote, "plays a very great part in these researches · · · . The essential element of this language is certain signs representing the several conjunctions—'if,' 'and,' 'or,' 'therefore.' It is possible that these signs may be convenient; but that they are destined to revolutionize all philosophy is another story." It was: the foundations of mathematics since at least the time of Kant had been considered a province of philosophy. Other departments of philosophy also are experiencing the impact of unambiguous symbolism at present.

Again, commenting upon Couturat's enthusiasm for Peano's pasigraphy as exemplified in the *Formulaire*, Poincaré observes: "I have the highest regard for Peano; he has done some very pretty things · · · . But after all he has not flown farther nor higher nor faster than the majority of wingless mathematicians, and would have done just as well on his legs." Exactly. It happened, however, that Peano and his successors were more interested in burrowing than in flying, and some of them have bored quite extensive tunnels into the foundations of mathematics. They have also, through their careful exploration of the postulates for groups, fields, and other constructs of rigidly technical mathematics, given to algebraists, at least, a wormseye view of the bases of their work, and a more thorough understanding of it than could have been obtained from a century of soaring in the vague empyrean of lofty speculation or pedestrian trudging along dusty highways.

In spite of significant applications of the new technique, principally by Peano's fellow countrymen, it had a grim struggle to rise in mathematical society; and when it did, shortly after the publication of Hilbert's *Grundlagen der Geometrie* in 1899, postulational analysis was stripped almost naked of logical symbolism in the works of professional mathematicians, to stand forth in a form which all could see and some admire. (In passing, it may be recalled that O. Veblen in 1904 did a much more thoroughgoing job in his system of axioms—not called postulates—for geometry.) Even at this comparatively advanced stage of respectability, the new method was not very cordially received by intuitionists. Poincaré praised Hilbert's geometrical effort with faint damns; and considerably later Klein looked back with nostalgic regret on the lush youth of group theory, when it proceeded on its carefree way untrammelled by any clear notion of what constitutes a group. Few working algebraists would claim that intuition plays no part or only a minor one in algebra. On the other hand, few who follow modern abstract algebra would admit that intuition is the whole play. The critical analysis of postulate systems in the past third of a century has not only rectified weaknesses in earlier intuitive work, but has also suggested profitable new fields for exploration, for example, the semigroups introduced by Dickson in 1905.

The earliest published contribution by an American to postulational methods is the paper by E. V. Huntington, *Simplified definitions of a group*, in April, 1902 (Bulletin of the American Mathematical Society, vol. 8, pp. 296–300). It is stated: "Up to the present time no attempt seems to have been made to prove the independence of the postulates employed to define a group, and as a matter of fact the definition usually given contains several redundancies." Huntington gave three postulates and proved their independence. In a subsequent paper (ibid., June, 1902, pp. 388–391), Huntington gave a second set, of four postulates. This second set was presented to the Society at its April meeting, 1902, where Moore also gave a set of six independent postulates, published in the Transactions of the American Mathematical Society, vol. 3 (1902), pp. 485–492. Moore analyzed his own postulates and those of Huntington in relation to them, adding to Huntington's first set the explicit statement of the closure postulate.

Moore (loc. cit., p. 488) mentions "earlier definitions of Pierpont and myself," and cites the report of J. Pierpont's lectures at the Buffalo Colloquium of September, 1896, on the Galois theory, subsequently published in the Annals of Mathematics, (2), vol. 2 (1900), especially p. 47, where a definition of finite groups by six postulates (compressed to three statements) is given. As no independence proof is offered, this earlier definition does not belong to modern postulational methods, as do the definitions of Huntington, Moore, and, later, Dickson. Thus Huntington's paper contains the earliest discussion of the *independence* of postulates for abstract groups. Huntington's papers of 1902 on complete sets of postulates for the theory of absolute continuous magnitude and for the theories of positive integral and rational numbers, contain the first definition of what Veblen later called "categorical." Those interested in the history of this topic may be referred to the papers of Dickson, Huntington, and Moore, in the Transactions of the American Mathematical Society, vol. 6 (1905). A recent remark by J. H. C. Whitehead (Science Progress, vol. 32 (1938), p. 495) that "The systematic study of abstract groups may be said to have been originated by L. E. Dickson," with a reference to the paper of 1905, would seem to require modification, if by "systematic study" is meant the explicit statement of a set of postulates with a proof of their independence. The interest here of this early work of Huntington, Moore, and Dickson is the impulse it imparted to abstract algebra in America.

The nature of the work on postulational analysis after the first papers already mentioned, can be seen from a series of samples, decade by decade. In practically all of the works cited, independence proofs were a major feature. In the decade 1902–1911, Huntington gave independent postulates for the integers and for the rational numbers, for real algebra, fields, ordinary complex algebra, two sets for abelian groups, and for the algebra of logic. A paper of his (Annals of Mathematics, 1906) on addition and multiplication in elementary algebra proposed a novel approach to the formal properties of numbers as operators. Dickson gave sets for groups, fields, and semigroups. Moore reconsidered his postulates for abstract groups.

Only that work in this field which is concerned more or less directly with algebra is noted. Thus no account is taken of the application of the postulational method to geometry, as in the work of Veblen and J. W. Young, nor of Moore's use of the method in his general analysis. Boolean algebra and its immediate neighbors (in so far as they concern algebra) are included, however, as from one historical aspect Boole's work in the algebra of logic is the original source. Boole, however, did not discuss independence, a characteristic feature of the modern work, nor did he give a set of postulates.

In the decade 1912–1921, two papers may be cited apart from the others for their interest beyond the special topics on which they were written. H. M. Sheffer's postulates for Boolean algebra, in which the now celebrated 'stroke' function was introduced, appeared in 1913. In 1921, E. L. Post published his *Introduction to a General Theory of Elementary Propositions*, one of the earliest papers on what are now called many-valued logics. This was done in complete independence of practically simultaneous work of a similar character in Europe. Another contrubution in this decade, B. A. Bernstein's determination in 1924 of all operations, with respect to which the elements of a Boolean algebra form a group, or more specially an abelian group, may be cited. The unique significance of the symmetric difference, appearing frequently today in topological algebra and elsewhere, is here first definitely pointed out.

A sufficient sample of postulational work in algebraic topics for the decade 1912–1921 shows several contributions by Bernstein to Boolean algebra, and an independence proof for Sheffer's postulates by J. S. Taylor, who wrote also on Boolean algebra. W. A. Hurwitz gave a concise set of postulates for abelian groups, proved independent by Bernstein. Taylor proved the independence of one of Bernstein's sets of postulates for abelian groups. Huntington continued as the most prolific contributor to postulational analysis. To this decade belong his analyses of cyclic order, serial order, and well ordered sets. N. Wiener investigated formal invariances in Boolean algebra, and defined fields in terms of the function $1 - x/y$.

In this period, and through the next decade to the present, there appear to have been two dominant aims: to abstract a given theory in a minimum set of independent postulates; to state for a given theory the most flexible set of postulates, necessarily an appeal to taste or intuition. Beginning shortly before 1930, many of the investigations began to be tinged with metamathematics and/or syntax. This more recent direction in postulational methods originated in attempts to evaluate the logic or/and mathematics of A. N. Whitehead's and Russell's *Principia Mathematica*. It is still at its beginning, and appears to be pointing from the domain of algebra to another that does not directly concern algebraic technicians. As before, a small sample, following the chronological development, must suffice to indicate the general trend from 1922 to the present.

Bernstein continued his researches in Boolean algebras, investigating the relations of such to groups, serial relations, the theory of functions of one variable, the representation of finite operations and relations, duality, fields (in Boolean algebras), and in 1934 gave a set of four postulates. In 1932 both Bernstein and Huntington discussed *Principia Mathematica*, the former in relation to Boolean algebra, the latter postulationally, work continued in 1934, when also the relation of C. I. Lewis' strict implication to Boolean algebra was investigated. Huntington (1935) showed the interdeducibility of the Hilbert-Bernays system and that of *Principia Mathematica*. H. B. Curry about 1930 began publishing his combinatorial logic. A. Church in 1925 introduced the concept of irredundancy of a set of postulates, distinct from Moore's complete independence. In 1935, detecting a subtlety overlooked by previous writers, R. Garver gave a remarkable set of three postulates for groups. In the same year, M. H. Stone gave postulates for generalized Boolean algebra, having applied this algebra to topology in 1934. In 1936 he developed the representation theory of Boolean algebra, in line with modern algebra. In still another direction, J. H. M. Wedderburn in 1934 developed Boolean linear associative algebra. Also in a new direction was the generation of an n-valued logic by one binary operation by D. L. Webb in 1935; for $n=2$ this is Sheffer's result of 1913. Finally, in 1936, returning to the topic which started the postulational method in America in 1902, Garver applied his discovery to special types of groups.

An inspection of the current literature shows no decline in the application of the postulational method. Much of the contemporary work has an ulterior motive, apparently, in topology or elsewhere; nevertheless, it is in the same broad tradition as that of the past thirty-six years. It may be said that American work in this general field has been sharper and clearer on the whole than that done elsewhere.

5. **Algebraic invariants.** In 1887 the second part of P. Gordan's *Vorlesungen über Invariantentheorie* was published. His finiteness theorem dates from 1868. In 1888 our Society was founded. This might have been an auspicious event for the future of algebraic invariants in the America where Sylvester had lavished much of his talent on the theory, had not Hilbert in the same year published his devastating proof of Gordan's theorem and his own basis theorem for an infinity of forms in any finite number of indeterminates.

It is sometimes said that Hilbert's attack slew the theory of algebraic invariants, and it is a fact that, with a few minor revivals, publication in the subject fell off rapidly. But why an encystment of existence theorems should be fatal to any body of mathematics is not clear: analysis is as tolerant of them as some share-croppers are of trichinae. Problems that were lively enough before Hilbert, slowly expired after he treated them.

In recent years the theory of algebraic invariants has experienced a sporadic resurrection. Part of this, in America, is due to a return to difficult problems left aside decades ago, as in the work of J. Williamson. Applications to atomic physics are also responsible for reviving interest, although the physicists do not seem very enthusiastic about mastering a new mathematical technique. The like is true for some aspects of permutation groups; and these quantal applications in both fields are sometimes urged as a teleological justification for the enormous labor of two generations of industrious tillers before the quantum theory even sprouted. This justification is difficult to comprehend, unless, of course, "time's arrow" points in the opposite direction from that in which the second law of thermodynamics invites it to point. However, if the new applications inspire algebraists to the invention of less inhuman algorithms than some of those in the classical literature, the debt of physics to algebra will have been discharged.

It is not feasible to give more than an almost random sample of the heterogeneous collection of results contributed by Americans to the theory of algebraic invariants during the fifty-year period. From the very nature of the subject, anything much to one side of the direction pointed out by Hilbert was bound to be detailed and special. An exception was the comprehensive theory of Dickson, *A Theory of Invariants*, published in 1909, in which the coefficients of the forms were taken in an arbitrary field, finite or infinite. This of course has contacts with modular invariants, not considered in this section.

Only two essentially new techniques (noted later) were applied to algebraic invariants during the fifty years. In the classical tradition, Bolza in 1888, at Klein's suggestion, investigated binary sextics with linear transformations into themselves, and Sylvester published his Oxford lectures on reciprocants in the journal he had founded, thus keeping touch with America and the older interests. Hilbert's ideas appear to have been first introduced into this country in 1892 by H. S. White, with a symbolic proof of Hilbert's method for deriving invariants and covariants of ternary forms.

In 1893, W. E. Story, who had been a pupil of Sylvester, simplified part of Hilbert's finiteness proof by extending the method used by Hilbert for two indeterminates to any finite number.

It is somewhat like witnessing a youthful indiscretion, in view of its author's subsequent achievements, to find W. F. Osgood expounding the symbolic notation of S. Aronhold and A. Clebsch (why not of A. Cayley?) in the same year for American readers, and calculating the system of two simultaneous ternary quadratics by the symbolic method. This, however, appears to have been only a temporary lapse, and Osgood never again fell from analytical grace.

The stream continued to flow, but it was only a trickle compared to what had swamped the American Journal during its first decade. Mc-Clintock in 1891 discussed lists of covariants and their computation. In 1894 F. Franklin, a leader in the earlier period, reviewed F. Meyer's exhaustive report on invariants. White in 1896 considered the cubic resolvent of a binary quartic. All through this period there were applications of the theory of invariants, mostly by the symbolic method, to geometry, particularly by A. B. Coble in the second half; but as the intent of these was not primarily algebraic, they are not included here.

To continue with the sample: in 1903, E. Kasner developed the cogredient and digredient theories of multiple binary forms; in 1909 D. D. Leib obtained the complete system of invariants for two triangles, and Dickson discussed combinants. E. D. Roe in 1911 presented a new invariantive function. Dickson's theory of modular invariants, developed during this period, is noted in another section. Glenn in 1914–1919, with a high degree of algebraic elegance, discussed finiteness theorems and gave a symbolic theory of finite expressions. H. B. Phillips in 1914 gave an example of what may be considered one of the innovations in technique, when he applied vector methods to the invariants and covariants of ternary collineations. I. H. Thomsen in 1916 wrote on the invariants of a ternary quantic, Dickson, in 1921, on those of a ternary cubic. C. C. MacDuffee in 1923 gave a theory of transformable systems and algebraic covariants of algebraic forms. J. Williamson in 1929, and later, obtained complete systems for certain simultaneous systems, for example, for two quaternary quadratics, also for two n-ary quadratics. Some of the items in the foregoing sample are on the borderline of other disciplines, or perhaps beyond it. Nevertheless, their algebraic content is high enough to justify inclusion. The same is true of the next.

Although its object was not the calculation of algebraic concomitants, the symbolic method devised by H. Maschke in 1904 for differential invariants has great interest as an algebraic algorithm. This was one of the essentially new techniques of the period.

Another new technique was the application of the tensor calculus to the derivation of algebraic invariants in 1928, and again in 1938, by C. M. Cramlet. The generalization of the deltas of L. Kronecker, which play a part in this work, appears to have occurred independently and almost simultaneously to Cramlet, Murnaghan, H. P. Robertson, and Veblen shortly after the advent of general relativity.

Whether the applications to physics are to induce any considerable revival in the theory of algebraic invariants in this country remains to be seen, and likely will be seen, one way or the other, within a decade. Physics also is subject to the fluctuations of fashion and necessity.

6. **Modular invariants.** One of the most interesting phenomena of the past thirty years of American algebra is the sudden rise and equally sudden decline of the theory of modular invariants. Activity in this field is at present in abeyance, apparently for lack of an extension (if there is one) to covariants of M. L. Sanderson's theorem on correspondences between modular and formal invariants, and of a proof of the conjecture that all congruent covariants admit symbolic representation. As the complete history of the topic up to 1922 is readily accessible in Dickson's *History of the Theory of Numbers* (vol. 3, 1923), and as only seven papers on the subject have been published by Americans since 1922, a few general remarks will suffice here.

Until E. Noether in 1926 applied her methods to a finiteness proof, modular invariants were practically an American preserve. As far as seems to be known, the first specimen of a modular invariant was the absolute invariant discovered in 1903 by Adolf Hurwitz (see his *Werke*, vol. 2, pp. 374–384) while investigating the number of roots of a congruence to a prime modulus. Unaware of Hurwitz' discovery at the time, Dickson in 1907 inaugurated the theory in what is now its classical form (Transactions of the American Mathematical Society, vol. 8, pp. 205–232). Of the 53 papers noted in the statistical data, 24, including the *Madison Colloquium Lectures* of 1914, were contributed by Dickson, 11 by Glenn, 5 by O. C. Hazlett, and 3 by W. L. G. Williams. The remaining contributors wrote their doctoral dissertations in the subject under Dickson.

It is of some interest to note that this field attracted two of the most active American women mathematicians of the period, Sanderson (1889–1914) and Hazlett. Miss Sanderson's single contribution (1913) to modular invariants has been rated by competent judges as one of the classics of the subject.

In conclusion, it may be said that the early expectations of some writers on the subject, that it would provide a powerful method of research in arithmetic, have yet to be realized.

7. **Theory of equations.** In an older day, algebra was almost synonymous with the theory of algebraic equations. Interest in the theory is still alive but apparently in a decline. During the period of the Society's existence, only about six per cent of all American contributions to algebra have been to the theory of equations, including expository articles on the Galois theory. Several textbooks on the elementary theory have been written by Americans, as the subject is still popular in colleges and universities. These need not be cited here.

Bolza's paper introducing the Galois theory to American students has already been noted; Pierpont in 1899 (Annals of Mathematics) presented a more detailed discussion. The theory became a standard part of the senior or graduate course in algebra, and by 1904 practically every Ph.D. graduated in mathematics from a reputable American university had at least a nodding acquaintance with the theory. The usual classical model of the theory was finally made available in accessible form by Dickson in his *Modern Algebraic Theories* (1926); a presentation of the newer approach was given ten years later by A. A. Albert in his *Modern Higher Algebra*. Remarkably little research in the Galois theory has been done by Americans, and there is even a dearth of significant applications to equations of special types. Possibly the theory was too abstract to afford a convenient mine for doctoral dissertations.

At the turn of the century, Moore was interested for a short time in the higher parts of the theory of equations, as a result of his work in groups and tactical problems. In 1899 he studied the resolvent of degree fifteen of the general equation of the seventh degree, and showed that the general equation of the eighth degree has a resolvent of degree fifteen.

As samples of contributions by other Americans to the theory of equations as a whole throughout the fifty-year period, the following may serve. In 1901 J. C. Glashan wrote on metacyclic quintics and B. G. Morrison on the removal of terms from an equation. Dickson in 1906 made a novel departure in the theory of equations in a finite field. O. Dunkel in 1909 discussed the imaginary roots of equations, and, in 1918, H. B. Mitchell investigated the imaginary roots of a polynomial. C. F. Gummer in 1922 wrote on the relative distribution of the real roots of systems of polynomials. Solutions of equations by infinite series were given in 1907 by P. A. Lambert, and in the same year Dickson investigated the Galois group of a reciprocal quartic. D. R. Curtiss in 1912 extended Descartes' rule of signs. J. L. Walsh in 1922–1923 discussed the location of roots, and gave inequalities for the roots of algebraic equations, either refining known methods or inventing new ones. In 1922 A. J. Kempner discussed the separation of the complex roots of algebraic equations. Glashan in 1923 investigated (what he called) isodyadic quintic equations, and, in 1924, isodyadic septimics. Kempner returned in 1935 to his topic of 1922. Possibly classifiable under this head are the researches of H. Blumberg (1916), O. Ore (1935), H. L. Dorwart (1935), and others, on criteria for the reduciblity of polynomials. The brevity of the foregoing list is no measure of the difficulty of some of the problems attacked and successfully solved.

Only one American writer of the period appears to have chosen algebraic equations as a major interest. Beginning about 1926, and continuing to his premature death in 1935 at the age of 34, Garver published a long and varied series of notes and papers on various topics in this field. These included investigations on the transformations of one principal equation into another, the binomial quartic as a normal form, Tschirnhaus transformations, cyclic cubics, the transformation of cubic equations, the Brioschi normal quintic, and many other investigations of a similar nature.

8. **Miscellaneous investigations.** This extensive division can be discussed only summarily, with mention alone of those topics out of the heterogeneous miscellany which attracted the largest numbers of investigators. The topics most frequently discussed appear to have been matrices, quadratic, Hermitian, and bilinear forms from the standpoints of reduction and equivalence, and determinants. The publication in 1907 of M. Bôcher's *Introduction to Higher Algebra* familiarized American undergraduates with the elements of these theories, and also with linear dependence and elementary divisors. The example of Bôcher's rigorous treatment did much to raise the standard of American instruction in algebra. Dickson's *Modern Algebraic Theories* of 1926 included a simplified and unified discussion of the forms mentioned, and was responsible for a considerable amount of research in this field.

The work in determinants has been as specialized as the nature of the subject would lead one to expect, with occasional interludes of novelty or generality. Moore in 1899 made "A Fundamental Remark concerning Determinantal Notations." When Moore called anything "fundamental," it was likely to be at least not trivial. The import of his "remark" was fully appreciated only when the tensor notations of general relativity became popular. Somewhat off the beaten track, polydimensional determinants occupied several writers. Thus in 1899, E. R. Hedrick gave a detailed treatment of three-dimensional determinants; L. P. Hall in 1917 discussed the general case; and L. H. Rice made the subject his own, contributing more to this field than any other American writer. In 1924, he obtained a generalization of Frobenius' theorem. Cramlet in 1927 reduced the theory of n-dimensional determinants to an exercise in tensor algebra. This does not imply, of course, that nothing remains to be done in the subject; but it appears to have been transformed.

Of papers in the classical tradition on ordinary determinants, the following may be cited as a sample. H. S. White in 1895 wrote on Kronecker's theorem, and W. H. Metzler in 1917 and 1924 on compound determinants; Dickson in 1903 generalized symmetric and skew symmetric determinants. L. M. Blumenthal in 1936 introduced new methods into the classical theory. A somewhat unusual problem claimed the attention of Dickson and some of his pupils, that of expressing certain forms as determinants and finding for what forms there is a rational solution. Thus Dickson in 1921 considered the case of cubic forms, also that of reducible cubic forms, and found all general homogeneous polynomials expressible as determinants with linear elements. H. S. Everett in 1922 considered the polynomial case. As regards the general classical theory as a whole, it appears that the most frequently useful properties of determinants are now best treated by elementary tensor methods. Much of the older theory seems to have become indeed classical, that is, dead.

A topic not yet exhausted is that of forms which repeat under multiplication (or which admit a rational composition). Dickson, Hazlett, and C. G. Latimer considered this (either in the general case, or in special instances) in 1920–1921, 1928, and 1929, respectively. The prime and composite polynomials defined and investigated in 1922 by J. F. Ritt, more in the spirit of iteration, are unrelated to these. The significance of the composition problem was pointed out by F. M. G. Eisenstein nearly a century ago.

A difficult type of tactical problem, originating in T. P. Kirkman's famous fifteen schoolgirls problem, has attracted a small group of American writers on account of its applications and its intrinsic interest. Moore was one of the earliest contributors; an application occurs in his paper (cited in the section on equations) on the general equations of degrees seven and eight. Cole in 1912 determined all the triad systems on thirteen letters, and in 1921 wrote on "Kirkman parades"—"crocodiles" would have been a more correct technical description than "parades," and one which Kirkman would have recognized. L. D. Cummings and White in 1914 discussed the groupless triad systems on fifteen letters; White, Cole, and Cummings determined the triads on fifteen letters in 1918, and in 1934, White those on thirty-one letters.

The theory of matrices has been, and is, a popular subject with many writers, no doubt on account of its numerous applications in other fields of algebra and elsewhere. MacDuffee compiled a useful tract in 1933 (in the Ergebnisse series), and Wedderburn in 1934 published his Princeton lectures on matrices in the Colloquium series of the Society. Other expositions are also readily accessible, so that the theory is now part of the standard equipment of every student of algebra, and has been for several years.

The evolution of this theory from its almost accidental beginning in Cayley's work, of about eighty years ago, into one of the most useful tools in algebra, suggests that there is but little rhyme and less reason in the historical development of algebra. It also suggests that other apparent trivia may be the germs of equally significant and useful theories. Now that the theory of matrices is full-blown before us, it is easy for any empirical historian to see the inevitability of the growth from seed to flower. But the familiar historical explanation through linear transformations, etc., explains precisely nothing, unless the explainer is able to validate himself and his explanation by making a prediction from the present phenomena of algebra for observers half a century hence to confirm or refute. The like applies to a good deal of the rest of algebra during the past fifty years. The solution of the implied problem may be left to social historians of mathematics.

A small sample of the more recent contributions by Americans to the theory will indicate the nature of present interests in matrices in this country. In 1914 Wedderburn considered the rank of a symmetric matrix, as did Dickson in 1917. Wedderburn in 1915 discussed matrices whose elements are functions of one variable, in 1925 the absolute value of the product of two matrices, and also matrices in a given field. H. B. Phillips investigated functions of matrices in 1919. MacDuffee in 1925 wrote on the nullity of a matrix with respect to a field. In 1928 E. T. Browne wrote on the characteristic equation of a matrix, and W. E. Roth gave a new discussion of matric equations. T. A. Pierce considered matrices with cyclic characteristic equations in 1930. In 1935 J. Williamson gave a method for the simultaneous reduction of matrices to canonical form, and N. H. McCoy gave a rational canonical form for a function of a matrix; M. M. Flood discussed matric polynomials; M. H. Ingraham and K. W. Wegner considered equivalent pairs of Hermitian matrices; Albert considered the principal matrices of a Riemann matrix, as one of his numerous contributions to a subfield of the theory of matrices in which he leads in this country. He had discussed Riemann matrices as early as 1929. In 1936 Roth investigated the characteristic values of certain functions of matrices; Williamson considered matrices with respect to their idempotent and nilpotent elements. In 1937 Brown, Flood, and Parker wrote respectively on conjugate sets of matrices, column normal matric polynomials, and the characteristic roots of matrices. From this sample it is evident that present interest in matrices is both lively and varied. Applications, as to matric algebras, or to physics, have not been included here, as their chief interest is in the applications rather than in the general theory of matrices.

American interest in the algebra of bilinear and Hermitian forms seems to have developed from the occurrence of such forms in linear algebra, and the theory of groups. Possibly the earliest American contribution to bilinear forms is Taber's discussion in 1885 of the automorphic of a bilinear form, a topic reconsidered by Wedderburn in 1921. In 1906 Dickson gave a simplified treatment of quadratic, Hermitian, and bilinear forms. J. I. Hutchinson considered Hermitian forms of zero determinant in 1907; Dickson in the same year discussed quadratic forms in a general field. M. I. Logsdon in 1922 considered the equivalence of pairs of Hermitian forms, and Dickson in 1927 treated the singular case of pairs of forms. In 1926 Dickson produced a new theory of the rational equivalence of linear transformations of bilinear forms, stressing the desirable rationality. In his book (already cited) of the same year, he gave an ingenious simultaneous discussion of parts of the theory of quadratic, Hermitian, and bilinear forms. O. E. Browne in 1931 considered equivalent triples of bilinear forms. Recent work of R. Oldenburger is concerned with similar equivalence problems from a general point of view.

Last may be mentioned the consideration of similar problems in Galois fields, which possibly are more arithmetical than algebraic in character. Some of this is abstracted by Dickson in his *History of the Theory of Numbers*. As specimens may be cited Dickson's (1908) reduction of quadratic forms in a Galois field of order a power of two; A. D. Campbell's

(1928, and later) development of geometry in a Galois field; and the work of L. Carlitz (1933–) on carrying over to Galois fields certain classical problems of algebra, such as the expression of a polynomial (when possible) as a sum of squares.

It has not been feasible to give more than a glimpse of the rich variety of fields successfully explored in this miscellaneous region of algebra during the past fifty years. Inventiveness is as frequent here as in other fields. For example, and to conclude with two specimens of things left aside because they do not fit any of the categories, there is O. Ore's paper of 1933 on noncommutative polynomials, and Wedderburn's of 1917 on continued fractions in noncommutative systems.

9. **Linear algebra; abstract algebra.** Great progress in linear algebras and in their general theory was made in Europe and America during the fifty-year period, and a considerable part of this progress was due to American algebraists. In the evolution of linear algebra in this country during the past thirty years is clearly seen the progression from the particular to the general. Another tendency is also evident in the latest period: parts of linear and abstract algebra now closely mimic parts of arithmetic, and concepts which first evolved in the theory of algebraic numbers are taking on a sort of protective coloration in the theory of algebras. This partial arithmetization of algebra belongs to the theory of numbers rather than to algebra, and is not considered here beyond the immediately following remarks, which do not apply to the arithmetics of specific algebras, such as that of generalized quaternions, investigated by Dickson and his pupils. These are not considered here, as their interest is arithmetical.

It has been reported that the reason for some of the more profound of these arithmetoid researches in algebra was an attempt to provide finite proofs for certain results in classical arithmetic obtained hitherto only analytically. If such is the fact, the attempt has not yet succeeded. The delayed success of this attempt is parallel to another, namely, the invention of the theory of algebraic numbers to aid in the solution of certain problems in classical arithmetic. If none of these successive generalizations of rational arithmetic has as yet attained its initial object, it is conceivable that no lack of competence in the devotees of these generalizations is responsible for the failure. A more imaginative generation may discover that, so far as arithmetic is concerned, close imitation of arithmetical concepts leads back to arithmetically barren reformulations of fundamental and difficult problems in arithmetic. What arithmetic seems to want at present is neither a parody of itself nor the sincere flattery of a close imitation but the solution of at least one of its outstanding classical problems. However, the advance in linear algebra during the past fifty years was but little concerned with the wants of arithmetic. The main progress was in another direction.

In America at the beginning of the fifty-year period, linear algebra was still in the tradition of Peirce; in Europe, Poincaré's connection between hypercomplex number systems and continuous groups, discovered in 1884, was already being exploited, notably by G. Scheffers. After the first phase waned (about 1905), what may be called the modern American tradition in linear algebra began to appear. This has had little to do with continuous groups, and has been essentially algebraic in character. The rapid and varied development of this tradition is readily traced to the work of three men, Dickson, Wedderburn, and Albert—in the chronological order of their entry into the field.

The relation of the contributions by American algebraists to "algebras" since about 1927 to the general progress in the subject, during the same period, can be seen by consulting M. Deuring's *Algebren* (1935). Dickson's *Algebras and their Arithmetics* (1923; German edition, 1927) will partly serve the same purpose for 1914–1923, and, for the period up to 1914, the same author's *Linear Algebras* (Cambridge Tract No. 16) may be consulted. A history of the subject has yet to be written.

As in previous sections, only a sample of the profusion of results, special and general, can be noted. Even this much presents serious difficulties of just exposition, as one author has frequently generalized the work of another, or of himself, soon after it was published, and what at the time seemed like several long steps forward turned out to be only half a step. In spite of this "dot and carry one" feature of the general advance, progress was nevertheless fairly coherent, due no doubt to the conscious direction of the three men mentioned. At the least, the progress appears to have been markedly less haphazard than was the case in the theory of groups.

As samples of the work up to 1905, the following may be offered. In 1899–1901, G. P. Starkweather discussed linear associative algebras of order six. H. Taber in 1904 extended Peirce's results concerning algebras of deficiencies, 0, 1 to those in which the domain of the coordinates is arbitrary. In the same year, H. E. Hawkes enumerated hypercomplex number systems in seven units, partly in defense of Peirce's methods against foreign critics (notably Cayley, Scheffers, and E. Study), who had been misled by Peirce's metaphysical propensities and occasional slips into the belief that his methods were inadequate for his specific purpose. In this paper and others (especially in the Transactions of the American Mathematical Society, vol. 3 (1902)), Hawkes removed the obscurities, and showed that "by using Peirce's principles as a foundation, we can deduce a method more powerful than those hitherto given for enumerating all number systems of the types Scheffers has considered." Hawkes thus placed Peirce's work (published first only in lithographed form, 1870, republished in the American Journal of Mathematics, vol. 4, (1881)) on a sound basis. He also evaluated Peirce's success in attaining his declared objective of exhaustively enumerating all types of number systems in a small number of units and of developing and applying calculi for some or all of these systems.

In a sense, this work of Hawkes balanced Peirce's account, and closed one chapter of the book opened by W. R. Hamilton and A. DeMorgan. Of the Hamilton-Peirce problem, the outstanding unsolved part is the somewhat vague project of devising "useful" applications; possibly the quantum theory, which has shown itself capable of swallowing even the eight-square imaginaries of Cayley without acute discomfort, may do what Hamilton and Peirce desired. While it is a question of applications, passing reference may be made to the ideas of J. W. Gibbs on multiple algebra. Up to the present, Gibbs' approach does not seem to have attracted professional algebraists. Whether this neglect is the fault of the algebraists or of Gibbs' ideas may be left to the judgment of posterity; the fact is that algebra has developed in other directions.

Still on the border of the newer tradition, W. M. Strong in 1901 wrote on nonquaternion number systems; S. Epsteen in 1903 on semireducible hypercomplex number systems; J. B. Shaw in 1903 on the theory of linear associative algebras, on nilpotent algebras, and on the application of matrices to algebras; Epsteen in 1904 on the definition of reducible hypercomplex number systems, and Shaw in the same year on algebras defined by finite groups. Dickson enters in 1905 with a more general discussion of hypercomplex number systems.

The year 1905 is also memorable in the subject for Wedderburn's proof that a Galois field is the only algebra with a finite number of elements that is a linear associative division algebra in the domain of real numbers, the analogue for finite algebras of the theorem of Frobenius and C. S. Peirce. The following year, Dickson made two contributions to a province of algebra in which he was to lead for over a quarter of a century, and in which he was to inspire many researches by his students, that of division algebras. In the first paper he found (among other things) new commutative algebras in which division is uniquely possible, and gave for division algebras a method of constructing an algebra of mk units from an algebra of m units when m exceeds two. He also determined the inequivalent, nonfield, commutative algebras in six units with coordinates in the same abstract field. In the second paper of 1906, Dickson exhibited commutative linear algebras in $2n$ units, with coordinates in a general field, n of the units defining a field subalgebra. In a later investigation (1910; published, 1912) in the same general direction, he found linear algebras containing a modulus in which neither the associative nor the commutative law of multiplication is postulated, such that every element of the algebra satisfies an equation analogous to the usual characteristic equation. Among many new results of this paper is the possibility of division in Cayley's eight-square algebra.

The year 1907 seasoned linear algebra in America with a pinch of irony.

In that year J. B. Shaw's monumental *Synopsis of Linear Associative Algebra* all but immortalized the subject like a perfectly preserved green beetle in a beautiful tear of fossilized golden amber. Had this exhaustive synopsis been the last word on linear associative algebra, it would have made a noble epitaph. Instead of submitting to premature mummification and honorific burial, however, the subject insisted on getting itself reborn, or its soul transmigrated immediately, in Wedderburn's paper *On hypercomplex numbers*, published in vol. 6 (1907) of the Proceedings of the London Mathematical Society. The object and point of view of this paper may be recalled in its author's words:

"My object throughout has been to develop a treatment analogous to that which has been so successful in the theory of finite groups. An instrument towards this lay to hand in the calculus developed by Frobenius, and used by him with great effect in the theory of groups. This calculus is, with slight additions, equally applicable to the theory of hypercomplex number-systems, or, as they will be called below, algebras."

The calculus referred to is that of complexes. Parts of Wedderburn's paper had been read before the Mathematical Seminar at the University of Chicago early in 1905, "and owe much to Professor Moore's helpful criticism." At Dickson's suggestion, "algebra" was adopted as equivalent to Peirce's "linear associative algebra." Algebra, after the assimilation of this paper, was a very different thing from what it was before. Much of it took on the graces of civilized generality and unity. The striking gain in simplicity of method, with its consequent greater ease in deduction, marked by this contribution can be seen by comparing some of the proofs of classical theorems as given in the paper with proofs by the older methods.

Dickson's earlier researches in division algebras have already been mentioned. The intensive investigation of such algebras, and the discovery of wide new classes of them, was one of the outstanding contributions to American algebra of the past thirty years. Although it is out of its chronological order here, special note may be made of Dickson's paper of 1926, *New Division Algebras*, in which the subject took a new direction. Stating that "the chief outstanding problem of linear algebras is the determination of all division algebras," Dickson proceeded to greatly extend existing knowledge by showing how to construct from any solvable group of order n at least one type of division algebra of order n^2. He recalled that until 1905, when he discovered a division algebra in n^2 basal units, fields and real quaternions were the only division algebras known; the results of 1926 generalized those of 1905. Apart from such particulars—sufficiently general in themselves—the main advance in this work was its pragmatic demonstration of the basic importance of the theory of finite groups in the theory of division algebras. In 1930 the work was continued in a paper on *Construction of Division Algebras*, in which methods were devised for greatly reducing the necessary computations.

To return to the chronological sampling: not all of the work of the period 1907–1938 was in the newer tradition; the older continued to give interesting results. As these seem to lie rather to one side of the advance toward generality, they will not be considered further here. In the main line, there were generalizations from special fields to an abstract field for the coordinates of hypercomplex numbers. On the borderline between algebra and arithmetic, the theory of certain finite algebras, constructed by H. S. Vandiver in 1912, abstracted and generalized the instances suggesting it in the residue classes of arithmetic. The work of E. Kircher in 1917, concerned in part with decompositions in rings, was in a similar direction. Generalizing results of Dickson, Wedderburn showed in 1914 that Dickson's algebra of the same year, connected with an abelian equation, can be made primitive. Shaw in 1915 investigated parastrophic algebras (one of the six possible types with multiplication tables derived from the table of a given algebra by permutation of the indices in the triple suffix of the multiplication constants), and showed that, when applicable, such algebras provided a short method of determining when a given algebra is semisimple. In passing, it seems fortunate that the names of the six types, such as antipreparastrophic and antipostparastrophic, reminiscent of the early Greek of the theory of elasticity, have not proved indispensable.

Hazlett's first contributions to the subject appeared in 1914–1916, the latter being the classification and invariantive characterization of nilpotent algebras. The following year and again in 1930 she discussed associative division algebras. Most of her further contributions were arithmetical in character; in particular, she modified Dickson's definitions for the arithmetic of an algebra. Wedderburn in 1924 opened a new field with his investigation of algebras without a finite basis. Cayley's eight-square algebra and generalized quaternions were discussed by Dickson in 1918, partly for their arithmetical interest. Carrying out a detail of the program in division algebras, Garver in 1927 produced a division algebra of order sixteen.

Albert in 1929 investigated normal division algebras in $4p^2$ units, p any odd prime, and determined all normal division algebras in sixteen units. In 1930 he showed how to construct all noncommutative rational division algebras of order eight, and found all normal division algebras in thirty-six units of particular types. Continuing his researches in this same general direction, he obtained normal division algebras of degree four over an algebraic field. Albert and H. Hasse in 1932 collaborated in a determination of all normal division algebras over an algebraic number field. In 1933 Albert investigated noncyclic algebras; in 1934 and 1936, normal division algebras, and also certain simple algebras. It is impossible here to give further indications of Albert's interests in linear algebra constituting, as stated previously, the third of the major surges in the subject as it has progressed in America since 1900.

Although the arithmetical aspects have been deliberately left aside, a word must be added on some work in this general field which is of algebraic interest apart from its arithmetical objective. In addition to his studies of 1929–1932 on the matrices of an algebra, MacDuffee investigated ideals (1931) in linear algebras, and, with G. Shover in 1933, defined ideal multiplication in a linear algebra. Shover in 1933 discussed the class number; Latimer in 1934 proved its finiteness in a semisimple algebra.

The most prolific contributors of twenty years ago are still active; thus, in 1935 Dickson gave a detailed investigation of algebras with associativity not assumed, and Wedderburn in 1937 extended certain of his previous methods so as to apply to algebras in modular fields. Among topics in which there is a new or revived interest, that of Lie algebras may be mentioned. G. Birkhoff and N. Jacobson are among the current workers in this topic. An investigation in a different direction from any so far indicated is cited here out of its chronological order to suggest that its possibilities have not, perhaps, been sufficiently explored: J. W. Young's *New Formulation of General Algebra*, of 1927.

As the fifty-year period closes, linear algebra is in a much livelier condition that it was half a century ago. The causes for this revival of interest have been sufficiently indicated in the foregoing samples. To judge by the number of young recruits entering the field, interest in linear algebra will persist for some time to come, although what is now called modern algebra is attracting many.

Modern abstract algebra, especially in America, is too close to the present to have acquired a long list of contributors. Nevertheless, the comparatively few in this vigorous young school who do cultivate the subject are sufficiently prolific to compensate for lack of numbers. There is, in fact, some indication that the next decade or two may experience a deluge from this quarter rivaling or even surpassing that of thirty years ago when the group-dam burst. There is no dearth of problems for competently trained men: practically the whole of algebra offers itself for remodelling in the streamlined patterns of the newer abstract algebra. The latest models of the Galois theory, for instance, also of the composition theorems in groups, are easier on the eyes than the old.

This latest phase of algebra is distinctly European in origin, and practically all German, if the ideas of Galois be excluded as too remote historically. Its roots are in Dedekind's work of 1900 on dual groups,* Steinitz' paper of 1910, and Emmy Noether's abstract school, trained by her either personally or through her writings from about 1922 to her death in 1935 at the age of 53.

A striking feature of the newer developments is the frequent use of

---

* And in work on modules as early as 1877: *Ueber die Anzahl der Ideal-classen in den verschiedenen Ordnungen eines endlichen Körpers.*

concepts, such as homorphism, residue classes, and ideals, which came into mathematics through arithmetic. These concepts are now abstracted and understood. The younger generation of American algebraists has been strongly attracted to this latest development. As an item of historical interest, Moore's early work (1893) on Galois fields was the first in this country to foreshadow the present trend.

The two most prolific of the many workers, all of whom are young, in this new field may be mentioned, so the reporter for the hundredth anniversary of the Society may be able to look back and see just how close to the mark our present aim comes. Nobody writing fifty years ago on linear algebra could have foreseen that within two decades the whole subject would be radically recast. Still less could anyone have foreseen who was to do the recasting. So, in any sample census at the present time, the probability of entirely missing the mark seems high. The very man who so far has contributed nothing or only one short abstract of his work to the Bulletin, and whose name is not even mentioned, may be the very one who will revise the tradition once more.

With a long record of achievement in algebraic numbers (among other things) behind him, O. Ore is at present engaged in elaborating his theory of structures in his work on the foundation of abstract algebra. "In the discussion of the structure of algebraic domains one is not primarily interested in the *elements* of these domains, but in the relations of certain *distinguished subdomains* like invariant subgroups in groups, ideals in rings and characteristic moduli in modular systems. For all of these systems there are defined the *two operations* of *union* and *cross-cut* satisfying the ordinary axioms. This leads naturally to the introduction of new systems, which we shall call *structures*, having these two operations." (Annals of Mathematics, vol. 36 (1935), p. 406.) Such is the bare indication of the program, already successfully carried out in numerous details. Some of the results obtained, as stated by Ore, are restatements of previous results due to Dedekind, and to G. Birkhoff in his paper *On the combination of subalgebras* (Proceedings of the Cambridge Philosophical Society, vol. 29 (1934)).

G. Birkhoff develops an abstract theory of what he calls lattices, which partially overlaps the earlier work of T. Skolem and Fritz Klein. (A Klein "Verband" is a finite lattice; there are further contacts with Klein's systems.) Many applications of lattice theory have been made. The theories of Birkhoff and Ore also overlap, and among other points not yet settled is that of which terminology is to survive, structure or lattice. Whichever does, it may be anticipated that there will be no dearth of attractive abstract theorems unifying numerous particulars of current theories, with many new algebraic facts and applications, all succinctly expressed in the ultimate language of the theory. Should this language prove to be the final one of algebra, algebra will be as dead as Cheops. But the experience of the past fifty years is against any such disastrous outcome of the present intensely interesting development of algebra par excellence, abstract algebra.

One root of the present development can be traced back to Boole, another to the G.C.D. and L.C.M. in rational arithmetic and in the theory of ideals in algebraic number rings, and still another to Euler and Gauss in rational arithmetic. In this connection it seems a pity that Dedekind did not take algebraists and arithmeticians into his confidence as to what he was really up to, and what false leads he abandoned—if he did—in his theory of dual groups, as he did in his account of how he created his theory of algebraic numbers and ideals. And if the algebra of structures and lattices is ever exhausted, there will remain the wider field of n-valued "connections" suggested by the current generalizations of parts of Boolean algebra. However, sufficient unto the day is the abstractness thereof—to transpose Moore's aphorism on mathematical rigor to the abstract temper of our times.

According to the mortality tables, many of the younger generation of American algebraists will be living in 1988, when the Society celebrates its first hundredth anniversary. If these survivors (provided human stupidity permits anything with brains in its head to survive) can look back at the algebra of 1938 and find some of it as quaint as some of that which we now recall from 1888, all will have been well from 1938 to 1988.

To conclude, a suggestion may be offered the officers of the Society who are to be responsible for the hundredth anniversary. Choose young men, preferably under thirty, to review the progress of American mathematics from 1938 to 1988. For if there is anything that will give a man, young or old, a decent humility and a sane humor regarding his own efforts, it is an acquaintance with the work of his predecessors and contemporaries. The earlier this acquaintance is gained, the better for all concerned, including mathematics.

California Institute of Technology,
Pasadena, Calif.

ALGEBRAIC ASPECTS OF THE THEORY OF DIFFERENTIAL EQUATIONS

BY

J. F. RITT

The theory of systems of algebraic equations is one of the most highly developed chapters of algebra. At the center of this theory stands the concept of polynomial in one or more letters. The formal properties of polynomials offer themselves first for investigation. One of the first results is that on the representation of a polynomial as a product of irreducible factors. Out of the factorization theorem grows, by a profound generalization, the theory of ideals of polynomials. There is furnished thus a basis for studying many aspects of algebraic manifolds, whose complete theory constitutes algebraic geometry. By the side of the theory of manifolds stands the theory of elimination, with algorithms for solving systems of equations and theorems for counting solutions. In elimination theory, resultants of systems of polynomials play a fundamental rôle. The key to the general theory of algebraic systems is Hilbert's famous theorem on the existence of finite bases of infinite systems of polynomials.

Algebraic equations may be regarded as differential equations of order zero, that is, as differential equations in which derivatives do not appear effectively. It is thus proper to ask whether the theory of differential equations can be developed in such a way as to yield, by specialization, the classic results on systems of algebraic equations. One would expect to be able to carry over certain algebraic results into the field of differential equations and, in the process, to find, for differential equations, properties with no counterpart in the algebraic theory. Naturally, one would begin with algebraic differential equations, proceeding from them to more general types.

The application of algebraic methods to differential equations is justified by more than the expectation of creating new links between algebra and analysis and of discovering novel problems in differential equations. For want of proper algebraic viewpoints, questions which date from the beginnings of mathematical analysis remained without systematic treatment. Thus, the older literature contains only fragmentary and heuristic indications on the elimination theory of a system of differential equations. The problem of the number of arbitrary constants in the solution of a system, that is, the problem of the *order* of a system, failed to receive even a sound formulation. The most striking condition of all is perhaps that in the literature on singular solutions. The greatest source of light on the nature of the singular solutions of an algebraic differential equation is probably the fact that the solutions of the equation separate, in a unique manner, into collections analogous to irreducible algebraic manifolds. The description of this decomposition, for a given equation, is the first step in the classification of the singular solutions of the equation. In writings of Laplace, Lagrange and Poisson on singular solutions,* one can discern a groping towards such a decomposition theorem as we have just mentioned. When they wrote, the time was not ripe for the exact investigation of such questions. It was a time when even proofs of the uniqueness of the representation of an integer as a product of primes and of the uniqueness of the representation of a polynomial as a product of irreducible polynomials were not generally known. Certainly, it was too much to expect a systematic investigation of the algebra of differential equations. It is in the light of what is now known that one can understand the direction of the efforts of the great analysts named above.

The construction of an algebraic theory of differential equations has, during the past several years, occupied the present writer and his colleagues H. W. Raudenbush, E. Gourin, and W. C. Strodt.† For systems, ordinary or partial, which are algebraic in the unknowns and their derivatives, the nucleus of a general theory has been secured and applications to special problems, such as the problem of singular solutions, have been made. The manifold theory for algebraic differential equations has already taken definite shape. Raudenbush has supplied a purely algebraic proof of the counterpart, for differential polynomials, of the Hilbert basis theorem. He has also constructed a restricted theory of ideals of differential polynomials. A theory of non-algebraic systems is already in process of development.

In what follows, we shall describe some of the principal results which have been secured and shall indicate some of the methods of proof. An analysis will be made of such early work, bearing on our topic, as has come to our attention. We shall restrict our discussion to ordinary differential equations; previous publications‡ will inform one as to what has been done for several independent variables. We shall leave untouched also the theory of algebraic difference equations which, reconnoitered in papers of J. L. Doob, F. Herzog, W. C. Strodt, and the present writer, still awaits intensive development.

---

* See §§17, 21, 22 below.

† One will understand that we are speaking of a theory constructed from the viewpoints of algebraic geometry and of the theory of elimination. Analogies between differential equations and algebraic equations have frequently been subjects of investigation. Similarities between linear differential equations and algebraic equations were observed by the early analysts. To this older work is related that of Landau, Loewy, Blumberg, Emmy Noether, Schmeidler, and Ore, who have studied the factorization of linear differential expressions. The Lie theory of differential equations was inspired by the Galois theory. The researches of Koenigsberger, Picard, Drach, and Vessiot have transformed the Lie theory into a closer analogue of the Galois theory.

‡ A bibliography is given at the end of the paper.

FORMS AND BASES

1. In constructing a theory of algebraic ordinary differential equations, it is natural to begin by studying the formal properties of polynomials in a set of unknown functions and their derivatives of various orders, the coefficients in the polynomials being functions of the independent variable. The nature of the coefficients should be specified with a view towards simplicity and generality for the resulting theory.

2. Let $\mathfrak{A}$ be an open region in the plane of the complex variable x. Let $\mathfrak{F}$ be a set of functions each of which is meromorphic in $\mathfrak{A}$ and at least one of which is not identically zero. We shall call $\mathfrak{F}$ a field if $\mathfrak{F}$ is closed with respect to rational operations and to differentiation. If f and g are functions in a field $\mathfrak{F}$, $f+g$, $f-g$ and fg are in $\mathfrak{F}$. If g is not identically zero, f/g is in $\mathfrak{F}$. Again, if f is any function in $\mathfrak{F}$, the derivative of f is in $\mathfrak{F}$. Thus is made explicit the meaning of the two types of closure.

3. Let n be any positive integer. Let $y_1, \cdots, y_n$ be unknown functions of the independent variable x. We denote by y_{ij} the jth derivative of y_i, $j=1, 2, \cdots$. We write, frequently, $y_i = y_{i0}$ and refer to y_i as its own derivative of order zero. By a *differential polynomial*, we shall mean a polynomial in a certain (eo ipso finite) number of the y_{ij}, with functions meromorphic in $\mathfrak{A}$ as coefficients. As a rule, we shall substitute the briefer term *form* for *differential polynomial*.

In every discussion, all forms which appear will be understood to have coefficients belonging to a given field $\mathfrak{F}$.

Raudenbush has employed *forms* in which the coefficients are not meromorphic functions, but rather abstract elements for which a differentiation process can be defined. This is certainly an excellent procedure from the point of view of abstract algebra. Nevertheless, the case of meromorphic coefficients contains most of what is vital for analysis, and allows the algebraic problems to be seen in their full proportions.

4. We shall use capital italic letters to denote forms, and large Greek letters to denote systems of forms. All forms will involve a definite set of unknowns $y_1, \cdots, y_n$.

One might conjecture, on the basis of Hilbert's theorem relative to the existence of finite bases for infinite systems of polynomials, that, in every infinite system Σ of forms, there is a finite system such that every form of Σ is a linear combination of the forms of the finite system, and of their derivatives of various orders, with forms for coefficients. Such a result does not hold. There exists, however, for infinite systems of forms, a theorem which may be regarded as an extension of Hilbert's theorem.

Let Σ be an infinite system of forms. Let Φ be a finite subset of the forms in Σ. We shall call Φ a *basis* of Σ if, for every form G in Σ, there exists a positive integer p, which depends on G, such that G^p is a linear combination of the forms in Φ and of derivatives of various orders of the forms in Φ, such that the coefficients in the linear combination are all of them forms.*

We are now ready to consider the fundamental theorem:†

THEOREM I. *Given a set of unknowns $y_1, \cdots, y_n$, every infinite system of forms in $y_1, \cdots, y_n$ has a basis.*

Theorem I is, for the case of forms with meromorphic coefficients, a consequence of two theorems which we shall proceed to explain.

By a *solution* of a system Σ of forms, we shall mean a solution of the system of equations obtained by equating the forms of Σ to zero. The totality of the solutions of a system of forms will be called the *manifold* of the system. The first of our theorems is the following:

THEOREM I'. *Let Σ be an infinite system of forms in $y_1, \cdots, y_n$. The system Σ contains a finite subsystem whose manifold is identical with that of Σ.*

The second theorem is as follows:

THEOREM II. *Let a form G vanish for every solution in the manifold of a finite system $H_1, \cdots, H_r$. Then some power of G is a linear combination of the H_i and of their derivatives of various orders, the coefficients in the linear combination being forms.*

Theorem I implies I', and I' and II together imply I. Theorem II will be recognized as an analogue of the well known *Nullstellensatz* of Hilbert and Netto. I' and II are due to the present writer, who gave an algebraic proof of I' and a proof of II depending on methods of analysis. Raudenbush gave a purely algebraic proof of I and also such a proof of an abstract version of II.

With respect to Theorem I, a first question which arises is the following. If $H_1, \cdots, H_r$ is a basis of Σ, does a positive integer p exist such that, for every form G in Σ, G^p is a linear combination of the H_i and their derivatives? Raudenbush furnished a negative answer to this question [12]. Let Σ be the totality of forms in the single unknown y which admit the solution $y=0$. By Theorem II, y^3 is a basis for Σ. Raudenbush showed that no p as above exists for the basis y^3.‡ It is proper now to ask whether there does not exist, for every infinite system Σ, some basis for which a single p as above can be found. This question is open at the present time.

5. The proof of Theorem I is much simpler for the case of a single unknown than for the case of many unknowns, particularly if one assumes the Hilbert basis theorem. It will possibly not be out of place for us to

---

* As was indicated in §3, all forms mentioned are understood to have their coefficients in a given field.

† See Ritt [14, p. 161], for a discussion of related work of Tresse. Our remarks on Tresse's work apply also to Drach's discussion mentioned below.

‡ A similar result holds for y^2, as Raudenbush has shown. The proof for y^3 is simpler.

present a proof for the case of one unknown here. Although I implies I′, the relative simplicity of the proof of I′ will justify starting with that theorem and passing from it to I.

6. We consider forms in a single unknown y, representing the jth derivative of y by y_j and y itself, at times, by y_0. Let A be a form which involves effectively one or more y_j, $(j = 0, 1, 2, \cdots)$. By the *order* of A, we shall mean the greatest j for which y_j appears effectively in A. A form which is merely a function of x will be considered to have the order zero.*

Let A be a form involving one or more y_j effectively. Let B be any form. If the order of A exceeds that of B, we shall say that A is *higher* than B. If A and B have the same order p and if the degree† in y_p of A is higher than that of B, we shall say, again, that A is higher than B. Two forms for which no difference in rank is created by what precedes will be said to be of the same rank. Thus, any two functions of x in $\mathfrak{F}$ are of the same rank.

Let A be any form which is not a function of x, and let A be of order p. We shall call the form $\partial A / \partial y_p$ the *separant* of A.

Let A be any form which is not a function of x. If G is a form whose order exceeds that of A, and if j is the difference of the orders of G and A, the jth derivative‡ A_j of A will have the same order as G. If p is the common order of G and A_j, A_j will involve y_p linearly, with S, the separant of A, for coefficient of y_p. Thus, if we multiply G by a suitable power S^q of S, and subtract a suitable multiple of A_j from $S^q G$, the remainder G_1 will be of lower order than G. If G_1 is of higher order than A, we give it the treatment accorded to G. We see thus that there is a positive integer q such that, when a suitable linear combination of derivatives of A is subtracted from $S^q G$, the remainder R is not of higher order than A. Using as small as possible a power of S at each stage of the reduction, we are led to a unique R. We call this R the *residue of G with respect to A*.

If G is given with an order not exceeding that of A, we take G itself as the residue of G with respect to A.

Considering now an infinite system Σ, let us call Σ *complete* if there is a finite subsystem of Σ whose manifold is that of Σ, and *incomplete* if there is no such finite subsystem.

Every system of forms in y which contains nonzero forms contains a nonzero form which is not higher than any other nonzero form of the system. We call any such nonzero form of lowest rank a *first form* of the system.

Suppose now that there exist incomplete systems. We consider the totality of such systems and select from them one, call it Σ, whose first forms are not higher than the first forms of any other incomplete system.

---

* Of course, there are forms of order zero which involve y_0.

† If $p = 0$ and if B is identically zero, the degree of B in y_0 is taken here as zero.

‡ In differentiating A, we consider y as a function of x.

Let A be a first form of Σ. Then A is not free of the y_i; otherwise, A and Σ would both be devoid of solutions, and this, by what one should read into the definition of completeness, would mean that Σ is complete. Let S represent the separant of A.

For every form G in Σ which is distinct from A, let a residue R with respect to A be found. The system Ω composed of A and of all the R involves no y_i higher than the highest y_i in A. By Hilbert's basis theorem, Ω has a finite subset Φ such that every form in Ω is a linear combination of the forms in Φ. The manifold of Ω is thus the manifold of Φ. We may and shall assume that Φ contains A.

Every R in Ω is obtained, by a subtraction, from some $S^q G$, where G is in Σ. Let Λ be the system composed of A and of the totality of the forms $S^q G$. It is easy to see that Λ is complete. In short, if Ψ is the finite system composed of A and of those $S^q G$ in Λ which furnish the R in Φ, Λ has the same manifold as Ψ.

Now, let

$$(1) \qquad S^{q_1} M_1, \cdots, S^{q_r} M_r,$$

where the M_i are forms in Σ, be any finite subsystem of Λ with the same manifold as Λ. We note that A is not prevented from figuring in (1). As Σ is incomplete, there is a K in Σ which does not have the property of vanishing for every solution of the system $M_1, \cdots, M_r$. Now some $S^q K$ vanishes for every solution of (1). This means that certain solutions of the system $S, M_1, \cdots, M_r$ are not solutions of K. Now the $M_1, \cdots, M_r$ in (1) may be taken so as to include any given finite subset of Σ, since the adjunction, to any set (1), of further forms of Λ produces a set with the same manifold as Λ. It follows that the set $\Sigma + S$, obtained by adjoining S to Σ, is incomplete.* Now S is lower than A. This contradicts the assumption that Σ is an incomplete system with lowest first forms, so that Theorem I' is proved for the case of one unknown.

7. Following Raudenbush, we shall now modify the foregoing proof so as to obtain Theorem I. We shall write

$$P \equiv Q \qquad\qquad (C_1, \cdots, C_r),$$

if $P - Q$ is a linear combination of the r forms C_i and their derivatives of various orders, with forms for coefficients. We prove the following lemma:

LEMMA. *If, for some positive integer g,*

$$(2) \qquad\qquad (PQ)^g \equiv 0 \qquad\qquad (C_1, \cdots, C_r),$$

then, if P' is the derivative of P,

$$(3) \qquad\qquad (P'Q)^{2g} \equiv 0 \qquad\qquad (C_1, \cdots, C_r).$$

---

* Note that, if $\Sigma + S$ were complete, any finite subset of $\Sigma + S$ with the same manifold as $\Sigma + S$ could be enlarged by the addition of any finite number of other forms of $\Sigma + S$.

We find from (2), by differentiation,*

(4) $$gP^{g-1}P'Q^g + gP^gQ^{g-1}Q' \equiv 0.$$

Multiplying (4) by Q/g, we have

(5) $$P^{g-1}P'Q^{g+1} \equiv 0.$$

If $g=1$, we have (3). If $g>1$, we differentiate (5) and multiply through by $P'Q$. We find (3) to hold for $g=2$. We continue to higher values of g, performing a differentiation and a multiplication by $P'Q$ at each step.

Let us suppose now that there exist infinite systems without bases. Let Σ be such a system whose first forms are as low as possible. We obtain Ω and Λ as above. By Hilbert's theorem, Λ has a basis. If this basis is taken so as to include A, the set of corresponding forms in Λ is easily seen to be a basis of Λ.

We say now that $\Sigma+S$ has no basis. Let this be false. Let (1) with the M_i in Σ, be a basis for Λ, and let us assume, as we evidently may, that $S, M_1, \cdots, M_r$ is a basis for $\Sigma+S$. Let K be any form in Σ. Then, for some g, we have

(6) $$K^g = LS + PM_1 + \cdots,$$

where the unwritten terms involve derivatives of S, or the M_i or their derivatives. Taking a positive integer t, we consider the expression for K^{tg} obtained from (6). If t is large, every term in this expression which is free of the M_i and their derivatives will involve S, or one of its derivatives appearing in (6), to a high power. Let S_j be any derivative of S which appears in (6). Because (1) is a basis for Λ, some power of SK is linear in the forms of (1) and their derivatives. By the lemma proved above, some power of S_jK is linear in the forms of (1) and their derivatives. Thus, if we take the expression for K^{tg} with t large and multiply it by an appropriate power of K, we shall secure a linear combination of the M_i and their derivatives. Then $M_1, \cdots, M_r$ is a basis of Σ. Thus $\Sigma+S$ has no basis, an absurdity which implies the truth of Theorem I for the case of one unknown.

The decomposition theorem

8. We deal with systems of forms in the n unknowns $y_1, \cdots, y_n$. Given two systems, Σ_1 and Σ_2, we shall say that Σ_1 *holds* Σ_2 if every solution of Σ_2 is a solution of Σ_1. A system Σ will be said to be equivalent to a finite set of systems, $\Sigma_1, \cdots, \Sigma_r$, if Σ holds each Σ_i and if every solution of Σ is a solution of some Σ_i.

A system Σ will be called *reducible* if there exist two forms G and H such that GH holds Σ while neither G nor H does. A system which is not reducible will be called *irreducible*. We now state the fundamental theorem:

---

* All congruences are with respect to $C_1, \cdots, C_r$.

THEOREM III. *Every system Σ is equivalent to a finite set of irreducible systems.*

Let a system Σ which contradicts our statement exist. Then Σ is reducible. Let $G_1 H_1$ hold Σ, while neither G_1 nor H_1 does. Σ is equivalent to the set $\Sigma + G_1$, $\Sigma + H_1$. Thus, one of the latter systems must lack the property of being equivalent to a finite set of irreducible systems. Let $\Sigma + G_1$ not have the property. We find now a G_2, which does not hold $\Sigma + G_1$, such that $\Sigma + G_1 + G_2$ does not have the mentioned property. We continue, finding a G_n for every n. We shall show that the system

$$(7) \qquad\qquad \Sigma + G_1 + G_2 + \cdots + G_n + \cdots$$

is incomplete. Let Φ be any finite subsystem of (7). For some n, Φ is contained in $\Sigma + G_1 + \cdots + G_n$; Φ thus holds the latter system. Hence G_{n+1} does not hold Φ. The incompleteness of (7) proves our theorem.

The pattern of the work in the present section is identical with that which Emmy Noether used in constructing her well known theory of ideals. The chief component of the pattern is a basis theorem. Actually, the idea of employing a basis theorem was derived by us from an earlier source, namely, from Drach's dissertation of 1898.* On the other hand, Raudenbush, in developing his theory of ideals which will be discussed below, was greatly influenced by Emmy Noether's work.

9. The decomposition of Σ into irreducible systems is unique in the following sense. From any finite set of systems to which Σ is equivalent, we can, by suppressing systems, obtain a set of systems, equivalent to Σ, in which no system holds any other. Now let Σ be equivalent to the set of irreducible systems $\Sigma_1, \cdots, \Sigma_r$, in which Σ_i does not hold Σ_j if $j \neq i$. If $\Omega_1, \cdots, \Omega_s$ is a second decomposition of Σ into irreducible systems none of which holds any other, then $r = s$ and each Σ_i is equivalent to some Ω_j. We omit the proof, which is perfectly simple.

10. We call the manifold of an irreducible system an *irreducible manifold*. Thus, *the manifold of a system of differential polynomials is composed of a finite number of irreducible manifolds.*

The analogy of this result to the fundamental theorem for algebraic manifolds is clear. However, differences between the two theories arise early. For instance, the manifold of an irreducible algebraic polynomial is an irreducible algebraic manifold. On the other hand, the manifold of an algebraically irreducible differential polynomial may easily be reducible. Let us consider, for instance, the equation

$$(8) \qquad\qquad y_1^2 - 4y = 0$$

in the single unknown y. Differentiating (8), we find

---

* Drach [2, pp. 292–296]. At other places in our work, we were guided by the literature inspired by Emmy Noether, especially by the writings of van der Waerden. This can be seen in Ritt [14].

$$2y_1(y_2 - 2) = 0.$$

The manifold of (8) is given by $y = (x+c)^2$, c constant. The form $y_2 - 2$ is annulled by the solutions $(x+c)^2$, but not by $y=0$. The form y_1 is annulled by $y=0$, but by no other solution of (8). Thus $y_1^2 - 4y$, which cannot be factored in any domain of rationality, is a reducible system. It is equivalent to a set of two irreducible systems, the first system composed of $y_1^2 - 4y$ and $y_2 - 2$, the second system composed of $y_1^2 - 4y$ and y_1.

11. Examples of algebraically irreducible differential polynomials which constitute reducible systems are plentiful in the first chapters of the formal theory of differential equations. In treating equations of the type

$$(9) \qquad y = f\left(x, \frac{dy}{dx}\right),$$

one differentiates (9) and considers the resulting equation as a differential equation of the first order for the unknown function dy/dx. Often the derived equation permits of a factorization. In many cases, such a factorization implies a reducibility from the point of view of differential equation theory. An illustration of this was seen in §10. As another example, consider the Clairaut equation

$$(10) \qquad y = x\frac{dy}{dx} + \left(\frac{dy}{dx}\right)^2.$$

We find, by differentiation,

$$(11) \qquad \frac{d^2y}{dx^2}\left(x + 2\frac{dy}{dx}\right) = 0.$$

The first factor in (11) is annulled by the non-singular solutions of (10) and the second factor by the singular solution.

What precedes is a sufficient hint of the bearing of the reducibility notion on the theory of singular solutions. We shall have more to say on this question later.

12. The simple examples treated above might lead one to suspect that the decomposition of a finite system of forms into irreducible systems can be effected by differentiating the forms a certain number of times and then performing algebraic operations. This is actually so. Only, no general principle exists at present for deciding how many differentiations of the given forms are necessary before algebraic combinations can be effected which will produce the irreducible systems. Even for a system composed of an algebraically irreducible form in one unknown, this is a complicated problem as soon as the order of the form exceeds unity. The complete treatment of this special case will apparently require a detailed study of the singular solutions of algebraic differential equations.

Theory of ideals

13. Behind the manifold theory which we have just considered, stands Raudenbush's elegant theory of ideals of differential polynomials [10].

A system Σ of forms in $y_1, \cdots, y_n$ is called an *ideal* if Σ has the following properties:

(a) If $A_1, \cdots, A_p$ is any finite set of forms of Σ, every linear combination of the A_i, with forms for coefficients, is contained in Σ.

(b) Given any form in Σ, the derivative of the form is contained in Σ.

Condition (a) states that Σ is an ideal in the sense in which such entities are defined in algebra. Condition (b) asks, in addition, that Σ be closed with respect to differentiation. As usual, we are dealing with forms whose coefficients lie in a given field.

An ideal Σ is called *perfect* by Raudenbush if, whenever a form G is such that some positive integral power of G is contained in Σ, G is contained in Σ. An ideal Σ is called *prime* if, for every pair of forms G and H with GH in Σ, at least one of G and H is in Σ.

We may now state the theorem of Raudenbush:

THEOREM IV. *Every perfect ideal of forms in $y_1, \cdots, y_n$ is the intersection of a finite set of prime ideals.*

Let a perfect ideal Σ exist for which our statement does not hold. Let AA', but neither A nor A', be contained in Σ. Let $H_1, \cdots, H_r$ be any basis of Σ. Let G be any form such that, for some g,

$$(12) \qquad\qquad G^g \equiv 0 \qquad\qquad (H_1, \cdots, H_r, A).$$

It is easy to see that the totality Σ_1 of such forms G is a perfect ideal of which Σ is a proper part. Using A' in place of A, we obtain similarly a perfect ideal Σ_1'. We shall now show that Σ is the intersection of Σ_1 and Σ_1'. We have to prove that every form G common to Σ_1 and Σ_1' is in Σ. Considering such a G, let g be such that one has (12) and also

$$(13) \qquad\qquad G^g \equiv 0 \qquad\qquad (H_1, \cdots, H_r, A').$$

We multiply the two expressions for G^g which are indicated by (12) and (13). We secure an expression for G^{2g} in which every term free of the H_i and their derivatives contains some term $A_i A_j'$, where subscripts indicate differentiation. A high power of G^{2g} will contain, in addition to terms involving the H_i or their derivatives, terms in which some $A_i A_j'$ appears to a high power. By the lemma of §7, we have, for t large,

$$G^{2gt} \equiv 0 \qquad\qquad (H_1, \cdots, H_r, AA'),$$

which means that G is in Σ.

This settled, we observe that at least one of Σ_1, Σ_1' is not the intersection of a finite set of prime ideals. Let this be the case for Σ_1. We treat Σ_1

as Σ was treated and continue, forming an infinite sequence of perfect ideals,

$$(14) \qquad\qquad \Sigma, \Sigma_1, \cdots, \Sigma_m, \cdots ,$$

each a proper part of its successor. Let Ω be the logical sum of the ideals (14), and let $H_1, \cdots, H_r$ be a basis of Ω. For some m, Σ_m contains every H_i. Such a Σ_m will contain Ω. This absurdity proves the decomposition theorem.

As to the uniqueness of the representation of Σ, it is easy to prove that Σ is the intersection of prime ideals none of which is contained in any other, and that this representation is unique.

The theorem of Raudenbush is adequate for those phases of the theory of manifolds which exist at present. One may properly hope, however, for a theory which will treat ideals of the most general type.

14. Let us see now, for the case of forms in one unknown y, how Raudenbush applies his ideal theory to the proof of Theorem II of §4. Let G hold the finite system $H_1, \cdots, H_r$, and suppose that no power of G is congruent to 0 for $(H_1, \cdots, H_r)$. We limit ourselves, as we evidently may, to the case in which the H_i are not all zero. The totality Σ of forms J for which a congruence as just described exists is a perfect ideal, and G is not in Σ. Hence, in the representation of Σ as an intersection of prime ideals, there is some prime ideal, call it Σ_1, not containing G. We consider the first forms of Σ_1. They cannot be functions of x, else Σ_1 would contain every form. As Σ_1 is prime, we can evidently find a first form of Σ_1 which is algebraically irreducible. Let A be such a first form of Σ_1, and let S be the separant of A. We shall show that every solution of A which does not annul S is a solution of Σ_1. Let K be any form in Σ_1. Let L be the residue of K with respect to A. Then L is in Σ_1. Now, if A is of order p in y, and if I is the coefficient of the highest power of y_p in A, we have a relation

$$(15) \qquad\qquad I^i L = PA + Q,$$

with Q, which is in Σ_1, lower than A. Thus $Q=0$, so that, because A is algebraically irreducible, and not a factor of I, L is divisible by A. This means that SK holds A, so that every solution of A which does not annul S is a solution of K, and indeed, of Σ_1. Now, because S, which is lower than A, is not in Σ_1, the residue H of G, with respect to A, is not in Σ_1. Hence H is not divisible by A. The form SH, whose order in y does not exceed that of A, is thus not divisible by A. Then SH does not hold A. This means that SG does not hold A. Then certain solutions of A which do not annul S are not solutions of G. Thus G does not hold Σ_1. But Σ holds Σ_1 and Σ is held by $H_1, \cdots, H_r$. This contradiction proves Theorem II for the case of forms in one unknown.

On the basis of Theorem II, we see that, if Σ is a prime ideal, Σ contains every form which holds Σ. The manifold of a prime ideal is therefore irreducible. The theorem on the decomposition of a system of forms into irreducible systems is thus seen to be contained in Raudenbush's ideal theory.

General solutions

15. To arrive at a thorough understanding of the nature of an irreducible manifold, we must acquaint ourselves first with the notion of the *general solution* of a single differential equation. Here we shall find ourselves developing an idea which existed in a rudimentary state in the work of Lagrange.

Let A be a form in the unknowns $y_1, \cdots, y_n$ which is algebraically irreducible; that is, A is not a function of x alone and A is not the product of two forms, with coefficients in the underlying field, neither of which is a function of x alone. Let y_j be an unknown such that A involves effectively either y_j or some derivative of y_j. Let S_j be the partial derivative of A with respect to the highest derivative of y_j (which may be y_j itself) appearing effectively in A. Let

$$(16) \qquad\qquad \Sigma_1, \cdots, \Sigma_s$$

be a decomposition of A into prime ideals none of which contains any other. It can be shown that *there is one and only one of the Σ_i which is not held by S_j*. The Σ_i which is thus determined is the same for every y_j described as above. Let us suppose that it is Σ_1 which is not held by the S_j. We shall call the manifold of Σ_1 *the general solution of A.*

For instance if A is the form $y_1^2 - 4y$ in the single unknown y, which appears in (8), the general solution of A is the set of solutions $(x+c)^2$. The manifold of A contains a second irreducible manifold, composed of the single solution $y = 0$.

We consider two other examples [19, part 2] which involve a single unknown y, the mth derivative of y being denoted by y_m.

Let

$$A = \left[\frac{d}{dx}(y_1^2 - y^3) \right]^2 - (y_1^2 - y^3).$$

In this case, A yields two irreducible manifolds, the general solution and the manifold given by

$$(17) \qquad\qquad y = \frac{4}{(x+c)^2}$$

with c constant. The manifold (17) is the solution of $y_1^2 - y^3$.

Again let

$$F = y(yy_2 + yy_1 - 2y_1)^2 - (y_1 - y)^2,$$

and let A be the algebraically irreducible form defined by

$$yA = y_1 F^2 - \prod_{i=0}^{4}\left(y_1 - y + \frac{y^2}{x+i}\right).$$

Here are the general solution and five other irreducible manifolds, the manifolds being the forms

(18) $$y_1 - y + \frac{y^2}{x+i}, \qquad i = 0, \cdots, 4.$$

The manifold of each form (18) contains the solution $y=0$, which also belongs to the general solution.

16. The phenomenon of the separation of the manifold of a single algebraically irreducible form A into a set of irreducible manifolds, one of which is the general solution of A, is possibly one of the most interesting effects encountered in the general theory which we are discussing. It reveals the great interest possessed by differential polynomials as algebraic entities. As has already been indicated, we have here a radical difference from what is found in the theory of algebraic polynomials, where an irreducible polynomial furnishes a single irreducible manifold. The algebraic structure of differential polynomials is a topic for investigation which may easily prove fruitful. The Newton polygons to which differential polynomials lead should figure prominently in such a study. The algebraic properties of a form become visible in the forms obtained from the given one by successive differentiations.

17. The concept of the general solution appears not to have caught the attention of mathematicians during the era of great progress which followed the appearance of the fundamental existence theorems of Cauchy. There is therefore all the more interest in putting the notion of general solution into a form which shows that some idea of its nature was possessed by Lagrange.

Let us consider again an algebraically irreducible form A and the various S_j associated with it. Let us call a solution of A *singular* if every S_j vanishes for the solution, and *non-singular* if at least one S_j does not vanish for it. The general solution contains all of the non-singular solutions. There arises the question: *Which singular solutions belong to the general solution?* The answer is: *A singular solution belongs to the general solution if and only if every form which vanishes for every non-singular solution vanishes for the singular solution.*

It follows directly from this that a singular solution $\bar{y}_1(x), \cdots, \bar{y}_n(x)$ of A certainly belongs to the general solution if the singular solution can be approximated uniformly in some area, with arbitrary closeness, by non-singular solutions. For instance, the non-singular solutions of

$$\left(\frac{dy}{dx}\right)^2 - y^3 = 0$$

are given by $y = 4(x+c)^{-2}$. Thus, the singular solution $y = 0$, which is approached uniformly by non-singular solutions, is contained in the general solution.

We turn now to work of Lagrange [6, §13, p. 25] published in 1774. Lagrange considers a differential equation (not necessarily algebraic) in the unknown y,

$$(19) \qquad\qquad V\left(x,\ y,\ \frac{dy}{dx}\right) = 0,$$

and a one-parameter family of solutions $y = f(x,\ a)$ which is supposed to have been determined for (19). Such a one-parameter family he calls the *complete integral* of (19). Referring to any special solution $y(x)$ of (19), he formulates conditions under which $y(x)$ will satisfy not only (19), but also "*à toutes les équations des ordres ultérieurs qui en seraient derivées.*"

The satisfaction by $y(x)$ of "all equations of higher orders" derived from (19) is offered, more or less, as a basis for considering $y(x)$ to be contained in the "complete integral."

The idea of "derived equation of higher order" is not made precise. It seems that one is expected to secure the derived equations from (19) by differentiations and eliminations. To secure precision, one would have to specify the nature of V in (19). One might, for instance, take V as an algebraically irreducible form. The derived equations might then be defined as those algebraic differential equations which are satisfied by all non-singular solutions of (19). A definition in algebraic terms would require the general theory which is the subject of the present article. One would be led to take all equations $U = 0$ where U is a form such that, S being the separant of A, some power of SU is linear in V and its derivatives, with forms for coefficients.

We thus see the concept of general solution, as presented here, taking form in Lagrange's work. The notion of irreducible manifold is missing, but there is present the idea of singular solutions which have the formal properties of the totality of non-singular solutions.

18. The remark made above on singular solutions which can be approximated uniformly by non-singular solutions suggests the investigation of the manner in which a singular solution which is contained in the general solution can be approximated by non-singular solutions. An answer to this question, useful for many purposes, is given by the following theorem [14, p. 101; 20, part 4]:

Let A be an algebraically irreducible form in $y_1, \cdots, y_n$. For a singular solution $\bar{y}_1, \cdots, \bar{y}_n$ of A to belong to the general solution of A, it is necessary and sufficient that there exist a value a of x, at which the $\bar{y}_i$ are analytic, such that, given any $\epsilon > 0$ and any positive integer m, A has a non-singular solution $\tilde{y}_1, \cdots, \tilde{y}_n$, analytic at a, such that, for $i = 1, \cdots, n$, each of the first $m+1$ coefficients in the Taylor expansion at a of $\tilde{y}_i - \bar{y}_i$ is less than ϵ in modulus.

The existence of a single point a as above is shown to imply the existence of a set of such points which is dense in the area in which the $\bar{y}_i$ are analytic. Strodt has shown that if there are points at which the $\bar{y}_i$ cannot be approximated by $\bar{y}_i$ as above, those points are either finite in number or countably infinite [23].

Whether the $\bar{y}_i$ of a singular solution in the general solution can always be approximated uniformly in some area by non-singular $\bar{y}_i$ is not known at present. It is known that the $\bar{y}_i$ may fail to be analytically embedded in a one-parameter family of $\bar{y}_i$ [20, part 4].

CLASSIFICATION OF SINGULAR SOLUTIONS

19. What precedes is enough to show the importance of the manifold theory for the study of the singular solutions of a differential equation in a single unknown function. A number of the early continental analysts, notably Euler, Lagrange, Laplace, and Poisson, undertook the study of such singular solutions. They succeeded, by heuristic methods, in revealing certain interesting situations, but rigorous results, giving a complete description of the phenomena involved, were beyond their reach. Let us say at once that, for equations of the first order, quite a good insight can be obtained into the nature of the singular solutions without the manifold theory. The older analysts secured a complete heuristic survey of the situation and a rigorous theory was supplied by Hamburger [4] in 1893. It is chiefly with equations of orders higher than the first that we shall be occupied here. We shall give an account of our principal results and shall compare them with the older work.

20. Let Σ be an irreducible system of forms in the single unknown y. Let us assume that Σ has solutions and contains at least one non-zero form. It is easy to show that the manifold of Σ is the general solution of an algebraically irreducible form.

On this basis, if A is an algebraically irreducible form in y, the manifold of A is composed of the general solutions of the forms of a certain finite set. As a first problem in the study of the singular solutions of A, one might propose the problem of determining a set of forms whose general solutions make up the manifold of A. There may be singular solutions which are contained in more than one of these general solutions. One would thus suggest as a second problem the determination, for any given singular solution of A, of those general solutions to which that singular solution belongs.

For the form A, one can obtain, by processes of elimination, a set of algebraically irreducible forms $B_1, \cdots, B_p$ whose general solutions make up the manifold of A [14, chap. 5]. It then becomes a matter of determining, for a given B_i, whether or not its general solution is an *essential* irreducible manifold in the manifold of A. By an *essential* irreducible manifold, we mean one which is not a proper part of some other irreducible manifold in the manifold of A.

This determination can be made with the help of a finite number of rational operations and differentiations [18, part 1]. In the special and interesting case of a B_i equal to y, a simple statement is possible. It is to the following effect. *Let A be an algebraically irreducible form in y, of order n in y. Let A vanish for $y=0$. For $y=0$ to be an essential irreducible manifold in the manifold of A, it is necessary and sufficient that A, considered as a polynomial in y, y_1, $\cdots$, y_n, contain a term in y alone, that is, a term free of y_1, $\cdots$, y_n, which is of lower degree than every other term of A.*

Thus, $y=0$ is an essential manifold for $y_1 y_2 - y$ but not for $y y_3 - y_2$ or for $y_2 y_3 - y^2$.

The problem of determining those irreducible manifolds to which a given singular solution of A belongs, has been solved for forms A of the second order in y [19, part 2]. In this problem, the following special question turns out to be of particular moment. *Let A, an algebraically irreducible form of the second order, vanish for $y=0$. It is required to determine whether $y=0$ belongs to the general solution of A.* This question can always be answered after there are performed a finite number of operations in which one examines certain polygons, of the Newton type, associated with A.

21. In a paper published in 1772, Laplace [7] considered a differential equation in y, of any order n. Laplace uses the term *general integral* to designate, apparently, a family of functions, satisfying the equation, which depends on n arbitrary constants. By a *solution* of the given equation, he understands an equation of order lower than n which "satisfies" the given equation. The precise meaning of "satisfy" is not given; nothing is said, for instance, in regard to the singular solutions of the second equation. A *particular integral* is a solution "contained in" the general integral and a *particular solution* is a solution which is not so contained. Laplace sets the following two problems:

Being given a differential equation of any order
(1) to determine whether an equation of lower order which satisfies it is contained or not contained in the general integral;
(2) to determine all of the particular solutions of the given equation.

Most of Laplace's work deals with his problem (2), which is a vague and incomplete formulation of the question, raised in §20, of determining whether the general solution of a B_i is essential. Laplace seeks to give a meaning to the concept, mentioned above, of particular integral. The point of view which he takes seems to be clear if one confines oneself to some simple examples, suitably chosen, but his ideas are far from being precise enough for the purposes of a general theory. His definition of particular integral suggests, in a distant way, the condition given in §18 for a singular solution to belong to the general solution.

What is possibly most interesting, in Laplace's paper, is a discussion of equations of the second order in which he treats "particular solutions without differences." [7, §9] The counterparts of these, in the theory of manifolds, are essential irreducible manifolds composed of one solution. Having regard to this relationship, one may attribute to Laplace the heuristic discovery of portions of the theorem of §20 which deals with the case of $B_i = y$. An example treated by Laplace suggests somewhat that his faith in his theoretical speculations was derived from calculations (not contained in his paper), which for that example, and for similar ones, would reveal reducibility in the sense in which we have been using that term.

Fragmentary as Laplace's work on this subject may be, one can see that he had derived, from a study of examples, the principle that the solutions of a differential equation separate into coherent families.

22. A paper by Poisson [8] in 1806 treats, in a somewhat different manner, the questions Laplace raised. Poisson's method is most easily understood from his discussion of Laplace's "particular solutions without differences," which Poisson calls "algebraic particular solutions." [8, §3]

Poisson considers that it is proper to call a solution $y(x)$ of a differential equation of any order an "algebraic particular solution" if and only if the equation does not have a one-parameter family of solutions $y(x) + \alpha z$, with α an arbitrary constant and z a function of x and α. More or less, an algebraic particular solution is, for Poisson, one which cannot be analytically embedded in a one-parameter family of solutions. With this definition, Poisson is able to state, for certain classes of equations, necessary and sufficient conditions for a given solution to be an algebraic particular solution. The results of Poisson, like those of Laplace, may be regarded as heuristic equivalents of portions of the theorem of §20. For instance, Poisson concludes that $y = 0$ is a particular solution of

$$\left(\frac{dy}{dx}\right)^m \frac{d^2y}{dx^2} = y^n$$

if and only if $m \geq n$. Actually, Poisson might have applied his method to perfectly general algebraic differential equations; his failure to do so would indicate that polynomials in several variables did not enjoy, in his day, the docility which is attributed to them now.

Poisson's ingenious formal work neglects convergence questions. His definition of "algebraic particular solution" is partially validated by the theory of manifolds. If a solution $\bar{y}$ of a form A is not an essential irreducible manifold, A is satisfied formally by a series

$$y = \bar{y} + \alpha\phi_1 + \alpha^2\phi_2 + \cdots$$

with α an arbitrary constant and the ϕ_i analytic functions of x. However, the series may diverge for every α distinct from 0.

One of Poisson's enunciations is even heuristically unsound [8, p. 89, lines 21–24]. It is a question of judging whether a solution of an equation of the second order is embedded in a one-parameter family or in a two-parameter family. Poisson's criterion would require one to conclude, for instance, that $y=0$ does not belong to the general solution (as defined here) of

$$\left(\frac{d^2y}{dx^2}\right)^2 + \frac{dy}{dx} + y = 0.$$

Actually, $y=0$ is so contained. The difficulty arises out of the stipulation which Poisson makes for the manner in which a given solution is to be embedded among other solutions. This stipulation is too strong for a sound description of phenomena, even on a heuristic basis.

One may conclude, from the work of Lagrange, Laplace and Poisson, that they had sensed the existence of such an algebraic theory of differential equations as we have been discussing. If they did not develop that theory, it was because a great drift in algebra and in analysis had to be awaited before the question became susceptible to treatment.

IRREDUCIBLE MANIFOLDS

23. The totality of sets of n analytic functions $y_1, \cdots, y_n$ is an irreducible manifold, the manifold of the form zero. Every other irreducible manifold in $y_1, \cdots, y_n$ may be considered as a birational map of the general solution of some form in n or fewer unknowns. This fact, which epitomizes the theory of irreducible manifolds, will now be discussed.

24. We shall say that a prime ideal Σ in $y_1, \cdots, y_n$ is *non-trivial* if Σ contains a form distinct from 0 and if Σ does not contain every form. Let Σ be a non-trivial prime ideal. It may be that, for every i from 1 to n, Σ contains a non-zero form involving only y_i. Let us suppose that this is not so. Let y_j be some unknown such that Σ has no non-zero form in y_j alone. We designate y_j by u_1. There may exist an unknown distinct from u_1 such that Σ contains no non-zero form involving only that unknown and u_1. If such unknowns distinct from u_1 exist, we choose any one of them and call it u_2. Continuing, we find a set $u_1, \cdots, u_q$, with $q < n$, such that Σ contains no non-zero form in the u_i alone, but contains, for every other unknown y_j, a non-zero form involving only y_j and the u_i. We now let $p = n - q$, and, changing the notation if necessary, designate the unknowns distinct from the u_i by $y_1, \cdots, y_p$. The unknowns $u_1, \cdots, u_q$ will be called *a set of arbitrary unknowns for* Σ.

The u_i are "arbitrary" in the following sense. One can take the u_i as any set of q analytic functions which does not annul a certain form, depending on Σ, which involves only the u_i. A set of differential equations then determines $y_1, \cdots, y_p$ in succession, to within arbitrary constants, so as to furnish a solution of Σ.

The integer q does not depend on the manner in which the u_i are selected. Σ may have many distinct sets of arbitrary unknowns, but all of the sets will contain the same number of unknowns.

25. We assume, as may be done without loss of generality, that the field underlying our work does not consist purely of constants. It is then possible to form a rational combination w of the* u_{ij} and y_{ij}, such that the system of equations obtained by equating the forms in Σ to zero determines each y_i, $(i=1, \cdots, p)$, as a rational combination of w, $u_1, \cdots, u_q$ and their derivatives of various orders. The coefficients in all of the rational combinations mentioned are functions of x in the underlying field.

Let us make clearer the nature of the birational relations just described. The expression for w is of the type Q/P, where P and Q are forms in the u_i and y_i. Let us now consider the system Λ of forms, in the $n+1$ letters u_i, y_i, and w, composed of Σ and of $Pw-Q$. We are now considering w as a new unknown, rather than as the rational combination mentioned above. Let Ω be the totality of forms, in the letters of Λ, which vanish for those solutions of Λ for which $P \neq 0$. It is easy to prove that Ω is a prime ideal. For every i from 1 to p, Ω will contain a form $R_i y_i + T_i$, where R and T involve only the u_i and w. This is the sense in which the birational relations exist.

Ω contains an algebraically irreducible form in w and the u_i alone, which is unique if one makes abstraction of multiplication by a function of x. Let A be such a form in Ω. We call the equation $A = 0$ a *resolvent* of Σ.

Given any solution

$$\bar{u}_1, \cdots, \bar{u}_q; \bar{y}_1, \cdots, \bar{y}_p; \bar{w}$$

of Ω, $\bar{u}_1, \cdots, \bar{u}_q; \bar{w}$ belongs to the general solution of A considered as a form in the u_i and w. This permits the manifold of Σ to be considered as a birational image of the general solution of A.

We have spoken as if the u_i exist. With a proper suppression of details, the discussion applies to the case where there are no u_i.

The rational combination for w may be chosen with great freedom. A prime ideal thus has many resolvents. It is a noteworthy fact, however, that the order, with respect to w, of the resolvent, that is, the order of the highest derivative of w present in A, depends only on Σ and on $u_1, \cdots, u_q$—not on the particular way in which w is formed.

26. The order of the resolvent in w is a measure of the number of arbitrary constants upon which the manifold of Σ depends after the arbitrary unknowns are selected.

We may thus consider the dimensionality of an irreducible manifold

---

* As in §3, the second subscript denotes differentiation.

to be measured by two numbers, the number q of arbitrary unknowns and the order h in w of the resolvent. The number q is unique for a given irreducible manifold, while h depends on the particular choice of the arbitrary unknowns.

27. In connection with the dimensionality of irreducible manifolds, Gourin [3] has obtained a theorem which parallels the theorem of algebraic geometry stating that if $\mathfrak{M}$ and $\mathfrak{N}$ are irreducible algebraic manifolds with $\mathfrak{N}$ a proper part of $\mathfrak{M}$, the dimensionality of $\mathfrak{M}$ exceeds that of $\mathfrak{N}$. Gourin's theorem is as follows. *Let Σ_1 and Σ_2 be non-trivial prime systems with the manifold of Σ_2 a proper part of that of Σ_1. Let $u_1, \cdots, u_q$ be a set of arbitrary unknowns for Σ_2. Then either Σ_1 has a set of arbitrary unknowns of which $u_1, \cdots, u_q$ is a proper subset, or $u_1, \cdots, u_q$ is a set of arbitrary unknowns for Σ_1 and the order in w of the resolvent of Σ_1, for $u_1, \cdots, u_q$, exceeds the corresponding order for Σ_2.*

Further work on the dimensionality of manifolds will be found in [16], [17], and [19].

With this we close our discussion. We have sought to point out some directions in which advances may be made. A study of the publications listed in the bibliography will reveal many others.

BIBLIOGRAPHY

1. DOOB, J. L., and RITT, J. F. *Systems of algebraic difference equations.* American Journal of Mathematics, vol. 55 (1933), pp. 505–514.

2. DRACH, J. *Essai sur la théorie générale de l'intégration et sur la classification des transcendantes.* Annales de l'École Normale Supérieure, (3), vol. 15 (1898), pp. 245–384.

3. GOURIN, E. *On irreducible systems of algebraic differential equations.* Bulletin of the American Mathematical Society, vol. 39 (1933), pp. 593–595.

4. HAMBURGER, M. *Ueber die singulären Lösungen der algebraischen Differenzialgleichungen erster Ordnung.* Journal für die reine und angewandte Mathematik, vol. 112 (1893), pp. 205–246.

5. HERZOG, F. *Systems of algebraic mixed difference equations.* Transactions of the American Mathematical Society, vol. 37 (1935), pp. 286–300.

6. LAGRANGE, J. L. *Sur les solutions particulières des équations différentielles.* Oeuvres Complètes, vol. 4, pp. 5–108.

7. LAPLACE, P. S. *Mémoire sur les solutions particulières des équations différentielles et sur les inégalités séculaires des planètes.* Oeuvres Complètes, vol. 8, pp. 326–365.

8. POISSON, S. D. *Mémoire sur les solutions particulières des équations différentielles et des équations aux différences.* Journal de l'École Polytechnique, vol. 6, no. 13 (1806), pp. 60–125.

9. RAUDENBUSH, H. W. *Differential fields and ideals of differential forms.* Annals of Mathematics, (2), vol. 34 (1933), pp. 509–517.

10. RAUDENBUSH, H. W. *Ideal theory and algebraic differential equations.* Transactions of the American Mathematical Society, vol. 36 (1934), pp. 361–368.

11. RAUDENBUSH, H. W. *Hypertranscendental extensions of partial differential fields.* Bulletin of the American Mathematical Society, vol. 40 (1934), pp. 714–720.

12. RAUDENBUSH, H. W. *On the analog for differential equations of the Hilbert-Netto theorem.* Bulletin of the American Mathematical Society, vol. 42 (1936), pp. 371–373.

13. RITT, J. F. *Manifolds of functions defined by systems of algebraic differential equations.* Transactions of the American Mathematical Society, vol. 32 (1930), pp. 369–398.

14. RITT, J. F. *Differential Equations from the Algebraic Standpoint.* American Mathematical Society Colloquium Publications, vol. 14. New York, 1932.

15. RITT, J. F. *Algebraic difference equations.* Bulletin of the American Mathematical Society, vol. 40 (1934), pp. 303–308.

16. RITT, J. F. *Systems of algebraic differential equations.* Annals of Mathematics, (2), vol. 36 (1935), pp. 293–302.

17. RITT, J. F. *Jacobi's problem on the order of a system of differential equations.* Annals of Mathematics, (2), vol. 36 (1935), pp. 303–312.

18. RITT, J. F. *Indeterminate expressions involving an analytic function and its derivatives.* Monatshefte für Mathematik, vol. 43 (1936), pp. 97–104.

19. RITT, J. F. *On the singular solutions of algebraic differential equations.* Annals of Mathematics, (2), vol. 37 (1936), pp. 552–617.

20. RITT, J. F. *On certain points in the theory of algebraic differential equations.* American Journal of Mathematics, vol. 60 (1938), pp. 1–43.

21. RITT, J. F. *Systems of differential equations.* I. *Theory of ideals.* American Journal of Mathematics, vol. 60 (1938), pp. 535–548.

22. STRODT, W. C. *Systems of algebraic partial difference equations.* Unpublished master's essay. Columbia University, 1937.

23. STRODT, W. C. *Sequences of irreducible systems of algebraic differential equations.* To appear in the Transactions of the American Mathematical Society (1939).

COLUMBIA UNIVERSITY,
NEW YORK, N. Y.

THE HISTORICAL BACKGROUND OF
HARMONIC ANALYSIS

BY

NORBERT WIENER

This address deals with certain aspects of the theory of Fourier series and integrals during the nineteenth century. The subject of Fourier series has been a central one both in the region of pure mathematical analysis and in mathematical physics. It is just because this subject faces two ways that its history is of especial interest. At each period in the history of mathematics, the relation between mathematics and physics has been viewed from an aspect somewhat peculiar to the period; and in tracing the history of this subject, we shall have in miniature a history of the larger relations between the two disciplines.

The first beginnings of Fourier series theory may be regarded as very ancient, for the musical theories of Pythagoras have already in them elements which later investigation has shown to be of trigonometric nature. The whole classical theory of cycles and epicycles as found in Ptolemaic astronomy is also something which a modern point of view would interpret as harmonic analysis. These two motives, that of the acoustical-optical wave theory, and that of astronomical and geophysical periodicities, united by Plato in the music of the spheres, have ever since furnished the chief stimuli of the natural sciences to the study of harmonic analysis. The motions of the planets, the tides, and the irregular recurrences of the weather, with their hidden periodicities, form a counterpart to the vibrating string and the phenomena of light.

However, it is probably a mere picturesque feat of the imagination to push harmonic analysis further back than Huygens. In Huygens' principle, which by the way was not correctly used by Huygens himself, we resolve a wave front into a set of centers of instantaneous disturbances, and by continuing these disturbances over a small interval of time we are in some way able to determine the new wave front.

While we can not extract from Huygens the Huygens principle in rigorous modern form, we at least find in his work a preoccupation with phenomena continuous over space and with their transportation from point to point by a process of expansion. It is not fanciful to see an extension of this point of view in the philosophy of Leibniz, who is under a heavy intellectual debt to Huygens, here and elsewhere. Leibniz regards space as a plenum, and considers that disturbances are transported from one region to another by a point to point transfer of energy, and not by an actual action at a distance.

The tool for the discussion of such plena was also formulated by Leibniz, and is the differential calculus. It was indeed the Leibnizian school, rather than Leibniz himself, which developed the theory of partial differential equations, or, as we should put it in the jargon of the present day, field theory. In this we must mention above all other names those of the Bernoulli family and of Euler. It is with Clairaut, d'Alembert, and Daniel Bernoulli that trigonometric expansions in the strict sense first come into prominence. Clairaut introduced them in the astronomical theory of the perturbing function, but their most famous application lies elsewhere. Among the simplest of partial differential equations is that of the vibrating string. It is one-dimensional and conserves energy, and it was observed by d'Alembert and Euler to possess a solution in the form of the pulse moving with a certain fixed velocity either to the right or to the left. This holds for the infinite string; in the case of the finite string the fastening at the ends serves to reflect an arriving pulse either with or without reversal of phase according to the nature of the constraint, and send it back along the line to meet and cross a similar pulse reflected from the other end. The solution of the string problem, given the initial displacement in velocity, is thus possible by means of extraordinary simplicity.

Besides the wave solution of the problem of the vibrating string, it was early seen that another solution of what may be called a vibration type is possible. Instead of looking for solutions whose geometrical character remains unchanged by bodily motion along the string, we look for solutions which remain unchanged except in scale by the passage of time. These represent what are called stationary vibrations of the string. Their analytic representation is that of a function of position alone multiplied by a function of time alone. Both functions are trigonometric in character. It will be found that neither the one nor the other is completely arbitrary, but on the other hand, that each one can assume only one of a discrete set of admissible frequencies, the so-called characteristic frequencies of the string.

The problem thus arises of synthesizing a solution of general type from these particular solutions. As the differential equation is linear, the natural means of synthesis is addition. It was realized very early—by Daniel Bernoulli, in 1753, for instance, as well as indirectly by d'Alembert—that solutions additively compounded from stationary solutions have a high degree of generality, and that they may be used in many cases interchangeably with the formally simpler wave solutions of the string problem.

However, the precise relations between these two types of solution still stood in need of elucidation. Series developments of particular numbers date well back into the seventeenth century, and the classical series development of a function—the power series of Taylor and Maclaurin—was known to Newton early in the eighteenth century. It was rediscovered about 1715 and soon was added to the repertory of any working mathematician. It is not surprising that certain highly special features of that development were taken as typical for series developments in general. In particular, the coefficients of a Taylor series are all obtained by successive differentiation in the neighborhood of a single point. It is thus a part of the very nature of such an expansion that it can represent only a function which is determined everywhere by its behavior in any single such neighborhood. The ordinary elementary functions of algebra and trigonometry, together with the logarithm and its inverse, the exponential function, are of this type. It was only natural that many mathematicians should expect that the series of stationary vibrations arising from the string problem might display a similar property.

On the other hand, the wave solution of the string problem is manifestly not confined to solutions with such a property of analyticity. A disturbance of any form, at least if it is smooth enough to have a slope, may be transported bodily along a string, reflected at the ends, transported back again, and so on; and the motion thus obtained is sufficiently perspicuous to make the verification of the fact that it satisfies the differential equation of the vibrating string a matter of trivial difficulty.

The early days of the Bernoulli vibration solution of the string problem were naturally stormy, even though neither Euler nor d'Alembert fully realized the degree of arbitrariness of the solution of the string problem which they had given, and in particular, did not believe the functions entering into their problem might coincide over one region and differ over another; they were not ready to believe that Bernoulli series could represent a motion of the degree of irregularity which fitted into their own solutions. Obviously no thoroughly satisfactory answer to this dilemma was possible until it was realized just how the coefficients of Bernoulli's trigonometric series depended on the functions represented. Lagrange made an attempt to arrive at this representation by a study of the vibrating string with equal concentrated masses distributed uniformly along it, and then proceeded to the limit as the points became sown more and more thickly. But his limit argument left much to be desired in rigor. The final formal representation of the coefficients of a trigonometric series is due to Fourier and, possibly independently, to Laplace.

Fourier's problem was closely analogous to that of the vibrating string, being, like it, the study of a partial differential equation with given initial conditions, although his equation was that of the flow of heat and was what we would now call of the parabolic type, as opposed to the equation of the string, which is of the hyperbolic type. Fourier represented his initial conditions by a trigonometric series in which the coefficients were given as definite integrals. This same representation of a function was employed by Laplace in connection with the use of the method of generating functions in his theory of probability. The moment this explicit representation was given, it became obvious that the method was formally applicable to a function made up of several discrete and independent pieces with angles or jumps between them. Thus a completely new idea of the nature of a function was originated, and perhaps the greatest step was taken in the theory which is now known as that of the functions of real variables.

We have mentioned that Laplace's study of trigonometric series arises in connection with the theory of generating functions. Generating functions were already known to Euler and applied by him to the theory of partitions and other similar combinatory problems. The basis of this whole theory is the formula which derives the coefficients of the product of two Taylor series from the coefficients of each series taken separately. It will be seen that the product coefficient is the sum of products of the coefficients from the two factor series taken in such a way that the sum of the exponents is fixed. Such a sum is very nearly what is known in modern terminology as the convolution or "Faltung" of the coefficients of the two series. This convolution is merely changed by a relabeling of its terms when one of the series is changed by multiplication by an integral power of a parametric variable. From another point of view, if we translate the coefficients of one series as a whole with respect to the coefficients of the other, we merely introduce a translation of the coefficients of the product series.

If we have a number of independent phenomena which combine additively, the distribution of the quantity representing the combined phenomena is derived by the successive convolution of the distribution functions of the components. This is the reason for introducing generating functions into the theory of probability. These functions represent a vital part of Laplace's contribution to the theory and dominate the theory at the present time, although the variables which we raise to a power in the series are generally now taken to be complex. In the light of this interpretation of the series a statement in a recent edition of the Encyclopedia Britannica, to the effect that Laplace's method of generating functions is obsolete, is not justifiable.

While the method of generating functions can be formulated for real Taylor or Laurent series, the problem of determining the coefficients of such a series is not physically natural enough to make this the most effective way of introducing generating functions. Laplace already knew that generating functions could be treated very effectively in the case in which the parametric variable is of absolute value 1. He was also aware of the advantages of replacing a discrete set of powers of the parametric variable combined in an ordinary sum by a continuum of such values combined in an integral. The so-called Laplace transform and its complex analogue now called the Fourier transform were both known to Laplace as well as to Fourier, who used them in connection with the problem of the conduction of heat in the half-plane, and so on.

Thus, at the very beginning of the theory of Fourier series, ideas belonging to a large number of related fields made their appearance. We have vibration problems, problems for the theory of the conduction of heat, combinatorial and other theory of number problems, and problems of probability. Nevertheless, the orthodox line of development of Fourier series theory went through the work of Fourier and, in so far as it was practically applied, it was chiefly to the boundary-value problems of the theory of partial differential equations as they occur in mathematical physics. Fourier himself, following along lines already laid out by Laplace, studied developments in spherical harmonics and Bessel functions and laid the groundwork for the general theory of orthogonal functions. The immediate followers of Fourier, such as Poisson, Sturm, Liouville, on the one hand, and Hamilton and Dirichlet on the other, partly devoted their efforts to a further exploration of this direction and partly to a more rigorous justification of the formulas which Fourier had attacked in a rough heuristic manner. This was a period when the exuberant fertility of the eighteenth century had already begun to give way to a more critical spirit, and when the influence of Cauchy had led mathematicians to make a much more careful examination of the convergence of their expansions. Thus it was no more than natural that an overwhelming part of the efforts of the students of Fourier series during the last century should have been devoted to questions of convergence.

We have already mentioned Cauchy. Besides his indirect influence on the theory of Fourier series from the point of view of rigor, his study of functions of a complex variable led to a better understanding of the relation between the Taylor series and the differential method of determining its coefficients on the one hand, and the Fourier series and the integral method of determining its coefficients on the other. It was seen that these two theories, widely discrepant as they seem to be when we remain in the real domain, form part of the same theory in the complex plane. The real part of a function of a complex variable is a harmonic function; this fact also led to a study of the relation between Fourier series and harmonic functions. This, it is true, may equally well be studied from the point of view of Fourier himself and the boundary-value problem on the circle. Both of these theories have a definite relation to the work of Poisson.

At the same time that the Fourier series theory was receiving this development either from the point of view of pure mathematics or from that of a rather rigidly formalized branch of applied mathematics in the case of boundary-value problems, other physical problems were familiarizing the physicists with the notion of trigonometric developments in a totally different direction. The old string problem received an enormously broad extension with the increasing popularity of wave theories, both in the domain of sound and in that of optics. This was particularly due to Young and to Fresnel. These theories borrowed much from the older string theory, but in view of the greater number of dimensions to which they applied, went far beyond it. The idea of white light as the additive combination of monochromatic vibrations was, of course, along the same lines as the theory of the Fourier integral, but there seems to be no evidence that any of the earlier writers saw that it demanded far more than had been developed explicitly by Fourier and Laplace.

To this same order of ideas belong questions of coherency and interference, of the different types of polarization, and so on. The astronomical motive in Fourier analysis, which had already appeared in the formal investigations of stability by Laplace, Lagrange, and Poisson, became the foundation of a new lunar theory in the hands of Hill and Brown. In all of this work, one can only wonder at the ability of the physicist working with the crudest of mathematical tools and total lack of rigor, to develop an intuition which, almost without exception, saves him from the apparently inevitable consequences of his mathematical sins.

It is a real tragedy of the mathematics of the nineteenth century that, on the one hand, its physical stimulus was continually schematized, reduced in breadth, thrown into the background, or even forgotten, while on the other the experimental work of the physicists gradually sundered itself from the fertilizing influence of the development of mathematical theory. For a long period the theory of Fourier series tended to contract itself to the scope of a mathematical game whose applications, whatever they might have been, were regarded as of little interest outside of mathematics. On the other hand, the harmonic analysis of the physicist gropingly developed its own technique as if the physicist had believed that the mathematical difficulties of principle had all been swept away somewhere obscurely in the literature by the pure mathematician, and that all he needed to do was to recreate crudely his own working formulas.

Within the limited field which the mathematicians have taken for their own, the first efforts of Poisson, Dirichlet, and their followers were directed to the purpose of finding some field, no matter how limited, in which the theory of the Fourier development could be carried out rigorously. The theory of functions of limited total variation and of uniform convergence are to a large extent by-products of this effort. Dirichlet's conditions represent the first important satisfactory achievement of the sort. The works of Riemann on the unicity of trigonometric developments attach themselves closely to this order of ideas, and foreshadow in certain respects the later theory of summable series.

On the other hand, once Fourier developments had been established on a sound basis in any region, no matter how narrow, mathematicians took upon themselves the problem of delimiting the exact bounds of this region. Inasmuch as the Fourier coefficients are defined by integration, this demanded a reinvestigation and a revision of the notions of measure and integral. It was soon seen that functions much more general than those of limited total variation could be given at least formal Fourier development, and what is much more important, that sets of coefficients much more general than those of functions satisfying the Dirichlet conditions determined, in some sense or other, the Fourier series of well defined functions.

In the course of time these activities led to numerous by-products. Parseval's relation between the sum of the squares of the coefficients of a Fourier series and the integral of the square of the function represented was a powerful stimulus to the investigation of the general question: under what circumstances can a function be determined by an arbitrary set of coefficients such that the sum of their squares converges. Far more recently, Hurwitz also studied this region of ideas. Again, the theory of the summability of series owes much of the interest which it has excited to its Fourier series applications. Here the work of Fejér is to be mentioned as the fountainhead of an important school of research. It became quite clear that the convergence theory, useful as it was in giving rigor to a limited region in Fourier analysis, was quite incapable of delimiting a sharp and well defined region in the theory of such series, and a great deal of Euler's work which had been buried under the wave of rigorism in the time of Cauchy was brought back to the light of day. We must mention Borel as one of the pioneers in this direction, as in so many that have helped to form the modern theory of harmonic analysis.

The ultimate triumph of this movement is to be found in the Riesz-Fischer theorem. Before we come to this theorem in detail, however, it is necessary to go back to the domain of mathematical physics and see what some of the leading ideas of statistical mechanics were in the last half of the nineteenth century. We have already seen the early connection of Fourier analysis and statistical theory in the work of Laplace. This connection is intimate and reappears on several different levels. Besides Laplace's problem of the composition of probabilities, the theory of light brought in the germs of a statistical theory of harmonic analysis itself. No one has ever seen an oscillograph of a ray of visible light. The evidence that this light is of a wave character is and can be only such evidence as is applicable to a statistical assemblage of vibrations, rather than to a single pure vibration. Thus the founders of wave optics were driven despite themselves, to invent a statistical harmonic analysis. Young, Fresnel, Goüy, and Schuster all did important work in this direction, as well as in the related field of partially polarized light. In the hands of Schuster, this range of ideas, together with ideas from meteorology and astronomy, led to the discovery of the periodogram, a theory for which the pure mathematical basis was defective for many decades. It was only in 1924 that a paper by Wiener established the precise connection between this and the rigorous modern theory of the Fourier integral. Another spectrum theory, earlier than that of Wiener and covering radically different aspects of singular distributions, was developed by Hellinger in order to analyze the unitary invariants of Hermitian transformations of Hilbert space.

Besides these two relations between harmonic analysis and statistics, the autonomous development of the theory of statistical mechanics has introduced yet a third, and this the most important. Statistical mechanics had its inception in Maxwell's theory of the distribution of the velocities of the particles in a gas. Its more mature form is due to Gibbs and concerns, instead of the distribution of quantities attached to the different particles of a single system, the distribution of all systems where the laws of force are given and only the initial conditions are allowed to vary. In any case, statistical mechanics makes no assertion about the individual particle or the individual system, but merely about what will happen except for a fraction of the particles or systems, which is so small that in some sense or other it may be neglected. If the Maxwell gas is taken as filling an infinite space, or if the Gibbs ensemble of systems is really taken as complete, these sets of negligible likelihood must be taken as in some sense or other of zero likelihood. We thus need for the complete justification of statistical mechanics a rigorous theory of measure in which sets of zero measure have a legitimate place. It is, of course, clear that a theory of sets of zero measure in rigorous form was not reached in a day. The fundamental assumption of Gibbs, for example, that an ensemble of dynamic systems in some way traces in the course of time a distribution of parameters which is identical with the distribution of parameters of all systems at a given time, was first stated in a form not merely inadequate, but impossible. This is the famous ergodic hypothesis. It is one of the greatest triumphs of recent mathematics in America, or elsewhere, that the correct formulation of the ergodic hypothesis and the proof of the theorem on which it depends have both been found by the elder Birkhoff of Harvard.

However, long before a really adequate formulation of the ergodic hypothesis was found, the notion of "almost all" had become an accepted part of the equipment of every physicist. It was under the influence of ideas belonging to this domain that Poincaré at the end of the last century developed the philosophy of questions in the theory of probability which marked the first really great progress in that theory since the days of Laplace. The ideas of statistical randomness and phenomena of zero probability were current among the physicists and mathematicians in Paris around 1900, and it was in a medium heavily ionized by these ideas that Borel and Lebesgue solved the mathematical problem of measure.

On the mathematical side, the problem of measure was absolutely vital to the foundation of a symmetrical theory of Fourier series. The formulas connecting a function and its Fourier coefficients are so symmetrical that it was early obvious that the problem of determining the coefficients of a function and the problem of determining a function from its coefficients were closely parallel. In any earlier theories of measure and integration, on the other hand, the problem of proceeding to a function from a set of coefficients enjoying some simple and very general property had no natural solution. The question of putting the theory of integration on a broad enough basis to allow a solution of these problems was attacked simultaneously by many mathematicians in many places. Besides Borel and Lebesgue in Paris and W. H. Young in England, we must mention the anticipatory work of Osgood and Pierpont in America which, if it did not lead completely to the goal of the new integration theory, at least did much to point to the direction in which that goal would be found. After the Lebesgue integral had been discovered, Daniell gave it an abstract form independent of dimensionality.

The Lebesgue theory of measure and integration produced an immediate and explosive expansion in the theory of harmonic analysis. The chief result was the Riesz-Fischer theorem, to the effect that there exists a perfect equivalence between the class of Lebesgue measurable functions with Lebesgue integrable square moduli, and the class of functions which can be represented by Fourier series for which the sum of the squares of the moduli of the Fourier coefficients converges. It is this theory which gives the motivation of the infinitely-many dimensional space of Hilbert. To this realm of ideas belong Weyl's lemma, to the effect that a sequence of functions of this class converging in the mean converges in the mean to a limit defined almost everywhere, and the Plancherel theorem as to the existence of Fourier transforms for an analogous class.

Both in the case of Fourier series and in that of the Fourier integral, there is an L^p theory analogous to the L^2 theory but less perfect. Here the chief names are Hölder, Hausdorff, Minkowski, Titchmarsh, and Paley.

Another block of related theorems includes the Lebesgue theorem that an integrable function is almost everywhere the derivative of its integral, and Lebesgue's other theorem that the Fourier series of an integrable function is almost everywhere Cesàro summable of the first order to the function. The whole theory of the convergence and summability of Fourier series was recast by a group of mathematicians working largely in England, among whom must be mentioned W. H. Young, Hobson, Hardy, Littlewood, and Chapman, together with the brothers Riesz, Szász, and Zygmund on the continent. The theory of summability in connection with trigonometric series, while anticipated by Abel and Poisson, was first consciously employed by Riemann. The study of convergence factors and exponents of convergence for Fourier series and even for general orthogonal series developed a literature of its own, particularly in the hands of the Polish school. Although no natural necessary and sufficient condition for the convergence of a Fourier series was forthcoming, such a condition was found by Hardy and Littlewood for summability of unspecified order.

It is impossible to follow the classical theory of Fourier series into all its ramifications, nor is it any easier to do so with the related theory of the Lebesgue integral. This latter theory, it is important to note, soon established relations with allied statistical theories. The work of Einstein and Smoluchowski on the Brownian motion had led in 1909 to the important investigations of Perrin in Paris, and it was not long before he was consulting his colleague Borel on the matter. Besides his work on measure, Borel was known for his investigations in the theory of probability, and was in close touch with the ideas of Poincaré. Perrin had noticed that the paths of particles subjected to the Brownian motion were suggestive of the non-differentiable continuous curves of Weierstrass. It is perhaps not too far-fetched to see in this suggestion a strong reinforcement of the motives which led Borel to apply the methods of the theory of probability—that is, of measure—to analytical problems. This is his theory of "probabilités denombrables," later studied by Steinhaus, Rademacher, Wiener, and others. In the hands of Paley and Zygmund, it became the nucleus of a fertile method for the devising of Gegenbeispiele in the theory of Fourier series. Wintner, first by himself and then in collaboration with Jessen, developed a parallel theory which yielded much information on the distribution of the values of the Riemann zeta function and other related functions. The Wiener theory of differential space is a direct development of the mathematical ideas behind the theory of the Brownian motion. It has led to a very general theory of continuous randomness, and is related to the work of Khintchine and Kolmogoroff, and to the theories of stochastic processes developed by these authors, Cramér, Lévy, and others. Through the work of Cramér, ideas of this order have been introduced into certain generalizations of number theory. Lastly, it now seems likely that a systematic study of such notions may lead to a really constructive systematization of the study of random ensembles in statistical mechanics, as, for example, in the theory of turbulence or in that of the statistical mechanics of liquids.

Besides the classical theories of Fourier series and integrals, a number of investigations have been made of trigonometric developments not falling strictly under either of these heads. Non-harmonic Fourier series are at least as old as Fourier, and the Dirichlet series of the student of analytic number theory give rise to trigonometric series, where the frequencies do not form an arithmetic progression. It was these number-theoretic series on the one hand, and the dynamical nonharmonic Fourier series of Bohl, on the other, which led Harold Bohr, in the early twenties, to formulate the notion of the almost periodic function. His original papers became the nucleus for a considerable literature. Bohr's fundamental theorems, to the effect that the Parseval theorem holds in a certain "mean" form for almost periodic functions, and that these functions are precisely those which admit a uniform approximation by trigonometric polynomials, were proved in widely different ways by Weyl, de la Vallée Poussin, and Wiener. The theory of Wiener was sufficiently general in scope to cover periodograms and the theory of white light. The class of almost periodic functions was generalized by Stepanoff, Weyl, Besicovitch, and Wiener. The definition of almost periodic functions was recast by Bochner into the form, "the class of all continuous functions, such that among any infinite sequence of translations of one of them, a uniformly convergent subset can be chosen." Bohr himself studied almost periodic functions in the complex domain, and was followed by Jessen, Favard, and Cameron in the investigation of the distribution of the values of an analytic almost periodic function in strips.

The more general question of the harmonic analysis of the orbits of particles in a dynamical system owes much to the work of Birkhoff. Birkhoff's work represents an essential refinement of the ideas of Poincaré on Poisson stability. Here we must mention the related physical theory of adiabatic invariants, as developed by Ehrenfest and Levi-Civita. Birkhoff's ergodic theory furnishes the necessary *point d'appui* of Wiener's generalized harmonic analysis. Indeed, it was for the purpose of such a harmonic analysis that the ergodic theorem was first applied. A concrete achievement in this direction is the theory of mean planetary motion of Wintner, von Kampen, Weyl, and others. Other forms of generalized harmonic analysis go back to the work of Hahn, and concern themselves with what should now be called the theory of Stieltjes-Fourier transforms being pursued so successfully by Wintner and his collaborators. Other writers who have contributed to the theory of generalized harmonic analysis are Bochner and Berry.

Almost periodic functions are characterized by a certain property of their translations, which is a property invariant under translation. This is related to the fact that the functions e^{iux} are the characteristic functions of the translation group. Harmonic analysis is thus the appropriate tool for the study of linear problems formally invariant under this group. As most physical phenomena are not attached to a fixed origin in time, and as indeed the existence of such an attachment would make it impossible to repeat an experiment, and to develop a consistent physics, harmonic analysis is indicated over a wide domain of practical problems. These group-theoretical aspects of harmonic analysis are foreshadowed in the work of Lagrange and Laplace on ordinary difference and partial differential equations with constant coefficients. The calculus of operations associated with the names of Arbogast and Boole, as well as the work of Heaviside on the electric circuit, represent further developments of this point of view. The example of Heaviside shows how directly it has remained in contact with physical and engineering practice. After Heaviside, obscure and intuitive as he was, an extensive interpretative literature developed, in which the names of Bromwich, Doetsch, Jeffries, and others are to be mentioned. The methods of Heaviside, as well as the alternative approach of Carson, have been pushed into the background by the conscious, explicit use of the Fourier integral, which has been much facilitated by the recent tables of Fourier transforms published by Campbell and Foster, of the Bell Telephone Laboratories.

The considerations which lie back of the operational calculus of Heaviside are clearly of group-theoretical nature, as we have seen. Other groups besides the translation-group possess characteristic functions, and a theory of expansions in terms of these functions. The characteristic functions belonging to the denumerable abelian group, all of whose operators are of period two, are the so-called Walsh functions, and they have as a basis the well known Rademacher functions. The functions of Haar and Franklin, while not characteristic, are closely related. It was a heuristic remark by Paley that the Walsh functions have expansion properties very nearly identical with those of the trigonometric functions, of which they form a good working model. This suggested to Paley and the author the formation of a bridge between the theory of Fourier developments and the theory of group measure of Haar and Pontrjagin. The work of von Neumann on almost periodic functions on groups represents a further development of this line of research, and in particular, the extension to the non-abelian case is an important advance. It has its inspiration in Weyl's approach to the theory of almost periodic functions, and in the earlier work of Hilbert and E. Schmidt.

While the theory of Tauberian theorems is not a Fourier theory in its origins, and while the original method of Hardy and Littlewood has nothing to do with trigonometric considerations, an early use of Tauberian methods was to establish the Poisson approach to Fourier series on a rigorous basis. However, there are other more intimate relations between the Tauberian theorems and harmonic analysis. Many of the most common theorems of Tauberian type or, in other words, inverse theorems concerning limit processes, deal with averages of a function which have a certain sort of invariance with respect to a multiplicative change in scale. The logarithmic transformation reduces this multiplicative change of scale to an additive change, and hence transforms Tauberian problems into a form suitable for the application of the methods of harmonic analysis. I repeat, the base of this application consists in the group-theoretical properties of the multiplication group. The earlier work of Hardy and Littlewood on these problems had no such group-theoretical justification, and it is in a paper of Wiener that a rational basis was found for introducing Fourier methods. Later on the author saw that the key theorem was one concerning the reciprocal of an absolutely convergent Fourier series. With the aid of these methods the solution of Tauberian problems has been reduced to a routine. The author's work was stimulated by the earlier work and personal suggestions of Robert Schmidt. The Toeplitz-Schmidt theory of gestrahlte Mittelbildungen bears the same relation to the author's work that the Laplace integral does to the Fourier transform.

Another closely related piece of work is that of Karamata, which, however, did not have in its inception any Fourier aspect whatever. With the aid of Tauberian theorems the author's pupil Ikehara and he have introduced simplifications into the proof of the prime number theorem, and these simplifications have led to subsequent work by Heilbronn, Landau, and others. This Tauberian work has found direct application in the theory of Fourier series and in other branches of harmonic analysis, and has also been turned by Paley and the author to the study of the behavior of entire functions of exponential type in the complex domain. Here their work joins with that of Pólya, Miss Cartwright, and others, and in its application to the study of gap series, with that of Mandelbrojt. A closely related field of harmonic analysis work is the theory of quasi-analytic functions, where the original introduction of trigonometric methods is due to de la Vallée Poussin, and where Paley, Mandelbrojt, and the author have carried the theory further. The recent very refined work of Levinson develops the theory in all these directions.

It is impossible in the time allotted me to take up all branches of harmonic analysis, and the motives which have played a rôle in forming the theories. The theory of the Laplace integral has been developed by Widder, Doetsch, S. Bernstein, Hille, Tamarkin, and others. In Japan, Izumi and his school have done much noteworthy work. The general theory of Watson transforms is also to be mentioned here. It will be seen that recent work in harmonic analysis is highly international, and that no inconsiderable part of it has been performed in this country.

While the historical facts in any concrete situation rarely point a clear-cut moral, it is worth while noting that the recent fertility of harmonic analysis has followed a refertilization of the field with physical ideas. It is a falsification of the history of mathematics to represent pure mathematics as a self-contained science drawing inspiration from itself alone and morally taking in its own washing. Even the most abstract ideas of the present time have something of a physical history. It is quite a tenable point of view to urge this even in such fields as that of the calculus of assemblages, whose exponents, Cantor and Zermelo, have been deeply interested in problems of statistical mechanics. Not even the influence of this theory on the theory of integration, and indirectly on the theory of Fourier series, is entirely foreign to physics. The somewhat snobbish point of view of the purely abstract mathematician would draw but little support from mathematical history. On the other hand, whenever applied mathematics has been merely a technical employment of methods already traditional and jejune, it has been very poor applied mathematics. The desideratum in mathematical as well as physical work is an attitude which is not indifferent to the extremely instructive nature of actual physical situations, yet which is not dominated by these to the dwarfing and paralyzing of its intellectual originality. Viewed as a whole, the theory of harmonic analysis has a very fine record of this sort. It is not a young theory, but neither is it yet in its dotage. There is much more to be learned and much more to be proved.

Massachusetts Institute of Technology,
    Cambridge, Mass.

RECENT DEVELOPMENTS IN THE CALCULUS OF VARIATIONS

BY

E. J. McSHANE

1. Since the somewhat indeterminate title of this lecture may have led someone to expect a complete history of the progress of the calculus of variations in the past half-century, I hasten to disclaim any such ambitious intention. My more modest aim is to present, in a manner which I hope will be intelligible to those of us whose chief interest does not lie in this field, a sketch of some of the most significant developments in the past twenty-five years. Moreover, I shall speak only of single integral problems, thereby passing by the recent solutions of the problem of Plateau [1–5];* and I shall not consider applications of the theory. I would feel quite uneasy about ignoring the applications to boundary value problems if the subject had not been so well reported on by W. T. Reid [6].

Let us then state the problems with which we shall be concerned. The simplest problem, often called the *free problem in non-parametric form*, is that of minimizing an integral

$$J[y] \equiv \int_{x_1}^{x_2} f(x, y, y')dx$$

in the class of all functions $y = y(x)$, continuous and having derivatives which are continuous except at a finite number of corners, for which $y(x_1)$ and $y(x_2)$ have assigned fixed values.† The problem as just stated is a plane problem. It becomes a problem in $(n+1)$-space if we choose to regard y as an n-tuple $(y^1, \cdots, y^n)$ and y' likewise.

The *free problem in parametric form* in n-space is that of minimizing an integral

$$J(C) \equiv \int_{t_1}^{t_2} F(y, y')dt,$$

where y denotes an n-tuple $(y^1, \cdots, y^n)$ and the curve

$$C: \quad y^i = y^i(t), \qquad t_1 \leq t \leq t_2, \ i = 1, \cdots, n,$$

has a tangent which turns continuously except at a finite number of corners. Since this integral is intended to be a function of the curve C alone

---

* Numbers in brackets refer to references at end of paper.

† Concerning differentiability requirements we shall agree that f and all other functions involved have as many derivatives as needed, unless there is some specific question as to such differentiability requirements.

and not of the particular parametric representation of it, we demand that $J(C)$ remain invariant under the change of parameter

(1.1) $t = t(\tau)$, $\tau_1 \leqq \tau \leqq \tau_2$; $t'(\tau) > 0$, $t(\tau_1) = t_1$, $t(\tau_2) = t_2$.

For this it is necessary and sufficient that the integrand $F(y, r)$ in $J(C)$ be positively homogeneous of degree 1 in r,

$$F(y, kr) = kF(y, r), \qquad\qquad k > 0.$$

Immediate consequences of this homogeneity are

(1.2) $r^i F_{r^i}(y, r) = F(y, r)$, $r^i F_{r^i r^j}(y, r)0$,

where the subscripts denote partial derivatives and the repetition of the affix i indicates as usual summation over the values $1, \cdots, n$ of i.

If instead of seeking to minimize an integral $J[y] = \int f(x, y, y')dx$ in the class of all functions with fixed end values we seek to minimize it in the subclass of such functions for which one or more integrals

$$G^i[y] = \int_{x_1}^{x_2} g^i(x, y, y')dx$$

have assigned constant values γ^i, the problem is called an *isoperimetric problem*. The analogous problem in parametric form is self-suggesting. The problem derives its name from the earliest problem of this type, that of finding the curve having a given length L and enclosing the greatest area. In our notation, we are to minimize

$$\int \tfrac{1}{2}(yx' - xy')dt$$

(the negative of the area integral) in the class of closed curves for which

$$\int [(x')^2 + (y')^2]^{1/2}dt$$

has the assigned value L.

Proceeding at once to the most inclusive variations problem involving single integrals, we state the *problem of Bolza*. In (x, y, r)-space (the y and r being n-tuples) a region R and functions $f(x, y, r)$, $\phi_\beta(x, y, r)$, $(\beta = 1, \cdots, m < n)$ are given and in $(2n+2)$-dimensional space a function $g(x_1, y_1, x_2, y_2)$. We seek to minimize the sum

$$J[y] = g(x_1, y(x_1), x_2, y(x_2)) + \int_{x_1}^{x_2} f(x, y, y')dx$$

in the class of functions

$$y^i = y^i(x), \qquad\qquad x_1 \leqq x \leqq x_2,$$

which satisfy the differential equations

$$\phi_\beta(x, y(x), y'(x)) \equiv 0,$$

and whose end points determine a point $(x_1, y(x_1), x_2, y(x_2))$ on a point set S in $(2n+2)$-space. This set S may be defined by equations of the form

$$\psi_\mu(x_1, y_1, x_2, y_2) = 0, \qquad\qquad \mu = 1, \cdots, p \leq 2n + 2,$$

or it may be represented parametrically,

$$x_s = x_s(\alpha_1, \cdots, \alpha_r), \qquad y_s^i = y_s^i(\alpha_1, \cdots, \alpha_r), \qquad s = 1, 2, r \leq 2n + 1.$$

This problem obviously reduces to a fixed end-point problem if the point set S consists of a single point (x_1, y_1, x_2, y_2). It becomes the simplest free problem if $g=0$ and the equations $\phi_\beta =0$ are omitted. The isoperimetric problem is brought into this form by introducing new variables z^i subject to the differential equations

$$x^{i'} - g^i(x, y, y') = 0$$

and end conditions

$$z^i(x_1) = 0, \qquad z^i(x_2) - \gamma^i = 0.$$

If $g\equiv 0$ we have the *Lagrange problem*, with variable or fixed end points according to the choice of the ψ_μ. If $f\equiv 0$, we have the *problem of Mayer*. If some of the functions ϕ_β are independent of y', the problem is one in which the curves $y=y(x)$ are required to lie on assigned surfaces.

While the problem of Bolza is thus easily seen to include all the other standard single integral problems of the calculus of variations, it obviously does not follow that an important theorem concerning this problem remains important in all of its specialized forms. As a rather crude example, a theorem in which one of the hypotheses is that the integrand f is not zero might be important for Lagrange problems, but it would have no immediate application to Mayer problems.

Thus far the word "minimum" has meant "absolute minimum." The classical calculus of variations has been much more concerned with relative minima. These are of two kinds. A function $y=\gamma(x)$ gives a *strong relative minimum* to an integral $J[y]$ if $J[\gamma]\leq J[y]$ for all functions $y(x)$ which differ from $\gamma(x)$ by less than some positive ϵ; it gives a *weak relative minimum* if $J[\gamma]\leq J(y)$ when $y(x)$ and $y'(x)$ differ from $\gamma(x)$ and $\gamma'(x)$ respectively by less than ϵ. Consider now the simplest problem. If $y=\gamma(x)$ gives a weak relative minimum to $J[y]$, and $y=y(x, t)$ is a family of curves passing through the given end points and containing the given curve for $t=0$, the function

$$J_t \equiv \int_{x_1}^{x_2} f(x, y(x, t), y_x(x, t))dx$$

will have a minimum at $t=0$. It follows that

$$(1.3) \qquad \frac{d}{dt} J_t = \frac{d}{dt} \int_{x_1}^{x_2} f(x, y(x, t), y_x(x, t)) dx = 0,$$

$$(1.4) \qquad \frac{d^2}{dt^2} J_t \geq 0,$$

for $t = 0$. Writing $\eta(x)$ for the "variation" $y_t(x, 0)$, the equation (1.3) becomes

$$\int_{x_1}^{x_2} (f_y \eta + f_{y'} \eta') dx = 0.$$

This must hold for all η vanishing at x_1 and x_2, for the family $y(x,t)$ $= \gamma(x) + t\eta(x)$ has $\eta(x)$ for its variation. By methods older than our Society we deduce two conclusions.

(i) *The Euler equation*

$$\frac{d}{dx} f_r(x, \gamma, \gamma') - f_y(x, \gamma, \gamma') = 0$$

holds between corners of the curve.

(ii) *At a value of x which defines a corner of the curve the Weierstrass-Erdmann corner condition*

$$f_r(x, \gamma(x), \gamma'(x - 0)) = f_r(x, \gamma(x), \gamma'(x + 0))$$

holds.

By definition, an *extremal* is a curve $y = \gamma(x)$ such that γ has continuous first and second derivatives and satisfies the Euler differential equation.

Somewhat more generally, the beginning point may vary on a curve $x = x_1(\alpha)$, $y = y_1(\alpha)$. If the integral represents arc length, it is obvious that the minimizing curve $y = \gamma(x)$ must meet the end-locus orthogonally. The easy generalization of this to general integrands takes the form that the minimizing curve must meet the end-locus *transversally*, by which we mean that the equation

$$(f - \gamma' f_r) x_1' + f_r y_1' = 0$$

must hold. Here the arguments of f and f_r are $(x_1, \gamma(x_1), \gamma'(x_1))$, while (x_1', y_1') is the vector tangent to the end-locus at the point of intersection.

Obvious analogues of these statements hold for parametric problems. For the Bolza problem, analogues hold, but they are no longer obvious or easily established. In place of the Euler equation, we have the *Lagrange multiplier rule*, which is as follows [7–9]: There is a number λ_0 and a set of functions $\lambda_1(x), \cdots, \lambda_m(x)$ (not all zero), continuous except perhaps at corners of the minimizing curve $y = \gamma(x)$, such that for the combination

$$F(x, y, r; \lambda) \equiv \lambda_0 f(x, y, r) + \lambda_\beta(x) \phi_\beta(x, y, r)$$

the Euler equations

$$\frac{d}{dx} F_{r^i} - F_{y^i} = 0, \qquad\qquad i = 1, \cdots, n,$$

hold between corners, while the Weierstrass-Erdmann condition holds at corners. Moreover a transversality condition holds which is a fairly direct generalization of that for the simplest case, but we shall not write it explicitly.

2. Returning to the simplest problem we will utilize the inequality (1.4). Straightforward differentiation shows that this can be written in the form

$$(2.1) \qquad I[\eta] = \int_{x_1}^{x_2} 2\omega(x, \eta, \eta')dx \geqq 0,$$

where

$$2\omega(x, \eta, \rho) = f_{rr}(x, \gamma(x), \gamma'(x))\rho^2 + 2f_{yr}(x, \gamma(x), \gamma'(x))\eta\rho$$
$$+ f_{yy}(x, \gamma(x), \gamma'(x))\eta^2.$$

It is not easy to verify whether or not inequality (2.1), as it stands, is satisfied along a given curve. Theoretically at least it would require the investigation of every function $\eta(x)$ vanishing at x_1 and at x_2. Therefore, just as in studying the first variation (1.3), we seek to bring the condition (2.1) into more usable form. The first method proposed for this is more than a century old. It involves a transformation of the second variation $I[\eta]$ into other forms [10, pp. 55, 61, 226, 619–634; 11]. This transformation is rather simple for the simplest problem. For the parametric problem, it already calls for ingenuity, and the complexity of the transformation increases rapidly with that of the original problem, reaching formidable proportions for the general Bolza problem. To avoid these analytic difficulties, Kneser developed a geometric method [12; 10, chap. 7; 13] which, at least in the simpler cases, was quite elegant, but which left some special situations undiscussed. The study of these special situations called for at least as much effort as that of the original case.

In 1916 Bliss [14–16] circumvented these troubles by remarking that the inequality $I[\eta] \geqq 0$ is equivalent to the statement that the function $\eta \equiv 0$ minimizes the integral $I[\eta]$ in the class of all functions $\eta(x)$ vanishing at x_1 and at x_2. Thus the discussion of the second variation becomes the study of a new variations problem, that of minimizing $I[\eta]$. The Euler equation for this "accessory" problem is called the Jacobi equation for the original problem; it is $d\omega_\rho/dx - \omega_y = 0$.

Two points x_3, x_4 are said to determine *conjugate points* on the extremal $E: y = \gamma(x)$ if there is a solution of the Jacobi equations which vanishes at x_3 and x_4 without vanishing identically. Jacobi's necessary condition is that, if the extremal E gives a weak relative minimum to $J[y]$ and along it $f_{rr} \neq 0$, there is no point $(x_3, \gamma(x_3))$ conjugate to the beginning point and having $x_1 < x_3 < x_2$. Suppose there were such a point x_3; we must show that E would not minimize the integral. Let $\eta(x)$ satisfy the Jacobi equations and vanish at x_1 and x_3 without vanishing identically. Let $u(x)$ equal

$\eta(x)$ for $x_1 \leq x \leq x_3$, while it vanishes identically for $x > x_3$. A simple calculation shows that $I[u] = 0$. But since $u[x]$ has a corner at x_3 the relation

$$\omega_p(x_3, a(x_3), u'(x_3 + 0)) - \omega_p(x_3, u(x_3), u'(x_3 - 0))$$

$$= f_{rr}(x_3, y(x_3), y'(x_3))(u'(x_3 + 0) - u'(x_3 - 0)) = 0$$

fails to hold. That is, the Weierstrass-Erdmann condition is *not* satisfied, and u does *not* minimize $I[\eta]$. So for some η_0 we must have $I[\eta_0] < 0$, violating the condition $I[\eta] \geq 0$ which is necessary for a minimum.

Bliss first set forth these ideas in connection with the parametric problem [14]. Here the situation is complicated by the fact that the Jacobi equations are not independent, so that there is a superfluity of solutions. In fact, if $y^i = \gamma^i(t)$ is an extremal, then for every continuously differentiable function $\rho(t)$ the product $\rho \gamma^{i'}$ satisfies the Jacobi equations. This lack of independence had been a source of annoyance in transformations of the second variation. Bliss disposed of it by considering only "normal" solutions $\eta(t)$ of the Jacobi equations, that is, solutions for which $\gamma^{i'} \eta^i$ vanishes identically. More recently, other devices for eliminating superfluous solutions have been proposed [17, 18, 19], designed so that the selected solutions $\eta(t)$ will be of a form suitable for some special purpose. Nevertheless, Bliss' original definition of normal solutions can, by a slight modification, be made to answer all special needs so far encountered.*

Since 1916, this method has been applied to variations problems of all degrees of generality with such consistency and success that now it is referred to as the "usual" or "classical" method. It is worthy of remark that a simple by-product of this line of reasoning is a derivation of a transformation of the second variation [15] without any of the massive analytical machinery of von Escherich and his predecessors.

3. In discussing the first and second variations for the simplest problem, it was most convenient that, for every function $\eta(x)$ vanishing at x_1 and x_2, there was a family $y(x, t)$ of functions, all having the assigned end values $y(x_1, t) = \gamma(x_1)$ and $y(x_2, t) = \gamma(x_2)$, containing the extremal E: $y = \gamma(x)$ for $t = 0$, and having $\eta(t)$ for its variation function $y_t(x, 0)$. All we had to do was to define

(3.1) $$y(x, t) = \gamma(x) + t\eta(x).$$

When side conditions are present, matters are not so simple. Consider for example, the Bolza problem. The simple definition (3.1) now fails for the functions $\gamma(x) + t\eta(x)$ will not in general satisfy the differential equations $\phi_\beta = 0$. In fact, if

(3.2) $$y = y(x, t), \qquad x_1(t) \leq x \leq x_2(t),$$

---

* Such as invariance of selected solutions under change of parameter and change of coördinates, and applicability to problems with end points variable on manifolds.

is a family of curves satisfying the differential equations

(3.3) $$\phi_\beta(x, y(x, t), y_x(x, t)) = 0$$

and the end conditions

(3.4) $$\psi_\mu(x_1(t), y(x_1(t), t), x_2(t), y(x_2(t), t)) = 0$$

for all t near 0, and if the given extremal E is defined by equations (3.2) with $t=0$, then by differentiating in (3.3) and setting $t=0$ we obtain

(3.5) $$\Phi_\beta(x, \eta, \eta') \equiv \phi_{\beta y^i}\eta^i + \phi_{\beta r^i}\eta^{i'} = 0,$$

where

(3.6) $$\eta^i(x) = y_t^i(x, 0).$$

Likewise, by differentiating in (3.4) and setting $t=0$, we obtain

(3.7) $$\Psi_\mu(\xi_1, \eta(x_1), \xi_2, \eta(x_2)) = 0,$$

where

(3.8) $$\xi_s = x_s'(0), \qquad\qquad\qquad s = 1, 2.$$

(We do not need the specific form of the functions Ψ_μ.)

Therefore in order that a set $(\xi_1, \xi_2, \eta(x))$ be the set of variations derived (by (3.6) and (3.8)) from a family of curves satisfying the differential equations and end conditions, it is necessary that equations (3.5) and (3.7) hold. Annoyingly, these conditions are still not sufficient. If we disregard the end conditions, we can show by theorems on differential equations that every set $\eta(x)$ satisfying the equations of variation (3.5) is derived (by (3.6)) from a family (3.2) of curves satisfying the equations $\phi_\beta = 0$. But this family may fail to satisfy the end conditions $\psi_\mu = 0$. If we try to determine the end points $x_1(t), x_2(t)$ in such a manner that the end conditions $\psi_\mu = 0$ hold, we are essentially trying to solve a set of equations for an unknown function. Recalling the implicit function theorem, we will not be astonished to find that in order to carry through the analysis it is necessary that a certain determinant be not zero. In this case, we need to have a system of sets

$$(\xi_{\nu,1}, \xi_{\nu,2}, \eta_\nu^i(x)), \qquad\qquad \nu = 1, \cdots, p,$$

such that the functions $\eta_\nu(x)$ satisfy equations (3.5) and the determinant

(3.9) $$\left| \Psi_\mu(\xi_{\nu,1}, \eta_\nu(x_1), \xi_{\nu,2}, \eta_\nu(x_2)) \right|, \qquad\qquad \mu, \nu = 1, \cdots, p,$$

is different from zero.

The case in which the determinant (3.9) can be made different from zero is thus obviously more tractable than that in which (3.9) vanishes identically. Moreover, we may reasonably expect it to be the usual case.

Accordingly, it has been named the "normal" case,* and in it the extremal E is said to be "normal with respect to the end conditions $\psi_\mu = 0$." It is evident that if E is normal with respect to the end conditions $\psi_\mu = 0$, it remains normal with respect to any subset of these conditions. Consequently, the most drastic type of normality requirement is that of normality with respect to fixed end points.

The distinction between normal and abnormal arcs was of course ignored in the days of Lagrange. After it was recognized, abnormal cases were systematically avoided, and rigid normality requirements imposed on all arcs considered. The necessary condition of Weierstrass was established, not for abnormal arcs, nor even for all normal arcs, but only for arcs such that every subarc is normal with respect to fixed end points [10, p. 603; 7]. Sets of sufficient conditions [10, §77; 7] included the even stronger hypothesis that the extremal $E: y = \gamma(x)$, $x_1 \leq x \leq x_2$, could be extended so as to be defined on a larger interval $x_1 - \epsilon \leq x \leq x_2 + \epsilon$, remaining normal with respect to fixed end points on every subarc of this extended arc.

Normality conditions of this type are undesirable for three reasons. First, we do not wish to restrict results by imposing somewhat artificial conditions designed to exclude the more refractory problems, if it is possible to avoid the use of such conditions. From this point of view it would be desirable to proceed without any use of normality. While this is beyond our reach at present, still we can hope to minimize normality requirements, and, in particular, to avoid the exceedingly drastic requirement of normality on every subarc. Second, even though the normal case is in a sense the usual case, still, in each separate instance, we must verify that the specific arc under consideration does not happen to be abnormal. This verification may be far from easy, especially when it must be made for every subarc. Third, the Mayer problem is a Bolza problem with $f(x, y, r) \equiv 0$; but, as remarked by Carathéodory [21, 22] and others, if $y = \gamma(x)$ is a minimizing curve for this Bolza problem, it cannot possibly be normal (with respect to fixed end points) on any subarc. Consequently, if the theory of the Bolza problem is to be developed to cover that of the more special problems, we must not restrict our attention to problems normal on all subarcs.

Craves [23] showed that the requirement of normality on subarcs is not needed in establishing the necessary condition of Weierstrass. He established the necessity of the Weierstrass condition under the hypothesis that the arc itself is normal with respect to the end conditions $\psi_\mu = 0$. Also, for a class of abnormal arcs, he gave a necessary condition analogous to that of Weierstrass, but more complex in its statement.

---

* The distinction between normal and abnormal cases appears already in the problem of minimizing a function $f(y)$ of the variable $y_1, \cdots, y^n$ subject to conditions $g_\mu(y) = 0$, $\mu = 1, \cdots,$ $p < n$. Bliss [20] has made use of this in presenting a highly readable and instructive introduction to the concept and uses of normality.

The first set of conditions not requiring normality and still sufficient to ensure a minimum was given by Hestenes [24]. His conditions were the following: (I') The functions $y^i = \gamma^i(x)$ are continuous with their first and second derivatives, and satisfy the Euler equations with continuously differentiable multipliers $\lambda_0 \neq 0$, $\lambda_\beta(x)$. (We can then take $\lambda_0 = 1$.) (II$_N'$) The strengthened Weierstrass condition holds along the curve $y = y_0(x)$. (III') The strengthened Clebsch condition holds; that is, the form

$$u^i F_{r_i r_i}(x, \gamma, \gamma') u^j$$

is positive definite. (IV') The second variation is positive. This last condition Hestenes showed to be a consequence of any one of three other hypotheses. Marston Morse [25] showed that (IV') is also a consequence of a hypothesis which is a direct generalization of the Jacobi condition, stated in terms of the zeros of solutions of the Jacobi equations.

A very different method of reaching the same results was used by W. T. Reid [26]. He made no use of fields or of any part of the Weierstrassian theory, returning instead to the venerable expansion proof. This style of proof is based on a Taylor expansion with an estimate of the remainder term. It had been attempted frequently, had yielded a sufficiency theorem for weak relative minima, and finally had been successfully applied by E. E. Levi [27] to establishing sufficient conditions for a strong relative minimum for problems involving no side conditions. Reid's proof uses a rather simple but important lemma on the existence of a system of solutions $\eta_1, \cdots, \eta_n$ of the Jacobi equations and equations of variation

$$\frac{d}{dx} \Omega_{\rho^i} - \Omega_{\eta^i} = 0, \qquad \phi_{\beta y^i} \eta^i + \phi_{\beta r^i} \eta^{i'} = 0,$$

which are conjugate in the sense that

$$\eta_k{}^i \Omega_{\rho^i}(x, \eta_j, \eta_j') - \eta_j{}^i \Psi_{\rho^i}(x, \eta_k, \eta_k') = 0, \qquad\qquad i, j = 1, \cdots, n,$$

and whose determinant $|\eta_j{}^i(x)|$ is not zero. This lemma was proved independently by Reid, Morse, and Hestenes. Except in this lemma, Reid's proof proceeds without any need of the concept of normality.

The proofs just mentioned apply to the case of separated end conditions, in which none of the functions $\psi_\mu(x_1, y_1, x_2, y_2)$ occurring in the end conditions $\psi_\mu = 0$ actually depend, both on (x_1, y_1) and on (x_2, y_2). The general problem is reducible to this by a device. More recently, Hestenes [28] and Reid [29] have given proofs which apply directly to general (not necessarily separated) end conditions.

It is to be remarked that if the problem is normal, every set of multipliers λ_0, $\lambda_\beta(x)$ has $\lambda_0 \neq 0$. The theorems under discussion require less than this. It is asked only that there exist at least one set of multipliers with $\lambda_0 \neq 0$. Thus the only case uncovered is what might be called the "pure abnormal" case, in which *every* system of multipliers λ_0, $\lambda_\beta(x)$ with which the

Euler equations hold is such that $\lambda_0 = 0$. This pure abnormal case seems to be hopelessly unmanageable at present. Recently, Bliss has shown [20] that in so far as sufficiency theorems are concerned, the only important distinction is between the pure abnormal and the normal cases. Problems which are abnormal, but still have multipliers λ_0, $\lambda_\beta(x)$ with $\lambda_0 \neq 0$, can be quite readily replaced by other problems, equivalent with respect to sufficiency conditions, which are normal with respect to the end conditions. Therefore, it is possible to simplify the proofs of Hestenes, Morse, and Reid by considering only normal extremals, and finally to recover the full generality of these theorems by using the device of Bliss.

Thus the treatment of the problem of Bolza from the classical point of view has now reached a state of completeness, at least in so far as normal arcs are concerned. For these, the necessary and the sufficient conditions are separated only by that gap which is already present in the simplest problem. For abnormal arcs not purely abnormal, the sufficiency theorems are essentially complete, but the same cannot be said of the necessary conditions. It does not seem likely that any simple and general results on such problems will soon be reached.

4. The problems which we have been discussing have required the finding of that one of a given class of functions or curves for which a certain integral assumes its least value. Heretofore we have considered functions or curves which give a *relative* minimum to the integral. It is quite another thing to ask if there actually exists a function or curve in the class for which the integral takes on its least value. Seventy-five years ago it was accepted that if the integrand were positive the existence of a minimum was evident. Weierstrass removed this misapprehension by a simple example. If we are to minimize the integral

$$J[y] = \int_0^1 |\, y' \,|^{1/2} dx$$

in the class of all functions having $y(0) = 0$ and $y(1) = 1$, we see that the lower bound of the values of the integral is zero; for it is never negative, and if $y = x^{2n+1}$, then $J[y] = (2n+1)^{1/2}(n+1)^{-1}$, which is arbitrarily close to zero. But $J[y]$ can never assume its lower bound zero; for if $J[y] = 0$ then $y' \equiv 0$, which is incompatible with the end conditions $y(0) = 0$, $y(1) = 1$.

A similar example in parametric form is not difficult to construct. We first observe that $2x(2^{1/2} - x) \leq 1$, so that $1/(2^{1/2} - x) \geq 2x$ if $x < 2^{1/2}$. Let us seek to minimize the integral $J(C) = \int F dt$ in the class of rectifiable curves C joining $(0, 0)$ and $(1, 0)$, where

(4.1) $F(x, y, \dot{x}, \dot{y}) = (1 + y^2)\, (\dot{x}^2 + \dot{y}^2) / [(2\dot{x}^2 + 2\dot{y}^2)^{1/2} - \dot{x}]$.

(The integral is a Lebesgue integral, and the dot denotes differentiation with respect to t.) It is convenient to choose the parameter t to be arc length, so that $\dot{x}^2+\dot{y}^2=1$ for almost all t. Then if $L(C)$ is the length of C we have

$$J(C) = \int_0^{L(C)} (1 + y^2)/(2^{1/2} - \dot{x})dt$$

(4.2)
$$\geq \int_0^{L(C)} 1/(2^{1/2} - \dot{x})dt$$

$$\geq \int_0^{L(C)} 2\dot{x}\, dt = 2x(L(C)) - 2x(0) = 2.$$

The value $J(C)$ is arbitrarily near 2 if evaluated along a polygon whose sides all have slopes ± 1 and which lies in a sufficiently narrow strip $|y| < \epsilon$. But there is no curve for which $J(C)=2$. If there were such a curve C: $x=x(t)$, $y=y(t)$, then for it all members of (4.2) would be equal. This would imply that for almost all t, $1+y^2=1$ and $1/(2^{1/2}-\dot{x})=2\dot{x}$. The first of these can hold only if $y\equiv 0$, so that $\dot{y}=0$ and $\dot{x}=\pm 1$. But this contradicts the second.

In 1900 Hilbert [30] published a short but suggestive paper expounding a method by which theorems on the existence of minimizing curves can be established for a very important class of problems. Consider the problem of minimizing an integral $J(C)=\int F\,dt$ (in parametric form) in the class of all curves lying in a bounded closed set A and joining two given points. We first assume that

(4.3)
$$F(y, r) \geq \epsilon |r|,$$

where ϵ is positive and $|r|$ denotes the length of the vector r. Then $J(C)\geq 0$; let μ be its lower bound. Let $\{C_n\}$ be a sequence of curves $y=y_n(t)$ for which $J(C_n)$ tends to μ. If we denote the length of C by $L(C)$, we have by (4.3)

$$L(C_n) = \int |\dot{y}_n|\, dt \leq \int (F/\epsilon)dt = \epsilon^{-1}J(C_n) \to \mu/\epsilon.$$

Hence the curves C_n have a bound on their lengths. We can therefore apply Hilbert's convergence theorem, which states that if C_n is a sequence of curves of uniformly bounded lengths lying in a bounded point set, it is possible to select a subsequence C_m and represent these curves C_m by equations $y^i=y_m^i(t)$, $(0\leq t\leq 1)$, in such a manner that the functions $y_m^i(t)$ converge uniformly to limit functions $y_0^i(t)$. Now we have a curve C_0: $y=y_0(t)$, $(0\leq t\leq 1)$, which is the limit of our minimizing sequence. It does not follow from our hypotheses that C_0 is a minimizing curve; our example (4.1) shows this. Let us now add the hypothesis that the integral $J(C)$ is *regular*, which by definition means that the quadratic form $F_{r^ir^j}(y, r)u^iu^j$ is positive for all y in A, all $r\neq 0$, and all u which do not satisfy the equations

$u^i = kr^i$. (If $u^i = kr^i$ the quadratic form necessarily vanishes, as follows from equation (1.2)). It is then possible to utilize the classical field construction on successive small arcs of C_0 in such a way as to show that C_0 actually minimizes $J(C)$. Hilbert gave this proof for plane problems. A similar discussion was applied by Carathéodory [31] to certain classes of non-regular integrals, and Bill [32] extended Hilbert's proof to space problems.

The situation can be described in topological terms by observing that the aggregate of all continuous curves $y = y(t)$, $(t_1 \leq t \leq t_2)$, lying in a euclidean space (or more generally, in a metric space) can be made into a metric space by a suitable definition of the distance $\|C_1, C_2\|$ between all pairs of curves C_1, C_2. Such a definition was given by Fréchet. For our purposes it is enough to observe that C_n tends to C_0, that is, $\lim \|C_n, C_0\| = 0$, if and only if each C_j, $(j = 0, 1, \cdots)$, can be parametrically represented by functions $y = y_j(t)$, $(0 \leq t \leq 1)$, in such a manner that $y_n(t)$ tends to $y_0(t)$ uniformly on the interval $0 \leq t \leq 1$.

Let us confine our attention to the (metric) subspace consisting of all curves C which are rectifiable (that is, have finite length) and whose points $y(t)$ lie in a given point set A. To each of these curves the integral $\int F \, dt$ assigns a functional value $J(C)$. We can now state our problem in the following form. Given a class K of rectifiable curves whose points lie in A, and a function $J(C)$ defined on K, we seek a curve C_0 in K such that $J(C) \geq J(C_0)$ for all curves C in the class K.

It is natural to approach this problem as before; we select first a sequence $\{C_n\}$ of curves of K such that $J(C_n)$ tends to the greatest lower bound μ of $J(C)$ on K. If the set A is bounded and closed, and $J(C)$ has some property which ensures that the C_n have uniformly bounded lengths (for instance, if $F(y, r) \geq \epsilon |r|$), then by Hilbert's convergence theorem there is a curve C_0 which is the limit of a subsequence of $\{C_n\}$. There is no loss of generality in supposing that this subsequence is the whole sequence $\{C_n\}$. The curve C_0 is a rectifiable curve and its points lie in A, but this alone does not imply that C_0 belongs to the class K. We therefore impose the hypothesis that K is a *complete* class, that is, that it contains all its rectifiable limit curves. For example, K may consist of all rectifiable curves in A joining two fixed points, or joining two fixed closed point sets; there are many other types of examples.

If now the function $J(C)$ were continuous, from the relations $C_n \to C_0$ and $J(C_n) \to \mu$ we would at once have $J(C_0) = \mu$, so that C_0 would be the minimizing curve sought. But it is easy to see that few of the interesting integrals of the calculus of variations yield continuous functions $J(C)$. Even the length integral is not continuous, for arbitrarily near any given curve C we can construct other curves so crinkly as to have lengths greatly in excess of the length of C. However, continuity is much more than we need. In fact, if $J(C)$ is lower semicontinuous, which by definition means that it satisfies the condition

(4.4) $$\lim_{n\to\infty} \inf J(C_n) \geqq J(C)$$

whenever C_n tends to C, then the curve C_0 is the minimizing curve sought. For then

$$\mu = \lim J(C_n) \geqq J(C_0)$$

by (4.4), while $J(C_0) \geqq \mu$ by the definition of μ. So $J(C_0) = \mu$, as was to be proved.

It was Tonelli [33] who first stressed the importance of this concept of lower semicontinuity in the calculus of variations, and used it to obtain powerful existence theorems. The integrals $J(C)$ which possess this property include all the regular integrals. In fact, if we consider only classes of curves of uniformly bounded lengths (and this restriction on lengths is necessary if we are to use Hilbert's theorem on convergence of curves), semicontinuity follows from the weaker condition that the inequality

(4.5) $$F_{r^i r^j}(y, r)u^i u^j \geqq 0$$

holds for all y in A, all $r \neq 0$ and all u. More than this, it even follows from the condition that for each fixed y in A the surface (called the *figurative*) defined by the equation

(4.6) $$z = F(y, r)$$

is convex. By the homogeneity of F, this surface is a cone with vertex at the origin; and for functions F which are twice differentiable, the figurative is convex if and only if (4.5) holds.

It is not very difficult to establish the theorem that the convexity of the figurative implies the lower semicontinuity of $J(C)$ on any class of curves of uniformly bounded lengths. Suppose that the curves $C_n: y = y_n(t)$, $(0 \leqq t \leqq 1)$, converge to $C_0: y = y_0(t)$, $(0 \leqq t \leqq 1)$, the functions y_n converging uniformly to y_0 and the derivatives y_n' being all less in absolute value than a constant M. If F is independent of y and $y_0'(t)$ is constant, we can apply Jensen's inequality to the convex function $F(r)$, obtaining

$$\int_0^1 F(y_n')dt \geqq F\left(\int_0^1 y_n' dt\right) = F(y_n(1) - y_n(0))$$

$$\to F(y_0(1) - y_0(0)) = F(y_0'(t)) = \int_0^1 F(y_0')dt.$$

That is,

(4.7) $$\lim \inf J(C_n) \geqq J(C_0).$$

(Observe that here we need the convergence of $y_n(t)$ to $y_0(t)$ only at $t = 0$ and $t = 1$.) If C_0 is not a line segment we can inscribe in it a polygon Π: $y = \pi(t)$, $(0 \leqq t \leqq 1)$, with sides short enough so that $J(\Pi)$ is arbitrarily near

$J(C_0)$. Although y_n does not tend to π for all t, we still have $y_n(t) \to \pi(t)$ whenever t defines a vertex of Π. So we can apply the previous proof to each side of Π and obtain

$$\lim \inf J(C_n) \geqq J(\Pi);$$

and since $J(\Pi)$ is arbitrarily near $J(C_0)$, inequality (4.7) still holds. We can extend these results to the general case, in which F depends on y, by the traditional device of subdividing the interval $0 \leqq t \leqq 1$ into short sub-intervals and using only large n, so that on each subinterval $F(y_j, y_j')$ is independent of y to within an arbitrarily small error $(j=0, 1, \cdots)$. This type of proof of semicontinuity does not even require F to have any partial derivatives; it is enough that it be continuous in (y, r) and convex in r for each y.

Tonelli's many contributions to this direct method in the calculus of variations up to 1922 are summed up in his book [33]. In it four types of problems (all in the plane) are considered; the free problem (without side conditions) both in parametric and non-parametric form, and the isoperimetric problem, also in both forms. Since then the development has been considerable in volume and varied in direction.

An early improvement was a weakening of the conditions needed to ensure the existence of a convergent minimizing sequence. The condition

$$(4.8) \qquad\qquad\qquad F(y, r) \geqq \epsilon |r|, \qquad\qquad\qquad \epsilon > 0,$$

used to keep a bound on the lengths of the curves C_n in a minimizing sequence, was replaced by a weaker condition by Hahn [34]. Hahn's theorem was improved by Carathéodory [35] and Tonelli [36], and extended to n-space by Graves [37] and McShane [38]. The result is that (4.8) can be replaced by the much weaker condition that the figurative (4.6) is convex and non-planar for each y, and there is a finite upper bound for the lengths of all curves C such that $J(C) \leqq 0$. This, with the semicontinuity theorem just discussed, yields a very strong existence theorem for problems in parametric form.

The problem in nonparametric form had been less exhaustively treated until five years ago. For such problems, the most straightforward approach is to show that the minimizing sequence $y = y_n(x)$ has an absolutely continuous limit function. This was the method used by Tonelli in his book. In order to control the behavior of the minimizing sequence, he assumed that there were positive constants a, b, ϵ such that

$$f(x, y, y') \geqq a |y'|^{1+\epsilon} - b$$

for all (x, y) in A and all y'. Nagumo [39] showed that it was sufficient to make the weaker hypothesis that

$$f(x, y, y')/|y'| \to \infty \qquad \text{as} \qquad |y'| \to \infty$$

uniformly in (x, y). The author [40] approached the problem indirectly. He restated the problem in parametric notation by defining

(4.9)
$$F(x, y, x', y') = x'f(x, y, y'/x'), \qquad x' > 0,$$
$$F(x, y, 0, y') = \lim_{x_r \to +0} F(x, y, x', y').$$

Then by methods appropriate to the more highly developed parametric problem he showed the existence of a minimizing curve $x = x(t)$, $y = y(t)$ for $\int F\, dt$ in the class of curves with $x'(t) \geqq 0$. Adding any of several hypotheses on $f(x, y, r)$ ensured $x'(t) > 0$ almost everywhere, permitting a return to the nonparametric form. A number of new theorems resulted. Tonelli [41] showed that all these theorems could also be obtained by his method, and added several new ones. The author [42] established a semicontinuity theorem for integrals $\int F\, dt$ where for each y the vectors r may be restricted in direction, the function $F(y, r)$ being merely assumed to be a lower semicontinuous function of its arguments. The analytical assumptions are weak enough so that the theorem can be applied to all the standard single integral problems, both in parametric and in nonparametric form. By use of this semicontinuity theorem he established rather general existence theorems [43] for problems in non-parametric form.

It would be natural to suppose that this relaxing of the continuity requirements on the integrand, so as to permit us to study problems in which the integrand is merely lower semicontinuous, is nothing more than analytic gymnastics. While it is true that most of the problems suggested by physics and chemistry have analytic or at least many times differentiable integrands, the extension is not really trifling. For one thing, when even an analytic and regular nonparametric problem is transformed by equations (4.9) into parametric form it will usually turn out that the transformed integrand is merely lower semicontinuous at points having $x' = 0$. For another, the principal existence theorems for nonparametric problems have hypotheses which do not permit the integrand $f(x, y, r)$ to vanish identically in r for any (x, y). Tonelli has established special theorems to cover certain classes of integrals in which this identical vanishing occurs. These theorems, even in generalized form, can be brought under the principal theorems by a suitable transformation of the independent variable x. But the problem when thus transformed has an integrand which is only lower semicontinuous, and in fact is $+\infty$ identically in r and y for some values of x. Thus the extension of the theory to discontinuous integrands has a rather noticeable unifying effect.

Another existence theorem which does not require continuity and to some extent even dispenses with lower semicontinuity of the integrand has been established by Menger [44–46]. The setting for the theorem is an abstract metric space. The integrand $F(y, r)$, which may be thought of as determined by the point y and the vector from the point $q = 0$ to the point

r, is replaced by a function $\phi(p; q, r)$. This generates a "ϕ-distance" between points, and thus defines the ϕ-lengths of polygons. The functional $J(C)$, now the ϕ-length of C, is defined by inscribing polygons; here the procedure is somewhat like that used by Weierstrass in defining the integral $J(C)$ on rectifiable curves in days when only the Riemann integral was available. Under a certain convexity assumption, the ϕ-length can be proved lower semicontinuous and existence theorems can be established.

Another extension of the calculus of variations to metric spaces was made by Frink [47], who showed that the Carathéodory linear measure was lower semicontinuous on the class of continua and thus established the existence of continua of least linear measure.

Problems with side conditions have as yet not been so completely treated. If the side conditions are in the form of differential equations linear in y' the theorems for free problems apply, as Graves [42, 48, 49] pointed out. The reason that such side conditions cause us no trouble is that the only property required of the class K of curves is completeness, or rather less than that; the class must be such that if C_n is a sequence of curves K having uniformly bounded lengths and converging to C_0, then C_0 must also belong to K. It is quite easy to prove that the class of all curves satisfying a set of linear differential equations has this property. This remark is not trivial, for such side conditions occur (1) when the curves are restricted to lie on a given surface (although here it is easy to see directly that such a class K of curves is complete); (2) in isoperimetric problems for which the integrands in the side integrals do not involve the derivatives; (3) when the problem under consideration is itself the second variation of another Lagrange problem; and (4) when the problem of minimizing an integral

$$\int f(x, y, y', \cdots, y^{(n)})dx$$

involving derivatives of y of higher order is set into Lagrange form. More recently, the problem with higher derivatives in the integrand has been studied in greater detail by Cinquini [50, 51] and the author [43], and now has been as completely solved as the nonparametric problem with only first derivatives in the integrand.

Since, ordinarily, the curves $y = y(x)$ satisfying a system of differential equations $\phi_\beta = 0$ do not form a complete class, the general Mayer, Lagrange, and Bolza problems require special treatment. Manià studied in detail two well known problems, the navigation problem of Zermelo [52] and the problem of finding that curve of descent of a particle through a resisting medium which shall maximize the final velocity [53, 54], and was led to an existence theorem for a class of Mayer and Lagrange problems [55, 56]. The most general theorem of this type, applicable to a class of Lagrange, Mayer, and Bolza problems, is due to Graves [57].

A restriction common to all the theorems mentioned in the preceding paragraph is that certain of the functions $y^i(x)$ must have their final values entirely unrestricted. This does not hinder their application to a number of interesting special problems, but fixed end-point problems are excluded. Among these excluded problems are all isoperimetric problems, so that these problems require special treatment. Some theorems for such problems were established by Tonelli [33] and slightly generalized by McShane [58]. These theorems apply to the problem

$$J(C) = \int F(y, y')dt = \min, \qquad G(C) = \int G(y, y')dt = \gamma,$$

and require a rather close relationship between the integrands F and G. It would seem that methods of proof based on lower semicontinuity are not well fitted to the discussion of these problems. Granted that we have a convergent sequence $\{C_n\}$ for which $J\{C_n\}$ tends to the lower bound μ while $G(C_n)$ tends to γ, it is not very helpful to find that at the limit curve C_0 we know only that $G(C_0) \leq \gamma$. In some papers as yet unpublished McShane [59] studies isoperimetric problems both in parametric and in nonparametric form without using semicontinuity. His method is an extension of one used by Lewy [60] for regular problems in the plane and later used by Manià [56] for a class of Mayer problems. First a particular type of minimizing sequence is found consisting of a sequence of polygons Π_n such that $J(\Pi_n) \to \mu$ and $G(\Pi_n) \to \gamma$. Each of these polygons Π_n has a minimizing property of its own, in that it minimizes $J(C)$ in the class of polygons having no more vertices than Π_n has and making $G(C)$ equal to $G(\Pi_n)$. From this minimizing property of the Π_n, it can be shown that these polygons satisfy certain relations which are approximations to the usual necessary conditions for a minimum. Two of these conditions are particularly useful. One is the Lagrange multiplier rule; there are numbers λ_0, λ_1 such that for the function $H(y, r) = \lambda_0 F(y, r) + \lambda_1 G(y, r)$ the Euler equations (in the integrated, or DuBois-Reymond, form)

$$H_{r^i}(y, y') = \int_a^t H_{y^i}(y, y')dt + c_i$$

are satisfied. The other is a corner condition established by Dresden [61]. The Dresden corner condition states that if t defines a corner of a minimizing curve $y = y(t)$, then

$$\Omega_H(y(t), y'(t - 0), y'(t + 0)) \leq 0,$$

where $\Omega_H(y, p, r) \equiv p_i H_{y^i}(y, q) - q^i H_{y^i}(y, p)$. From the information which these relations yield concerning the derivatives of the functions $y_n(t)$ defining the polygons Π_n, it can be shown that under suitable hypotheses a minimizing sequence exists such that $y_n(t)$ converges uniformly to a limit function $y_0(t)$, while $y_n'(t)$ converges almost everywhere to $y_0'(t)$. It follows at once that for the curve $C_0: y = y_0(t)$ the equations

$$J(C_0) = \lim J(\Pi_n) = \mu, \qquad G(C_0) = \lim G(\Pi_n) = \gamma$$

hold.

It is evident that this style of proof does not require semicontinuity of the integrals involved. More than that, the hypotheses are not strong enough to imply semicontinuity. Thus even for free problems existence theorems are established which are new in that they apply to problems in which the figurative is not convex. (Some such theorems had already been established by Carathéodory.) The existence theorems thus established for isoperimetric problems in non-parametric form are the first of any generality.

5. Although many elementary problems in the differential calculus require the minimizing of a function, there are many other problems in which it is required to find a stationary point of a function. Consider, for example, a rigid convex body. At each point P of its surface we define $f(P)$ to be the distance from the center of mass C of the body to the plane tangent to the surface at P. In other words, if the body is placed on a horizontal table with the point P resting on the table, $f(P)$ is the height of the center of gravity above the table. In order that the body be in equilibrium when placed with the point P_0 touching the table, the function $f(P)$ must be stationary at P_0. If P_0 minimizes $f(P)$, the equilibrium is stable.

Likewise, in the calculus of variations, many important applications require the determination of a curve along which the first variation of a certain integral is zero. Such a curve is an extremal, at least if it is twice continuously differentiable. For instance, the principle of "least" action is of this type; what is sought is a curve of *stationary* action, that is, an extremal curve. In optics, Fermat's principle of "least" time is again of this type. This suggests the importance of studying the stationary points of functions and the extremal curves of integrals quite apart from their minimizing properties.

That such a study is really profitable was definitely established in 1917, when Birkhoff [62] enunciated his minimax principle and utilized it in establishing the existence of new classes of periodic orbits in dynamical problems. Birkhoff defined the minimax points of a function J as follows. *If J_0 is the value of J at a point P_0 and if the inequality $J < J_0 - \epsilon$ where ϵ is small and positive defines more than one region near the point P_0, then P_0 will be called a point of minimax. If the inequality defines k regions in the neighborhood of P_0, that point will be said to be of multiplicity $k-1$.* It is easily seen that such a point P_0 is a *critical point* of J, by which we mean that all first partial derivatives of the function vanish at P_0; but P_0 is not a minimum point of the function. In fact, if we introduce a coordinate system $(x^1, \cdots, x^n)$ with origin at P_0 and represent the function J as a function $f(x)$, then (assuming that f has continuous partial derivatives of order up to 3)

(5.1) $$f(x) = f(0) + \tfrac{1}{2}f_{x^i x^j}(0)x^i x^j + R_3,$$

where R_3 is an infinitesimal of the third order with respect to $|x|$. The quadratic form in (5.1) governs the behavior of f near 0. If it is nonsingular, the critical point is called *nondegenerate*. In this case, by means of a linear transformation to new variables y, the quadratic form in (5.1) can be brought into the form

(5.2) $$- (y^1)^2 - \cdots - (y^k)^2 + (y^{k+1})^2 + \cdots + (y^n)^2.$$

Birkhoff showed [62] that the critical point is a minimax point if and only if $k = 1$ in the quadratic form (5.2). (Recall that this is under the assumption that the critical point is nondegenerate.)

Morse observed [63] that among nondegenerate critical points the minimum and minimax points represent two classes out of a total of $n+1$. For if at a nondegenerate critical point the second-order terms are brought into the form (5.2), then k (the *index* of the quadratic form $f_{x^i x^j} x^i x^j$) can have any one of the values $0, 1, \cdots, n$. If we say that k is the *type* of the critical point, then a critical point of type 0 is a minimum point, a critical point of type 1 is a minimax point, and there still remain critical points of type $2, 3, \cdots, n$, a critical point of type n being a maximum point. Morse investigated the interrelations between the numbers of critical points of different types and the Betti numbers of the point set R on which the function is defined. Suppose first that R is compact and without boundary, each point of R having neighborhoods which can be mapped topologically on the interior of a sphere in n-space. For example, if $n = 2$ the set R can be the surface of a sphere or of a torus. If $p_0, p_1, \cdots, p_n$ are the Betti numbers of R, and f has only non-degenerate critical points (necessarily finite in number), and M_k is the number of critical points of type k, the following relationships must hold, as Morse proved:

$$M_0 \geqq p_0,$$
$$M_1 - M_0 \geqq p_1 - p_0,$$
$$M_2 - M_1 + M_0 \geqq p_2 - p_1 + p_0,$$

(5.3) $$\cdots\cdots\cdots\cdots\cdots\cdots\cdots\cdots\cdots\cdots\cdots\cdots\cdots,$$

$$M_{n-1} - M_{n-2} + \cdots + (-1)^{n-1}M_0 \geqq p_{n-1} - p_{n-2} + \cdots + (-1)^{n-1}p_0,$$
$$M_n - M_{n-1} + \cdots + (-1)^n M_0 = p_n - p_{n-1} + \cdots + (-1)^n p_0.$$

The first of these is obvious; in each separate portion of R the function has at least one minimum. The second expresses Birkhoff's minimax principle; it was established by him for analytic functions without assuming that the minimax points are nondegenerate. The final equation was known to

Poincaré [64], at least for $n=2$; a closely related theorem on the sum of the indexes of fixed points of transformations was established by Lefschetz [65] and by Hopf [66] at about the same time that Morse established the relations (5.3).

It might be interesting to look at a rather crude and heuristic sketch of a proof of these inequalities for the case $m=2$. Assume that all the critical points $P_1, \cdots, P_n$ are non-degenerate and therefore finite in number, and that the critical values $f(P_i)$ are distinct. For purposes of visualization think of $f(P)$ as represented by a sort of relief map on K, and for a real number c consider the part of K on which $f(P) < c$ as inundated. This flooded portion has Betti numbers $p_0(c)$, $p_1(c)$, $p_2(c)$; and for $k=0, 1, 2$ $M_k(c)$ is defined as the number of critical points of type k under water, that is, having $f(P_i) < c$. We now proceed to establish

$$M_0(c) \geq p_0(c),$$

(5.4) $$M_1(c) - M_0(c) \geq p_1(c) - p_0(c),$$

$$M_2(c) - M_1(c) + M_0(c) = p_2(c) - p_1(c) + p_0(c),$$

for all c.

If c is just a little greater than the absolute minimum of f, then $M_0(c) = 1$, $M_1(c) = M_2(c) = 0$. The inundated portion consists of one small nearly elliptical lake, with Betti numbers 1, 0, 0. Hence (5.4) holds. It is intuitively plausible (and also true) that as c increases from one value c_1 to another c_2 such that no critical value lies in the interval $c_1 \leq c \leq c_2$ the Betti numbers $p_j(c)$ do not change, and by definition the numbers $M_k(c)$ remain constant. Therefore it remains only to investigate the behavior of these functions as c increases from a value c_1 slightly less than a critical value $f(P_r)$ to a value c_2 slightly greater than that critical value.

If the critical point P_r happens to be of type 0 the result is easily seen. Except near P_r, there is essentially no change; around P_r a new small lake appears. This introduces no new nonbounding one-cycle or two-cycles, but the Betti number $p_0(c)$ increases by unity. So does $M_0(c)$; and we verify at once that the relationships (5.4), if valid for $c=c_1$, are still valid for $c=c_2$. If P_r is a critical point of type 2, then for $c=c_1$ the point P_r is surrounded by a small island which is flooded when $c=c_2$. Consider a small circle Γ drawn in the flooded region about the island. There are two possibilities. Either Γ bounds a flooded region, which is only possible if the island is the last unflooded land; or it does not. In the first case the whole of K is flooded at $c=c_2$, so that $p_2(c_2)$ is the two-dimensional Betti number of K, which is 1, while $p_2(c_1)$ is zero. Then the right-hand member of the equation in (5.4) increases by 1; so does its left-hand member, since one new critical point of type 2 is flooded. So the equality remains valid; the inequalities are unaffected. In the second case the circle Γ was at $c=c_1$ a nonbounding cycle while at $c=c_2$ it is bounding, since its whole interior is flooded. Then $p_1(c)$ diminishes by unity, since one nonbounding one-cycle is lost. Here, too, we verify that relations (5.4) retain their validity.

Finally, let P_r be a critical point of type 1. By suitable choice of co-ordinates near P_r, the function $f(P)$ is approximately represented in the neighborhood P_r by the equation

$$f(P) = f(P_r) - (y^1)^2 + (y^2)^2.$$

This yields the diagram

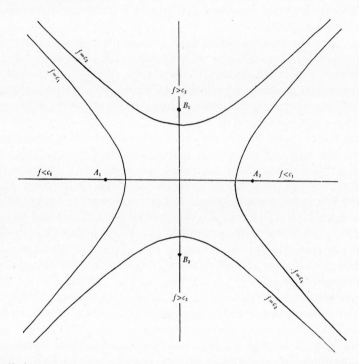

As c goes from c_1 to c_2, the number $M_1(c)$ increases by 1, while $M_0(c)$ and $M_2(c)$ are unchanged. Consider the points A_1, A_2, of the region $f < c_1$. Either they can be joined by an arc lying in $f < c_1$, or they cannot. In the first case this arc, with the segment $A_1 A_2$, constitutes a closed curve lying in $f < c_2$; it is nonbounding in $f < c_2$, for a portion of K bounded by it would have to contain either B_1 or B_2, and neither is in $f < c_2$. Hence the number $p_1(c)$ of nonbounding one-cycles has increased by 1. We verify that relations (5.4) retain validity. In the second case, the pair of points A_1, A_2 constitute in $f < c_1$ a nonbounding zero-cycle. In the set $f < c_2$ they bound the segment $A_1 A_2$. So one nonbounding zero-cycle is lost, and $p_0(c)$ has decreased by 1. Otherwise stated, for $c = c_1$ the pieces containing A_1 and A_2 are separate, while for $c = c_2$ they are united, and the number $p_0(c)$ of pieces has diminished by 1. In this case, too, we see that (5.4) retains validity.

Since it is now true that (5.4) is valid for all c greater than the absolute minimum of f, we assign c a value greater than the absolute maximum of f. Then relations (5.4) reduce to Morse's relationships (5.3).

The Betti numbers of a sphere are $p_0 = 1$, $p_1 = 0$, $p_2 = 1$. So on a globe which shows elevations in relief, the number M_2 of peaks plus the number M_0 of valley-bottoms equals 2 plus the number M_1 of passes. (This works better on a globe than on the earth itself, since such phenomena as natural bridges alter the Betti numbers of the earth's surface and complicate the notions of pass, etc.)

In stating the Morse relationships, we assumed for simplicity that the set R on which f is defined has no boundary. If it has a boundary, and at each boundary point the derivative of f in the direction of the outwardly-drawn normal is positive, the relations still hold [63]. Without the assumption about the directional derivative, the relations still hold, if the numbers M_k are properly reinterpreted [67].

If we try to apply the theory of critical points to the calculus of variations we encounter an obvious difficulty. The class of rectifiable curves C lying in a manifold constitutes a metric space, and on it an integral of the type considered in the calculus of variations defines a function $J(C)$. But the space is not finite-dimensional, and the function $J(C)$ is not in general continuous; even if the integral is regular and positive definite we can only say that $J(C)$ is lower semicontinuous, as we saw in §4. Thus in each application of the critical point theory it is necessary either to simplify the formulation of the variational problem, to generalize the theory, or to do some of both.

There are some questions in the calculus of variations to which the critical point theory can be readily applied by means of a simple device [68]. Suppose that we are studying the values of an integral taken along a class of curves lying in a manifold R and having the initial and terminal points in submanifolds Z_1, Z_2, respectively. If E is an extremal $y = \gamma(t)$, $(t_1 \leq t \leq t_2)$, belonging to this class of curves and meeting Z_1 and Z_2 transversally, cut it by $(n-1)$-dimensional manifolds $T_1, \cdots, T_p$. In Z_1, Z_2 and each T_j we choose coordinate systems. Then if $(A, P_1, \cdots, P_p, B)$ is a sequence of points with A in Z_1, P_j in T_j and B in Z_2, we can represent the whole sequence by a single μ-tuple (z), by writing first the coördinates of A in Z_1, then those of P_1 in T_1, etc. Under everyday hypotheses, if the manifolds T_j divide E into small enough arcs and the points $A, P_1, \cdots, P_p, B$ are near enough to E, they can be joined in that order by uniquely determined short extremal arcs. Thus (z) determines an extremaloid, or broken extremal, with vertices as indicated. We may suppose that (0) determines E itself. The integral along the extremaloid determined by (z) we denote by $J(z)$.

A simple calculation shows that a point (z) is a critical point of $J(z)$ if and only if the extremaloid determined by (z) is free of corners (and is therefore an extremal) and cuts Z_1 and Z_2 transversally, this last condition being considered vacuously satisfied at an end locus Z_i which consists of a single point. In particular, (0) is a critical point. If Z_1 and Z_2 both reduce to single points, the nature of the critical point is expressed by the *index theorem* [71]: *The critical point* $(z) = (0)$ *is degenerate if and only if the beginning and end points of E are conjugate. If they are not conjugate, the type of the critical point is equal to the number of points on E conjugate to the beginning, each counted according to its multiplicity.* A like result holds if only one end manifold reduces to a point; the type of the critical point is the number of points of E which are focal points of the other end manifolds.

From this we deduce several results of interest in the calculus of variations. For example, there is a well known theorem, due to Bliss, concerning the order of focal points along a minimizing curve in the plane problem with two variable end points. By use of broken extremals, Currier [72] extended this theorem to the problem of minimizing an integral on a family of curves in $(n+1)$-space joining two n-dimensional manifolds. He obtained both necessary conditions and sufficient conditions for a minimum. Morse [73] extended this by permitting the end manifolds to be of arbitrary dimensionality. Again, by use of similar concepts, Morse [69] established the following result. Let the terminal manifold Z_2 be a single point not focal to any point of Z_1. Suppose that each point P of Z_1 can be joined to Z_2 by a unique continuously varying extremal. The numbers M_k of such extremals cutting Z_1 transversally and containing k focal points are connected with the Betti numbers of Z_1 by the relations (5.3).

Consider next the aggregate of all extremals joining two fixed points A and B on a manifold R. We can proceed nearly as before. For any large number p, we can choose points $A, P_1, P_2, \cdots, P_p, B$, subject only to the restriction that the distances between successive points be small enough, and then join these by extremal arcs. Again, we can determine the sequence of points by a single np-tuple (z) consisting of the coordinates of P_1, followed by those of P_2, etc. Denoting by $J(z)$ the value of the integral along the extremaloid determined by (z), we find that (z) is a critical point of $J(z)$ if and only if the extremaloid has no corners. But this precludes the possibility of isolated critical points. For if we cut any extremal in any manner into short arcs, the points of division yield a critical point (z), so that each critical point belongs to an n-dimensional spread of such points.

This is harmless if we are using Birkhoff's minimax principle, since that principle is valid without assumptions of nondegeneracy of critical points. In this manner, Birkhoff was able to prove, for example, that on every surface of the topological type of the sphere there exists at least one closed geodesic [62]. However, if we wish to apply the entire set of Morse relations to such problems, the theory of critical points must be extended.

Such an extension was made by Morse [70], who thereby arrived at esti-
mates of the numbers of extremals of different types joining two fixed
points.

Thus we see that even in a rather simple variational problem, there is a
need for generalization of the critical point theory. This need increases
with the complexity of the problem discussed. Particularly, in discussing
the problems (first investigated by Poincaré) concerned with the existence
and behavior of closed geodesics on a surface we encounter the space of
closed curves; and this space presents such topological complications that
it is most undesirable to have also to keep guard against the analytical
complication arising from the degeneration of critical points.

But if the general theory is to be extended to functions with degenerate
critical points, the definition of the type of a critical point must be changed,
and some reasonable method of assigning multiplicities must be devised.
Our crude sketch of proof of the Morse relations contains a hint as to how
this might be done. In the course of the proof it was shown that as c increased through a critical value $f(P_r)$, where P_r is a critical point of type
k, ($k=0$, 1 or 2), then either $p_k(c)$ increased by 1 or $p_{k-1}(c)$ decreased by 1.
So we can say that the "multiplicity" of P_r as a critical point of type j
(which for this simple case should obviously be 0 if $j \neq k$ and 1 if $k=j$) is
the sum of the number of new nonbounding j-cycles and the number of
$(j-1)$-cycles which become bounding as c increases through $f(P_r)$. Such a
topological definition clearly can be applied to degenerate critical points,
and even to functions without derivatives. It conforms with Birkhoff's
definition [62] of the multiplicity of a minimax point. As a simple example,
consider a flat-topped mountain (not the highest in the world). At every
point of the top all first partial derivatives of the height $f(x)$ are zero.
But as c increases through the height of the mountain top, the number of
nonbounding one-cycles in a maximal independent set will diminish by
just one, so the whole mountain top is to be regarded as the equivalent of
a single critical point of type 2 (maximum type). The "type number sums"
for the critical set formed by the mountain top are: 0 for type 0, 0 for type
1, 1 for type 2.

In 1929 W. M. Whyburn [74] established some properties of functions
with nonisolated critical points, which in essence were a generalization of
the minimax principle. A year later A. B. Brown [75, 76]* extended the
critical point theory to analytic functions with isolated critical points.
Morse [71] further extended the theory so as to permit its use in treating
the Poincaré problem on closed geodesics. He obtained theorems of which
the following is a sample. Let R be a Riemannian manifold which is the
nonsingular, analytic homeomorph of the unit m-sphere. Then there exists a set G of closed geodesics on R such that the kth type number sum of

* The theory is extended in [76] to critical sets which are complexes. There is a lacuna in
one of the proofs in [75] (cf. footnote [76, p. 512]).

the geodesics of G is at least the number of principal ellipses of index k on any ellipsoid $E_m(a)$ for which the principal semi-axes are distinct and sufficiently near unity.*

But the movement toward generalizing the critical point theory did not stop with the papers cited. As we have already mentioned, it is possible to define critical points of various types by means of purely topological concepts without mention of derivatives. Recently the theory has been reinvestigated from the topological aspect, and as a result of the researches of Morse, Birkhoff, and Hestenes it has been extended so as to apply to functions defined and lower semicontinuous on metric spaces [71, 78–80].

While the theory of critical sets is thus extended to a wide class of spaces and functions, we cannot expect that the work in this direction is completed nor that it has assumed its final form. And if it were completed, the theory of the calculus of variations in the large would still be far from being a closed chapter. For we may reasonably hope to see it extended to larger classes of problems, including double integral problems, and we may expect new and significant applications of the general theory, for example, to problems in dynamics.

6. The idea, presented in the preceding paragraphs, of embedding the problems of the calculus of variations in a more general class of problems, is not a new one. Volterra considered the integrals of the calculus of variations as a particular class of functions of lines, and more recently there have probably been many who have regarded these integrals as functions on metric spaces [81]. We have already seen that the existence theorems gain in clarity when regarded from this point of view, and that Menger has studied the problems of the calculus of variations entirely within the framework of semimetric spaces. Moreover we have seen that the critical point theory can be profitably extended to functions defined on metric spaces. However, the same concept can also be used in deriving necessary conditions for a minimum. LeStourgeon [82] studied the problem of minimizing functionals of a certain type, and by use of the differential, established necessary conditions which specialized to the Euler equation and Jacobi condition for free problems. More recently, Lusternik [83] considered the problem of minimizing a functional f on that part of a linear space A which is carried by a differentiable transformation into the origin of another linear space B. He obtained a necessary condition which generalizes the Lagrange multiplier rule for Lagrange problems. Graves [84] applied theorems developed in general analysis to establish the Euler equations for Lagrange problems in a degree of generality which, at least for parametric problems, seems to leave nothing to be desired. Goldstine [85, 86] set up a problem of which the Bolza problem is a special case, and

---

* By different methods, depending on the introduction of a new topological invariant could the "category," Lusternik and Schnirelmann earlier established the existence of at least three non-self-intersecting closed geodesics on surfaces of genus zero [77].

for it deduced the analogues of the Euler equations and the Legendre and Weierstrass conditions. The problem of developing the methods of abstract spaces far enough to include with profit a large central portion of the calculus of variations is very far from completion. But in view of the widespread trend in analysis toward the general and abstract, we may well expect to see the program pushed forward in the next few years.

UNIVERSITY OF VIRGINIA
CHARLOTTESVILLE, VA.

BIBLIOGRAPHY

1. RADÓ, T. *On the Problem of Plateau*. Ergebnisse der Mathematik und ihre Grenzgebiete. 1933.

2. DOUGLAS, J. *Some new results in the problem of Plateau*. Journal of Mathematics and Physics, vol. 15 (1936), pp. 55–64.

3. DOUGLAS, J. *Minimal surfaces of general topological structure with any finite number of assigned boundaries*. Journal of Mathematics and Physics, vol. 15 (1936), pp. 105–123.

4. COURANT, R. *Plateau's problem and Dirichlet's principle*. Annals of Mathematics, (2), vol. 38 (1937), pp. 679–724.

5. COURANT, R. *The existence of a minimal surface of least area bounded by prescribed Jordan arcs and prescribed surfaces*. Proceedings of the National Academy of Sciences, vol. 24 (1938), pp. 97–101.

6. REID, W. T. *Boundary value problems of the calculus of variations*. Bulletin of the American Mathematical Society, vol. 43 (1937), pp. 633–666.

7. BLISS, G. A. *The problem of Lagrange in the calculus of variations*. American Journal of Mathematics, vol. 52 (1930), pp. 674–744.

8. MORSE, M., and MYERS, S. B. *The problems of Lagrange and Mayer with variable end points*. Proceedings of the American Academy of Arts and Sciences, vol. 66 (1931), pp. 235–253.

9. BLISS, G. A. *The Problem of Bolza in the Calculus of Variations*. Mimeographed notes of lectures delivered at the University of Chicago, 1935.

10. BOLZA, O. *Vorlesungen über Variationsrechnung*. Leipzig, Teubner, 1909.

11. VON ESCHERICH, G. *Die zweite Variation der einfachen Integrale*. Sitzungsberichte der Akademie der Wissenschaften zu Wien, (2A),vol. 107 (1898), pp. 1191–1250, 1267–1326, 1381–1428; vol. 108 (1899), pp. 1269–1340.

12. KNESER, A. *Lehrbuch der Variationsrechnung*. Braunschweig, Vieweg, 1900.

13. MASON, M., and BLISS, G. A. *The properties of curves in space which minimize a definite integral*. Transactions of the American Mathematical Society, vol. 9 (1908), pp. 440–466.

14. BLISS, G. A. *Jacobi's condition for problems of the calculus of variations in parametric form*. Transactions of the American Mathematical Society, vol. 17 (1916), pp. 195–206.

15. BLISS, G. A. *The transformation of Clebsch in the calculus of variations*. Proceedings of the International Congress at Toronto, 1924, vol. 1, pp. 589–603.

16. BLISS, G. A. *Some recent developments in the calculus of variations*. Bulletin of the American Mathematical Society, vol. 26 (1919), pp. 343–361.

17. HESTENES, M. R. *A note on the Jacobi condition for parametric problems in the calculus of variations*. Bulletin of the American Mathematical Society, vol. 40 (1934), pp. 297–302.

18. BIRKHOFF, G. D., and HESTENES, M. R. *Natural isoperimetric conditions in the calculus of variations*. Duke Mathematical Journal, vol. 1 (1935), pp. 198–286. (Cf. in particular, p. 264.)

19. MORSE, M. *The index theorem in the calculus of variations*. Duke Mathematical Journal, vol. 4 (1938), pp. 231–246.

20. BLISS, G. A. *Normality and abnormality in the calculus of variations*. Transactions of the American Mathematical Society, vol. 43 (1938), pp. 365–376.

21. Carathéodory, C. *Die Theorie der zweiten Variation beim Problem von Lagrange*. Sitzungsberichte der Bayerischen Akademie der Wissenschaften, 1923, pp. 99–114.

22. Carathéodory, C. *Über die Einteilung der Variationsprobleme von Lagrange nach Klassen*. Commentarii Mathematici Helvetici, vol. 5 (1933), pp. 1–19.

23. Graves, L. M. *On the Weierstrass condition for the problem of Bolza in the calculus of variations*. Annals of Mathematics, (2), vol. 33 (1932), pp. 747–752.

24. Hestenes, M. R. *Sufficient conditions for the problem of Bolza in the calculus of variations*. Transactions of the American Mathematical Society, vol. 36 (1934), pp. 793–818.

25. Morse, M. *Sufficient conditions in the problem of Lagrange without assumptions of normalcy*. Transactions of the American Mathematical Society, vol. 37 (1935), pp. 147–160.

26. Reid, W. T. *Sufficient conditions by expansion methods for the problem of Bolza in the calculus of variations*. Annals of Mathematics, (2), vol. 38 (1937), pp. 662–678.

27. Levi, E. E. *Sui criterii sufficienti per il massimo e per il minimo nel calcolo delle variazioni*. Annali di Matematica Pura ed Applicata, (4), vol. 21 (1913), pp. 173–218.

28. Hestenes, M. R. *A direct sufficiency proof for the problem of Bolza in the calculus of variations*. Transactions of the American Mathematical Society, vol. 42 (1937), pp. 141–154.

29. Reid, W. T. *A direct expansion proof of sufficient conditions for the non-parametric problem of Bolza*. Transactions of the American Mathematical Society, vol. 42 (1937), pp. 183–190.

30. Hilbert, D. *Über das Dirichletsche Prinzip*. Jahresbericht der Deutschen Mathematiker-Vereinigung, vol. 8 (1900), pp. 184–188.

31. Carathéodory, C. *Über die starken Maxima und Minima bei einfachen Integralen*. Mathematische Annalen, vol. 62 (1906), pp. 449–503.

32. Bill, E. S. *An existence theorem for a problem of the calculus of variations in space*. Transactions of the American Mathematical Society vol. 13 (1912), pp. 50–58.

33. Tonelli, L. *Fondamenti di Calcolo delle Variazioni*. Zanichelli, Bologna, vol. 1, 1921, and vol. 2, 1923.

34. Hahn, H. *Über ein Existenztheorem der Variationsrechnung*. Sitzungsberichte der Akademie der Wissenschaften zu Wien, (2A), vol. 134 (1925), pp. 437–447.

35. Carathéodory, C. *Über die Existenz der absoluten Minima bei regulären Variationsproblemen auf der Kugel*. Annali della Scuola Normale Superiore di Pisa, (2), vol. 1 (1932), pp 79–88.

36. Tonelli, L. *Sull'esistenza del minimo in problemi di calcolo delle variazioni*. Annali della Scuola Normale Superiore di Pisa, vol. 1 (1932), pp. 89–99.

37. Graves, L. M. *On an existence theorem of the calculus of variations*. Monatshefte für Mathematik und Physik, vol. 39 (1932), pp. 101–104.

38. McShane, E. J. *Remark concerning Mr. Graves' paper "On an existence theorem of the calculus of variations."* Monatshefte für Mathematik und Physik, vol. 39 (1932), pp. 105–106.

39. Nagumo, M. *Über die gleichmässige Summierbarkeit und ihre Anwendung auf ein Variationsproblem*. Japanese Journal of Mathematics, vol. 6 (1929), pp. 173–182.

40. McShane, E. J. *Existence theorems for ordinary problems of the calculus of variations*. Annali della Scuola Normale Superiore di Pisa, (2), vol. 3 (1934), pp. 183–211, 287–315.

41. Tonelli, L. *Su gli integrali del calcolo delle variazioni in forma ordinaria*. Annali della Scuola Normale Superiore di Pisa, (2), vol. 3 (1934), pp. 401–450.

42. McShane, E. J. *Semi-continuity of integrals in the calculus of variations*. Duke mathematical Journal, vol. 2 (1936), pp. 597–616.

43. McShane, E. J. *Some existence theorems for problems in the calculus of variations*. Duke Mathematical Journal, vol. 4 (1938), pp. 132–156.

44. Menger, K. *Metrische Geometrie und Variationsrechnung*. Fundamenta Mathematicae, vol. 25 (1935), pp. 441–458.

45. Menger, K. *Die metrische Methode in der Variationsrechnung*. Ergebnisse eines Mathematischen Kolloquiums, vol. 8. Vienna, 1937.

46. Menger, K. *Metric methods in the calculus of variations*. Proceedings of the National Academy of Sciences, vol. 23 (1937), pp. 244–250.

47. FRINK, O. *Geodesic continua in abstract metric space.* American Journal of Mathematics, vol. 58 (1936), pp. 514–520.

48. GRAVES, L. M. *On the existence of the absolute minimum in space problems of the calculus of variations.* Annals of Mathematics, vol. 28 (1927), pp. 153–170.

49. GRAVES, L. M. *On the existence of the absolute minimum in problems of Lagrange.* Bulletin of the American Mathematical Society, vol. 39 (1933), pp. 101–104.

50. CINQUINI, S. *Sopra l'esistenza della soluzione nei problemi di calcolo delle variazioni di ordine n.* Annali della Scuola Normale Superiore di Pisa, (2), vol. 5 (1936), pp. 169–190.

51. CINQUINI, S. *Nuovi teoremi di esistenza dell'estremo in campi illimitati per i problemi di calcolo delle variazioni di ordine n.* Annali della Scuola Normale Superiore di Pisa, (2), vol. 6 (1937), pp. 191–209.

52. MANIÀ, B. *Sopra un problema di navigazione di Zermelo.* Mathematische Annalen, vol. 113 (1936), pp. 584–599.

53. MANIÀ, B. *Esistenza dell'estremo assoluto in un classico problema di Mayer.* Annali della Scuola Normale Superiore di Pisa, (2), vol. 2 (1933), pp. 343–354.

54. MANIÀ, B. *Sulla curva di massima velocità finale.* Annali della Scuola Normale Superiore di Pisa, (2), vol. 3 (1934), pp. 317–336.

55. MANIÀ, B. *Sui problemi di Lagrange e di Mayer.* Rendiconti del Circolo Matematico di Palermo, vol. 58 (1934), pp. 285–310.

56. MANIÀ, B. *Sopra una classe di problemi di Mayer considerati come limiti di ordinari problemi di minimo.* Rendiconti del Seminario Matematico della Università di Padova, 1934, pp. 99–121.

57. GRAVES, L. M. *The existence of an extremum in problems of Mayer.* Transactions of the American Mathematical Society, vol. 39 (1936), pp. 456–471.

58. McSHANE, E. J. *Semi-continuity in the calculus of variations, and absolute minima for isoperimetric problems.* Contributions to the Calculus of Variations, 1930. University of Chicago, 1931.

59. McSHANE, E. J. *Some existence theorems in the calculus of variations.* A sequence of five notes to appear in the Transactions of the American Mathematical Society.

60. LEWY, H. *Über die Methode der Differenzengleichungen zur Lösung von Variations- und Randwertproblemen.* Mathematische Annalen, vol. 98 (1928), pp. 107–124.

61. DRESDEN, A. *The second derivatives of the extremal integral.* Transactions of the American Mathematical Society, vol. 9 (1908), pp. 467–486. (Cf. in particular, p. 486.)

62. BIRKHOFF, G. D. *Dynamical systems with two degrees of freedom.* Transactions of the American Mathematical Society, vol. 18 (1917), pp. 199–300.

63. MORSE, M. *Relations between the critical points of a real function of n independent variables.* Transactions of the American Mathematical Society, vol. 27 (1925), pp. 345–396.

64. POINCARÉ, H. *Sur les courbes définies par les équations différentielles.* Journal de Mathématiques Pures et Appliqués, (4), vol. 1 (1885), pp. 167–244.

65. LEFSCHETZ, S. *Continuous transformations of manifolds.* Proceedings of the National Academy of Sciences, vol. 11 (1925), pp. 290–292.

66. HOPF, H. *Vektorfelder in n-dimensionalen Mannigfaltigkeiten.* Mathematische Annalen, vol. 96 (1927), pp. 225–250.

67. MORSE, M., and VAN SCHAACK, G. B. *The critical point theory under general boundary conditions.* Annals of Mathematics, (2), vol. 35 (1934), pp. 545–571; Duke Mathematical Journal, vol. 2 (1936), pp. 220–242.

68. MORSE, M. *The foundations of a theory in the calculus of variations in the large.* Transactions of the American Mathematical Society, vol. 30 (1928), p. 213–274.

69. MORSE, M. *The foundations of the calculus of variations in the large in m-space.* I. Transactions of the American Mathematical Society, vol. 31 (1929), pp. 379–404.

70. MORSE, M. *The foundations of a theory of the calculus of variations in the large in m-space.* II. Transactions of the American Mathematical Society, vol. 32 (1930), pp. 599–631.

71. MORSE, M. *Functional topology and abstract variational theory*, Annals of Mathematics. (2), vol. 38 (1937), pp. 386–449.

72. CURRIER, A. E. *The variable end point problem of the calculus of variations including a generalization of the classical Jacobi conditions*. Transactions of the American Mathematical Society, vol. 34 (1932), pp. 689–704.

73. MORSE, M. *The Calculus of Variations in the Large*. American Mathematical Society Colloquium Publications, vol. 18, pp. 64–70 New York, 1934.

74. WHYBURN, W. M. *Non-isolated critical points of functions*. Bulletin of the American Mathematical Society, vol. 35 (1929), pp. 701–708.

75. BROWN, A. B. *Relations between the critical points of a real analytical function of N independent variables*. American Journal of Mathematics, vol. 52 (1930), pp. 251–270.

76. BROWN, A. B. *Critical sets of an arbitrary real analytical function of n variables*. Annals of Mathematics, (2), vol. 32 (1931), pp. 512–520.

77. LUSTERNIK, L., and SCHNIRELMANN, L. *Topological Methods in the Calculus of Variations*. Gosudarstvennoe Izdatelstvo, Moscow, 1930. (In Russian.) [*Méthodes topologiques dans les problèmes variationnels*. Actualités Scientifiques et Industrielles, no. 188. 1934. (French translation of first part of book.)]

78. MORSE, M. *Analysis in the Large*. Lithoprinted notes of lectures delivered at the Institute for Advanced Study, 1935–1936.

79. BIRKHOFF, G. D., and HESTENES, M. R. *Generalized minimax principle in the calculus of variations*. Duke Mathematical Journal, vol. 1 (1935), pp. 413–432.

80. HESTENES, M. R. *Minimax principle for functions*. Proceedings of the National Academy of Sciences, vol. 22 (1936), pp. 115–119.

81. SANGER, R. G. *Functions of lines and the calculus of variations*. Contributions to the Calculus of Variations, 1931–1932. University of Chicago, 1933.

82. LeSTOURGEON, F. E. *Minima of functions of lines*. Transactions of the American Mathematical Society, vol. 21 (1920), pp. 357–383.

83. LUSTERNIK, L. A. *Sur les extrêmes relatifs des fonctionelles*. Recueil Mathématique de Moscow, vol. 41 (1934), pp. 390–400. (In Russian.)

84. GRAVES, L. M. *On the problem of Lagrange*. American Journal of Mathematics, vol. 53 (1931), pp. 547–554.

85. GOLDSTINE, H. H. *Conditions for a minimum of a functional*. Contributions to the Calculus of Variations, 1933–1937. University of Chicago, 1937.

86. GOLDSTINE, H. H. *The minima of functionals with associated side conditions*. Duke Mathematical Journal, vol. 3 (1937), pp. 418–425.

RECENT TRENDS IN GEOMETRY

BY

T. Y. THOMAS

Generally speaking, the subject of geometry falls into two main categories: the intrinsic theory of space and the theory of configurations existing in space. In this latter category we have the projective differential geometry of curves and surfaces which is largely devoted to the study of the differential invariants of these configurations which are left unaltered by transformations of the projective group and which, in this country, is usually associated with the names of Wilczynski and Lane. Usually however in dealing with problems in this category one is concerned with the purely metric theory, for example, the differential properties of configurations in a euclidean metric space which are unaltered by the group of orthogonal transformations of this space. In this connection one must think of the work of C. Burstin and W. Mayer who obtained for the first time the system of invariants for the general surface in a space of constant curvature by which the surface is characterized to within a rigid displacement in the imbedding space. Here, also, belong the recent researches of E. Kasner on conformal geometry, the investigations of W. C. Graustein, and the earlier work of L. P. Eisenhart.

But it is chiefly the intrinsic theory of spaces that has been the center of attention in recent years due to the influence of Einstein's theory of relativity and the attempts of many of the most distinguished mathematicians of the present time to devise a unified field theory of gravitation and electricity. While these investigations have so far fallen short of the physical requirements they have resulted in a number of elegant mathematical theories of abstract spaces and in this form they will undoubtedly survive. Owing to these and other researches we have today a rather extended abstract theory of various generalized spaces existing as a separate mathematical discipline and occupying a very definite place in the mathematical literature. It is this theory to which I have previously referred as the intrinsic theory of spaces or intrinsic geometry and with which I intend to occupy myself exclusively in this report. By thus restricting the domain of our considerations so as to permit a more detailed discussion and in view of the fact, also, that my own investigations have been primarily in the field of the intrinsic geometry I have hoped to make this report in some sense a scientific contribution.

1. By a geometry we shall understand the theory of a space and by a space a set of undefined objects, called points, on which a structure has been imposed by assuming that the points and certain subsets, usually said to be open, satisfy a prescribed number of conditions (structural

properties). For example, if we define the neighborhood of a point P of the space as any of the above open subsets containing P we may suppose that the points and the neighborhoods satisfy the four well known axioms of Hausdorff. In such a space one may define the concepts of limit point, complement, nowhere dense set, connected set, compact set, continuous function, and so on, which have become commonplace in the language of present day mathematics.

We arrive at the spaces of differential geometry by a fundamental restriction of the Hausdorff spaces, namely, by the requirement that the neighborhoods be homeomorphic to the n-dimensional number space, that is, the totality of ordered sets of n real numbers $x^1, \cdots, x^n$ with the ordinary arithmetic definition of neighborhood. Such a space is commonly called a topological manifold. Thus the differential geometer is provided with one of his essential tools, namely the use of coordinate systems which can be introduced into the various neighborhoods of the topoligical manifold owing to the above homeomorphisms. By a coordinate system is here meant a $(1, 1)$ continuous correspondence between the points of a neighborhood of the manifold and a region (open point set) of the arithmetic space of n dimensions. Suppose now that it is possible to define in each of a set of neighborhoods covering the topological manifold a system of coordinates in such a way that the coordinate relationships which are defined in the intersections of any two coordinate neighborhoods are of class C^r, that is, are continuous and have all continuous partial derivatives to the order r inclusive where r is zero or a positive integer; these relations are regular if $r \geq 1$, that is, if the jacobian is everywhere different from zero. We shall understand, moreover, that any point set U which is homeomorphic to a region of the n-dimensional number space and in which a system of coordinates $x^1, \cdots, x^n$ can be defined (one to one continuous correspondence between the coordinates of the system and points of the set) such that the coordinates of U are related by transformations of class C^r (with non-vanishing jacobians if $r \geq 1$) to the coordinates of the above systems in the manifold is likewise admissible as a coordinate system in the topological manifold. We shall say that the topological manifold having as neighborhoods the coordinate regions so defined is an n-dimensional manifold of class C^r. In particular if the above coordinate relationships possess derivatives of all orders without restriction we shall speak of an n-dimensional manifold of class C^∞ and still more particularly if these relationships are analytic we have the analytic manifold or manifold of class C^ω, to use a notation suggested by Veblen and Whitehead in their Cambridge Tract on *The Foundations of Differential Geometry* [54].*

In the above paragraph we have given a hasty description of the manifold of class C^u (where $u = r \geq 0$, ∞, or ω) by a process of specialization

---

* Numbers in square brackets refer to the bibliography at the end of the paper.

having its beginning in the Hausdorff space. Veblen and Whitehead [54] have devised an axiomatic characterization of these manifolds in terms of an undefined class of allowable coordinate systems. Their axioms fall into three groups A, B, and C. The axioms A define the local structure completely, the axioms B define the class of allowable coordinate systems, while the axioms C impose certain general restrictions on the topology of the space of such a nature that A and C together characterized the space as a topological manifold. This tract by Veblen and Whitehead is worthy of serious study as the most complete and carefully thought out work that has appeared to date on the foundations of differential geometry defined as the general theory of manifolds of class C^u with $u \neq 0$. The influence of this work can easily be discerned in the present account of the intrinsic theory of differential geometry.

The above coordinate neighborhoods in a manifold $\mathfrak{M}$ of class C^u will also be called proper coordinate neighborhoods. An open set S which is the continuous map of a (proper) coordinate neighborhood of the n-dimensional number space will be said to be an improper coordinate neighborhood of $\mathfrak{M}$ with respect to the coordinates $x^1, \cdots, x^n$ which are thus introduced in S if any point $T \subset S$ is contained in a (proper) coordinate neighborhood $N(T)$ having $x^1, \cdots, x^n$ as coordinates. Thus the coordinates of an improper coordinate neighborhood S are *locally* in (1, 1) correspondence with points of $\mathfrak{M}$ but not necessarily over the entire neighborhood S.

It is often convenient to consider such coordinate systems the coordinates of which are not in (1, 1) correspondence with the points of the space. Indeed by a coordinate system we shall mean quite generally a correspondence $P \rightarrow x$ between a set of points $[P]$ of the space and a set of arithmetic points $[x]$, that is, points of the n-dimensional arithmetic space. Any arithmetic point x which corresponds to P in this correspondence may be called an image of P in $P \rightarrow x$ and P may be called an image of x. The numbers $x^1, \cdots, x^n$ which constitute an image of P are called the coordinates of P. An example of an important system of coordinates not in (1, 1) correspondence with the points of the space is the system of homogeneous coordinates used in the classical projective geometry.

The above discussion may be extended to the case where the set of coordinate relationships considered in the manifold is restricted to belong to a particular pseudo-group of transformations of class C^u (not identical with the set of all regular coordinate transformations of class C^u) and in the following such pseudo-groups will indeed appear (see, for example, the end of §11). In such cases the pseudo-group cannot be entirely arbitrary since there is evidently some connection between it and the topology of the manifold.

2. Before proceeding further let us pause to consider the beginning

which has already been made in the study of manifolds of class C^u where $u \neq 0$. I have in mind in particular the work of Hassler Whitney [63] who has shown, among other things, that an n-dimensional manifold of class C^r, where r is different from zero or ω, can be embedded in a euclidean space of $2n$ dimensions and that this embedding can be made without intersections in a euclidean space of $2n+1$ dimensions. The method here used by Whitney is closely related to one employed by Hurewicz [18] in purely topological embedding problems. An immediate consequence of this theorem is that there can be defined over the manifold a Riemann metric (§6). Generally speaking, the results which have been established for nonanalytic manifolds cannot be extended to the case of the analytic manifold. Thus one has so far not succeeded in showing that an analytic manifold can be embedded analytically in a euclidean space, that any two points of an analytic manifold connected in the topological sense can be joined by an analytic arc, or that any analytic arc in an analytic manifold can be covered by an allowable coordinate system. Another problem in this connection would be that of showing whether or not one can define along any analytic arc in an analytic manifold a vector whose components are analytic functions of the parameter of the arc, other than the trivial case of the tangent vector. Of course such questions are primarily questions of analysis but they are likewise of interest from the standpoint of differential geometry.

Another contribution is the demonstration by S. S. Cairns [4] that any manifold of class C^1 can be triangulated, a result which has important applications, for example in the proof of the generalized theorem of Stokes [5]. However the methods employed by Cairns are rather complicated as are also, for that matter, those used by Whitney and it would be extremely desirable to obtain the results of these authors by simpler procedures.

3. In a sense the general manifold of class C^u is a rather amorphous affair and to arrive at the spaces which one habitually considers in the intrinsic theory one must add other elements of space structure. These additional elements of space structure are of primary importance in the theory of the space and on this account one usually speaks of this part of the structure briefly as the structure of the space. There are many ways of introducing this additional structure which lead to interesting spaces and we shall wish to examine some of these in detail. But first I should like to present an important definition applying quite generally to any space defined as a set of points with definitely specified structural properties. Two spaces U and V are said to be *equivalent* or *isomorphic* if there exists a $(1, 1)$ correspondence between their points which carries the space U into the space V, that is, which carries the structural properties of U into those of V, and conversely. In particular, if $U = V$, the isomorphic correspondence is called an automorphism. Of course this general form of the concept of isomorphism must be somewhat vague without additional clarification.

Instead of attempting to enlarge on this idea in its general aspect we shall attempt to supply the needed clarification in connection with several particular but important spaces to which we next turn our attention.

4. One way in which additional elements of structure may be added to a manifold is by means of a special class of coordinate systems called *preferred coordinate systems*. Denoting by G a set of transformations of arithmetic points into arithmetic points, we define the structure of a space by means of the following set of axioms in which points and preferred coordinate systems enter as undefined terms.

A_1. *Each preferred coordinate system is a* (1, 1) *transformation of the space into the arithmetic space of n dimensions.*

A_2. *Any transformation of coordinates from one preferred coordinate system to another belongs to G.*

A_3. *Any coordinate system obtained from a preferred coordinate system by a transformation belonging to G is preferred.*

A_4. *There is at least one preferred coordinate system.*

It follows from the above axioms (we omit the details) that G is a group. Now let S and S' be two spaces satisfying the axioms A for the same group G. When we denote by $P \rightarrow x$ a preferred coordinate system for S and by $P' \rightarrow x'$ a preferred coordinate system for S' the relation $x = x'$ defines a (1, 1) correspondence C between the points of S and S'. It is easily seen that any preferred coordinate system for S is carried by C into a preferred coordinate system for S' and conversely. We have here an illustration of a (1, 1) point correspondence between two spaces which carries the structural properties (determined by the totality of preferred coordinate systems) of either one into the structural properties of the other as demanded by the general definition of isomorphism in the preceding section. Hence two spaces which satisfy the axioms A with the same group G are isomorphic.

If G is the affine group, any space satisfying the axioms A is an affine space and the preferred coordinate systems are then called cartesian coordinate systems. If G is the group of similarity transformations, a space satisfying the axioms A is a euclidean space. Also if G is the euclidean metric group, a space satisfying the axioms A is a euclidean metric space. In the last two cases the preferred coordinate systems are called rectangular cartesian coordinate systems.

An automorphism $P \rightarrow \bar{P}$ of a space satisfying the axioms A is evidently represented in any preferred coordinate system $P \rightarrow x$ by a transformation $x \rightarrow \bar{x}$ belonging to the group G. Conversely any transformation $x \rightarrow \bar{x}$ belonging to G in a preferred coordinate system $P \rightarrow x$ defines an automorphism $P \rightarrow \bar{P}$ of the space. It is clear in fact that the group of automorphisms G^* of the space is isomorphic (in the group-theoretic sense) to the group G. Now the group G^* provides a method of classification of configurations (sets of points) of the space into congruent or non-congruent configurations. Two configurations are said to be *congruent* if one can be carried into the other by a transformation belonging to G^*. It is important to emphasize that the definition of congruence here introduced pertains to a space whose structure is defined by a group of coordinate transformations in accordance with the above axioms A.

The concept of congruence as determined by a group of point transformations was proposed by Klein [20] as the defining property of a space in his Erlanger Program (1872). When the structure of a space is defined by the totality of congruence relationships existing in the space, which is, strictly speaking, the point of view of Klein, the group of point transformations which enters into the determination of these congruence relationships will be a subgroup (and in certain cases a proper subgroup) of the group of automorphisms of the space. But this view point is of very restricted application since many of the spaces which have been the object of recent study have as their group of automorphisms the identity and this is evidently insufficient for their characterization. The idea of the coordinate transformation and not Klein's idea of the point transformation or automorphism of a space is fundamental in the modern space concept.

5. Projective and conformal spaces may be defined by sets of axioms analogous to the above axioms A. As a matter of interest in itself and also for future reference in this report we state the axioms for the projective space. The axioms are given in terms of homogeneous coordinate systems in which a point P corresponding to an arithmetic point $(x^1, \cdots, x^{n+1})$ also corresponds to the point $(\lambda x^1, \cdots, \lambda x^{n+1})$, where λ is any non-zero factor and no point of the space corresponds to the origin of the $(n+1)$-dimensional arithmetic space. The undefined terms are the point and the preferred homogeneous coordinate system.

B_1. *In a preferred homogeneous coordinate system each point is represented by at least one arithmetic point in the arithmetic space of $n+1$ dimensions, and each arithmetic point other than the origin represents just one point.*

B_2. *Two arithmetic points represent the same point if, and only if, they lie on the same arithmetic straight line through the origin.*

B_3. *Any preferred coordinate system can be transformed into any other by a linear homogeneous transformation.*

B_4. *Any homogeneous coordinate system obtained from a preferred coordinate system by a linear homogeneous transformation is a preferred coordinate system.*

B_5. *There is at least one preferred coordinate system.*

It follows from the axioms B_1 and B_2 that each preferred coordinate system is a (1, 1) correspondence between the points of the projective space and the arithmetic straight lines through the origin of the $(n+1)$-

dimensional arithmetic space. The group of automorphisms of a projective space is called the *n*-dimensional projective group.

6. One of the most important types of space is that known as the Riemann space which may be said to have had its origin in Riemann's *Habilitationsschrift* [30]. From the general point of view which we have adopted, a Riemann space is defined as a manifold of class C^u with an additional element of structure consisting of a positive definite quadratic differential form defined over the manifold and on the basis of which the metric relationships existing in the space are determined. The existence of the quadratic differential form implies that its coefficients, which are functions of the coordinates $x^1, \cdots, x^n$ in any particular coordinate neighborhood, have the tensor law of transformation in the transition from one coordinate neighborhood to another—these coefficients are the components of a tensor called the fundamental metric tensor of the space. We may suppose the components of the fundamental metric tensor to be of class C^r, where $r < u$ and $u \geq 1$, since their class will then be preserved under allowable coordinate transformations in the manifold. Ordinarily we suppose the integer r to have its greatest value consistent with the value of u, that is, $r = u - 1$. In such a case we may speak of a Riemann space of class C^r with the understanding that the underlying coordinate manifold is of class C^{r+1}; correspondingly, we may speak of an analytic Riemann space or Riemann space of class C^ω when the components of the fundamental metric tensor are analytic functions defined over an analytic manifold.

In the theory of the Riemann space one is usually not concerned with the particular quadratic differential form which enters in the definition of its structure. In other words one deals with properties which are common to all such spaces. Accordingly, by the Riemann space we frequently understand the class of all Riemann spaces whose structure is determined by particular quadratic differential forms. Whether the designation Riemann space refers to a (particular) Riemann space as above defined or to the class of all such spaces must usually be decided in the light of the context. Analogous remarks apply to the various generalized spaces which we shall consider in the following sections.

Much of the formal local theory of Riemann spaces into which we do not enter here is independent of the fact that the quadratic differential form is positive definite and for this part of the theory it suffices to assume merely that the discriminant of the form does not vanish. A direct incentive to the treatment of such indefinite quadratic differential forms has moreover been furnished by the theory of relativity. On this account many authors do not insist that the above quadratic differential form be positive definite (as originally formulated by Riemann) in their definition of the Riemann space. However, in certain investigations, account must be taken of the signature of this form and, in particular, this is the case when dealing with properties of the space in the large where the signature must of necessity play an important rôle. We would suggest, therefore, that the designation "Riemann space" be used in the strict sense here considered owing to the especial mathematical interest of these spaces; and that a coordinate manifold over which an indefinite but non-degenerate quadratic differential form is defined be called generally a pseudo-Riemann space or a Riemann space of signature $s(<n)$ when the actual value of the signature is of significance. Of course one may also consider spaces for which the discriminant of the quadratic differential form vanishes at exceptional points, or even becomes infinite, for example over a set of points nowhere dense in the underlying manifold, and such spaces would appear to offer the possibility of interesting investigations.

Two Riemann or pseudo-Riemann spaces of the same class C^u are isomorphic if, and only if, there exists a (1, 1) point correspondence between the spaces which is representable by coordinate relationships of class C^u and which transforms the quadratic differential form of one of the spaces into that of the other. An automorphism of such a space is sometimes referred to as a motion. Correspondingly, the group of automorphisms is referred to as the group of motions and under this heading has been extensively treated in the literature. Since the group of automorphisms of a Riemann or pseudo-Riemann space is in general the identity these spaces fall outside the scope of the Erlanger Program (see end of §4).

7. The concept of infinitesimal parallel displacement, formulated by Levi-Civita in 1917, was of the utmost importance in the development of the theory of generalized spaces and led directly to the discovery of spaces generalizing those of Riemann [22]. Starting with an n-dimensional surface S immersed in a euclidean space E of m dimensions, Levi-Civita so defined the parallel displacement of a vector ξ along a curve of class C^1 in S with reference to the enveloping space E that the change in the components of the vector ξ along C proceeded in accordance with the equations

$$(1) \qquad \frac{d\xi^\alpha}{dt} + L^\alpha_{\beta\gamma}\xi^\beta \frac{dx^\gamma}{dt} = 0,$$

where t denotes the parameter of the curve and the L's are a set of symbols previously defined by Christoffel [8] and depending on the coefficients of the quadratic differential form which determines the element of arc length in S as a subspace of the euclidean space E. In the case of a two-dimensional surface S in a three-dimensional euclidean space, where the idea of Levi-Civita has its strongest intuitive appeal, the procedure, in brief, may be described as follows. Let F be a developable surface tangent to S along C (envelope of the one-parameter family of tangent planes to S along C). Let ξ_P be a vector in the tangent plane to S at a point P on C. Roll F on a plane so that C becomes a curve C' in the plane, P a point P' on C', and ξ_P a vector $\xi_{P'}$ at P'. Displace $\xi_{P'}$ along C' by parallel displacement in the

ordinary sense (parallel displacement in a euclidean plane). We thus define
vectors $\xi'(t)$ along C' parallel in the ordinary euclidean sense. Now wrap
the plane about the surface S along C to secure the original developable
surface F. Thereby the vectors $\xi'(t)$ go into vectors $\xi(t)$ tangent to S
along C. We define the vectors $\xi(t)$ which are in the surface S, that is, in
the tangent planes to S along C, to be parallel with respect to C and in
fact to result from the original vector ξ_P at P by parallel displacement
along C. Levi-Civita's definition of parallel displacement of a vector in a
surface S generalizes the ordinary euclidean concept of parallel displacement in the sense that if S is a plane (in general an n-dimensional euclidean
space) the parallel displacement is identical with the ordinary euclidean
displacement.

Soon after the work of Levi-Civita, a significant contribution was made
to the idea of parallel displacement by H. Weyl [55] in his search for a
combined theory of gravitation and electricity. Weyl's contribution consisted primarily in removing the enveloping euclidean space. He furthermore generalized the functions $L^{\alpha}_{\beta\gamma}$ appearing in the above differential
equations to functions of the coordinates $x^1, \cdots, x^n$ of class C^u with a
definite law of transformation, namely,

$$(2) \qquad \bar{L}^{\sigma}_{\beta\gamma} \frac{\partial x^{\alpha}}{\partial \bar{x}^{\sigma}} = \frac{\partial^2 x^{\alpha}}{\partial \bar{x}^{\beta} \partial \bar{x}^{\gamma}} + L^{\alpha}_{\mu\nu} \frac{\partial x^{\mu}}{\partial \bar{x}^{\beta}} \frac{\partial x^{\nu}}{\partial \bar{x}^{\gamma}},$$

which is uniquely determined by the requirement of the invariance of the
equations (1). Weyl called the space in which the concept of parallel displacement was so defined by means of the equations (1) an affinely connected space and spoke of the functions $L^{\alpha}_{\beta\gamma}$ appearing in these equations
as the components of the affine connection. As Weyl assumed the functions
$L^{\alpha}_{\beta\gamma}$ to be symmetric in their lower indices a further generalization, more
or less trivial, remained; namely, the extension to a space with a non-
symmetric affine connection. We thus arrive at the concept of the general
affinely connected space with structure that of a manifold of class C^u plus
an affine connection L having definitely determined components $L^{\alpha}_{\beta\gamma}(x)$ of
class C^r in the various coordinate neighborhoods which transform by the
law (2) in the transition from one coordinate neighborhood to another
and in which the parallel displacement of an arbitrary vector along a curve
of class C^1 is defined by (1). It is here to be assumed in accordance with
the transformation (2) that $u \geq 2$ (or that the underlying manifold is
analytic) and that $r \leq u - 2$ (that $r \geq 0$ or $r = \omega$ in the analytic case) since
the class C^r of the components $L^{\alpha}_{\beta\gamma}$ is then unaltered by coordinate transformations.

One may apply the calculus of Ricci in the extended and technically
improved form in which it exists today in developing the theory of the
affinely connected space. We shall speak of such investigations later in
this report.

An automorphism of an affinely connected space is also called a collinea-tion and the local theory of the collineation group (as well as the group of isomorphisms of certain other spaces which we shall later discuss) has been investigated by M. S. Knebelman [21]. In this connection we may mention an interesting result due to L. P. Eisenhart [12] who has shown that a non-symmetric affine connection can be defined in the group mani-fold of a simply transitive continuous group as well as a number of non-degenerate quadratic differential forms with respect to each of which the group manifold becomes a Riemann (or pseudo-Riemann) space admitting the given group as a transitive group of motions. Further developments of this idea of Eisenhart have been made by Cartan and Schouten [7].

8. A curve of class C^1 which possesses the property that its tangents are parallel to the curve itself is given as a solution of the equations

$$(3) \qquad \frac{d^2 x^\alpha}{dt^2} + \Gamma^\alpha_{\beta\gamma} \frac{dx^\beta}{dt} \frac{dx^\gamma}{dt} = 0,$$

where the $\Gamma^\alpha_{\beta\gamma}$ are the symmetric part of the components of the affine connection. Such curves are a generalization of the straight lines of a euclidean space and may be thought of as affording a means by which one may find his way about in a space with affine connection. A curve defined by (3) is called a path and on any path the parameter t is determined to within a linear (affine) transformation since the equations (3) are in-variant under such, and only such, transformations of the parameter. When the structure of a space is defined by the totality of such paths it is called an affine space of paths. In a sense the affine space of paths so de-fined is but another name for a space with symmetric affine connection Γ since one can pass from this later space via (3) to an affine space of paths and, conversely, from (3) one can pass to the equations defining the parallel displacement of vectors, that is, to the equations (1) with $L^\alpha_{\beta\gamma} = \Gamma^\alpha_{\beta\gamma}$ or in other words to a space with symmetric affine connection. However the concept of the path as the fundamental structural element of a space which was initiated by Eisenhart and Veblen [11] has been the stimulus of several interesting investigations.

9. When the structure of a space is defined by the totality of paths given as solutions of (3) apart from any particular parametrization of the paths, the space is called a projective space of paths. The theory of this space or the projective geometry of paths thus consists in the body of theorems expressing properties of the paths as such, that is, independent of a particular parametric representation. As an illustration of a theorem of the projective geometry of paths we may mention Whitehead's con-vexity theorem which states that any point of a projective space of paths is contained in a simple convex neighborhood, that is, a neighborhood any two points of which can be joined by one and only one path lying in the neighborhood [60]. This theorem was later extended by Whitehead [61]

to the more general spaces considered in §13 and a new proof of this generalized theorem possessing some merit has recently been given by R. E. Traber [48].

The question arises as to whether or not there is more than one affine connection on the basis of which the paths of a projective space of paths are determined. The answer to this question is that two affine connections Γ and Λ will determine the same system of paths if, and only if, the components of these connections are related by the equations

$$(4) \qquad \Lambda_{\beta\gamma}^{\alpha} - \Gamma_{\beta\gamma}^{\alpha} = \delta_{\beta}^{\alpha}\phi_{\gamma} + \delta_{\gamma}^{\alpha}\phi_{\beta},$$

where the ϕ's are functions of the coordinates $x^1, \cdots, x^n$ to which the covariant vector law of transformation may be ascribed. The conditions (4) were originally found by Weyl [57] who also showed the possibility of defining a curvature tensor in the projective space of paths which is now usually referred to as the Weyl projective curvature tensor. As a matter of fact, the realization of the existence of the projective theory, the precise equations (4) and certain other results were discovered at a later date independently by Veblen [49] to whom Weyl's work was not available.

10. The fact that the structure of a projective space of paths may be defined by a multiplicity of affine connections, the components of which are related by (4), appears as an obstacle in the analytical development of the theory of this space. To overcome this difficulty Thomas [37] introduced the projective connection Π whose components $\Pi_{\beta\gamma}^{\alpha}$ defined by

$$(5) \qquad \Pi_{\beta\gamma}^{\alpha} = \Gamma_{\beta\gamma}^{\alpha} - \frac{\delta_{\beta}^{\alpha}}{n+1}\Gamma_{\sigma\gamma}^{\sigma} - \frac{\delta_{\gamma}^{\alpha}}{n+1}\Gamma_{\sigma\beta}^{\sigma}$$

have a unique determination in any coordinate neighborhood and in which, in fact, they appear as one of the above sets of functions $\Lambda_{\beta\gamma}^{\alpha}$ defining the system of paths. From (5) and the transformation law of the components $\Gamma_{\beta\gamma}^{\alpha}$ it follows that under changes of coordinates the quantities $\Pi_{\beta\gamma}^{\alpha}$ transform in accordance with the equations

$$(6) \qquad \begin{aligned} \overline{\Pi}_{\beta\gamma}^{\sigma}\frac{\partial x^{\alpha}}{\partial \bar{x}^{\sigma}} &= \frac{\partial^2 x^{\alpha}}{\partial \bar{x}^{\beta}\partial \bar{x}^{\gamma}} + \Pi_{\mu\nu}^{\alpha}\frac{\partial x^{\mu}}{\partial \bar{x}^{\beta}}\frac{\partial x^{\nu}}{\partial \bar{x}^{\gamma}} \\ &\quad - \frac{1}{n+1}\frac{1}{(x\bar{x})}\left[\frac{\partial(x\bar{x})}{\partial \bar{x}^{\beta}}\frac{\partial x^{\alpha}}{\partial \bar{x}^{\gamma}} + \frac{\partial(x\bar{x})}{\partial \bar{x}^{\gamma}}\frac{\partial \bar{x}^{\alpha}}{\partial \bar{x}^{\beta}}\right], \end{aligned}$$

where $(x\bar{x})$ stands for the jacobian of the coordinate transformation. Thus the system of paths may be defined by

$$\frac{d^2 x^{\alpha}}{dp^2} + \Pi_{\beta\gamma}^{\alpha}\frac{dx^{\beta}}{dp}\frac{dx^{\gamma}}{dp} = 0,$$

in which the parameter p, called the projective parameter, is determined in any coordinate neighborhood to within a linear transformation and changes, when the coordinates are changed, by a definitely determined law. The projective space of paths may therefore be regarded as a space whose structure is defined by a projective connection and the theory of such a projectively connected space is the projective geometry of paths.

11. The possibility of applying the elegant methods of the tensor analysis to the treatment of the theory of an affinely connected space depends essentially on the existence of a set of equations of the form (2) for the transformation of the components of the affine connection. This happy state of affairs may be realized if we restrict the structure of the projective space by a set of coordinate neighborhoods such that $(x\bar{x}) = 1$ and then limit ourselves to coordinate transformations for which the jacobian is equal to unity since then in (6) the last two sets of terms will disappear (equi-projective geometry of paths). To obtain an analogous result without this restriction on the structure of the space Thomas [38] introduced a fictitious coordinate x^0 and augmented correspondingly the set of components of the projective connection. Suppose that Greek indices take on the values $1, \cdots, n$ and Latin indices the values $0, 1, \cdots, n$ in the remainder of this section. Define a set of quantities $\Pi_{jk}^i(x)$ in the coordinate neighborhoods of the projective space of paths by the requirement that the Π_{jk}^i are identical with the components $\Pi_{\beta\gamma}^\alpha$ of the projective connection when the indices i, j, k have the values $1, \cdots, n$ and for the remaining quantities Π_{jk}^i put

$$\Pi_{j0}^i = \Pi_{0j}^i = -\frac{\delta_j^i}{n+1}, \qquad \Pi_{\beta\gamma}^0 = \Pi_{\gamma\beta}^0 = \left(\frac{n+1}{n-1}\right)\mathfrak{L}_{\beta\gamma\alpha}^\alpha,$$

where $\mathfrak{L}_{\beta\gamma\delta}^\alpha$ are the components of the curvature tensor of the equi-projective theory. Then

(7)
$$\overline{\Pi}_{jk}^l \frac{\partial x^i}{\partial \bar{x}^l} = \frac{\partial^2 x^i}{\partial \bar{x}^j \partial \bar{x}^k} + \Pi_{pq}^i \frac{\partial x^p}{\partial \bar{x}^j} \frac{\partial x^q}{\partial \bar{x}^k},$$

where the derivatives in these equations are calculated from the relations

(8)
$$x^\alpha = \phi^\alpha(x^1, \cdots, x^n), \quad x^0 = \bar{x}^0 + \log(x\bar{x}) + \text{const.},$$

the first set of which denotes the coordinate transformation between the coordinates of two neighborhoods of the projective space of paths. In case the indices i, j, k in (7) have values $1, \cdots, n$ these equations are identical with the equations of transformation of the components of the projective connection given by (6). In case j or k has the value zero the equations (7) reduce immediately to an identity. The remaining case $i=0$, and $j, k \neq 0$ gives the equations of transformation of the components of the contracted equi-projective curvature tensor. As only the derivatives of $\log(x\bar{x})$ occur in (7) it is immaterial whether or not the jacobian $(x\bar{x})$ is positive or negative; however, in order that the relations (8) shall be strictly real, we shall now suppose that $(x\bar{x})$ stands for the absolute value of the Jacobian of the coordinate transformation in the projective space of paths.

The projective space of paths may now be defined as a space whose structure is given by the above extended connection Π, the components of which transform by (7), under transformations of the coordinates in the underlying n-dimensional manifold. Owing to the form of the relations (7), the formal theory of the affinely connected space may be carried over without modification to the projective space of paths. Thus we may construct the curvature tensor B by the ordinary method and we may define the repeated covariant derivatives of the curvature tensor. It is interesting to observe that the above curvature tensor B yields the Weyl curvature tensor when the indices appearing on the symbol of its components are restricted to the range $1, \cdots, n$ and that in the two dimensional case, where Weyl's curvature tensor vanishes identically, it provides us with a tensor analogous to the curvature tensor of Weyl. It should be emphasized here that the components Π_{jk}^{t} are independent of the variable x^0 and the same is therefore true of the curvature tensor B and its covariant derivatives. Defining the components of a tensor field (for example, T_j^i) to depend only on the coordinates $x^1, \cdots, x^n$ of the underlying manifold and to transform by the ordinary tensor law under transformations (8) the covariant derivatives of the tensor will have the same property. Although the extra coordinate x^0 is in some sense analogous to the factor of proportionality in the classical projective geometry, the vanishing of this coordinate in the above theory, contrary to the situation in the classical projective geometry, is the occasion of no especial concern since it does not enter explicitly in any of the invariant relationships of the projective geometry.

The generalized n-dimensional projective space is defined in the following manner. We generalize the relations (8) to the relations of the form

$$(9) \qquad x^\alpha = \phi^\alpha(x^1, \cdots, x^n), \quad x^0 = \bar{x}^0 + \log (x\bar{x})^m + \text{const.},$$

where m is an arbitrary (but fixed) constant and the remaining designations in these relations have their previous significance. We furthermore consider a connection, which we likewise denote by Π, having components Π_{jk}^{t} which may be arbitrary functions of the coordinates $x^1, \cdots, x^n$ of the coordinate neighborhoods of a manifold of class C^u subject to conditions on their class of the sort specified in §8 and which transform by the equations (7) in which the derivatives are determined by (9) when the coordinates $x^1, \cdots, x^n$ of the underlying manifold undergo a transformation given by the first set of these equations. By a generalized n dimensional projective space we mean an n dimensional manifold of class C^u whose (additional) structure is defined by the above connection Π. This space is of course a generalization of the projective space of paths and its theory is the generalized *n*-dimensional projective geometry.

Two points of view are now possible: We may either adopt the above point of view in which we adhere to the underlying *n*-dimensional space of the projective geometry or we may associate with this space an $(n+1)$-dimensional affinely connected space having coordinates $x^0, x^1, \cdots, x^n$ and affine connection II the components of which transform by (7) under transformations (9) of the coordinates. This latter viewpoint provides a direct $(n+1)$-dimensional affine representation of the generalized projective space and lends itself very readily to interesting geometrical interpretations, some of which have been given by Whitehead [59].

12. We shall now consider a generalization of the classical projective space due to Veblen [51]. While the point of view of Veblen was purely local his work can be extended without serious difficulty so as to apply to spaces in the general sense here adopted. We shall present the theory in its extended form and remark that the details of this extension into which we do not enter may be found in the planographed *Lectures on Differential Geometry* [45].

Consider the *n*-dimensional projective space as defined in §5 by the axioms B. As we have already remarked, the points of this space are in (1, 1) correspondence with the straight lines through the origin of the $(n+1)$-dimensional arithmetic space. If we denote by $z^0, z^1, \cdots, z^n$ the coordinates of points in the arithmetic space, the points of the projective space are in (1, 1) correspondence with the points of the sphere $z^\alpha z^\alpha = 1$, where points at opposite extremities of a diameter are considered as identical. Denoting by $\mathfrak{P}$ the point set consisting of the points of this sphere with the above identifications, we shall use the concrete representation of the points of the projective space which is given by the set $\mathfrak{P}$ as an aid in the following discussion. The *n*-dimensional projective space under consideration may be regarded (to within an isomorphism) as the point set $\mathfrak{P}$ having the structural properties defined by the axioms B. It is possible to cover the point set $\mathfrak{P}$ by coordinate neighborhoods having coordinates $x^1, \cdots, x^n$ related analytically to one another and in consequence of which the point set $\mathfrak{P}$ becomes an analytic manifold $\mathfrak{M}$. We can now define over $\mathfrak{M}$ a set of $n+1$ analytic scalars $f^0, f^1, \cdots, f^n$ such that the determinant

$$
\Delta = \begin{vmatrix} f^0 & f^1 & \cdots & f^n \\[2mm] \dfrac{\partial f^0}{\partial x^1} & \dfrac{\partial f^1}{\partial x^1} & \cdots & \dfrac{\partial f^n}{\partial x^1} \\[2mm] \cdot & \cdot & \cdots & \cdot \\[2mm] \dfrac{\partial f^0}{\partial x^n} & \dfrac{\partial f^1}{\partial x^n} & \cdots & \dfrac{\partial f^n}{\partial x^n} \end{vmatrix}
$$

vanishes at no point of the manifold and possessing the property that in a definite preferred homogeneous coordinate system the coordinates z^α of any point of the projective space are given by $z^\alpha = f^\alpha(x^1, \cdots, x^n)\sigma$, where the factor σ is different from zero but otherwise arbitrary. In accordance with the axioms B the coordinates of points of the projective space in any preferred homogeneous coordinate system are then $z^\alpha = p_\beta{}^\alpha f^\beta \sigma$ where the $p_\beta{}^\alpha$ are constants such that the determinant $|p_\beta{}^\alpha|$ is different from zero. For the analytical requirements of the theory it is convenient to represent this last set of relations in the form $z^\alpha = \pm p_\beta{}^\alpha e^{x^0} f^\beta$ which automatically takes account of the fact that the above factor σ is different from zero.

To free ourselves from the special rôle played by the above scalars f^α we now put

$$(10) \qquad\qquad z^\alpha = p_\beta{}^\alpha A^\beta, \qquad\qquad (A^\beta = \pm e^{x^0} f^\beta),$$

and eliminate the constants $p_\beta{}^\alpha$ from these equations. When we observe that quantities $a_\beta{}^\gamma$ may be defined by writing $a_\beta{}^\gamma \partial A^\alpha/\partial x^\gamma = \xi_\beta{}^\alpha$, since $\Delta \neq 0$, this elimination leads to the equations

$$(11) \qquad\qquad \frac{\partial^2 z^\alpha}{\partial x^\beta \partial x^\gamma} = \Pi_{\beta\gamma}^{\sigma} \frac{\partial z^\alpha}{\partial x^\sigma}, \qquad \left(\Pi_{\beta\gamma}^{\sigma} = a_\tau^{\sigma} \frac{\partial A^\tau}{\partial x^\beta \partial x^\gamma}\right).$$

The $\Pi_{\gamma\beta}^{\sigma}$ are functions of the coordinates $x^1, \cdots, x^n$ having a unique determination in each of the coordinate neighborhoods covering the manifold $\mathfrak{M}$ if we suppose that the identity transformation $x^0 = \bar{x}^0$ is combined with the transformation $x \to \bar{x}$ of the coordinates of the neighborhoods. Assuming the scalar character of the z^α and the invariance of the above equations (11) and making use of the fact that the determinant $|\partial z^\alpha/\partial x^\beta|$ does not vanish, which is a consequence of $\Delta \neq 0$, it follows that the functions $\Pi_{\beta\gamma}^{\alpha}$ transform by the equations

$$(12) \qquad\qquad \overline{\Pi}_{\beta\gamma}^{\sigma} \frac{\partial x^\alpha}{\partial \bar{x}^\sigma} = \frac{\partial^2 x^\alpha}{\partial \bar{x}^\beta \partial \bar{x}^\gamma} + \Pi_{\mu\nu}^{\alpha} \frac{\partial x^\mu}{\partial \bar{x}^\beta} \frac{\partial x^\nu}{\partial \bar{x}^\gamma}$$

under an arbitrary regular analytic transformation of all the variables $x^0, x^1, \cdots, x^n$. We shall not, however, consider such arbitrary transformations of these variables but shall limit ourselves to transformations of the form

$$(13) \qquad x^i = \phi^i(\bar{x}^1, \cdots, \bar{x}^n), \quad x^0 = \bar{x}^0 + \log \rho(\bar{x}^1, \cdots, \bar{x}^n),$$

where the first set of these equations represents an allowable analytic transformation of the coordinates of our manifold and where $\rho(\bar{x})$ is a positive analytic function, in consequence of the fact that under such transformations the form of the scalars z^α as given by (10) is unaltered. In particular, we speak of the transformation $x^i = \phi^i(\bar{x})$, $x^0 = \bar{x}^0$ as a coordinate transformation and of the transformation $x^i = \bar{x}^i$, $x^0 = \bar{x}^0 + \log \rho(\bar{x})$ as a gauge transformation. The general transformation (13) is called a representation (Darstellungs) transformation. Owing to the possibility of gauge transformations there exists an infinite number of sets of the functions $\Pi^\alpha_{\beta\gamma}$ in any coordinate neighborhood of the projective space.

The above considerations lead to the generalized projective space in the sense of Veblen which may be defined as follows: The *generalized n-dimensional projective space* is a space whose structure is defined by a (projective) connection Π having components $\Pi^\alpha_{\beta\gamma}$ which are functions of the coordinates $x^1, \cdots, x^n$ of class C^r and which transform in accordance with the equations (12) under representation transformations (13). The above form of the functions A^α gives the motivation of Veblen's definition of projective tensor in the generalized projective space. Veblen defines the projective scalar as a geometrical object (see §14) having components $e^{x^0} f(x^1, \cdots, x^n)$ in any representation and which is a scalar in the ordinary sense under transformations of the representation; more generally a projective scalar of index M is the object having the components $e^{Mx^0} f(x^1, \cdots, x^n)$ in any representation where M is a constant. Similarly the contravariant vector of index M is defined as the object having components $e^{Mx^0} \xi^\alpha(x^1, \cdots, x^n)$ in any representation and transforming under transformations of the representation as the components of an ordinary contravariant vector. The general projective tensor of index M is defined in an analogous manner and its (repeated) covariant derivatives can be constructed by the usual procedure. Likewise a projective curvature tensor can be defined as well as its successive covariant derivatives on the basis of the equations (12). The equations of transformation of the components of vectors and tensors have an interesting decomposition in view of the special form of the representation transformation (13) but it seems inadvisable to enter here into such detailed considerations.

In the case of the classical projective space having the (analytic) projective connection Π defined by the above equations (11) the following three conditions are satisfied:

(a) The connection is symmetric, that is, $\Pi^\alpha_{\beta\gamma} = \Pi^\alpha_{\gamma\beta}$;

(b) The conditions $\Pi^\alpha_{\beta 0} = \Pi^\alpha_{0\beta} = \delta_\beta{}^\alpha$ hold;

(c) The curvature tensor vanishes identically.

Conversely, it can undoubtedly be shown that a generalized n-dimensional analytic projective space, the points of which are in (1, 1) correspondence with the straight lines through the origin of the $(n+1)$-dimensional arithmetic space, and for which the above conditions (a), (b), (c) hold is a realization of the classical projective space of n-dimensions in the sense that preferred homogeneous coordinate systems can be defined such that the axioms B in §5 are satisfied. The corresponding local result was established by O. Veblen [52]. If we use the procedure employed by Veblen, it should be possible to work out the remaining details necessary to prove the above converse theorem and so obtain the precise conditions under which the generalized projective space becomes the space of the classical projective geometry.

It is immediately clear from its formulation on the basis of the axioms B of §5 that the generalized projective space of Veblen is indeed a generalization of the classical projective space. That the generalized projective space of §11 is likewise a generalization of the classical projective space is perhaps not so immediately evident but that such is the case is easily seen by the following very simple consideration. In the case of the classical projective space, where the components $\Pi^\alpha_{\beta\gamma}$ have the form given by (11) and the above conditions (a), (b), (c) are satisfied, the transformation relations (12) yield, for gauge transformations, the following conditions

$$\overline{\Pi}^i_{ik} = \frac{\partial \log D}{\partial x^k} + (n+1)\frac{\partial \log \rho}{\partial x^k}, \qquad \left(D = \text{absolute value of } \left|\frac{\partial A^\alpha}{\partial x^\beta}\right| \right).$$

Hence $\overline{\Pi}^i_{ik}$ vanishes if ρ is taken equal to $1/D^{n+1}$. It is therefore possible to cover the projective space with coordinate neighborhoods in each of which the condition $\Pi^i_{ik}=0$ is satisfied. It now follows readily from the equations (12) which give the relations between the components of the connection Π in the intersection of any two such coordinate neighborhoods (we omit the details of the calculation) that $\rho = c(x\bar{x})^{-1/n+1}$, where c is an arbitrary positive constant and, as above, $(x\bar{x})$ denotes the absolute value of the jacobian of the coordinate transformation. Hence for the above covering by coordinate neighborhoods (13) becomes

$$x^i = \phi^i(\bar{x}^1, \cdots, \bar{x}^n), \quad x^0 = \bar{x}^0 + \log (x\bar{x})^{-1/n+1} + \text{const.},$$

and is therefore identical with (9) when $m = -1/n+1$. In other words, the classical projective space may be thought of as a special case of the generalized projective space defined in §11 and this latter projective space becomes the classical projective space under the same conditions as the generalized projective space in the sense of Veblen.

The above consideration indicates clearly that there is no essential difference between the generalized projective space defined in §11 and the generalized projective space as defined by Veblen in this section. It might appear at first sight that the definition of the generalized projective space of §11 is preferable owing to the uniqueness of the determination of the components of the projective connection and the components of tensors in any coordinate neighborhood but on the other hand the multiplicity of these determinations in Veblen's formulation of the generalized projective space arises from the gauge transformation, and this transformation appears as an important element in the projective theory of relativity [52].

It may likewise be pointed out here that the later formulations of generalized projective spaces by the Dutch school and in particular the generalized projective space of van Dantzig based on the use of homogeneous coordinates has led to nothing essentially different from the projective spaces above discussed.

13. We have seen that the parameter of any path in the affine space of paths was determined to within a linear or affine transformation (§8) and that in the projective space of paths there was no such limitation on the allowable parameter transformations (§9). The significance of such parameter transformations in the determination of the structure of a space was clearly brought out by Jesse Douglas [9]. A general space of paths in the sense of Douglas is a space whose structure is defined by a system of curves or paths such that through each point P of the space there is one and only one path having an arbitrarily prescribed direction at P. We understand here, following Douglas, that the vectors $\lambda\xi$, where ξ is a particular non-zero vector at P and λ is an arbitrary non-zero constant, define the same direction at P and that any direction at P can be so defined (an extension of this definition of direction will result if we require λ to be a positive constant). We shall understand also that if the underlying manifold is of class C^u the paths are of class C^r, where $r \leq u(\neq \omega)$ and where r is completely arbitrary if $u = \omega$, since under these conditions the class C^r of the paths is preserved under allowable coordinate transformations in the manifold. The requirement $u \geq 2$ or $u = \omega$ is furthermore necessitated by the following analytical procedure.

By the specification of a definite group of allowable parameter transformations Douglas imposes an additional structural property on the general space of paths and treats in detail three cases which are thus distinguished by their group of parameter transformations, namely:

(a) *The affine space of paths*: on each path the parameter is determined to within a linear or affine transformation, that is, only transformations of the type $\bar{t} = at + b$ are allowed where $a(\neq 0)$ and b are arbitrary constants.

(b) *The descriptive space of paths*: any parameter transformation of class C^r is allowed on a path.

(c) *The metric space of paths*: only parameter transformations of the form $\bar{t} = t + b$ are allowed, where b is an arbitrary constant.

In the case of the affine space of paths a set of n functions $x^\alpha(at+b)$ will represent the path through an arbitrary point P of the space and having at P a specified direction. If we choose a particular non-zero vector ξ to represent the direction at P, the requirement that the first derivatives $(dx^\alpha/dt)_P = \xi^\alpha$ will fix the value of the constant a and determine uniquely the second derivatives at the point P. Hence in any coordinate neighborhood of the affine space of paths there exists a unique set of functions $H^\alpha(x, \xi)$ such that the paths are solutions of the equations

$$(14) \qquad \frac{d^2x^\alpha}{dt^2} = H^\alpha(x, \xi), \qquad \left(\xi^\alpha = \frac{dx^\alpha}{dt}\right).$$

We refer to (14) as the differential equations of the paths of an affine space of paths.

By the above consideration the functions $H^\alpha(x, \xi)$ are defined only for non-zero vectors ξ. Let us therefore put $H^\alpha(x, 0) = 0$ to complete the definition of these functions. Evidently if we replace the vector ξ by $\lambda\xi$, where λ is not equal to zero but otherwise arbitrary, we must change the parameter from t to t' where $t = \lambda t' + b$ in the definition of the functions H^α. This leads to the relations $H^\alpha(x, \lambda\xi) = \lambda^2 H^\alpha(x, \xi)$ which are thus seen to hold for all values of λ including zero in view of the above complete definition of the functions H^α. Hence the functions $H^\alpha(x, \xi)$ are homogeneous of the second degree in the variables ξ^α (in case the above extended definition of direction and corresponding modification of the group of parameter transformations are adopted, the functions H^α to which we are led will be positively homogeneous of the second degree in these variables). The invariance of (14) under affine transformations of the parameter is an immediate consequence of this homogeneity property.

To derive the relation between the H^α in different coordinate systems we have only to differentiate the transformation equations $x^\alpha = \phi^\alpha(\bar{x})$ with respect to the parameter of a path. We thus obtain

$$(15) \qquad \xi^\alpha = \bar{\xi}^\beta \frac{\partial x^\alpha}{\partial \bar{x}^\beta}, \quad H^\alpha(x, \xi) = \bar{H}^\beta(\bar{x}, \bar{\xi}) \frac{\partial x^\alpha}{\partial \bar{x}^\beta} + \bar{\xi}^\beta \bar{\xi}^\gamma \frac{\partial^2 x^\alpha}{\partial \bar{x}^\beta \partial \bar{x}^\gamma},$$

and on the basis of these equations we can give an immediate formal proof of the invariance of (14) under coordinate transformations.

With the existence of the functions $H^\alpha(x, \xi)$ established we may now reverse our point of view and consider these functions as the fundamental structural element of the space. From this point of view, we consider a space whose structure is defined by a unique set of n functions $H^\alpha(x, \xi)$ in each coordinate neighborhood, these functions being homogeneous of the second degree in the variables ξ^α and transforming by the law (15) under coordinate transformations. For the requirements of the differential geometry it is furthermore desirable to assume certain differentiability properties of the functions $H^\alpha(x, \xi)$, for example, that these functions are of class C^1 for values of the x's in any coordinate neighborhood and for unrestricted values of the ξ's. Under these conditions the differential equations (14) have a solution $x^\alpha(t)$ uniquely determined in any coordinate neighborhood by arbitrary initial values t_0, x_0^α, and ξ_0^α of these variables. Also $x^\alpha(at+b)$ will be a solution of (14) on account of the homogeneity property of the functions $H^\alpha(x, \xi)$ and this solution corresponds in fact to the initial values t_0', x_0^α, $a\xi_0^\alpha$, the value of t_0' (which may be arbitrary) being determined by the value of the constant b. Hence the parameter on any curve given as a solution of (14) is determined to within an affine transformation and it follows that if we take these curves as our paths the space is an affine space of paths in the sense of Douglas.

If we assume that the $H^\alpha(x, \xi)$ have a sufficient number of derivatives with respect to the x's and ξ's, we can develop the theory of the space in a manner which corresponds closely to the theory of the affine space of paths as defined in §8. In fact we can define functions

$$\Gamma^\alpha_{\beta\gamma}(x, \xi) = \frac{1}{2} \frac{\partial^2 H^\alpha(x, \xi)}{\partial\xi^\beta \partial\xi^\gamma}$$

which, because of the relations (15), have the same transformation law as the components of the affine connection, namely (2). We can thus define a curvature tensor and we can develop a theory of covariant differentiation analogous to the theory of covariant differentiation in the ordinary affine space of paths (§8). We can also define the parallel displacement of a vector along a curve by means of equations analogous to (1) and those curves possessing the property that their tangent vectors are parallel with respect to the curves are easily seen to be the paths of the space. It is an interesting and easily demonstrated fact in this connection that if the above differentiability properties of the functions $H^\alpha(x, \xi)$ are such that these functions are, in the neighborhood of the values $\xi^\alpha = 0$, of class C^2 in the ξ's, then the $H^\alpha(x, \xi)$ will be homogeneous polynomials of the second degree in the ξ's, in consequence of which the above functions $\Gamma^\alpha_{\beta\gamma}$ will be independent of the ξ's and the space will revert to the ordinary affine space of paths.

Just as the affine space of paths in the sense of Douglas is a generalization of the ordinary affine space of paths so is Douglas' descriptive space of paths a generalization of the projective space of paths (§9). On the other hand the metric space of paths when the parameter t is taken as the arc length becomes identical with the space of the calculus of variations or Finsler space as it is sometimes called [14]. While the treatment of these spaces by Douglas is very interesting and worthy of a more detailed account we must pass on to a discussion of other topics. We should, however, mention that our treatment of the affine space of paths in the sense of Douglas is not, strictly speaking, the same as that given by Douglas who has, for example, assumed the existence of a definite number of parameters $a^1, \cdots, a^{2n-2}$ determinative of the paths of the space and has then attempted to deduce the differential equations (14) as the result of an elimination of these parameters from a system of equations in which they enter instead of deriving these equations, as we have done, as a direct logical consequence of the fundamental postulate on the determination of the paths of the space. The procedure which we have here employed for the case of the affine space of paths can of course be applied likewise to the descriptive and metric spaces of paths, and for further details in this connection reference may be made to *Lectures on Differential Geometry* [45].

14. In developing the ideas leading to the theories of the generalized affine, projective, and other spaces it came to be realized that one was in

each case concerned essentially with the theory of an invariant of the space and that in this sense the theory of each of these spaces was the theory of an appropriate invariant. For example, in the case of the Riemann space this invariant is a quadratic differential form (or what amounts to the same thing a symmetric covariant tensor of the second order), in the general affinely connected space (§7) it is the affine connection L and in the projective space of paths it is the projective connection Π defined in §10, and so on.

The idea of a geometry as the theory of an invariant was first stated in its full generality by O. Veblen in his Bologna address on *Differential invariants and geometry* [50]. As an alternative to the word invariant, the term *geometric object*, which appears likely to come into general use, was introduced by J. A. Schouten and E. R. van Kampen [36] and we shall likewise adopt their terminology. By a geometric object we shall mean precisely (regardless of possible variations in the use of this term by other writers) an abstract object having a *unique* set of components, depending on the coordinates and their differentials to a specified order, in any coordinate neighborhood of a topological manifold. In this definition of the geometric object the topological manifold may be a manifold of class C^u or the set of coordinate transformations considered in the manifold may be restricted further by the condition that they belong to a specified pseudo-group of transformations, for example, transformations of class C^u such that the jacobian is equal to unity or again transformations of class C^u belonging to the family (9), and so on. A geometric object such that its components in any coordinate neighborhood of the manifold depend only on the coordinates will be called a simple geometric object. The Riemann space is an example of a space with structure defined either by a geometric object which is not a simple object (quadratic differential form) or by a simple geometric object (fundamental metric tensor). Strictly speaking the projective connection Π of the generalized n-dimensional projective space in the sense of Veblen (§12) is not a geometric object since it admits a multiplicity of components in any coordinate neighborhood but this circumstance can be avoided (if we desire) by considering the $(n+1)$-dimensional representation obtained after the manner mentioned at the end of §11 by adjoining the variable x^0 to the n coordinates of the generalized n-dimensional projective space. The structure of each of the other generalized spaces which we have discussed can be described directly in terms of an appropriate geometric object (at least under suitable continuity and differentiability conditions) and in each case this object has been clearly exhibited.

In the case of the classical projective space the structure of the space can be defined by means of a particular geometric object as follows from the result given in §12 on the characterization of this space. The classical affine, euclidean, and euclidean metric spaces defined by means of the axioms A in §4 may likewise be defined by suitable geometric objects (see §17).

It must be emphasized that we do *not* say *any* geometry is the theory of a geometric object but rather that we *may* say that the geometry is the theory of a geometric object under certain circumstances, namely, when the structure of the space in question can be shown to be defined by an appropriate geometric object. For example the general affine space of paths of Douglas, when the paths are curves of class C^0, cannot, apparently, be defined by a geometric object in the above sense but the geometric object having the components $H^\alpha(x, \xi)$ may define the structure of such an affine space of paths under certain conditions as was shown in §13. Again, it is not immediately clear that the structure of the projective space of paths as defined in §9 can likewise be defined by a geometric object but it was later shown (§10) that the projective connection II was capable of defining the structure of this space and in this sense the theory of this geometric object, that is, the projective connection II, can be identified with the projective geometry of paths.

When one has discovered a geometric object in terms of which the structure of a given space can be defined (in case the structure of the space is not defined directly by a geometric object) one has obtained an unexcelled means for the exploitation of the theory of the space and this is especially true when the object is of the general nature of an affine connection as determined by the transformation law of its components under coordinate transformations in the space (for example the projective connections II defined in §11 and §12). It is conceivable that a generalization of the definition of the geometric object may be desirable for certain purposes but it is likewise evident that if this generalization is pushed too far, the geometric object will lose its above significance in the development of the theory of a space defined as a point set with definitely specified structural properties.

15. We have now discussed a fair number of the more important spaces and we have developed a point of view which would appear to be adequate to describe those theories which are nowadays grouped under the heading of differential geometry. It remains, largely as a matter of record, to mention certain other spaces which have been the subject of more or less recent investigation. Chief among those is, perhaps, the conformal Riemann space which may be defined as the theory of a relative symmetric covariant tensor of the second order and weight $-2/n$ (geometric object). A very complete formal theory of this space is to be found in the various notes on this subject which have appeared between the years 1925 and 1935, in the Proceedings of the National Academy of Science. It would be interesting however to develop this theory along more geometrical lines starting perhaps with the set of axioms which define the classical conformal space analogous to the axioms A (§4) and B (§5) and to proceed to the con-

formal Riemann space or indeed to a generalization of this space. In this connection there is an interesting result on conformal spaces (which we shall not state here explicitly) by J. A. Schouten and J. Haantjes [35] which will undoubtedly find its place in such a development of the conformal space.

There is also the space originated by Weyl in his theory of gravitation and electricity which may be described roughly as a cross between an affine and a conformal space. Mention may also be made of the space of distant parallelism (or teleparallelism) in terms of which Einstein at one time hoped to find the solution to the space-time problem. This is a space where the structure is given by an ennuple of n independent vectors and in which it is possible, as the name implies, to define parallel displacement in such a way that the parallelism of vectors at distant points of the space is independent of the route of displacement. Of various other spaces which might be mentioned we shall say only a word concerning the Finsler space which we already encountered in connection with the work of Douglas (§13). The formal theory of the Finsler space is closely analogous to that of the Riemann space and has been considerably over-emphasized in the literature; on the other hand, those investigations which are not of a formal nature and which are undeniably of interest are usually treated in a special branch of differential geometry called the calculus of variations. Finally we signalize without further comment the analogues involving functional and Banach spaces which have been developed principally by the Pasadena school under the leadership of A. D. Michal.

16. The importance of the characterization of a space by means of its invariants by which one arrives at the idea of a complete set of invariants of the space seems to be recognized by the topologists but the significance of the corresponding characterization of the spaces of differential geometry does not appear to be so clearly recognized by the differential geometers. We shall say that a set of differential invariants of a generalized space is complete if conditions, algebraic in the components of the invariants, can be found by means of which the space is characterized to within an isomorphism. In dealing with the question of equivalence or isomorphism of the spaces of differential geometry attention has so far been confined to the local aspect of the problem and it has been shown that the various spaces which we have discussed can all be characterized locally by sets of tensor differential invariants in the above sense.

As an illustration we take the Riemann space. Let S and $\bar{S}$ denote n-dimensional Riemann spaces of class C^r, the value of the integer r to be determined by the requirements of the following discussion. Then S and $\bar{S}$ are isomorphic if, and only if, there exists a $(1, 1)$ point correspondence between these spaces which is representable by coordinate relationships $x^\alpha = \phi^\alpha(\bar{x})$ of class C^{r+1} and transforms the fundamental quadratic differential form of one of the spaces into that of the other, that is, such that

(16) $$\bar{g}_{\alpha\beta}(\bar{x}) = g_{\mu\nu}(x) \frac{\partial x^{\mu}}{\partial \bar{x}^{\alpha}} \frac{\partial x^{\nu}}{\partial \bar{x}^{\beta}}$$

over S or $\bar{S}$ (cf. §6). The integrability conditions of (16) when combined with the equations (16) themselves give the following sequence

$$\bar{g}_{\alpha\beta} = g_{\mu\nu} u_{\alpha}^{\mu} u_{\beta}^{\nu} \; ; \; \overline{B}_{\alpha\beta\gamma\delta} = B_{\mu\nu\sigma\tau} u_{\alpha}^{\mu} \cdots u_{\delta}^{\tau} \; ; \; \overline{B}_{\alpha\beta\gamma\delta,\epsilon} = B_{\mu\nu\sigma\tau,\eta} u_{\alpha}^{\mu} \cdots u_{\epsilon}^{\eta} \; ; \; \cdots \; ,$$

where the u_{β}^{α} stand for the corresponding derivatives of the above co-ordinate relationships. Suppose that there exists an integer M such that the first M sets of the above equations are algebraically consistent as equations for the determination of the x^{α} and u_{β}^{α} as functions of the co-ordinates $\bar{x}^{\alpha}$ of a neighborhood $\overline{N}$ of the space $\bar{S}$. It can be proved that this condition is necessary and sufficient for the isomorphism of a neighborhood N of the space S and some neighborhood $N' \subset \overline{N}$ of the space $\bar{S}$ (theorem of local isomorphism). Under the conditions of this theorem the equations (16) will admit a solution $x^{\alpha} = \phi^{\alpha}(\bar{x})$ of class C^{r+1} defined in some neighborhood $\tilde{N} \subset \overline{N}$ in which the jacobian will not vanish in view of the fact that the determinants $\left| g_{\mu\nu} \right|$ and $\left| \bar{g}_{\alpha\beta} \right|$ are different from zero by hypothesis. Hence there exists a regular $(1, 1)$ correspondence of class C^{r+1} between neighborhoods N and $N' \subset \tilde{N}$ of the spaces S and $\bar{S}$, respectively, satisfying (16) by which the isomorphism of these neighborhoods is established. It is evident that the maximum value which can be assumed by the integer M in the above theorem is given by the sum of the variables x^{α} and u_{β}^{α} or, in other words, is equal to $n(n+1)$. Hence the above theorem gives necessary and sufficient conditions for the local isomorphism of n-dimensional Riemann spaces of class C^{r} where $r \geq n(n+1)+1$ but may likewise furnish a test of isomorphism for smaller values of r in case the above maximum value of M is not attained in the process of attempting to satisfy the conditions of the theorem. The above theorem can be extended to analytic Riemann spaces and analogous theorems of isomorphism can be given for the various generalized spaces.

E. B. Christoffel [8] was the first to give an equivalence theorem of the above type. He considered, however, the case when the first M sets of the above equations admit a single independent solution and so arrived only at sufficient conditions for the equivalence of two quadratic differential forms. The fundamental existence theorem for systems of differential equations which is now commonly used in the proof of the above theorem of local isomorphism seems to have had a rather lengthy history. It is, for example, essentially the same as a theorem given by J. E. Wright [64] and T. Levi-Civita [23], but the form of this theorem which is best adapted to our purpose is due to Veblen and J. M. Thomas [53] who used it to prove a theorem of local isomorphism for the projective space of paths. The question of the extent to which such theorems of local isomorphism can be carried to furnish necessary and sufficient conditions for the isomorphism of generalized spaces in the large has, as far as I am aware, never been considered.

Whitehead [59] has proved that under certain restrictions the general affine equivalence of the $(n+1)$-dimensional affine representations of two generalized projective spaces in the sense of Veblen implies the equivalence of the projective spaces. The nature of the restrictions imposed by Whitehead are sufficiently weak to permit one to say that the equivalence of two projective spaces of paths is always a consequence of the general affine equivalence of their $(n+1)$-dimensional affine representations [39].

It follows from the definition of the complete set of invariants of a space that any local condition on the space can be expressed directly in terms of the invariants of the complete set without the necessity of further differentiation. Moreover, it would appear that these invariants furnish the simplest possible means of expressing such conditions when they are of tensor character. It is evident that such is the case in dealing with the problem of the local isomorphism of spaces. As a further illustration of the advantages attending the use of the tensor differential invariants of a space one may point to the researches on the problem of the determination of the absolute scalar differential invariants of a Riemann space by means of the integration of complete systems of differential equations. Earlier writers beginning with Sophus Lie (1884) and K. Zorawski (1892) made direct use of the components $g_{\alpha\beta}$ of the fundamental metric tensor and their ordinary partial derivatives as the basis for expressing the scalar invariants. All this work has been greatly simplified and extended by Michal and Thomas [26] by use of the tensor differential invariants of the space. Now the quantities $g_{\alpha\beta}$ and their partial derivatives to a specified order constitute the components of a spatial invariant (geometric object) and in fact a non-tensor invariant the components of which have a linear homogeneous transformation law. The use of invariants whose components have the general linear homogeneous law of transformation should be discarded whenever possible in favor of invariants of simple tensor character.

17. If the structure of a space S can be regarded as a component part of the structure of a space S' of lesser generality, the space S will under certain conditions *reduce* to the space S'. Thus the generalized projective space may reduce to the classical projective space and the conditions for this reduction have in fact already been given in §12. Similarly the general n-dimensional affine space with symmetric affine connection Γ will reduce to the classical affine space if, and only if, it is homeomorphic to the n-dimensional number space and the curvature tensor vanishes identically. Under corresponding conditions the Riemann space reduces to the euclidean metric space and the conformal Riemann space to the classical or euclidean conformal space. Likewise the euclidean space is a special case of the generalized conformal-affine space whose structure is defined by a

composite geometric object consisting of a positive definite relative covariant tensor K of the second order and weight $-2/n$ and a symmetric affine connection Γ. In fact the n-dimensional conformal-affine space reduces to the euclidean space if, and only if, it is homeomorphic to the n-dimensional number space and two invariants of the space vanish, namely, the covariant derivative of the tensor K and the curvature tensor; that is, under these conditions preferred coordinate systems can be defined for the conformal-affine space which satisfy the axioms A of §4 where G is the group of euclidean similarity transformations. As far as I am aware, the proof of these theorems is not to be found in the literature but their demonstration should be a comparatively easy matter.

Usually one considers the question of the local reducibility of spaces. For example, a general affinely connected space with symmetric affine connection, but without regard to its topological properties, is said to reduce locally to the classical affine space or to be locally flat if the curvature tensor vanishes identically. In this case any point P of the space is contained in a coordinate neighborhood $N(P)$ with respect to which the components $\Gamma^{\alpha}_{\beta\gamma}$ of the affine connection vanish and in consequence of this the neighborhood $N(P)$ can be mapped upon a neighborhood of the classical affine space in such a way that the paths in $N(P)$ go into the straight lines of this latter space. Similar theorems of local reducibility with corresponding geometrical interpretations can be stated for the various generalized spaces for which curvature tensors can be constructed and indeed any such theorem expresses the characteristic property of the curvature tensor for the space under consideration.

As another illustration, selected from among many which might be given, of a theorem on the local reducibility of a space let us consider the problem of finding conditions for an affine space of paths to reduce to a Riemann space. In other words, we seek necessary and sufficient conditions for the paths to be the extremals of an integral $\int (g_{\alpha\beta}(x)dx^{\alpha}dx^{\beta})^{1/2}$, where the expression in parentheses is a positive definite quadratic differential form. This is one of the inverse problems of the calculus of variations. The problem is equivalent to the problem of finding a solution $g_{\alpha\beta}(x)$, such that the form $g_{\alpha\beta}(x)dx^{\alpha}dx^{\beta}$ is positive definite, of the system of equations

$$(17) \qquad \frac{\partial g_{\alpha\beta}}{\partial x^{\gamma}} = g_{\sigma\beta}\Gamma^{\sigma}_{\alpha\gamma} + g_{\alpha\sigma}\Gamma^{\sigma}_{\beta\gamma},$$

in which the $\Gamma^{\alpha}_{\beta\gamma}$ are the components of the affine connection of the given space. To solve this problem we consider the following sequence of integrability conditions of (17), namely,

$$g_{\sigma\beta}B^{\sigma}_{\alpha\gamma\delta} + g_{\alpha\sigma}B^{\sigma}_{\beta\gamma\delta} = 0; \; g_{\sigma\beta}B^{\sigma}_{\alpha\gamma\delta,\epsilon} + g_{\alpha\sigma}B^{\sigma}_{\beta\gamma\delta,\epsilon} = 0; \; \cdots .$$

Suppose that (a) there exists an integer M such that the first M sets of equations of the above sequence are algebraically consistent as equations for the determination of the symmetric quantities $g_{\alpha\beta}$ in a neighborhood N of the affinely connected space, (b) all the above solutions satisfy the $(M+1)$th set of equations of the sequence, and (c) there exists one solution $g_{\alpha\beta}(x)$ of the first M sets of equations defined in N such that the form $g_{\alpha\beta}(x)dx^{\alpha}dx^{\beta}$ is positive definite. The following theorem may be proved: *A necessary and sufficient condition for the affinely connected space to reduce to a Riemann space in some neighborhood $N' \subset N$ is that the above conditions* (a), (b), *and* (c) *be satisfied.* Since the maximum value which it is necessary to take for the integer M is easily seen to be $n(n+1)/2$, the above theorem gives the conditions for the local reducibility of an affine space of paths for which the components of the affine connection are of class C^r with $r \geq n(n+1)/2+1$. A theorem of this type giving sufficient conditions only for the reducibility was first proved by Eisenhart and Veblen [11]. The basis of the proof of the above stated theorem is the existence theorem on systems of differential equations mentioned in the preceding section. In the usual statement of this theorem the above condition (c) is omitted and this is a rather serious omission since the equations (17) may have solutions and only such solutions $g_{\alpha\beta}(x)$ for which the determinant $\left| g_{\alpha\beta}(x) \right|$ vanishes identically. We remark also that the statement of the above theorem has been carefully phrased so as to avoid the difficulties occasioned by possible singular points in the affine space (that is, points analogous to the singular points defined in §19). For a detailed proof in which these questions are considered reference may be made to the *Lectures on Differential Geometry* [45].

18. When one deals with problems of differential geometry having to do with the existence of specified properties of a space, one is invariably confronted with the integration of a system of differential equations. It is sometimes possible to reduce this system—frequently the defining equations of the property in question—to an equivalent system of differential equations exhibiting greater simplicity in certain respects. When this has been done, the reduced system is usually said to furnish a solution of the problem although in no fundamental sense is this correct since these latter conditions are likewise of differential character. Now it can be shown under very general conditions that the question of the existence of a solution of a system of differential equations can be reduced to the question of the existence of a solution of a system of algebraic equations to which can be applied the highly developed theory of algebraic elimination. This procedure of algebraic elimination will lead to a set of conditions involving polynomials in the fundamental structural functions of the space (in case the structure of the space is defined by one or more geometric objects) which will be necessary and possibly sufficient for the existence of the property under consideration. We embody precise types of such conditions

which are of especial interest in the following definition of the algebraic characterization.

We shall say that the conditions $F_1=0$, $F_2\neq0$, $F_3>0$, $F_4\geqq0$ constitute an algebraic characterization of a property P of a space, where the F's denote polynomials in the fundamental structural functions of the space and their derivatives to a definite order, provided that these conditions are necessary and sufficient for the existence of the property P. A simple example of an algebraic characterization of the type $F_1=0$ is afforded by the equations expressing the vanishing of the curvature tensor of any one of the various generalized spaces for which such tensors have been found, these equations giving in fact necessary and sufficient conditions for the space in question to be locally flat. Other examples only slightly more complicated have been given in a paper by J. Levine and the present writer [46]. In a Riemann space of class one the rank of the matrix of the second fundamental quadratic differential form can be shown to be an intrinsic invariant of the space and this invariant has been called the type number of the space. As an intrinsic invariant the type number of a Riemann space is definable regardless of whether the space is of class one or not. It has been shown by Thomas [42] that an $n(\geqq3)$ dimensional Riemann space of class C^3 and type number $\tau\geqq3$ is of class one if, and only if, conditions of the form $F_1=0$, $F_3>0$, and $F_4\geqq0$ are satisfied, the inequalities expressing the conditions of reality involved in the solution of the problem. This algebraic characterization of Riemann spaces of class one has been extended to Riemann spaces of class p by C. B. Allendoerfer [2].

The conditions given in the preceding section for the local reducibility of affinely connected spaces to Riemann spaces constitute what may be called an *algebraic test* of reducibility rather than a true algebraic characterization. As a matter of fact it can be proved that there exists no algebraic characterization of the class of affinely connected spaces which reduce to Riemann spaces [41, 43]. These facts, namely, the existence of the algebraic test and non-existence of the algebraic characterization, suggest the desirability of a critical discussion of the possible types of conditions for the various properties of spaces that have been treated.

It is therefore of significance to inquire concerning the existence or nonexistence of an algebraic characterization for any specified property P of a space and this question gives rise to a host of interesting and difficult problems in differential geometry. For example, one may consider the question of the algebraic characterization of Riemann spaces of class one without the above supplementary condition on the type number. One might also consider the question of the existence of an algebraic characterization of Riemann spaces admitting an n-tuply orthogonal system of hypersurfaces [47].

19. Since the structure of an affinely connected space is determined

essentially by the definition of parallel displacement a fundamental class of problems in the theory of this space has to do with questions concerning the parallel displacement of vectors. We may mention here the well known theorem on the parallel displacement of a vector around an infinitesimal closed circuit. This problem was first considered by J. A. Schouten [34] and Schouten's work was later extended and perfected by H. Weyl [56].

A field of vectors in a domain D of an affinely connected space is said to be *parallel* if the vectors of the field are parallel in the sense of §7 with respect to any curve of class C^1 in D. The necessary and sufficient condition for a field of contravariant vectors $\xi(x)$ to be parallel in the domain D is that the equations

$$(18) \qquad\qquad \frac{\partial \xi^\alpha}{\partial x^\beta} + L^\alpha_{\mu\beta}\xi^\mu = 0$$

be satisfied in this domain. A rather general investigation of the existence of fields of parallel vectors defined over open point sets in an affinely connected space was made by Mayer and Thomas [24] under the hypothesis that the components $L^\alpha_{\beta\gamma}$ (not necessarily symmetric) of the affine connection were of class C^s, where $s \geq n+1$ and n is the dimensionality of the space. In consequence of this hypothesis the equations (18) admit the following sets of integrability conditions

$$(E_0)\xi^\mu B^\alpha_{\mu\beta\gamma} = 0, \; (E_1)\xi^\mu B^\alpha_{\mu\beta\gamma,\delta_1} = 0, \cdots, (E_n)\xi^\mu B^\alpha_{\mu\beta\gamma,\delta_1,\ldots,\delta_n} = 0,$$

where the B's denote the components of the curvature tensor and its successive covariant derivatives. A point P of the space will be said to be regular (called regular or non-essential singular in above paper) if there exists a neighborhood $U(P)$ in which the rank of the matrix M formed from the coefficients B of the system $(E_0) + \cdots + (E_{n-1})$ is constant. Other points of the space will be said to be singular (called essential singular in above paper). It can be shown that the set R of regular points is open and the set S of singular points is nowhere dense. By the component of a point $P \subset R$ is meant the greatest open connected point set $K(P)$ in R which contains the point P. Thus the set R is divided into a finite or infinite number of components $K(P)$ with boundaries composed of singular points. It can be proved that the rank of the above matrix M is constant in any component $K(P)$ and that this rank determines the number of independent fields of parallel vectors in $K(P)$. In fact, in any connected and simply connected open point set O contained in any component $K(P)$ the parallel displacement of any solution vector ξ of the system $(E_0) + \cdots + (E_{n-1})$ at a point Q to any other point Q' of O will be independent of the path of the displacement and hence will give rise to a field of parallel vectors in O.

A necessary condition for the existence of a field of parallel vectors

$\xi(x)$ over the above affinely connected space $\mathfrak{M}$ is that the system (E_0) $+ \cdots +(E_{n-1})$ shall possess a non-trivial solution at any point of $\mathfrak{M}$ and this condition can be expressed by the vanishing of the resultant system $\mathcal{R}$ of $(E_0)+ \cdots +(E_{n-1})$ over $\mathfrak{M}$. If now, conversely, $\mathcal{R}=0$ over $\mathfrak{M}$, a field of parallel vectors will exist in the open point sets O in any component $K(P)$. In particular, if all the components $K(P)$ are simply connected, a field of parallel vectors will exist in each of these components, but it may not be possible to choose these fields so that discontinuities will not arise at the singular points in $\mathfrak{M}$, that is, at the boundaries of the various components $K(P)$. Whether or not the space $\mathfrak{M}$ is itself simply connected appears to be without especial significance in this connection. Here arises one of the essential differences in the problem of characterizing spaces admitting a field of parallel vectors under the non-analytic and analytic hypotheses. For in the analytic case the equations $\mathcal{R}=0$ give an algebraic characterization of those (topologically) simply connected spaces $\mathfrak{M}$ over which a field of parallel vectors can be defined [44]. In a non-analytic affinely connected space the various components $K(P)$ play the same role as that of the entire space under the analytic hypothesis.

It is known that if p independent fields of parallel vectors can be defined in a neighborhood of a Riemann space, it is possible to introduce in this neighborhood a system of coordinates with respect to which the fundamental quadratic differential form becomes $(dx^1)^2+ \cdots +(dx^p)^2+g_{\mu\nu}dx^\mu dx^\nu$, where the last set of terms is independent of the variables $x^1, \cdots, x^p$. This result admits a natural extension when the fields of parallel vectors are replaced by the more general concept of the parallel vector space as has been shown by W. Mayer [10]. The corresponding reduction of the fundamental form of a pseudo-Riemann space in which null parallel vector fields may arise has recently been investigated by L. P. Eisenhart [13].

20. This report would not be complete without some mention of the theory of the tangent or associated spaces which can be defined at the points of a manifold of class $C^u (u \neq 0)$. Consider the totality of contravariant vectors ξ at any point P of such a manifold. These vectors, regarded as abstract objects, constitute the points of a space called the tangent space to the manifold at the point P. We can introduce a coordinate system in this tangent space in the following manner. If $U(P)$ is a coordinate neighborhood of the manifold containing the point P, we define the components ξ^α with respect to the coordinates of $U(P)$ of any contravariant vector ξ at P to be the coordinates of the corresponding point ξ of the tangent space. As so defined, a coordinate system in the tangent space is determined to within a linear homogeneous transformation. With these coordinate systems as preferred coordinate systems the axioms A of §4 are satisfied, where G is the group of linear homogeneous transformation, that is, the tangent space is a *centered* affine space, the center being determined by the zero vector at P. This tangent space may be thought

of as having contact with the manifold at P, the center of the tangent space coinciding with the point P of the manifold. Any centered affine space determines uniquely an affine space in which the center is regarded as equivalent to any other point. The affine space determined in this way by the above tangent centered affine space at any point P of the manifold is called the tangent affine space at P.

The definition of parallel displacement in a (topologically connected) space with affine connection L determines a mapping of the tangent affine space at any point P on the tangent affine space at any other point Q. Join P to Q by a curve $C(t)$ of class C^1 where $t_0 \leq t \leq t_1$ with $P = C(t_0)$ and $Q = C(t_1)$. By the existence theorem for systems of differential equations, the general solution of (1) along the curve C has the form $\xi^\alpha = a_\beta{}^\alpha(t, t_0)\xi^\beta(t_0)$, where the $\xi^\beta(t_0)$ are arbitrary constants, $a_\beta{}^\alpha(t_0, t_0) = \delta_\beta{}^\alpha$ and the determinant $|a_\beta{}^\alpha(t, t_0)| \neq 0$ for $t_0 \leq t \leq t_1$. It is easily seen that these equations define a geometrical or point correspondence between the tangent affine space at P, referred to coordinates $\xi^\beta(t_0)$, and the tangent affine space at Q, referred to coordinates $\xi^\alpha(t_1)$, and that this correspondence is independent of the parametrization of the curve C. By this correspondence, the zero vector in the tangent space at P is carried into the zero vector in the tangent space at Q. But this property may be lost under a more general definition of the mapping between tangent spaces. For example, this will be the case if we determine the correspondence between tangent spaces by integration of the system of equations obtained by adding the quantities $B_\beta{}^\alpha dx^\beta/dt$ to the left-hand members of (1) as we may do in a space whose structure is defined by a composite geometric object consisting of an affine connection L and a mixed tensor B of the second order. Various modifications can be made in the system of differential equations used to define the correspondences between tangent spaces, and some of these may be worthy of serious study [54]. This process of mapping tangent spaces on one another may be expected to apply whenever the underlying space contains a geometric object having the general properties of an affine connection. In particular, it has been used in the theory of the generalized projective space by Veblen [52].

A general theory of the correspondences between associated spaces may be based on the following abstract formulation: With each point P of a manifold of class C^u there is associated a space $S(P)$, all these spaces being isomorphic. By a family of correspondences we shall mean a set of transformations $S(P) \rightarrow S(Q)$, such that:

(a) Any correspondence $S(P) \rightarrow S(Q)$ is an isomorphic transformation of $S(P)$ into $S(Q)$;

(b) If P and Q are any two points of the manifold, there exists at least one correspondence $S(P) \rightarrow S(Q)$;

(c) The resultant of a correspondence $S(P) \rightarrow S(Q)$ followed by a correspondence $S(Q) \rightarrow S(R)$ is a correspondence $S(P) \rightarrow S(R)$;

(d) The inverse of any correspondence $S(P) \to S(Q)$ is a correspondence $S(Q) \to S(P)$.

A family of correspondences is therefore a pseudo-group of isomorphisms between associated spaces. If P is any point in the manifold, the set of correspondences which carries $S(P)$ into itself is obviously a group contained in this pseudo-group. It is a sub-group of the group of automorphisms of $S(P)$ and is called the *holonomic* group at P [6]. It is easily seen that the holonomic groups at any two points P and Q are (simply) isomorphic. Hence, if the holonomic group reduces to the identity at any point, it reduces to the identity at every point of the manifold. In such a case the pseudo-group of correspondences between the associated spaces is said to be *holonomic*. The pseudo-group of correspondences is necessarily holonomic if the group of automorphisms of $S(P)$ is the identity. For a further discussion of this general theory see Veblen and Whitehead [54].

E. Cartan has attempted, in a succession of papers extending from 1923 to 1937, to use the associated spaces and their correspondences in a definition of generalized affine, conformal, and projective geometries. Apparently his procedures require some sort of relation between the associated spaces and the underlying manifold and the lack of such a relation has been referred to by H. Weyl as a blemish in the theory [58]. Cartan has likewise failed to set up an isomorphic correspondence between the pseudo-group of coordinate transformations relative to coordinate neighborhoods $U(P)$, with P fixed, and the group of coordinate transformations in the associated space $S(P)$ in consequence of which any coordinate neighborhood $U(P)$ determines a unique coordinate system in $S(P)$. Such an isomorphic correspondence was established at the beginning of this section for the case of the tangent vector spaces and its importance has been emphasized by H. P. Robertson [32] and H. Weyl [33]. Briefly stated, the general problem with which one is here concerned is the problem of finding a geometric object defined in a manifold of class C^u which can be used to establish a pseudo-group of isomorphic correspondences between a given set of isomorphic associated spaces A by the process of integrating a system of differential equations along curves in the manifold. The space S whose structure is defined by this geometric object may be thought of as constituting a generalization of the associated spaces A if, in the holonomic case, S is isomorphic to A. I am not sure whether this is an accurate description of the point of view which Cartan has adopted in his treatment of generalized spaces and so it is best that I present this formulation of the problem on my own responsibility.

21. There is an interesting and difficult class of problems which have to do with the relation between the structure of a space and its topology. One of these is the Clifford-Klein space problem. Historically, this problem had its beginning in the discovery by Clifford in 1873 of a surface having zero curvature in three dimensional elliptic space. Klein in 1890 drew

attention to Clifford's result and formulated the general problem of the topology of Riemann spaces of constant curvature K. This problem has since come to be known as the Clifford-Klein space problem and was studied by Killing in his book *Grundlagen der Geometrie* (1893) where it was shown that the determination of all Clifford-Klein space forms can be carried back to the determination of the discontinuous groups of motions without fixed points of the euclidean, spherical and hyperbolic spaces. A recent investigation of this problem from the standpoint of modern topological theory has been made by H. Hopf [15].

As a significant concept in the investigation of Riemann spaces in the large, H. Hopf and W. Rinow [17] defined the non-continuable analytic Riemann space and this concept has an immediate extension to the case of any generalized space whose structure is determined by an analytic geometric object. An analytic Riemann space S is said to be continuable if there exists an analytic Riemann space S' such that S is isomorphic to a proper part of S'; otherwise S is non-continuable. Evidently the continuability or non-continuability of a space S is an intrinsic property of this space, although Hopf and Rinow did not succeed in finding an intrinsic characterization of this property. However, any one of the following four intrinsic conditions is sufficient for the space S to be non-continuable and each of these can be proved to be equivalent to the other three conditions:

(a) Every geodesic can be continued to infinite length.

(b) Every divergent line is infinitely long (a single valued continuous image in S of a euclidean ray is called a divergent line in S if to every divergent sequence of points on the ray corresponds a divergent sequence of points in S).

(c) Every Cauchy sequence converges.

(d) Every bounded set of points has a limit point.

An analytic Riemann space S satisfying any one of the above conditions is said to be *complete*. It can be shown, for example, that any two points of a complete space can be joined by a curve of shortest length (geodesic) and this property does not persist in non-continuable Riemann spaces. The complete spaces constitute a rather large subclass of the non-continuable Riemann spaces which is worthy of separate investigation.

The general problem of the relation between the metric structure and the topology of an analytic Riemann space was divided by H. Hopf [16] into two separate problems, namely, the *metrization* problem and the *continuation* problem (evidently corresponding problems can be framed for any generalized space with structure defined by an analytic geometric object). The metrization problem has to do with the extent to which the metric structure is determined or conditioned by the underlying topological manifold. In a sense, the metrization problem is the converse of the continuation problem since in the latter, one is concerned with the question of the possibility of continuing an arithmetic n-cell in which an analytic

positive definite quadratic differential form (Riemann element) is defined
to a non-continuable or more particularly a complete space. Going out
from this general point of view, Hopf has proved a number of very interesting special results and has, moreover, mentioned as many problems for
investigation, some of which have recently been solved by S. B. Myers
[27]. A fundamental result in the theory of spatial continuation has been
proved by W. Rinow [31], namely, that two simply connected and complete spaces S and S', each of which is the continuation of the same Riemann element, are isomorphic (isometric).

A number of new results have recently been obtained by S. B. Myers
and J. H. C. Whitehead on the minimum point locus with respect to an
arbitrary point P of a Riemann or Finsler space. A point M on a geodesic
ray g issuing from P is said to be a minimum point with respect to P on g
if M is the last point on g such that PM furnishes an absolute minimum to
the arc length of curves joining P to M. This locus was originally introduced by Poincaré [29] who considered it only for closed simply connected
surfaces of positive curvature. Whitehead [62] treats this locus, which he
calls a cut locus, for an n-dimensional Finsler space subject to a completeness condition. He obtains the theorem that such a space can be decom-
posed into an n-cell and the cut locus which forms the singular boundary
of the n-cell. A study of the topology of the minimum locus was made by
Myers [28] for two-dimensional compact Riemann spaces. Myers showed
that in the case of the analytic Riemann space the minimum locus is a
linear graph and obtained certain additional properties of this locus. He
also made a brief study of the minimum locus for non-analytic Riemann
spaces and showed that for such a space this locus turns out to be a continuous curve (not necessarily a linear graph) under the assumption that
the space is compact and possesses certain properties of regularity. One
could proceed quite naturally from these results to many others which are
usually treated under the heading of the calculus of variations.

It is known that over certain types of topological manifolds it is not
possible to have a continuous vector field without singular points. For
example, Brouwer [3] and J. W. Alexander [1] have shown that such a field
cannot be defined over an n-dimensional spherical surface if n is an even
integer. It follows from this fact and the theorem on the algebraic characterization of spaces admitting a field of parallel vectors in §19 that it is
not possible to define an affine connection L with analytic components over
a spherical surface of even dimensionality such that the conditions $\mathcal{R} = 0$
are satisfied; in particular the affine connection cannot be such that the
curvature tensor will vanish at all points of this surface. Quite generally,
one may consider the topological character of any generalized space over
which is satisfied a specified system of invariant differential equations in
the fundamental structural functions of the space (components of the
geometric object defining the space). One extreme of this class of problems

is reached when no such structural conditions are imposed on the space. Here one must expect little or no restriction on the underlying topological manifold as indicated by the researches of H. Whitney (§2). At the other extreme the structural conditions are so restrictive as to characterize the space locally to within an isomorphism. As an example of this extreme we may mention the Riemann space of constant curvature (Clifford-Klein space problem). Between these two extremes there is a large class of exceptionally difficult problems. A particularly interesting problem belonging to this last category and one which is, in fact, a direct extension of the Clifford-Klein space problem is the problem of the topological nature of Riemann spaces of constant *mean* curvature. In this connection one might investigate a question corresponding to Hopf's metrization problem with supplementary conditions; namely, to what extent is the metric of a Riemann space of constant mean curvature zero and dimensionality $n \geqq 4$ determined by the requirement that its manifold be homeomorphic to the n-dimensional number space and that it be flat at infinity? The euclidean metric space satisfies the above conditions and, although it seems likely that the euclidean metric space is the only such Riemann space of constant mean curvature zero, this has never been established. With regard to the general problem a result has been proved by Thomas [40] which can roughly be described by saying that a compact Riemann space S of positive constant mean curvature, but not of constant curvature, cannot differ infinitely little in its metric relationships from a space of constant curvature S' when the two spaces S and S' are considered in their entirety. In other words, the transition from S to S' corresponds to a jump or discontinuous process. While this is a rather special result it would appear to indicate that a thorough investigation of Riemann spaces of constant mean curvature in the large would lead to some interesting discoveries.

BIBLIOGRAPHY

1. ALEXANDER, J. W. *On transformations with invariant points.* Transactions of the American Mathematical Society, vol. 23 (1922), pp. 89–95.

2. ALLENDOERFER, C. B. *The imbedding of Riemann spaces in the large.* Duke Mathematical Journal, vol. 3 (1937), pp. 317–333.

3. BROUWER, L. E. J. *Ueber eindeutige stetige Transformationen von Flächen in sich.* Mathematische Annalen, vol. 69 (1910), pp. 176–180, 592.

4. CAIRNS, S. S. *Triangulation of the manifold of class one.* Bulletin of the American Mathematical Society, vol. 41 (1935), pp. 549–552.

5. CAIRNS, S. S. *The generalized theorem of Stokes.* Transactions of the American Mathematical Society, vol. 40 (1936), pp. 167–174.

6. CARTAN, E. *Les groupes d'holonomie des espaces généralisés.* Acta Mathematica, vol. 48 (1926), p. 1.

7. CARTAN, E., and SCHOUTEN, J. A. *On the geometry of the group-manifold of simple and semi-simple groups.* Proceedings, Koninklijke Akademie van Wetenschappen te Amsterdam, vol. 29 (1928), pp. 803–815.

8. CHRISTOFFEL, E. B. *Transformation der homogenen Differentialausdrücke zweiten Grades.* Journal für die reine und angewandte Mathematik, vol. 70 (1869), pp. 46–70, 241.

9. DOUGLAS, J. *The general geometry of paths.* Annals of Mathematics, (2), vol. 29 (1927), pp. 143–168.

10. DUSCHEK-MAYER. *Lehrbuch der Differentialgeometrie.* II. *Riemannsche Geometrie.* Leipzig, Teubner, 1930, p. 152.

11. EISENHART, L. P., and VEBLEN, O. *The Riemann geometry and its generalization.* Proceedings of the National Academy of Sciences, vol. 8 (1922), pp. 19–23.

12. EISENHART, L. P. *Linear connections of a space which are determined by simply transitive continuous groups.* Proceedings of the National Academy of Sciences, vol. 11 (1925), pp. 246–250.

13. EISENHART, L. P. *Fields of parallel vectors in a Riemann space.* Annals of Mathematics, (2), vol. 39 (1938), pp. 316–321.

14. FINSLER, P. *Ueber Kurven und Flächen in allgemeinen Räumen.* Dissertation, Göttingen, 1918.

15. HOPF, H. *Zum Clifford-Klein Raumproblem.* Mathematische Annalen, vol. 95 (1926), pp. 313–339.

16. HOPF, H. *Differentialgeometrie und topologische Gestalt.* Jahresbericht der Deutsche Mathematiker Vereinigung, vol. 41 (1932), pp. 209–229.

17. HOPF, H., and RINOW, W. *Ueber den Begriff der vollständigen differentialgeometrischen Fläche.* Commentarii Mathematici Helvetici, vol. 3 (1931), pp. 209–225.

18. HUREWICZ, W. *Über Abbildungen von endlichdimensionalen Räumen auf Teilmengen cartesischer Räume.* Sitzungsberichte der Preussische Akademie der Wissenschaften, Berlin, 1933, pp. 754–768.

19. *Killing, W. Grundlagen der Geometrie.* Paderborn, F. Schöningli, 1893.

20. KLEIN, F. *Gesammelte Mathematische Abhandlungen.* Vol. 1. Berlin, 1921, p. 460.

21. KNEBELMAN, M. S. *Collineations and motions in generalized spaces.* American Journal of Mathematics, vol. 51 (1928), pp. 527–564.

22. LEVI-CIVITA, T. *Nozione di parallelismo in una varietà qualunque e consequente specificazione geometrica della curvatura Riemanniana.* Rendiconti del Circolo Matematico di Palermo, vol. 42 (1917), pp. 173–204.

23. LEVI-CIVITA, T. *The Absolute Differential Calculus.* London, Blackie and Son, 1927, pp. 29–33.

24. MAYER, W., and THOMAS, T. Y. *Fields of parallel vectors in non-analytic manifolds in the large.* Compositio Mathematica, vol. 5 (1938), pp. 192–207.

25. MICHAL, A. D. *Affinely connected function space manifolds.* American Journal of Mathematics, vol. 50 (1928), pp. 473–517. *Abstract covariant vector fields in a general absolute calculus.* Ibid., vol. 59 (1937), pp. 306–314, where other references may be found.

26. MICHAL, A. D., and THOMAS, T. Y. *Differential invariants of relative quadratic differential forms.* Annals of Mathematics, (2), vol. 28 (1927), pp. 631–688.

27. MYERS, S. B. *Riemannian manifolds in the large.* Duke Mathematical Journal, vol. 1 (1935), pp. 39–49.

28. MYERS, S. B. *Connections between differential geometry and topology.* Duke Mathematical Journal, vol. 1 (1935), pp. 376–391; ibid., vol. 2 (1936), pp. 95–102.

29. POINCARÉ, H. *Sur les lignes geodesiques des surfaces convexes.* Transactions of the American Mathematical Society, vol. 6 (1905), p. 243.

30. RIEMANN, B. *Gesammelte Mathematische Werke.* Leipzig, 1876, p. 254.

31. RINOW, W. *Ueber Zusammenhänge zwischen der Differentialgeometrie im Grossen und im Kleinen.* Mathematische Zeitschrift, vol. 35 (1932), pp. 512–528.

32. ROBERTSON, H. P. *Note on projective coordinates.* Proceedings of the National Academy of Sciences, vol. 14 (1928), pp. 153–154.

33. ROBERTSON, H. P., and WEYL, H. *On a problem in the theory of groups arising in the foundations of infinitesimal geometry.* Bulletin of the American Mathematical Society, vol. 35 (1929), pp. 686–690.

34. SCHOUTEN, J. A. *Die direkte Analysis zur neueren Relativitätstheorie.* Verhandelingen, Koninklijke Akademie van Wetenschappen te Amsterdam, vol. 12 (1918), no. 6, p. 64.

35. SCHOUTEN, J. A., and HAANTJES, J. *Ueber allgemeine konforme Geometrie in projektiver Behandlung.* Proceedings, Koninklijke Akademie van Wetenschappen te Amsterdam, vol. 38 (1935), p. 706; vol. 39 (1936), p. 27. *Beiträge zur allgemeinen (gekrümten) conformen Differentialgeometrie.* Mathematische Annalen, vol. 112 (1936), p. 594; ibid., vol. 113 (1936), p. 568.

36. SCHOUTEN, J. A., and VAN KAMPEN, E. R. *Zur Einbettungs- und Krümmungs-theorie nichtholonomer Gebilde.* Mathematische Annalen, vol. 103 (1930), pp. 752–783.

37. THOMAS, T. Y. *On the projective and equi-projective geometries of paths.* Proceedings of the National Academy of Sciences, vol. 11 (1925), pp. 199–203.

38. THOMAS, T. Y. *A projective theory of affinely connected manifolds.* Mathematische Zeitschrift, vol. 25 (1926), pp. 723–733.

39. THOMAS, T. Y. *The Differential Invariants of Generalized Spaces.* Cambridge University Press, 1934, p. 59.

40. THOMAS, T. Y. *On the variation of curvature in Riemann spaces of constant mean curvature.* Annali di Matematica, vol. 13 (1934–1935), pp. 227–238.

41. THOMAS, T. Y. *Algebraic characterizations in complex differential geometry.* Transactions of the American Mathematical Society, vol. 38 (1935), p. 508.

42. THOMAS, T. Y. *Riemann spaces of class one and their characterization.* Acta Mathematica, vol. 67 (1936), pp. 169–211.

43. THOMAS, T. Y. *On the metric representations of affinely connected spaces.* Bulletin of the American Mathematical Society, vol. 42 (1936), p. 77.

44. THOMAS, T. Y. *Fields of parallel vectors in the large.* Compositio Mathematica, vol. 3 (1936), pp. 453–468.

45. THOMAS, T. Y. *Lectures on Differential Geometry.* Princeton Lecture Notes, 1937.

46. THOMAS, T. Y., and LEVINE, J. *On a class of existence theorems in differential geometry.* Bulletin of the American Mathematical Society, vol. 40 (1934), pp. 721–728.

47. THOMAS, T. Y., and LEVINE, J. *Simple tensors and the problem of the invariant characterization of an N-tuply orthogonal system of hypersurfaces in a V_n.* Annals of Mathematics, (2), vol. 35 (1934), pp. 735–739.

48. TRABER, R. E. *A fundamental lemma on normal coordinates and its applications.* Quarterly Journal of Mathematics, vol. 8 (1937), pp. 142–147.

49. VEBLEN, O. *Projective and affine geometry of paths.* Proceedings of the National Academy of Sciences, vol. 8 (1922), pp. 347–350.

50. VEBLEN, O. *Differential invariants and geometry.* Atti del Congresso Internazionale dei Matematici, vol. 1 (1928), pp. 181–189.

51. VEBLEN, O. *Generalized projective geometry.* Journal of the London Mathematical Society, vol. 4 (1929), pp. 140–160.

52. VEBLEN, O. *Projektive Relativitätstheorie.* Berlin, Springer, 1933.

53. VEBLEN, O., and THOMAS, J. M. *Projective invariants of affine geometry of paths.* Annals of Mathematics, (2), vol. 27 (1926), pp. 279–296.

54. VEBLEN, O., and WHITEHEAD, J. H. C. *Foundations of Differential Geometry.* Cambridge Tract No. 29, 1932.

55. WEYL, H. *Reine Infinitesimalgeometrie.* Mathematische Zeitschrift, vol. 2 (1918), pp. 384–411.

56. WEYL, H. *Raum, Zeit, Materie.* 5th edition. Berlin, Springer, 1921.

57. WEYL, H. *Zur Infinitesimalgeometrie: Einordnung der projektiven und der conformen Auffassung.* Göttingen, Nachrichten, 1921, pp. 99–112.

58. WEYL, H. *On the foundations of general infinitesimal geometry.* Bulletin of the American Mathematical Society, vol. 35 (1929), p. 719.

59. WHITEHEAD, J. H. C. *The representation of projective spaces.* Annals of Mathematics, (2), vol. 32 (1931), pp. 327–360.

60. WHITEHEAD, J. H. C. *Convex regions in the geometry of paths.* Quarterly Journal of Mathematics, vol. 3 (1932), pp. 33–42.

61. WHITEHEAD, J. H. C. Ibid., vol. 4 (1933), pp. 226–227.

62. WHITEHEAD, J. H. C. *On the covering of a complete space by the geodesics through a point.* Annals of Mathematics, (2), vol. 36 (1935), pp. 679–704.

63. WHITNEY, H. *Differentiable manifolds.* Annals of Mathematics, (2), vol. 37 (1936), pp. 645–680.

64. WRIGHT, J. E. *Invariants of quadratic differential forms.* Cambridge University Press, 1908, pp. 15–17.

PRINCETON UNIVERSITY,
    PRINCETON, N. J.

THE SPHERE IN TOPOLOGY

BY

R. L. WILDER

INTRODUCTION

Probably no branch of mathematics has experienced a more surprising growth than has, during the past two decades, that field known variously as Topology or Analysis Situs. Originating in the work of many mathematicians of the past century, including Cantor, Riemann, and Kronecker, it won recognition as a distinct branch of mathematics largely through the writings of Poincaré about the beginning of the present century. Although having many ramifications, it has progressively become a unified subject, and due to its foundation in the theory of abstract spaces, has come to collaborate with abstract group theory as a unifying force in mathematics as a whole. It has provided a tool for classification and unification, as well as for extension and generalization, in algebra, analysis, and geometry. Considered as a most specialized and abstract subject in the early 1920's, it is today almost an indispensable equipment for the investigator in modern mathematical theories.

It is with pardonable pride that one can point to the part which American mathematicians have played in this development. Although his name will not appear again in this monograph, we may well ponder how much this was due to that great American mathematician, E. H. Moore, by whose students, particularly R. L. Moore and O. Veblen, the actual beginnings of Topology in this country were made.

The writer was tempted to give the chief rôle in this monograph to the historical aspects of Topology. More careful reflection, based on limitations of space and ideals of coherence, seemed to point to a different task. There exist several modern treatises in Topology, as well as numerous special monographs; and besides these an almost overwhelming number of original papers, many of which are very lengthy. To the average mathematician who would like to gain some acquaintance with the subject, from either cultural or utilitarian motives, the literature probably presents a confusing aspect; he may select two books with identical titles, but with almost no overlapping of material—indeed, a casual glance at their contents may make him wonder if the printer has not erred in imprinting of titles on the jackets. It is perhaps not strange, under these circumstances, that the writer decided to subordinate the historical to the expository. More specifically, it is the intention of this monograph to furnish, first of all, a brief introduction to Topology in all its aspects, abstract, set-theoretic, and combinatorial. There seems no reason, a priori, why such an introduction cannot be given which will at the same time incorporate

136

to some extent, in its development from the simple to the more complex, the various stages of historical progress. This is the key to what the writer has tried to accomplish. The choice of subject, *The sphere in topology*, was dictated by a consideration of what material could best achieve these objectives.

It may as well be frankly stated that what appears herein has been hastily conceived and executed for the purposes of this semicentennial celebration. The writer makes no apologies for what in some sections, may seem a rather naive presentation; nor for errors or omissions unintentionally made. The first three sections are quite elementary, and should be readily handled by a first-year graduate student. The subject matter is necessarily limited, but is at least self-sufficient, and with the accompanying bibliography will, it is hoped, prove a reasonable introduction to the huge literature which it is supposed to represent. The only extraneous material required of the reader is some elementary knowledge of abstract group theory.

No more has been included in Chap. I than is needed in the later development. The axiomatic set-up of Chap. II and the statements of theorems without proof were motivated by the feeling that the doing of mathematics is the only safe road to real appreciation and rigor. Although the material in Chap. III is limited to the 2-sphere, symbols and terminology have been so arranged as to adapt themselves to immediate generalization later on. Chap. V is admittedly a sop to the writer's own predilections in Topology; but possibly we can plead that the justification for inclusion here lies in its nature as a sample of the direction indicated by Schoenflies. Chaps. IV, VI, and VII are intended to develop some of the more recent tendencies, and will possibly give an indication of the present status of Topology.

I. The space concept

1.1. **Set-theoretic remarks.** If M is any collection or *set* of elements, then $x \, \varepsilon \, M$ will be read "x is an element of M." More generally, $x_1, x_2, \cdots, x_n \, \varepsilon \, M$ will be read "$x_1, x_2, \cdots, x_n$ are elements of M." A set A will be called a *subset* of a set M, in symbols $A \subset M$, or $M \supset A$, if $x \, \varepsilon \, A$ implies $x \, \varepsilon \, M$. Negations of these relationships are indicated in the usual way, thus $\not\subset$ and $\notin$, respectively. If $A \subset M$ and there exists x such that $x \notin A$ and $x \, \varepsilon \, M$, then A will be called a *proper* subset of M. It is convenient and customary to introduce the *null* (empty or *vacuous*) set 0, which is defined as being the set such that for no x does the relation $x \, \varepsilon \, 0$ hold. As a logical consequence of its definition, 0 is an element of most classes of sets; for example, the class of all subsets of a given set, of all connected sets (§1.3), of all open sets (§1.2), etc.

If A and B are sets, then $A + B$ (*sum* of the sets A and B) is the set of all elements x such that at least one of the relations $x \, \varepsilon \, A$, $x \, \varepsilon \, B$ holds. The set $A \cdot B$ (*common part* of the sets A and B) is the set of all elements x such that both of the relations $x \,\varepsilon\, A$, $x \,\varepsilon\, B$ hold. If $A \cdot B = 0$, then A and B are called *mutually exclusive*. Finally, the set $A - B$ is the set of all elements x such that $x \,\varepsilon\, A$ and $x \,\notin\, B$.

1.2. **Spaces.** Generally speaking, any set M in which the "structural" concept of *limit point* has been established may constitute a *space* in Topology. Most of the early work in Topology was confined to euclidean spaces or their subsets, but it gradually became apparent that subsets of euclidean spaces were of themselves types of general spaces. The method of defining limit point in a given set M is quite arbitrary. One may proceed [1] by giving for each set $A \subset M$ the set A' (*derived set*) of all its limit points. Or one may prefer first to introduce *neighborhoods* of points and then define limit points in terms of neighborhoods. When one is studying the topology of an n-dimensional euclidean space E_n, the latter method is the more natural.

The simplest system or collection of neighborhoods for a euclidean space is that obtained by letting the set of points interior to a sphere be a neighborhood of any point in the set; more specifically, if x is a point and ϵ a positive number, the set $S(x, \epsilon)$ of all points y such that the distance $\rho(x, y)$ from x to y is less than ϵ is a neighborhood of any $y \,\varepsilon\, S(x, \epsilon)$. Thus, in E_1, the neighborhoods are intervals minus end points, and in E_2 they are interiors of circles. Finally, a point x is called a *limit point* of a set of points M, or M is said to *have x as a limit point*, provided that for every $\epsilon > 0$ the set $M \cdot S(x, \epsilon) - x \neq 0$; in words, every neighborhood of x contains at least one point of M distinct from x. It must be noted that M may have x as a limit point no matter whether $x \,\varepsilon\, M$ or not.

Now all we have just done is to set up a *neighborhood system* based on, or in agreement with, the euclidean *metric*. Suppose that we have an abstract set M on which there is defined a *single-valued, real* function $\rho(x, y)$ satisfying the following conditions: (1) $\rho(x, y) = 0$ if and only if $x = y$; (2) for any $x, y, z \,\varepsilon\, M$, distinct or not, $\rho(x, y) \leq \rho(x, z) + \rho(y, z)$. Then if limit points are defined as above, M is called a *metric space*, the function $\rho(x, y)$ being its *metric*. (It follows readily from the definition that $\rho(x, y)$ is nonnegative and symmetric.) If a neighborhood system for a metric space is set up exactly as was done in the preceding paragraph for E_n, such a system is said to be in agreement with the metric.

If S is a given space, hence a set in which limit points have been defined either by a metric or otherwise, and $A \subset S$, then by $\overline{A}$ (*closure of A*) we denote the set $A + A'$, where A' is the set of all limit points of A. If $A = \overline{A}$, the set A is called *closed*. If $A \subset S$ is a closed set, then $S - A$ is called *open*; thus open sets are the *complements* of closed sets. Ordinarily, as for instance in a metric space, neighborhoods are special cases of open sets, and it is easy to see that a necessary and sufficient condition that a point x be a limit point of a set of points $M \subset S$ is that for every open set U containing x, the set $M \cdot U - x \neq 0$; in other words, that x be a limit point of M as given by the neighborhood system consisting of all open sets of S. Thus in a metric space we have defined two neighborhood systems, that consisting of its spherical neighborhoods $S(x, \epsilon)$ and that consisting of all its open sets. As a corollary of the statement just made above, if a point x is a limit point of a set A in a metric space M in terms of its spheres, then x is a limit point of A in terms of its open sets, and conversely.

This brings us to the notion of equivalent neighborhood systems of a set S: Two neighborhood systems of S are called *equivalent* if, given a neighborhood U of a point x in either system, there is a neighborhood V of x in the other system such that $V \subset U$. It follows immediately that if Σ_1 and Σ_2 are equivalent neighborhood systems of S, and a subset M of S has a limit point x in terms of neighborhoods of Σ_1, then x is a limit point of M in terms of Σ_2; and conversely. In a metric space the system Σ_1 of spheres $S(x, \epsilon)$ is equivalent to the system Σ_2 of open sets. It is important to note that by the imposition of nonequivalent neighborhood systems, the same set S may constitute different spaces in an essential sense (see §1.3 below). Hereafter when a space is defined in terms of a certain neighborhood system, we call the latter the *defining system* of neighborhoods.

In a metric space S, we may extend the symbol $\rho(x, y)$ to the form $\rho(X, Y)$, where $X \subset S$, $Y \subset S$; it will denote the greatest lower bound of the set of all numbers $\rho(x, y)$ such that $x \varepsilon X$, $y \varepsilon Y$. Also, if $M \subset S$, we shall find useful the notion of the *diameter* of M, to be denoted by $\delta(M)$, which is the least upper bound of the set of all numbers $\rho(x, y)$ where $x \varepsilon M$ and $y \varepsilon M$.

1.3. **Homeomorphisms, invariants.** If S_1 and S_2 are two spaces, then a *continuous mapping* of S_1 into S_2 is a single-valued function $y = f(x)$ such that (1) $x \varepsilon S_1$ and f is defined for all $x \varepsilon S_1$, (2) $y \varepsilon S_2$, and (3) f is continuous; that is, if $y = f(x)$ and $U \subset S_2$ is a neighborhood of y, then there is a neighborhood $V \subset S_1$ of x such that $f(V) \subset U$. In an expression of the sort $Y = f(X)$ as used here we interpret the symbol Y simply as the set of all $y \varepsilon S_2$ such that for some $x \varepsilon X$, $y = f(x)$, and as such we call it the *image set* of X (in S_2, rel. f).

There is another sense in which the symbol Y in the expression $Y = f(X)$ may be interpreted, and in which it signifies a duplicate of X in S_2 wherein for $y = f(x_1) = f(x_2)$, $(x_1 \neq x_2)$, we consider the values $f(x_1), f(x_2)$ as two points which coincide on y, and in this sense we call Y the *image* of X (in M, rel. f). Two mappings of X into M may have the same image sets but different images [68]. The set X will be called the counter image of Y. When Y is considered as the image set of X (in M, rel. f), then for $y \varepsilon Y$, the counter image of y is the set of all $x \varepsilon X$ such that $y = f(x)$, and this set is denoted by $f^{-1}(y)$.

If f is such that every point of S_2 is in the image set, then f is called a mapping *on* S_2. Finally, if f is a mapping of S_1 on S_2 and the inverse function $x = f^{-1}(y)$ is single valued and constitutes a continuous mapping of S_2

on S_1, then f (or f^{-1}) is called a *homeomorphism* (or topological mapping). The *topology* of a space S is the study of those properties that remain invariant under homeomorphisms of S. It is easy to show that a necessary and sufficient condition that a $(1-1)$-correspondence T between two spaces S_1, S_2 be a homeomorphism is that the neighborhood system of S_1 be equivalent to the system consisting of the image sets (in S_1, rel. T) of the elements of the neighborhood system of S_2.

In metric spaces, there is associated with the notion of continuous mapping that of *uniformly continuous mapping*, whose definition is like that of the special case of uniform continuity for real functions. And if, between two metric spaces M_1, M_2, there exists a homeomorphism f such that both f and f^{-1} are uniformly continuous, then f is called a *uniformly bicontinuous mapping*. The following theorem, whose proof is left to the reader, is of importance later on.

THEOREM. *If A_1 and A_2 are subsets of the compact* (definition in next paragraph) *metric spaces M_1 and M_2, respectively, such that $\overline{A}_i = M_i$, $(i=1, 2)$, and f is a uniformly bicontinuous mapping between A_1 and A_2, then f may be extended to a homeomorphism between M_1 and M_2.*

One of the most important topological invariants is compactness; a space is called *compact* if every infinite subset has a limit point. As in the case of most topological invariants, this property may be *localized*: A space S is called *locally compact* if for every $x \, \varepsilon \, S$ there exists a neighborhood U of x such that the closure of U is compact. Thus the space E_n is locally compact, but not compact. Another important invariant is *separability*: A space S is called *separable* if it has a denumerable subset A such that $\overline{A} = S$. A stronger invariant is that of perfect separability: A space S is called *perfectly separable* if it has a denumerable neighborhood system which is equivalent to the defining system. We introduce one more invariant at this stage: Let us call two subsets A and B of a space S *separated* if $A \neq 0 \neq B$ and $\overline{A} \cdot B = A \cdot \overline{B} = 0$; then a space S is called *connected* if it is not the sum of two separated sets. By way of example, the space E_n is connected and perfectly separable. As an example of a space which is separable but not perfectly separable, consider, in the coordinate plane, the set M_1 of all points (x, y) such that $x^2 + y^2 < 1$ and the set M_2 such that $x^2 + y^2 = 1$; let $M = M_1 + M_2$. Thus far, M is only a *set* and not a *space*. Now for $p \, \varepsilon \, M_1$, let each neighborhood of p consist of all points of M_1 interior to a circle with center p; for $q \, \varepsilon \, M_2$, let each neighborhood of q consist of q together with all points of M_1 interior to a circle with center q. The space M so defined is separable, since if A consists of all points of M_1 both of whose coordinates (as points of the coordinate plane) are rational, $\overline{A} = M$; it is not, however, perfectly separable. The reader may also note that M is connected but not locally compact; and that the space M is not *metrizable* in that there does not exist a metric such that the system of spherical neighborhoods defined thereby is equivalent to the system of neighborhoods defining M above. (In regard to metrization problems, see [2].)

1.4. Subspaces, imbedding. Let A be a subset of a space S. Since limit points are defined in S, the set A may be considered as a space whose limit points are defined as in S (thus, if in S, $x \varepsilon A$ is a limit point of $M \subset A$, then x is a limit point of M in A). We then call A a *subspace* of S, or, which is equivalent, say that A is *imbedded in* S. The set M described in the preceding paragraph is a subset of the plane E_2, but is *not* a subspace of E_2 since in E_2 the point $(1, 0)$ is a limit point of M_2, whereas in M this is not the case. A natural way to consider a subset A of a space S as a subspace of S is to let the neighborhoods in A be the "overlappings" of A with neighborhoods of S; more specifically, if U is a neighborhood in S of $x \varepsilon A$, let the set $U \cdot A$ be a neighborhood of x in A.

More generally, suppose S_1 and S_2 are spaces. If there exists a subspace A of S_2 such that A and S_1 are homeomorphic, then S_1 is said to be imbeddable in S_2. There exists, for example, a complete characterization of the compact Peano spaces (Chap. II) that are imbeddable in the 2-sphere [3], and in the Menger-Urysohn dimension theory [4] it is known, for example, that every n-dimensional compact metric space is imbeddable in E_{2n+1}. When a space S_1 is imbeddable in a space S_2, we shall often denote any homeomorph of S_1 in S_2 by the same symbol S_1.

The invariants defined in §1.3 may now be applied to subsets A of a space S; we speak of "connected subsets," "separable subsets," etc. It should be noted, however, that a majority of authors call a set $A \subset S$ compact if every infinite subset of A has a limit point *in* S, and introduce the term *self-compact* to denote compactness of A as a *subspace* of S; we use the term compact in this sense hereafter. However, for metric spaces, sets which are compact and closed are self-compact, and conversely, so that for closed sets in metric spaces the distinction is not significant. When a point set consisting of more than one point is both closed and connected, we call it a *continuum*. The reader will note that a connected space S_1 containing more than one point is a continuum, but that if it is embedded in a space S_2 it may fail to be a continuum in S_2, due to the non-invariance of the closure property (thus the segment $0 < x < 1$ of the space of real numbers is a continuum in itself as space, but not in the complete real number system). For this reason, when using either of the terms closed, continuum, the space relative to which these properties are used must be evident (in Chap. II below, for example, these terms will be used relative to C).

1.5. Some important special spaces. A. The real number continuum E_1. This section is basic in all that follows, since it contains the fundamental connecting link with ordinary analysis. Thus, the material in Chap. III is ultimately dependent on the structure of E_1, as also are the definitions of E_n and S_n below which are basic in the later discussions. Furthermore, particular pains have been taken in Chap. II to establish the homeomorphism between any set satisfying the arc definition used therein and the *bounded* real number continuum E_1^* consisting of all real numbers x such that $0 \leq x \leq 1$. Of course, the ordinary conception of the real number continuum is not topological; probably the Cantor-Huntington [5] axioms best express the usual intuitive conception, namely, a simply ordered set satisfying the Dedekind cut axiom, having a denumerable separating set, but no first and no last point (for E_1^* the last condition is replaced by the assumption of both a first and a last point). To consider E_1 as a space we may let, for any $x \, \varepsilon \, E_1$, a neighborhood of x consist of all points y such that $a < y < b$, where a and b are any points such that $a < x < b$. In terms of such neighborhoods one may show that E_1 is a locally compact, connected, perfectly separable space. In E_1^* neighborhoods would be similarly defined, except for 0 and 1; thus for $x = 0$ a neighborhood would consist of all y such that $0 \leq y < b$.

The following example is instructive: In the cartesian plane let M be the set of points consisting of $(0, 0)$ and all points (x, y) such that $y = \sin (1/x)$, $(0 < x \leq 1)$. The set M may be linearly ordered in obvious fashion, and with neighborhoods defined as in the preceding paragraph is homeomorphic with E_1^*. However, as a subspace of the cartesian plane, the set M is not homeomorphic with E_1^*, inasmuch as the set K of points whose ordinates equal 1 has no limit point in M, whereas E_1^* is compact. What happens here is that the point $(0, 0)$, which is a limit point of K when neighborhoods are defined in M as on the linear continuum, is no longer a limit point of K when the metric on the cartesian plane is used to define neighborhoods of M. This example will perhaps also make clear later the significance of Theorem 12 in Chap. II.

B. The euclidean n-dimensional space E_n. This is a metric space whose points are the ordered n-tuples $(x_1, x_2, \cdots, x_n)$, where x_i, $(i = 1, 2, \cdots, n)$, takes on all possible values in the real number continuum E_1, and whose metric is defined thus: if $x = (x_1, x_2, \cdots, x_n)$ and $y = (y_1, y_2, \cdots, y_n)$, then $\rho(x, y) = (\sum_{i=1}^{n}(x_i - y_i)^2)^{1/2}$. This is a special case of a *product space* (although as a product space the neighborhoods are parallelopipeds forming a system equivalent to the spherical neighborhood system given by the above metric). The fact that E_n is locally compact, connected, and perfectly separable follows from the same properties of E_1.

C. The n-sphere, S_n. This is the subspace of E_{n+1} consisting of all points $(x_1, x_2, \cdots, x_{n+1})$ such that $x_1^2 + x_2^2 + \cdots + x_{n+1}^2 = 1$. This space is compact.

Since our point of view is to be topological, any space homeomorphic with one of the above spaces will receive the same name. For example, if $x \, \varepsilon \, S_n$, then the subspace $S_n - x$ is an E_n. When we speak of an S_n imbedded, say, in some E_k, the set of points constituting S_n is not in general a "sphere" in the sense of euclidean geometry, and, indeed, its relations to the complementary set $E_k - S_n$ may be greatly different from those of the euclidean sphere to its complement [6]. The 1-sphere S_1 is ordinarily called the *simple closed curve* or Jordan curve, and (Chap. III, Theorems J_1, J_2 [7]) an essential part of the proof of the Jordan curve theorem is to show that the complement of an S_1 imbedded in S_2 is exactly two components, just as in the analytically demonstrable case of the circle $x_1^2 + x_2^2 = 1$, $x_3 = 0$, in the 2-sphere $x_1^2 + x_2^2 + x_3^2 = 1$. We remark here that in general, if A and B are metric spaces, and $B' = f(B)$, f a homeomorphism, $B' \subset A$, then the distance $\rho(x, y)$ for $x, y \,\varepsilon\, B'$ will be that given by the metric of A rather than that of B.

D. The Hilbert fundamental cube, Q_ω. This is the space whose points are all sequences $(x_1, x_2, \cdots, x_n, \cdots)$ of real numbers x_n, where $0 \leq x_n \leq 1/n$, and where $\rho(a,b), a = (x_1, x_2, \cdots, x_n, \cdots), b = (y_1, y_2, \cdots, y_n, \cdots)$ is the number $(\sum_{n=1}^{\infty}(x_n - y_n)^2)^{1/2}$.

E. Group-space. [8]. If a given set forms both a space and a group, then, if certain continuity conditions relating the limit point notion to the group operation are satisfied, the set is called a group-space (topological group, continuous group). In terms of neighborhoods, these continuity conditions usually imply that, given a neighborhood $U(c)$ of c and $a \cdot b = c$, then there exist neighborhoods $U(a)$, $U(b)$ such that $U(a) \cdot U(b) \subset U(c)$; and there exists $U(c^{-1})$ such that $(U(c^{-1}))^{-1} \subset U(c)$. In a metric space, where a limit point of a set is a limit point of a sequence of points of that set, these conditions may be stated in terms of limits of sequences.

II. LOCALLY COMPACT METRIC SPACES AND PEANO SPACES

We give in this section what may be considered an introduction to the material and methods exploited so effectively by the set-theoretic topologists. We list a set of five axioms. From two of these we derive (in §2.1) a number of fundamental theorems which include topological characterizations of E_1^* and S_1, the Cantor product theorem, the Borel theorem, and so on.

The complete set of five axioms serves to define a Peano space, and the theorems given in §2.2 are true for any such space. Historically, this material originates in the "continuous curves" of Jordan's *Cours d'Analyse* [9], defined for the coördinate plane by continuous functions of a real parameter. It is probably true that the investigation of these curves owes its liberation from the confines of analysis to the attention accorded them in connection with the so-called "space-filling curve" of Peano [10], and partly for this reason, as well as to avoid confusion with the term "Jordan curve" (S_1), the name Peano space has been applied in recent years to their topological analogues (although the terms "continuous curve," "Jordan continuum," are still used by some authors). However, the topological possibilities of these "curves" were first discovered by Schoenflies [11], whose set-theoretic researches culminated in their topological characterization among the subspaces of the euclidean plane. (See Chap. V.)

This type of work, concerning the relations between a continuous curve in the plane and its complement, was not, except for certain isolated papers, systematically continued and extended until taken up by R. L. Moore and his students and the Polish school of topologists. The material given here on Peano spaces actually relates, however, to the later development in point of view, which considers the curve as a space in itself, without reference to any larger space in which it may be imbedded, and particularly from the structural point of view introduced by G. T. Whyburn, which regards this space as being made up of certain subspaces called "cyclic elements." This material was selected not only for its importance as a powerful tool, but because it furnishes a convenient basis for the proof that the only compact Peano space which can satisfy the Jordan curve theorem non-vacuously is the 2-sphere.

Axiom 4 embodies the so-called "connectedness im kleinen" or local connectedness property of Peano spaces, and characterizes, among the compact, connected metric spaces, those which are image sets relative to continuous mappings of E_1^* (§1.5). Regarding the more detailed history of the property, the reader is referred to [12]; it will suffice to remark here that it embodies an internal characteristic of image-sets of E_1^*, dependent in no way on dimensionality or imbedding, whereas the Schoenflies characterization embodies an external characterizing property, relative only to sets imbedded in E_2. Our assumption in Axiom 1 of local compactness instead of compactness in no way complicates the proofs of theorems, and allows sufficient greater generality to achieve our purposes. We shall, in general, leave the details to the reader, but will, in the case of more difficult proofs, give references to the literature. The aim, as explained in the introduction, is to encourage the reader to supply his own proofs.

We consider a set C, whose elements we call points, satisfying:

AXIOM 0. *C contains at least two distinct points.*

AXIOM 1. *C is a metric space.*

AXIOM 2. *C is locally compact.*

AXIOM 3. *C is connected.*

AXIOM 4. *If $x \varepsilon C$ and ϵ is a positive number, then there exists an open connected subset U of C such that $x \varepsilon U$ and $U \subset S(x, \epsilon)$.*

A set C satisfying these axioms we call a Peano space.

2.1. Some consequences of Axioms 1 and 2; topological characterizations of E_1^* and S_1. In the following theorems all point sets mentioned are assumed to lie in a space C satisfying Axioms 1 and 2.

THEOREM 1. *If x is a limit point of a set of points M, then every open set which contains x also contains infinitely many points of M.*

COROLLARY. *No finite set of points has a limit point.*

THEOREM 2. *If x is a limit point of the sum of two point sets A and B, then x is a limit point of at least one of the sets A, B.*

THEOREM 3. *If A is a connected subset of a connected set M, and M − A = B + D where B and D are separated, then both sets B + A, D + A are connected.*

DEFINITION. *If a and b are distinct points of a connected set I such that no connected proper subset of I contains both a and b, then I is said to be irreducibly connected from a to b. In the theorems below, I will be a set irreducibly connected from a to b* [13].

THEOREM 4. *If N is a connected subset of I which contains a or b, then I − N is connected.*

THEOREM 5. *If N is a connected subset of I which contains neither a nor b, then I − N is the sum of two separated connected sets containing a and b respectively.*

THEOREM 6. *If M and N are connected subsets of I each of which contains a, then either M ⊂ N or N ⊂ M.*

THEOREM 7. *Every x ε I determines in unique fashion a decomposition of I into two sets $A(x)$ and $B(x)$ such that* (1) $A(x)$ *is irreducibly connected from a to x, and* $B(x)$ *is irreducibly connected from x to b;* (2) $A(x) \cdot B(x) = x = A(x) \cdot \overline{B}(x) + \overline{A}(x) \cdot B(x)$.

THEOREM 8. *If for distinct points x, y ε I such that $A(x) \subset A(y)$ there is set up the binary relation $x < y$, then the set I is simply ordered in terms of the relation <.*

THEOREM 9. *For every x ε I, the set $A(x)$ consists of those points y ε I such that $y \leq x$.*

DEFINITION. *A subset M of I is called a portion of I if every element of I which is between (in terms of the relation <) two elements of M is itself an element of M.*

DEFINITION. *An x ε I is called a lower bound of a set M ⊂ I if $x \leq M$ and there exists no y ε M such that $x < y \leq M$.*

(We write $x \leq M$ if for every y ε M, $x \leq y$.) Upper bound is defined in an obvious way.

THEOREM 10. *If a point x of a portion M of I is not an upper bound or a lower bound of M, then x is not a limit point of I − M.*

THEOREM 11. *In terms of the relation <, the set I satisfies the Dedekind cut axiom.*

THEOREM 12. *A closed I is compact.*

146   R. L. WILDER

Definition. *Let Σ_1 denote the set of all $S(x, \epsilon)$, $x \in C$. Then if $M \subset C$, a collection Σ of subsets of C will be said to be equivalent to Σ_1 relative to M if for every $x \in M$ and $U \in \Sigma$ such that $x \in U$, there exists $\epsilon > 0$ such that $S(x, \epsilon) \subset U$; and conversely, given an $S(x, \epsilon)$ there exists $U \in \Sigma$ such that $x \in U \subset S(x, \epsilon)$.*

Theorem 13. *If M is a compact point set, there exists a denumerable collection Σ of neighborhoods $S(x_n, \epsilon_n)$ such that Σ is equivalent to Σ_1 relative to M.*

Corollary. *Every compact point set is separable.*

Theorem 14. *A closed set I contains a sequence of points $x_1, x_2, \cdots, x_n, \cdots$ such that for any $x, y \in I$ and $x < y$, there exists an n such that $x < x_n < y$.*

Theorem 15. *Every closed set I is homeomorphic with E_1^*.*

Theorem 15 embodies a topological characterization of those subsets of locally compact metric spaces that are homeomorphic with E_1^*, since it is obvious that every homeomorph of E_1^* is a set I. Hereafter, we shall call any homeomorph of E_1^* an *arc*.

Theorem 16. *In order that a connected set M be irreducibly connected between two of its points a and b, it is necessary and sufficient that if $x \in M$ and $a \neq x \neq b$, $M - x$ is the sum of two separated sets neither of which contains both a and b.*

Corollary. *Among the continua, the arc is characterized by the condition of Theorem 16.*

Definition. *If a set M is the sum of two I's, say I_1, I_2, such that $I_1 \cdot I_2 = a + b = \bar{I}_1 \cdot I_2 = I_1 \cdot \bar{I}_2$, then M is called a quasi-closed curve.*

Theorem 17. *In order that a connected set M be a quasi-closed curve, it is necessary and sufficient that (1) for every $x \in M$, $M - x$ be connected, and (2) for $x, y \in M$, $x \neq y$, the set $M - (x + y)$ be not connected.*

Corollary, *In order that a continuum M be an S_1, it is necessary and sufficient that conditions (1), (2) of Theorem 17 hold. [14].*

Theorem 18 (Cantor product theorem). *If $M_1, M_2, M_3, \cdots$ form an infinite sequence of compact sets such that $M_n \supset \bar{M}_{n+1}$, (§1.2), $n = 1, 2, 3, \cdots$, then the product $\Pi_{n=1}^{\infty} M_n$ is nonvacuous and closed.* (See definition of compact, §1.3, §1.4.)

Definition. *If M is a point set and G is a set of point sets such that for every $x \in M$ there exists at least one $g \in G$ such that $x \in g$, then G is said to cover M.*

THEOREM 19 (Denumerable to finite Borel theorem). *If M is a closed and compact point set and G is a denumerable set of open sets covering M, then there exists a finite subset of G which covers M.*

(Consider the sets $M - M \cdot \sum_{i=1}^{n} g_i$, where $g_i \varepsilon G$.)

Now from Theorem 13 above it follows easily that if G is a collection of open sets covering a compact and closed set M, then a denumerable subset of G covers M. From this and Theorem 19 we have the following theorem.

THEOREM 20 (Borel). *If G is a collection of open sets covering a compact and closed point set M, then a finite subset of G covers M.*

THEOREM 21. *Under the hypothesis of Theorem 18, with the additional assumption that each set M_n is connected, the product $\prod_{n=1}^{\infty} M_n$ is connected.*

DEFINITION. *If $x, y \varepsilon C$, then a finite sequence of sets $M_1, M_2, \cdots, M_n$ will be said to form a simple chain of sets from x to y if (1) $x \varepsilon M_1$ if and only if $i = 1$, (2) $y \varepsilon M_i$ if and only if $i = n$; and (3) $M_i \cdot M_j \neq 0$, $(i < j)$, if and only if $j = i + 1$.*

THEOREM 22. *If M is a connected point set and G is a collection of open sets covering M, then for any two points $x, y \varepsilon M$ there exists a simple chain of elements of G from x to y.*

2.2. **Some properties of Peano spaces; topological characterization of** S_2.

THEOREM 23. *If each connected open subset of C is called a neighborhood of each of its points, then the system Σ_2 of all such neighborhoods is equivalent to Σ_1.*

Hereafter we call each element of Σ_2 a *domain*. By Theorem 1 and Axiom 3, every domain contains infinitely many points.

If a set M is an arc, and a, b are the points of M corresponding to 0, 1 of E_1^*, then we shall often denote M by ab. If M is a point set such that for every $a, b \varepsilon M$ there exists an arc ab in M, then M will be called *arcwise connected*.

Related to the following so-called "arc theorem," there exists a not inconsiderable literature. For a proof that can be adapted to the present framework, the reader is referred to [15].

THEOREM 24. *The space C is arcwise connected.*

COROLLARY. *Every domain is arcwise connected.*

(For the Axioms $0-4$ all hold for every domain; that is, every domain is itself a Peano Space.)

Remark. For reference in Chap. VI, we note here that it now follows readily that in order that a locally compact, connected metric space S containing more than one point be a Peano space, it is necessary and sufficient that for every $x \, \varepsilon \, S$ and $\epsilon > 0$ there exist a $\delta > 0$ such that for every pair $a, b \, \varepsilon \, S \, (x, \delta)$ there is an arc ab in $S(x, \epsilon)$.

DEFINITION. *If M is a point set and $p \, \varepsilon \, M$, then the component of M determined by p is the set of all points $x \, \varepsilon \, M$ such that both p and x lie in a connected subset of M. It may be shown directly from the definition of connectedness that if L is the component of M determined by $p \, \varepsilon \, M$, then for every $q \, \varepsilon \, L$, the component of M determined by q is again L, so that every point set possesses a unique decomposition into its components.*

THEOREM 25. *A necessary and sufficient condition that a subset R of C be a domain is that it be a component of an open subset of C.*

DEFINITION. *If R is a domain, then the boundary of R is the set of points $\overline{R} - R$.*

THEOREM 26. *If R is a domain not identical with C, then the boundary B of R is a nonvacuous, closed point set. Furthermore, if $C - \overline{R} \neq 0$, then $C - B$ is the sum of the separated sets R and $C - \overline{R}$.*

DEFINITION. *A point p is called an end point of C if for every $\epsilon > 0$ there exists a point x such that $C - x = C_1 + C_2$, where C_1 and C_2 are separated and $p \, \varepsilon \, C_1 \subset S(p, \epsilon)$* [16].

DEFINITION. *If M is a connected set and $x \, \varepsilon \, M$ is such that $M - x$ is not connected, then x is called a cut point of M. If an $x \, \varepsilon \, M$ is not a cut point of M, it is called a non-cut point of M* [17].

DEFINITION. *If M is a metric space and $x \, \varepsilon \, M$, $\epsilon > 0$, then by $F(x, \epsilon)$ we denote the set of all $y \, \varepsilon \, M$ such that $\rho(x, y) = \epsilon$.*

THEOREM 27. *If x is a non-cut point of C and ϵ a positive number such that $F(x, \epsilon)$ is compact, then there exists a $\delta > 0$ such that for any $a, b \, \varepsilon \, F(x, \epsilon)$ there is an arc ab in $C - S(x, \delta)$.*

COROLLARY. *If x is a non-cut point of C and ϵ a positive number, then there exists a $\delta > 0$ such that all points of $C - S(x, \epsilon)$ lie in one component of $C - S(x, \delta)$.*

DEFINITION. *With every non-cut point p of C, we associate a set C_p which consists of all points x of C such that for no $y \, \varepsilon \, C$ is $C - y = C_1 + C_2$ where C_1 and C_2 are separated sets containing p and x, respectively. By a cyclic element of C will be meant either a cut point of C or a set C_p.*

By way of examples, the end points of E_1^* are sets C_p and the other points of E_1^* are cut points, so that each point of E_1^* is a cyclic element of E_1^*. The 1-sphere S_1 is a cyclic element of S_1. The set M consisting of two tangent circles in E_2 has just three cyclic elements consisting respectively of the point of tangency and the two sets of points lying on the respective circles; this example shows, incidentally, that cyclic elements are not in general mutually exclusive point sets [18].

THEOREM 28. *A $C_p = p$ only if p is an end point.*

THEOREM 29. *Every C_p is a closed point set.*

THEOREM 30. *A C_p has the property that each component of $C - C_p$ has just one limit point in C_p.*

THEOREM 31. *If M is a connected set, then for any C_p the set $M \cdot C_p$ is connected.*

DEFINITION. *A set which has more than one element will hereafter be called nondegenerate.*

THEOREM 32. *Every nondegenerate C_p is a Peano space having no cut point.*

THEOREM 33. *If M is a set C_p and A_1, A_2 are closed, mutually exclusive, nondegenerate subsets of M, then there exist in M two arcs $a_{1i}a_{2i}$, $(i = 1, 2)$, such that $a_{1i} \varepsilon A_1$, $a_{2i} \varepsilon A_2$, and $(a_{11}a_{21}) \cdot (a_{12}a_{22}) = 0$.*

LEMMA. *If M is a nondegenerate C_p (and consequently a Peano space), D is a domain of M, and x is a non-cut point of D, then the set C_x of the Peano space D is nondegenerate.*

THEOREM 34. *If M is a C_p and a, b, $c \varepsilon M$, where a, b, and c are distinct, then there exists in M an arc ac which contains b.*

DEFINITION. *A Peano space C is called cyclicly connected if each pair of points of C lie together on some 1-sphere of C.*

THEOREM 35. *Every C_p is cyclicly connected.*

DEFINITION. *If M is a connected set, $A \subset M$ and $B \subset M - A$, and $M - A$ is the sum of two separated sets, each of which contains points of B, then we say that A separates B in M.*

THEOREM 36. *If K is a nondegenerate subset of C such that no point of C separates K in C, then K lies in a single C_p of C.*

THEOREM 37. *If p is a non-cut point of C, then the set C_p may be defined as the maximal, cyclicly connected subset of C that contains p.*

DEFINITION. *A Peano space C will be said to satisfy the Jordan curve theorem nonvacuously if there exists at least one 1-sphere in C, and if for every 1-sphere S_1 of C, it is true that $C - S_1$ consists of two mutually exclusive domains each of whose boundaries is S_1.*

THEOREM 38. *If C is compact and satisfies the Jordan curve theorem non-vacuously, then C is a 2-sphere.*

THEOREM 39. *If C is compact and contains at least one 1-sphere, and every 1-sphere of C separates C but no subarc of a 1-sphere separates C, then C is a 2-sphere.*

For history and proof of Theorems 38 and 39 (originally due to Zippin), the reader is referred to [19].

III. ELEMENTARY COMBINATORIAL TOPOLOGY; THE JORDAN CURVE THEOREM

In the Introduction it was stated that we would try to introduce notions in as simple a form as feasible, proceeding gradually to the more refined concepts embodied in generalizations and extensions, with the double purpose (1) of building up that intuitive background so necessary to an understanding and appreciation of the abstract formulations and (2) of observing the historical side of the development of topology. It is in accordance with this purpose that the present section is included.

The mode of development here is obviously inspired by [20], which seemed best adapted to our scheme. Except for what seems a restriction to topology on the 2-sphere (which is apparent rather than real, since concepts such as chain, homology, and so on, are phrased in terms and symbols which extend immediately to higher dimensional cases), the material is supposed to present a sample of the activity of the combinatorial school of thought, as represented particularly by Veblen and Alexander, during the decade approximately from 1915 to 1925. The simple modulo 2 topology is used throughout this section. Where orientation is not essential, this apparatus is most convenient. Of course, without orientation, certain topological invariants are missed, the most obvious one of which is perhaps the notion of orientability of manifolds (in terms of which and the Betti numbers, for instance, the 2-dimensional manifolds may be entirely classified).

As an application of the restricted theory developed in this section, we give a proof of the Jordan curve theorem, again adapted from [20]. It is accurate, we believe, to say that the earliest topological activity in this country was devoted to proofs of this theorem, and today the literature on the subject is immense. The first statement and proof were given by Jordan in [9]. In the opening words of a paper [21] which many consider as presenting the first completely rigorous and satisfactory proof of the theorem, Veblen states: "Jordan's explicit formulation of the fundamental theorem that a simple closed curve lying in a plane decomposes this plane into an inside and an outside region is justly regarded as a most important step in the direction of a perfectly rigorous mathematics."

As we shall see later, the Jordan curve theorem is now recognized to be, in its essential parts, only an instance of a general topological duality which in turn is an instance of a general group-theoretic theorem. It is hoped, by the way, that the reader will observe that whereas much emphasis is laid on the fundamental analytic basis of the real number system in these early sections, we gradually become more immersed in geometric considerations, and from there we fall inevitably into the algebraic (see Chap. IV).

It is also noteworthy that, with the close of the present chapter we shall have, as by-products of Chaps. II and III, a complete proof of this theorem:

THEOREM. *A necessary and sufficient condition that a Peano space be a 2-sphere is that it satisfy the Jordan curve theorem nonvacuously.*

3.1. **Geometric basis.** Choose an S_2 represented in E_3 by the equation $x^2 + y^2 + z^2 = 1$. The intersection of this S_2 with the plane $z = 0$ is a 1-sphere S_1, which separates S_2 into two open hemispheres E_1^2, E_2^2. Similarly the plane $y = 0$ intersects S_1 in two points E_1^0, E_2^0 forming a 0-sphere S_0 which separates S_1 into two open arcs E_1^1 and E_2^1. The geometric configuration Q_1 consisting of the elements E_i^k, $(k = 0, 1, 2; i = 1, 2)$, we call an *elementary subdivision* of S_2. Pairwise, these elements have no common points, and we call E_i^k a k-dimensional cell, or simply a *k-cell* (the 0-cells may also be called *vertices*). Write

$$(3.1) \qquad\qquad E_i^k \rightarrow E_1^{k-1} + E_2^{k-1}, \qquad\qquad k = 1, 2,$$

a so-called "boundary relation," where the $\rightarrow$ may be read "is bounded by."

From the elementary subdivision Q_1 we pass to the *derived subdivisions* of S_2. These are obtained by further intersections with planes through $(0, 0, 0)$. For example, we may first consider the plane $x = 0$, which intersects E_1^1 in a point E_3^0, *subdividing* E_1^1 into open segments one of which we continue to denote by E_1^1, the other by E_3^1; the configuration consisting of the new cells E_i^k, $(k = 0, 1, 2)$, we call the *first derived subdivision* Q_2. Then Q_3 may consist of the new configuration in S_2 resulting from subdivisions of E_2^1 by the same plane $x = 0$; Q_4 of the configuration on S_2 resulting from subdivision of E_1^2 into two new 2-cells and a new 1-cell; and so on. In an obvious manner we may define, inductively, a sequence of *subdivisions* $Q_1, Q_2, \cdots, Q_n, \cdots$ such that (1) for each natural number n, Q_{n+1} is derived from Q_n by the subdivision of a single cell as above, and (2) for arbitrary $\epsilon > 0$, there exists an integer m such that for $n > m$, all cells of Q_n are of diameter less than ϵ (where diameter is the set-theoretic diameter obtained from the metric on E_3). For each Q_n we may write a set of bounding relations such as (3.1), except that the right-hand member usually contains symbols of more than two $(k-1)$-cells.

A collection K of cells E_i^k of Q_n will be called a *complex* if, for $E_i^k \, \epsilon \, K$, and $E_i^k \rightarrow \cdots + E_h^{k-1} + \cdots$, each cell E_h^{k-1} is in K. If we denote the set of all points in cells of K by (K), then the latter condition is equivalent to requiring that (K) be a closed point set. If, moreover, there is a fixed integer m such that for the cells E_i^k of K, (1) $k \leq m$, and (2) there is at least one $E_i^m \in K$, then K is called an m-dimensional complex, or simply an *m-complex*. Thus Q_n is itself a 2-complex, and any complex whose cells are elements of Q_n is a *subcomplex* of Q_n. If K_1 and K_2 are subcomplexes of Q_n and Q_{n+h}, respectively, and $(K_1) \equiv (K_2)$, then we call K_2 a subdivision of K_1.

3.2. **Algebraic basis; homology groups.** Let K be a complex, and denote the cells of K by E_i^k, $(k=0, 1, \cdots, m; i=1, 2, \cdots, \alpha_k)$. With K we associate certain abelian groups $C^k(K)$ whose elements are polynomials of the type

$$(3.2) \qquad\qquad \sum_{i=1}^{\alpha_k} c^i E_i^k, \qquad\qquad c^i = 0 \text{ or } 1, \ E_i^k \in K,$$

and whose operation is ordinary addition modulo 2. The polynomials (3.2) are called *k-chains*. If C^k is a k-chain, denote by $|C^k|$ the smallest subcomplex of K containing all cells E_i^k for which $c^i = 1$, and we call $|C^k|$ the complex associated with C^k. In particular, each symbol E_i^k is a k-chain, a *cell-chain*; however, in this case we shall continue to let E_i^k denote both a k-chain and a k-cell (except where confusion may result).

As in (3.1), let us denote the boundary relations for K thus:

$$(3.1)' \qquad\qquad E_i^k \to \sum_{h=1}^{\alpha_{k-1}} e_{ik}^h E_h^{k-1}, \qquad\qquad e_{ik}^h = 0 \text{ or } 1, \ k > 0.$$

Then we may interpret (3.1)′ as an association of a unique $(k-1)$-chain with each cell-chain E_i^k. This may be extended as follows:

$$(3.3) \qquad\qquad \sum_{i=1}^{\alpha_k} c^i E_i^k \to \sum_{i=1}^{\alpha_k} \sum_{h=1}^{\alpha_{k-1}} c^i e_{ik}^h E_h^{k-1}.$$

Then by (3.3) there is associated with each k-chain, a unique $(k-1)$-chain; the latter we call the *boundary-chain* of the former. The reader may prove the following theorem.

THEOREM 1. *The boundary-chain of the sum of two chains is identical with the sum of their boundary-chains.*

Hence relations (3.3) may be added termwise, and we have this corollary:

COROLLARY 1. *The relations* (3.3) *establish a homomorphism of the group* $C^k(K)$ *into a subgroup* $H^{k-1}(K)$ *of* $C^{k-1}(K)$.

If $C^k \to 0$, where 0 is the identity of $C^{k-1}(K)$, then the chain C^k is called a *cycle*, or when we wish to indicate dimension, a *k-cycle*. We also have another corollary:

COROLLARY 2. *The set of all k-cycles, $k > 0$, consists of the elements of that subgroup $Z^k(K)$ of $C^k(K)$ that is mapped by (3.3) into the identity of $C^{k-1}(K)$.*

In Theorem 1 and its corollaries, we have assumed $k > 0$, since relation (3.1)' is not defined otherwise. We now make the convention that any 0-chain which has an even number of non-zero coefficients is a 0-cycle. Then the set of all such 0-cycles is an abelian group $Z^0(K)$.

Since, as is easily shown, the right-hand member of (3.1)' is a cycle, we have another corollary of Theorem 1.

COROLLARY 3. *Every boundary chain is a cycle, hence $H^{k-1}(K)$ is a subgroup of $Z^{k-1}(K)$.*

DEFINITION. *For any $k \geq 0$, the factor group of $Z^k(K)$ modulo $H^k(K)$ is called the kth homology group of K modulo 2, or the kth Betti group of K modulo 2, and will be denoted by $B^k(K)$. The number of linearly independent generators of this group is called the kth Betti number of K modulo 2, and is denoted by $p^k(K)$.*

The relation $\gamma^k \varepsilon H^k(K)$ is usually expressed by a relation

$$(3.4) \qquad\qquad \gamma^k \sim 0,$$

to be read "γ^k is homologous to zero." Thus two cycles γ_1^k, γ_2^k lie in the same coset of $B^k(K)$ if and only if $\gamma_1^k + \gamma_2^k \sim 0$. In general, if cycles $\gamma_1^k, \gamma_2^k, \cdots, \gamma_n^k$ satisfy a relationship $\gamma_1^k + \gamma_2^k + \cdots + \gamma_n^k \sim 0$, we call them linearly dependent with respect to homologies on K. Evidently the number $p^k(K)$ is the maximal number of k-cycles linearly independent with respect to homologies on K.

Remark. Since it may be shown that any two 0-cells of a connected complex are the end points of an arc of that complex made up of 0-cells and 1-cells, this theorem follows readily:

THEOREM 2. *The number $p^0(K) + 1$ is the number of components in (K).*

3.3. **Invariance under subdivision.** Suppose K_2 is a subdivision of K_1, as defined in the final paragraph of §3.1. Then the passage from K_1 to K_2 consists of a series of steps, each step consisting of a subdivision of a single cell. It is easily shown that this operation leaves $p^k(K)$ unchanged.

THEOREM 3. *The numbers $p^k(K)$ are invariant under subdivision.*

Since $p^k(Q_1) = 0$ for $k < 2$, and equals 1 for $k = 2$, we have the following corollary:

COROLLARY 4. *The Betti numbers $p^k(Q_n)$ are all 0 if $k < 2$, and 1 if $k = 2$.*

3.4. **Open subsets of S_2.** Let U be an open subset of S_2, and let U_n denote the set of all cells E_i^k of Q_n such that the closure of $(E_i^k) \subset U$. Then

U_n is a complex, and furthermore $(U_n) \subset (U_{n+1})$. We define chain-groups $C^k(U)$ of U, whose elements are the chains in $C^k(U_n)$ for $n = 1, 2, 3, \cdots$, making the convention that if the complex $|C_2^k|$, where $C_2^k \; \varepsilon \; C^k(U_{n+h})$, is a subdivision of $|C_1^k|$, where $C_1^k \; \varepsilon \; C^k(U_n)$, then the chains C_1^k, C_2^k are the same element of $C^k(U)$. To add two elements of $C^k(U)$, it is necessary only to find n great enough so that the two chains are elements of $C^k(U_n)$; their sum in the latter group determines their sum in $C^k(U)$.

Groups $Z^k(U)$, $H^k(U)$, $B^k(U)$, and numbers $p^k(U)$ are defined analogously as for the case of a complex K; the essential difference here is that we are actually dealing with U as an infinite complex.

THEOREM 4. *The number $p^0(U) + 1$ is the number of domains in U.*

(Theorems of Chap. II are applicable in the proof of this theorem.)

3.5. **Miscellaneous theorems.** Hereafter, if C is a chain, (C) denotes the set of points $(|C|)$.

THEOREM 5. *A 1-cycle γ^1 of Q_n is the boundary-chain of exactly two different chains K_1^2, K_2^2 of Q_n, and $(K_1^2) \cdot (K_2^2) = (\gamma^1)$.*

(For proof, use Corollary 4 and Theorem 1.)

COROLLARY 5. *If $x \; \varepsilon \; S_2$ and $\gamma^1 \; \varepsilon \; Z^1(S_2 - x)$, then $\gamma^1 \; \varepsilon \; H^1(S_2 - x)$.*

COROLLARY 6. *If a subset M of S_2 consists of exactly two points, then $p^1(S_2 - M) = 1$.*

The following theorem is an example of a so-called "addition theorem":

THEOREM 6. *Let A, B be closed subsets of S_2, and suppose that for a given $\gamma^0 \; \varepsilon \; Z^0(S_2 - A - B)$ there exist chains $K_A^1 \; \varepsilon \; C^1(S_2 - A)$, $K_B^1 \; \varepsilon \; C^1(S_2 - B)$, $K^2 \; \varepsilon \; C^2(S_2 - A - B)$ such that $K_A^1 \to \gamma^0$, $K_B^1 \to \gamma^0$ and $K^2 \to K_A^1 + K_B^1$. Then $\gamma^0 \sim 0$ in $S_2 - A - B$.*

(For proof see [20, Corollary W^i].)

THEOREM 7. *If t is an arc of S_2, then $p^k(S_2 - t) = 0$ for $k = 0, 1$.*

As t is an E_1^*, it is the sum of arcs t_1, t_2 where t_1 corresponds to the interval $0 \leq x \leq \frac{1}{2}$, and $t_1 \cdot t_2$ is a single point a. By Corollary 5 and Theorem 6 a $\gamma^0 \; \varepsilon \; Z^0(S_2 - t)$ which is nonbounding in $S_2 - t$ is also nonbounding in at least one of the sets $S_2 - t_1$, $S_2 - t_2$, say the former; subdivide t_1, etc. Continuing in this manner one shows the existence of a sequence T of arcs such that (1) each arc of T contains its successor, and the product of all arcs of T is one point x; (2) γ^0 is nonbounding in $S_2 - t'$ for all $t' \; \varepsilon \; T$. But (Theorem 4) $p^0(S_2 - x) = 0$; hence every γ^0 bounds a chain K' of $S_2 - x$. The remainder of the proof is left to the reader.

3.6. **The Jordan curve theorem.**

THEOREM J₁. *If J is an S_1 imbedded in S_2, then $p^0(S_2 - J) \geqq 1$.*

Proof. Let $a, b \, \varepsilon \, J$; then $J = A + B$, where A and B are arcs having only a and b in common. By Corollary 6, there exists a 1-cycle γ^1 of $S_2 - a - b$ which is nonbounding in the latter set, and by application of Theorem 7, $A \cdot (\gamma^1) \neq 0$ and $B \cdot (\gamma^1) \neq 0$.

Now $\gamma^1 = K_A{}^1 + K_B{}^1$, where $(K_A{}^1) \cdot A = 0 = (K_B{}^1) \cdot B$. Let $K_A{}^1 \to \gamma^0$. Then γ^0 is a cycle in $S_2 - J$ and is nonbounding in the latter set. For suppose we have an $L^1 \to \gamma^0$ in $S_2 - J$. Then not both $K_A{}^1 + L^1 \sim 0$, $K_B{}^1 + L^1 \sim 0$, hold in $S_2 - a - b$, else the sum would. Hence $K_A{}^1 + L^1$, say, is nonbounding in $S_2 - a - b$. But then by Theorem 7, $(K_A{}^1 + L^1) \cdot A \neq 0$.

THEOREM J_2. *If J is an S_1 imbedded in S_2, then $p^0(S_2 - J) \leqq 1$.*

Proof. Suppose $p^0(S_2 - J) \geqq 2$. Then for n large enough, there exist in Q_n cycles $\gamma_1{}^0$, $\gamma_2{}^0$ that are independent with respect to homologies in $S_2 - J$. Using the notation A, B of the above proof, and applying Theorem 7, there exist chains $K_A{}^1$, $K_B{}^1$ in $S_2 - A$, $S_2 - B$ respectively, such that

$$(3.5) \qquad\qquad K_A{}^1 \to \gamma_1{}^0 , \quad K_B{}^1 \to \gamma_1{}^0 ,$$

and by Theorem 6, the cycle $K_A{}^1 + K_B{}^1$ is nonbounding in $S_2 - a - b$. Similarly, there exist chains $L_A{}^1$ and $L_B{}^1$ in $S_2 - A$ and $S_2 - B$ respectively, such that

$$(3.6) \qquad\qquad L_A{}^1 \to \gamma_2{}^0 , \quad L_B{}^1 \to \gamma_2{}^0 ,$$

and $L_A{}^1 + L_B{}^1$ is nonbounding in $S_2 - a - b$.

By Corollary 6, the cycles $K_A{}^1 + K_B{}^1$, $L_A{}^1 + L_B{}^1$ cannot be independent with respect to homologies in $S_2 - a - b$, hence their sum bounds in $S_2 - a - b$. But from (3.5) and (3.6) we have $K_A{}^1 + L_A{}^1 \to \gamma_1{}^0 + \gamma_2{}^0$ in $S_2 - A$ and $K_B{}^1 + L_B{}^1 \to \gamma_1{}^0 + \gamma_2{}^0$ in $S_2 - B$, and then by Theorem 6, the cycle $\gamma_1{}^0 + \gamma_2{}^0$ bounds in $S_2 - J$.

THEOREM J_3. *If J is an S_1 imbedded in S_2, then $S_2 - J$ is the sum of two mutually exclusive domains whose common boundary is J.* (For definitions see Chap. II.)

Proof. Since by Theorems J_1, J_2, $p^0(S_2 - J) = 1$, there are just two components in $S_2 - J$. Select Q_n so that there exists a cycle γ^0 of Q_n associated with two 0-cells $E_1{}^0$, $E_2{}^0$ and nonbounding in $S_2 - J$, and let $x \, \varepsilon \, J$. Consider any $S(x, \epsilon)$ (the metric in E_3 may be used here). By continuity of the homeomorphism defining J, and using the notation introduced above, A and B exist such that $x \, \varepsilon \, A \subset S(x, \epsilon)$. By Theorem 7, there exists in $S_2 - B$ a chain $K^1 \to \gamma^0$. But since γ^0 is nonbounding in $S_2 - J$, $(K^1) \cdot A \neq 0$.

Now the point set (K^1) contains an arc $E_1{}^0 E_2{}^0$ (see Remark preceding Theorem 2), and the common part of this arc and A is a closed point set M. From the "I-theorems" of Chap. II, there exist portions of the arc $E_1{}^0 E_2{}^0$ in each domain of $S_2 - J$ that lie in $S(x, \epsilon)$. Hence J is the common boundary of these domains.

IV. Generalizations; duality theorems

From the elementary formulation of the combinatorial method in Chap. III, the reader has probably guessed the great possibilities of generalization. That the geometric set-up of §3.1 may be paralleled on an S_n in E_{n+1} is obvious, and the modulo 2 algebraic machinery of §3.2 has been so phrased for general k that it applies immediately to the higher-dimensional case. It was with such a basis as this that Alexander established his celebrated duality theorem [20]:

Theorem. *If K is a complex imbedded in S_n, then $p^k(K) = p^{n-k-1}(S_n - K)$.*

Applied to the $(n-1)$-sphere and $(n-1)$-cell so as to parallel the results at the end of Chap. III, this duality yields immediately the extension to S_n of the Jordan theorem (first established by Brouwer [23]).

Historically, the modulo 2 coefficients of §3.2 were preceded by the integer coefficients used in Poincaré's fundamental work; a systematic exposition has been given [24] by Veblen who in the same connection develops the modulo 2 theory for complexes introduced earlier [25]. One of Poincaré's most notable results was his duality theorem for orientable manifolds:

Theorem. *If M is an orientable n-manifold, then $p^k(M,G_0) = p^{n-k}(M, G_0)$.*

(These symbols will be explained below.) Cell-orientation was essential in Poincaré's theory, as well as in the general theory described below. General modulo m coefficients were introduced by Alexander [26] and rational coefficients together with the useful notion of relative chains by Lefschetz. The latter made a most notable advance in the enunciation of a general duality which generalized both the Poincaré and Alexander dualities, as well as establishing the intimate relationship between these two theorems [27]. More recently, Pontrjagin demonstrated that these dualities were consequences of a group-theoretic theorem [28]. Our exposition in §4.4 and §4.5 below is based on the later more refined and conclusive papers [29].

4.1. **General homology theory of a complex.** If K is a subcomplex of some subdivision of an S_r, we may associate with K the abelian chain-groups $C^k(K,G)$ whose elements are again polynomials (3.2), but where now the coefficients c_i are elements of some given abelian group G. In Chap. III we dealt exclusively with the case where G is the modulo 2 group of integers. The most important special cases of G with which we shall be concerned later on are (1) the finite additive groups of integers modulo m, to be denoted by G_m, $m>1$; (2) the additive group of integers G_0, often called the integer group modulo 0; (3) the group of rotations of the 1-sphere, or additive group of real numbers modulo 1, which we denote by R; (4) the additive group of rational real numbers G_r. It will be noted that if the usual multiplication is introduced, the groups $G_m(m$ prime) and G_r are algebraic fields; all G_m are rings, but R is not even a ring. Except for considerations of a special nature, however, these facts are largely irrelevant. It is important chiefly that it be possible to associate with K certain abelian groups which have geometric significance in the sense of yielding topological invariants.

Simplicial ("barycentric") subdivision. Denote the cells of K by E_i^k, $(i=1, 2, \cdots, \alpha_k; k=0, 1, \cdots, n)$, denote E_i^0 temporarily by P_i^0, and let P_i^k denote a point in the cell E_i^k. Hereafter, if in any complex a cell E_j^h is in the complex $\left| E_i^k \right|$, $(h<k)$, we shall call the cells E_j^h, E_i^k *incident* to one another, and indicate this incidence by the relation $E_j^h < E_i^k$. Now there can be set up a new complex K', the *simplicial subdivision* of K, each of whose k-cells has $k+1$ vertices $P_{i_0}^a$, $P_{i_1}^b$, $\cdots$, $P_{i_{k-1}}^l$, $P_{i_k}^h$, where, $E_{i_0}^a < E_{i_1}^b < \cdots < E_{i_k}^h$ and where the points of the k-cell are the points (excepting $P_{i_k}^h$ itself, and, in case $k=1$, excepting $P_{i_0}^a$) of S_r on geodesics joining $P_{i_k}^h$ to the points of the cell whose vertices are $P_{i_0}^a$, $P_{i_1}^b$, $\cdots$, $P_{i_{k-1}}^l$ (such a "cell," no longer obtained as were the original cells, is nevertheless like the latter homeomorphic with the set of points $x_1^2 + x_2^2 + \cdots + x_k^2 < 1$ in E_k, hence with the space E_k itself; *hereafter a cell is characterized by this property*). It will be noted that in the point set-theoretic sense, each cell E_i^k is the sum of all cells of K' in E_i^k having P_i^k as a vertex. And a simple argument shows that in each cell E_i^k, the $(k-1)$-cells of K' are incident with exactly two k-cells of K'. Furthermore, the set of points in $\left| E_i^k \right| - E_i^k$ is an S_{k-1}.

Orientation. If, in a complex, a k-cell has exactly $k+1$ vertices, we call it a *simplex*. A simplex may be assigned positive and negative *orientations* as follows: A certain simple ordering of its vertices, $v_0, v_1, \cdots, v_k$ is selected, and the symbol $v_0 v_1 \cdots v_k$, or any even permutation of the v's therein, regarded as an algebraic symbol associated with the simplex and its positive orientation; the symbol derived from $v_0 v_1 v_2 \cdots v_k$ by any odd permutation of the v's, or the symbol for a positive orientation preceded by a minus sign, is associated with a negative orientation. We usually denote a positive orientation, $v_0 v_1 v_2 \cdots v_k$, by a single symbol such as σ, and let $-\sigma$ denote the negative orientation; of course $-(-\sigma) = \sigma$.

We define a function (or linear operator) F as follows:

$$(4.1) \qquad F(v_{i_0} v_{i_1} \cdots v_{i_k}) = \sum_{s=0}^{s=k} (-1)^s v_{i_0} v_{i_1} \cdots v_{i_{s-1}} v_{i_{s+1}} \cdots v_{i_k}$$

and, more generally,

$$(4.2) \qquad F\left(\sum_i \eta^j \sigma_j^k \right) = \sum_i \eta^j F(\sigma_j),$$

the algebraic operations being commutative, associative and distributive.

Returning to K', all of whose cells are simplexes, we assign orientations to all its cells a_j^k, denoting their positive orientations by τ_j^k. Each cell will be oriented independently of all others of the same or different dimension, except as follows: If $E_i^k \varepsilon K$, denote the k-cells of K' in $|E_i^k|$ by a_{ij}^k, and to a_{i1}^k assign a positive orientation τ_{i1}^k. Then to the other cells a_{ii}^k of E_i^k we assign orientations τ_{ij}^k such that the terms with non-zero coefficients in $F(\Sigma_j \tau_{ij}^k)$ are associated with the cells of K' on $|E_i^k| - E_i^k$; of course, the latter fact holds also for $F(\Sigma_j(-\tau_{ij}^k))$. We call τ_{i1}^k the *indicatrix of* E_i^k, and associate with E_i^k and τ_{i1}^k, a positive orientation σ_i^k.

If we formally set $\sigma_i^k = \Sigma_j \tau_{ij}^k$, then we note that $F(\sigma_i^k) = \sum \eta^m \sigma_m^{k-1}$. In this manner we can extend F to the σ's, and write a relation in the σ's analogous to (4.2). That F^2 operating on the τ's gives 0, and hence also on the σ's gives 0, is readily shown.

Finally, if G is any abelian group, we let $C^k(K, G)$ denote the abelian group whose elements are polynomials of type $\sum_{i=1}^{\alpha_k} c^i \sigma_i^k$. By defining

$$(4.3) \qquad F\left(\sum_i c^i \sigma_i^k \right) = \sum_i c^i F(\sigma_i^k),$$

algebraic operations being as before commutative, associative, and distributive, and with $c^i \cdot (-1) = -c^i$, and so on, we obtain a homomorphism of $C^k(K, G)$ onto a subgroup $H^{k-1}(K, G)$ of $C^{k-1}(K, G)$. Denoting the identity of $C^k(K, G)$ by 0, it turns out that the group $Z^k(K, G)$ of $C^k(K, G)$ which maps into 0 by (4.3) contains $H^k(K, G)$ as subgroup.

The elements of $C^k(K, G)$, $Z^k(K, G)$, $H^k(K, G)$ we call respectively *k-chains, k-cycles, bounding k-cycles*, all *over G*. The factor group of $Z^k(K, G)$ modulo $H^k(K, G)$ we call the *kth Betti group of K over G*. For the case $k = 0$, one has to adopt, as was done in Chap. III, a convention regarding what is to constitute a 0-cycle. The reader will recognize the connection of all this with the material in §3.2, and perhaps supply the notion of homology and Betti number over G (number of linearly independent generators of the corresponding Betti group); the use of the $\rightarrow$ of Chap. III instead of the operator F may, of course, be introduced if desired.

4.2. Dual complexes. Suppose that the structure of the n-complex K is such that there exists a complex D, the *dual* of K, defined as follows: The 0-cells B_i^0 of D are the points P_i^n of K'; in general, the $(n-k)$-cells B_i^{n-k} of D are, in a point set sense, the sum of all cells of K' with vertices $P_i^k, P_j^l, \cdots, P_s^h$ such that $E_i^k < E_j^l < \cdots < E_s^h$; in particular, each n-cell B_i^n is the sum of all cells of K^1 having P_i^0 as a vertex. Then if (K) is connected, we call K a closed n-manifold. Cells such as E_i^k, B_i^{n-k} are called *dual*; note that $(E_i^k) \cdot (B_i^{n-k}) = P_i^k$. Also, if $E_i^k < E_j^{k+1}$, then $B_j^{n-k-1} < B_i^{n-k}$.

Suppose, now, that the structure of the n-manifold K is such that, starting with an indicatrix for a particular n-cell of K, say the indicatrix τ_{11}^n of E_1^n, it is possible so to orient the other cells E_i^n, $(i = 2, \cdots, \alpha_n)$, that $F(\sum_{i=1}^{\alpha_n} \sigma_i^n) = 0$. There being, from the definition, two and only two

n-cells $E_p{}^n$, $E_q{}^n$, incident with a given cell $E_i{}^{n-1}$, this means that $\sigma_p{}^n$ and $\sigma_q{}^n$ are so defined that $\sigma_i{}^{n-1}$ occurs in $F(\sigma_p{}^n)$ and $F(\sigma_q{}^n)$ with opposite signs. We then call K a closed *orientable n-manifold*, and when oriented so that $F(\sum_{i=1}^{\alpha_n}\sigma_i{}^n) = 0$, we call it *coherently* oriented relative to the indicatrix $\tau_{11}{}^n$.

Let K be an orientable n-manifold coherently oriented relative to some indicatrix. We may orient its dual, D, as follows: $B_i{}^{n-k}$ being a cell of D, we choose an indicatrix b^{n-k} in $B_i{}^{n-k}$ with vertices $P_i^k, P_i^{k+1}, \cdots, P_i^n$, and let $\eta_1 P^0 P^1 \cdots P_i^k$ (where η_1 is $+1$ or -1) be a positive orientation of a cell of K' in E_i^k. Let $\sigma^n = \eta_2 P^0 P^1 \cdots P_i^k P_j^{k+1} \cdots P_s^n$, the η_2 having been determined in K' during the orientation of K. Then we let $\beta_i{}^{n-k} = \eta_1 \eta_2 P_i^k P_j^{k+1} \cdots P_s^h$ be the positive orientation of b^{n-k}. As K' is a simplicial subdivision of D, this indicatrix determines the positive orientation of $B_i{}^{n-k}$, which we denote by $\delta_i{}^{n-k}$.

4.3. Intersection numbers in an orientable n-manifold. We define a number $\chi(\sigma_i{}^k, \delta_j{}^{n-k})$ as follows: If $i \neq j$, its value is zero; if $i = j$, let $\tau_{i1}{}^k = \eta_1 P^0 P^1 \cdots P_i^k$, and let $\eta_3 P_i^k P^{k+1} \cdots P^n$ be the indicatrix of $\delta_j{}^{n-k}$. If we choose η_2 as above so that $\eta_2 P^0 P^1 \cdots P_i^k P^{k+1} \cdots P^n$ is a positive orientation of the n-cell indicated, then $\chi(\sigma_i{}^k, \delta_i{}^{n-k}) = \eta_1 \eta_2 \eta_3$. Obviously $\chi(\sigma_i{}^k, \delta_i{}^{n-k}) = 1$. It may be shown that any of the τ's or β's in E_i^k, $B_i{}^{n-k}$ would yield the same result. Furthermore, $\chi(-\sigma_i{}^k, \delta_j{}^{n-k})$, may be defined in an obvious manner. We call $\chi(\sigma_i{}^k, \delta_j{}^{n-k})$ the *intersection number* or Kronecker index of σ_i^k, $\delta_j{}^{n-k}$.

Since K is the dual of D, the numbers $\chi(\delta_i{}^{n-k}, \sigma_i^k)$ are defined, and it may be shown by counting transpositions that

$$\chi(\delta_i{}^{n-k}, \sigma_i^k) = (-1)^{k(n-k)} \chi(\sigma_i^k, \delta_i{}^{n-k}).$$

Consider $\sum_{i=1}^{\alpha_k} c^i \sigma_i^k = C^k \varepsilon C^k(K, G')$ and $\sum_{i=1}^{\alpha_k} d^i \delta_i{}^{n-k} = D^{n-k} \varepsilon C^{n-k}(D, G'')$. If we can attach a suitable meaning to the product $c^i \cdot d^i$, we may define

$$(4.4) \qquad \chi(C^k, D^{n-k}) = \sum_{i=1}^{\alpha_k} c^i d^i \chi(\sigma_i^k, \delta_i{}^{n-k}).$$

For example, if $G' = G'' = G_m$ (see §4.1), the number χ is defined and may be called the *intersection number* of the chains C^k, D^{n-k}; in Chap V, where we use G_2 exclusively as coefficient group, the intersection numbers will all be 0 or 1. For the general case, we introduce the notions below.

4.4. Character groups. Consider three additive abelian groups X, G, and R, whose identities we denote by 0, and suppose that to each ordered pair x, g, $x \varepsilon X$, $g \varepsilon G$, there corresponds a unique $r \varepsilon R$; we write $xg = r$. If this operation satisfies the distributive laws $(x_1 + x_2)g = x_1 g + x_2 g$, $x(g_1 + g_2) = x g_1 + x g_2$, then we say that X and G form a *group pair*. If H is a subgroup of G, denote by (X, H) the set of all $x \varepsilon X$ such that for all $h \varepsilon H$, $xh = 0$; we call (X, H) the *nullifier* of H in X. This nullifier is a subgroup of X.

Similarly, we define the nullifier (G, Y) of Y in G. Finally, if $(X, G) = 0 = (G, X)$, we call G and X *orthogonal*.

Suppose now that R is the group R of §4.1 and G is any, at most denumerable, discrete group. The set of all homomorphisms h of G into R forms a group X, whose operation is defined by the rule $h = h_1 + h_2$ if for all $g \varepsilon G$, $h(g) = h_1(g) + h_2(g)$, and which is continuous in the sense that $\lim h_n = h$ if for all $g \varepsilon G$, $\lim h_n(g) = h(g)$. We call X the *group of characters* of G; it is a compact metric space [29(a)]. In case G is finite it is isomorphic to G[29(a)]. The groups X and G form an orthogonal group pair rel. R, where $hg = h(g)$ for all $h \varepsilon X$, $g \varepsilon G$.

Reversing the above procedure and starting with a continuous group X there is obtained a discrete group G of continuous homomorphisms (homomorphisms that preserve limits) of X into R, and in similar fashion G, is called the group of characters of X. In general, it may be shown [29 (a)] that if a compact metric topological group X and a discrete group G are orthogonal, then each is the group of characters of the other.

4.5. **Linking numbers; dualities.** If the groups G', G'' determining the chains C^k, D^{n-k} of (4.4) form an orthogonal group pair, then the number $\chi(C^k, D^{n-k})$ is defined by (4.4) in an obvious manner. Suppose, finally, that $\Gamma^k \varepsilon H^k(K, G)$, $\Gamma^{n-k-1} \varepsilon H^{n-k-1}(D, X)$, where G, X form an orthogonal group pair, and consider any $C^{n-k} \varepsilon C^{n-k}(D, X)$ such that $F(C^{n-k}) = \Gamma^{n-k-1}$. Then the number $\chi(\Gamma^k, C^{n-k})$ is called the *linking number* of Γ^k and Γ^{n-k-1} (in K) and is denoted by $\nu(\Gamma^k, \Gamma^{n-k-1})$. It is dependent only on the Γ's, being the same for all chains C^{n-k} as well as for successive (concordantly oriented) subdivisions of K.

It was shown by Pontrjagin in [29(b)], to which we refer the reader for proofs, that if K is an S_n, and M a complex imbedded [22] in S_n, then the Betti groups $B^k(M, X)$, $B^{n-k-1}(S_n - M, G)$ form an orthogonal group pair, if for Γ^k, Γ^{n-k-1} as cycles in elements of these respective groups we define the product as yielding the linking number $\nu(\Gamma^k, \Gamma^{n-k-1})$ and let this be the product of those elements. (In order to apply the above definitions, chains in M are approximated by chains in the basic subdivisions Q_m of S_n, and chains of $S_n - M$ are obtained relative to complexes dual to the basic subdivisions of S_n.) The duality thus obtained, establishing as a by-product the invariance of the Betti groups of the complement of a complex in S_n (under homeomorphisms of that complex) is of course a generalization of the Alexander duality. It holds, moreover, under suitable restrictions as to cycles employed [27] for the case of a general orientable closed manifold instead of S_n, as well as for the case where M is any closed point set. (See Chap. VI.)

With the geometric and algebraic background which we hope has been furnished in this section, the reader who is interested in these particular aspects of topology is urged to pursue the matter further, particularly with reference to the generalizations of the notions of cell and manifold [30] as well as the abstract approach in terms of cell-spaces [31] and the formulation in terms of cohomology groups [32] (also see Chap. VI).

V. The S_{n-1} imbedded in S_n, $(n = 2, 3)$

In his fundamental work on point sets imbedded in S_2, Schoenflies showed that not only is the complement of a point set M, which is an S_1 imbedded in S_2, the sum of exactly two domains of which M is common boundary, but that if D is either one of these domains, then every point of M is *accessible* from D (that is, given $x \varepsilon M$, $y \varepsilon D$, there exists an arc xy such that $xy - x \subset D$). He then proceeded to show that the Jordan curve theorem, extended in this manner, allows a converse. Using the characterization of S_1 in the corollary to Theorem 17 (§2.1), we give below a simple proof of this converse, using an hypothesis weaker than that of Schoenflies [11, Chap. V].

As we have pointed out elsewhere [33], it was Schoenflies' feeling that when a suitable theory of connectivity for polyhedrals became available, such results as this could be extended to higher dimensions. Using the homology and duality theory developed above, as well as the material on Peano spaces in Chap. II, we give a sample in Theorem 2 below of such a result (see also §7.1). We include the proofs, adapted to present circumstances, as examples of the use to which the preceding material may be put. Since orientation has no advantages in these problems, we use modulo 2 chains exclusively.

5.1. The S_1 in S_2. We shall first prove the following theorem:

THEOREM 1. *In order that a point set M in S_2 should be an S_1, it is necessary and sufficient that it be a common boundary of two domains D_1 and D_2 from each of which every point of M is accessible.*

Proof. As for the necessity, besides the obvious application of the Jordan curve theorem, we may proceed in a manner which is quite uniform for all cases of S_{n-1} in S_n, and which we prefer to exemplify in the proof below of the u.l.0-c. property in Theorem 2; since it is easily shown that the u.l.0-c. property as defined below is stronger than the accessibility property.

Suppose that M is a common boundary of domains D_1 and D_2. That M is closed follows from Theorem 26 (§2.2). Suppose M not connected. Then in some subdivision Q of S_2, the closed 2-cells of Q that contain points of M form a complex K such that $p^0(K) \geqq 1$. By the duality of Chap. IV there exist cycles γ^1 of $S_2 - (K)$ and γ^0 of K such that $\nu(\gamma^0, \gamma^1) = 1$. The cycle γ^1 is the sum of cycles $\gamma_i{}^1$, $(i = 1, 2, \cdots, k)$, such that for each i, $(\gamma_i{}^1)$ is a component of (γ^1). Since, from the definition of ν,

$$\nu(\gamma^0, \gamma^1) = \sum_{i=1}^{k} \nu(\gamma^0, \gamma_i{}^1), \qquad \text{(mod 2)},$$

at least one linking number $v(\gamma^0, \gamma_i{}^1)$, say $v(\gamma^0, \gamma_1{}^1)$, is 1. The set $(\gamma_1{}^1)$, being connected, lies wholly in one component of $S_2 - M$. And since $(\gamma_1{}^1)$ must separate (K) in S_2, it also separates M. But every point of M is a limit point of both A and B, so that each of these domains contains points of $(\gamma_1{}^1)$, contradicting the fact that $(\gamma_1{}^1)$ lies in one component of $S_2 - M$.

No point of M separates M. For if $x \varepsilon M$ were such that $M - x = M_1 + M_2$, where M_1, M_2 are separated, and γ^0 a cycle based on a single pair of 0-cells one from each of the domains D_1, D_2, then γ^0 would have to be nonbounding in $S_2 - (M_1 + x)$ (see first part of proof of Theorem 7 (§3.5)).

Finally, every two points of M separate M. For, using the accessibility property, if $x, y \varepsilon M$ there exists an S_1, say J, consisting of two arcs t_i such that $t_i - (x+y) \subset D_i$ and x, y are the end points of t_i. By Theorem J_3 (§3.6), $S_2 - J$ is the sum of two domains A, B having J as common boundary. Each of the sets A, B contains points of M. For consider the point set $A + s_1 + s_2$, where $s_i \varepsilon t_i - (x+y)$; A is connected and both s_1, s_2 are limit points of A, and hence $A + s_1 + s_2$ is connected. But a connected set which contains points of both D_1 and D_2 is easily shown to contain points of M. Thus $M - (x+y) = M_1 + M_2$ where $M_1 \subset A$, $M_2 \subset B$ and hence M_1, M_2 are separated sets.

That M is an S_1 now follows from the corollary to Theorem 17 (§2.1).

Further properties of the complement of an S_1 in S_2 will be given when the general case is discussed in Chap. VII.

5.2. The S_2 in S_3. In one of those papers of Brouwer [34] that seem to have been inspired by Schoenflies' work, he pointed out that accessibility is not a sufficient tool to characterize simple surfaces in S_3. In the same connection he proved that the domains complementary to surfaces, among which in S_3 the S_2 is a particular case, have a stronger property (*Unbewalltheit*) which we call *uniform local 0-connectedness* (u.l.0-c.), and this property, as we shall see, is enough to "smooth out" the boundary of a domain in a manner not effected by accessibility.

A domain D is called u.l.0-c. if for every $\epsilon > 0$ there exists a $\delta > 0$ such that any 0-cycle γ^0 of D such that $\delta(\gamma^0) < \delta$ bounds a chain K^1 of D such that $\delta(K^1) < \epsilon$.

THEOREM 2. *A necessary and sufficient condition that a point set M in S_3 be an S_2 is that it be a common boundary of two u.l.0-c. domains A and B such that $p^1(A) = 0$.* [35].

Proof of necessity. Let M be an S_2 imbedded in S_3. Then, by the Alexander duality theorem (Chap. IV), $p^0(S_3 - M) = p^2(M) = 1$ (Corollary 4, §3.3), and hence $S_3 - M$ consists of just two domains A, B. That M is the common boundary of these domains follows from the duality theorem and an argument similar to that used in Theorem J_3 (§3.6).

The domain A is u.l.0-c. Consider an $x \varepsilon M$ and $\epsilon > 0$. From the continuity of the homeomorphism defining M, there exists in M an S_1, say J, which lies in $S(x, \epsilon)$ and such that if C and R are the domains in M whose common boundary is J, then $x \in C \subset S(x, \epsilon)$, and C and R are 2-cells. Let $\delta > 0$ be such that $M \cdot S(x, \delta) \subset C$, and consider any cycle γ^0 of $A \cdot S(x, \delta)$. There exists a chain K_1^1 of $S(x, \delta)$ such that $K_1^1 \to \gamma^0$; hence we may write

$$(5.1) \qquad K_1^1 \to \gamma^0 \quad \text{in} \quad S_3 - [\overline{R} + F(x, \epsilon)].$$

Also, since (γ^0) lies in the component A of $S_3 - M$, there is a K_2^1 such that

$$(5.2) \qquad K_2^1 \to \gamma^0 \quad \text{in} \quad S_3 - [\overline{C} + F(x, \epsilon)].$$

The cycle $\gamma^1 = K_1^1 + K_2^1$ bounds a chain of $S_3 - J$. For γ^1 is also a cycle of $S_3 - \overline{R}$, and $\overline{R}$ being the closure of a 2-cell, we have by the Alexander duality that $p^1(S_3 - \overline{R}) = p^1(\overline{R}) = 0$. Then by Theorem 6 (§3.5), which extends immediately to S_3, γ^0 bounds a chain of $S_3 - [\overline{C} + \overline{R} + F(x, \epsilon)]$, and hence in $A \cdot S(x, \epsilon)$.

The property just established holds for all points of $\overline{A}$, its proof being trivial for $x \in A$, and employing the Borel theorem 20 (§2.1) the u.l.0-c. property of A follows at once.

Since $p^1(M) = 0$ (Corollary 4, §3.3), it follows from the Alexander duality that $p^1(A) = 0$.

Proof of sufficiency. Let M be a common boundary of two u.l.0-c. domains A and B in S_3, such that $p^1(A) = 0$. We shall show that M satisfies the hypothesis of Theorem 39 (§2.2). That M is a continuum follows as in the proof of Theorem 1.

The set M satisfies Axiom 4 of Chap. II. Consider any $x \in M$ and $\epsilon > 0$, and let $C(x, \epsilon)$ denote the component of $M \cdot S(x, \epsilon)$ determined by x. If $C(x, \epsilon)$ is an open subset of M, Axiom 4 is satisfied. Suppose this is not the case. Then there exists $y \in C(x, \epsilon)$ such that y is a limit point of $M - C(x, \epsilon)$. Then if η_1 is such that $0 < \eta_1 < \epsilon - \rho(x, y)$, there exists in $S(y, \eta_1)$ an $x_1 \in M - C(x, \epsilon)$. The component $C(x_1, \epsilon)$ has no limit point in $C(x, \epsilon)$, hence there exists $\eta_2 < \eta_1$ such that $0 < \eta_2 < \rho(y, C(x_1, \epsilon))$. Suppose $x_2 \in [M - C(x, \epsilon)] \cdot S(y, \eta_2)$. Continuing in this manner, with $\lim \eta_i = 0$, it is shown that there exist mutually exclusive components $C(x_i, \epsilon)$, $(i = 1, 2, \cdots, n, \cdots)$, such that y is a limit point of the set of all points x_i.

Let δ be such that $\overline{S}(y, \delta) \subset S(x, \epsilon)$. Then no two points x_i are in the same component of $M \cdot S(y, \delta)$. As A is u.l.0-c., there exists a $\delta_1 > 0$ such that any 0-cycle of $A \cdot \overline{S}(y, \delta_1)$ bounds a chain of $A \cdot S(y, \delta)$; and such that a similar statement holds for B. Let $x_k, x_j \in S(y, \delta_1)$. By adapting the procedure used above to the present case, there can be shown to exist a cycle γ^2 of $S_3 - M \cdot S(x, \delta)$ such that (γ^2) is connected and separates x_k and x_j in S_3. Let T_1 be the sum of those components (finite in number) of $(\gamma^2) \cdot S(y, \delta)$ that have points in $S(x, \delta_1)$. Then $(\gamma^2) \cdot S(y, \delta) = T_1 + T_2$, where $T_2 = (\gamma^2) \cdot S(y, \delta) - T_1$. The set $N = F(y, \delta) + T_1 + T_2$ separates x_k and x_j in S_3. It follows readily from the extension to S_3 of Theorem 6 (§3.5) that

$N - T_2$ separates x_k and x_j in S_3, and finally that $C_1 + F(y, \delta)$, where C_1 is the symbol for a single component of T_1, separates x_k and x_j.

But x_k and x_j are boundary points of both A and B, hence in some subdivision Q of S_3 can be found cycles γ_1^0, γ_2^0 of A and B, respectively, which lie in $S(y, \delta_1)$ and fail to bound a chain of $S_3 - [C_1 + F(y, \delta)]$. But there exist chains $L_i^1 \to \gamma_i^0$, $(i = 1, 2)$, in $A \cdot S(y, \delta)$ and $B \cdot S(y, \delta)$, respectively. Both sets $(L_i^1) \cdot C_1$ are therefore nonvacuous, and, consequently, C_1 contains points of both A and B, and $C_1 \cdot M \neq 0$. But this is impossible since $C_1 \subset (\gamma^2) \cdot S(y, \delta)$ and $(\gamma^2) \cdot S(y, \delta) \cdot M = 0$. We must therefore conclude that M is a Peano space.

By hypothesis, $p^1(A) = 0$; we now prove that $p^1(B) = 0$. Assume γ^1 a cycle nonbounding in B. In each complex Q_i of a sequence of subdivisions $\{Q_i\}$ of S_3, let P_i denote the complex composed of all closed 3-cells of Q_i that contain points of M. Then for i large enough, γ^1 is a nonbounding cycle of $S_3 - P_i$ and by the duality theorem is linked with a cycle z^1 of P_i. Now every vertex v of the complex associated with z^1 is a vertex of a closed 3-cell of P_i that contains at least one point of M; hence if every cell of Q_i is of diameter $< \epsilon_i$, where $\lim_{i \to \infty} \epsilon_i = 0$, there is a point v' of A whose distance from v is $< \epsilon_i$. Then for i large enough, there exists, by virtue of the fact that A is u.l.0-c., a cycle Γ^1 of A composed of a set of chains of A bounded by 0-cycles associated with the v''s, and such that $\Gamma^1 \sim z^1$ in $S_3 - (\gamma^1)$. Thus there exists a chain $K_1^2 \to \Gamma^1 + z^1$ in $S_3 - (\gamma^1)$. Now by hypothesis $p^1(A) = 0$, hence there exists a chain $K_2^2 \to \Gamma^1$ in A. Let $K^2 = K_1^2 + K_2^2$; then $K^2 \to z^1$ in $S_3 - (\gamma^1)$, $\chi(\gamma^1, K^2) = 0$, and $\nu(\gamma^1, z^1) = 0$. This contradiction establishes that $p^1(B) = 0$.

No arc of M separates M. The proof of this is like that used in the third paragraph of the proof of Theorem 1.

Finally, every S_1 in M separates M. For suppose J an S_1 in M such that $M - J$ is connected. By the duality theorem, there exists a cycle γ^1 of $S_3 - J$ which is nonbounding in $S_3 - J$, and such that for i large enough, there exist cycles z_i^1 in the dual of Q_i approximating J such that $\nu(\gamma^1, z_i^1) = 1$. The set $(\gamma^1) \cdot M$ is a closed subset F of $S_3 - J$. Letting $\rho((\gamma^1), J) = 4\epsilon$, every $x \in F$ is in a domain of M of diameter $< \epsilon$, since M is peanian. By the Borel theorem, a finite number of these domains, say $U_1, U_2, \cdots, U_k$ contain all points of F. For each i, let $a_i \in U_i$. Since $M - J$ is a domain, there exists in $M - J$ an arc $a_1 a_i$ for each $i > 1$, by the corollary to Theorem 24 (§2.2). The point set H formed by the closure of the set

$$\sum_{i=1}^{k} U_i + \sum_{i=2}^{k} a_1 a_i$$

is a subcontinuum of $M - J$.

Letting $\rho(H, J) = \epsilon_1$, suppose η is a positive number less than both ϵ and ϵ_1. Using the u.l.0-c. of A and B, there exist, for i great enough, cycles Z_A^1 and Z_B^1 of A and B respectively, approximating z_i^1 and such that there exists a $K^2 \rightarrow Z_A{}^1 + Z_B{}^1$, every point of whose intersection $(K^2) \cdot M$ with M lies at a distance $< \eta$ from J, and for which $\nu(\gamma^1, Z_A{}^1) = \nu(\gamma^1, Z_B{}^1) = 1$. Since $p^1(A) = p^1(B) = 0$, there exist chains $K_A{}^2 \rightarrow Z_A{}^1$, $K_B{}^2 \rightarrow Z_B{}^1$ lying in A and B respectively. We have the relations

$$K_A{}^2 \rightarrow Z_A{}^1 \quad \text{in} \quad S_3 - [(\gamma^1) - (\gamma^1) \cdot A],$$

$$K^2 + K_B{}^2 \rightarrow Z_A{}^1 \quad \text{in} \quad S_3 - (\gamma^1) \cdot \overline{A}.$$

By the extension to S_3 of Theorem 6 (§3.5), the 2-cycle $M^2 = K_A{}^2 + K^2 + K_B{}^2$ must be nonbounding in $S_3 - (\gamma^1) \cdot M$, else $Z_A{}^1$ would bound in $S_3 - (\gamma^1)$. But this implies that the point set (M^2) separates points of H in S_3. However, H is a continuum and $H \cdot (M^2) = 0$, so that this is impossible.

Thus M is a Peano space satisfying the hypothesis of Theorem 39 (§2.2), and, consequently, M is a 2-sphere.

VI. Continuous mappings

Mapping spaces. In Chap. I we have defined the notion of continuous mapping of one space into another. Hereafter we drop the word "continuous"—it will be understood that all mappings are continuous. If A and M are spaces, there exist in general many different mappings of A into M; for example, the trivial "constant" mappings of type $f(A) = x$ where $x \, \varepsilon \, M$. The set of all mappings of A into M we denote by the customary symbol M^A. If M is compact [36] metric, the set M^A becomes a metric space (which we continue to denote by M^A) if, given f, $g \, \varepsilon \, M^A$, we define $\rho(f, g) = \text{LUB}_{x \varepsilon A} \rho[f(x), g(x)]$ (LUB = least upper bound).

6.1. Homotopy and mapping classes. Consider f, $g \, \varepsilon \, M^A$. We call f *homotopic to* g if there exists a continuous function $\phi(x, t)$, $x \, \varepsilon \, A$, $(0 \leqq t \leqq 1)$, whose "values" are points of M and such that $\phi(x, 0) = f(x)$, $\phi(x, 1) = g(x)$ for all $x \, \varepsilon \, A$. The fact that f is homotopic to g may also be expressed by saying simply that f and g are *homotopic*, since the relationship is plainly symmetric. Furthermore, being also reflexive and transitive, the relationship constitutes an equivalence relation in the set M^A, and the corresponding classes [37] are called the *mapping classes* of M^A. Where it will cause no confusion and f, $g \, \varepsilon \, M^A$ are homotopic, we shall sometimes speak of the images themselves as being homotopic; for example, if $K = f(S_1)$ is the image of a circle S_1 in M, we may say that K is homotopic to a point x in M meaning thereby that f is homotopic to the mapping $g(S_1) = x$.

6.2. Special cases of mapping spaces. We shall often be concerned below with particular, but important, choices of M or A. The case where M or A is the n-sphere S_n or the euclidean n-space E_n will be of special interest. One of the earliest examples of the latter type is due to Brouwer [38] (to whom, indeed, the notion of mapping classes is due), who took $M = E_1$ and A as any compact closed subset of E_n and showed the existence of an $f \, \varepsilon \, E_1{}^A$ where each $f^{-1}(x)$ is vacuous or a component of A. From R. L.

Moore's study of upper-semicontinuous collections of continua in the plane [39], it follows that if $f \varepsilon S_2^{S_2}$ such that each counter image $f^{-1}(x)$ is non-vacuous and connected and does not separate S_2, then the image set is S_2 itself, and as a matter of fact, using terminology to be explained below, f is a mapping of degree one.

The spaces $S_n^{S_m}$ for general values of m and n have been given considerable attention, particularly by Hopf. When $m < n$, the space $S_n^{S_m}$ is connected—indeed, arcwise connected, since every two mappings are homotopic. Likewise, $S_1^{S_m}$ for $m > 1$ is connected. For $m = n$, $S_n^{S_m}$ has infinitely many components as shown by Hopf, who has also shown that the space $S_2^{S_3}$ has infinitely many components [40]. For $m > n > 2$ very little is known concerning the structure of the space $S_n^{S_m}$. We return to these matters later on.

The more general case where either M or A is assumed merely to be peanian has also received considerable attention, especially by American topologists. In 1921 Hahn showed that a decomposition of a continuum C that is irreducibly connected between two points into its "prime parts" generates an $f \varepsilon E_1^{*C}$. Following out this idea, R. L. Moore in 1925 showed that a decomposition of any compact metric continuum K into its prime parts generates a mapping of K onto a compact Peano space C such that for every $x \varepsilon C, f^{-1}(x)$ is a prime part of K (unless of course K has only one prime part). This procedure has been made abstract and considerably extended both as to breadth of application and results by G. T. Whyburn and the present author [41]. The case A and M both Peano spaces has been studied extensively of late by topologists in this country, usually, however, with attention confined to special subspaces of M^A, as for instance the subspaces of arc-preserving mappings, interior mappings, etc. [42].

But to return to our main interest—the case where M or A is an S_n—it will simplify our exposition if we treat separately the cases where (1) M is an S_n and (2) A is an S_n. In accomplishing this, it will be necessary for us to broaden our basis of discussion, particularly with reference to the extension of the notion of Peano space.

6.3. **Some extensions of the notion of Peano space.** We remarked in §2.2 that in order for a locally compact, metric, connected space M to be peanian, it is necessary and sufficient that for any $x \varepsilon M$ and $\epsilon > 0$ there exist a $\delta > 0$ such that any two points of $S(x, \delta)$ are the end points of an arc in $S(x, \epsilon)$. In terms of homotopy, this is equivalent to requiring that there exists $\delta > 0$ such that any image of S_0 in $S(x, \delta)$ be homotopic in $S(x, \epsilon)$ to a point.

Following this line of thought, we may define [43] a metric space M as n-*dimensionally locally connected* (n-LC) if, given any $x \varepsilon M$ and $\epsilon > 0$, there exists $\delta > 0$ such that any image of S_n in $S(x, \delta)$ is homotopic in $S(x, \epsilon)$ to a point. If M is n-LC for $n = 0, 1, \cdots, p$, we call M an LC^p, and if M is n-LC for all non-negative integers n, we call M an LC$^\infty$. In this terminology a Peano space is an LC^0. But we may go further. Let us call a subcomplex L of a complex K dense in K if all vertices of K are in L. A partial mapping of K into M will be any $f \ \varepsilon \ M^L$ where L is any complex dense in K. The mesh of such a mapping will be the maximum $\delta(f(E))$ for all cells E of L. Then we call M an LC if for every $\epsilon > 0$ there exists a $\delta > 0$ such that for every complex K and partial mapping of K into M of mesh less than δ, the mapping can be extended to a mapping of K of mesh less than ϵ. As an example (Borsuk) of a set which is LC$^\infty$ but not LC, consider in Q_ω the closed segment L joining the origin to the point $(1, 0, 0, \cdots)$. Let $x_p = (1/p, 0, 0, \cdots)$, $(p = 2, 3, 4, \cdots)$, and let S_p be a p-sphere of center x_p and diameter less than $[\rho(x_p, x_{p+1})]/2$. The set of all such spheres together with the points of L not on diameters of any of these spheres is an LC$^\infty$ but not an LC. Finally, M is an LC* if it is an LC and for all n every image of an S_n in M is homotopic in M to a point.

Below we shall point out other types of local connectedness; but first we shall define certain spaces, which, while the fact is not at all apparent at first, are intimately related to the various types of spaces LC.

6.4. **Retracts.** Following a line of thought suggested by the notion of homotopy, suppose $M \subset A$ and that there exists $f \ \varepsilon \ M^A$ such that $M = f(A)$ and $f[f(x)] = f(x)$ for all $x \ \varepsilon \ A$; then we call M a *retract* of A [44]. Those sets which are retracts of Q_ω turn out to be identical with those sets that are retracts of every metric space in which they are imbedded, and are called, by Borsuk, *absolute retracts* (AR-set). The AR-sets are peanian, satisfy a fixed point theorem (see §6.9), and do not separate any E_n containing them; when imbedded in E_2, they are identical with those Peano continua that do not separate E_2.

Related to the AR-sets are the *absolute neighborhood retracts* (ANR-sets) [45]: If $M \subset A$, and M is a retract of some open subset of A containing it, then M is called a neighborhood retract of A; if, moreover, M is a neighborhood retract of every metric space in which it is imbedded, then it is an ANR-set; such sets are identical with the neighborhood retracts of Q_ω. Apart from their many interesting intrinsic properties, it is interesting to note that if $M \subset E_n$ is an ANR-set, then $E_n - M$ is the sum of a finite number of domains each of whose boundaries is peanian and accessible from the corresponding domain.

We come directly, below, to the relations of the sets just defined to local connectedness. Before this, however, we define another related notion, that of *local contractibility*. A metric space M is called *locally contractible* if, given $x \ \varepsilon \ M$ and $\epsilon > 0$, there exists $\delta > 0$ such that the set $S(x, \delta)$ is homotopic to a point in $S(x, \epsilon)$. It is immediately obvious that a locally contractible space is n-LC for all n. *Among the finite dimensional spaces, the ANR-sets are identical with the compact metric spaces that are locally contractible*

[45]; *and identical with the compact metric spaces that are n-LC for all n.* Furthermore, as shown by Lefschetz [43], *the properties ANR and LC are equivalent; and the properties AR and LC* are equivalent.*

Aside from these relationships, these sets have many interesting intrinsic properties—for instance, if M is an ANR-set there exists a complex K such that all Betti groups (§6.5) of M as well as the fundamental group (§6.7) are homomorphic mappings of the corresponding groups of K [46]— but it is necessary to refer the reader to the works cited for these, and return to the main line of thought.

6.5. Betti groups of abstract spaces. In Chapter IV we defined Betti groups $B^k(M, G)$ where M is a complex and G an abelian group. We consider now the possibility of setting up like groups for the case of an abstract space M, the nature of these groups being such that in case K is a complex, $B^k(K, G)$, $B^k((K), G)$ are isomorphic. This problem was first attacked from a standpoint closely allied to the approach outlined in Chaps. III and IV above. It should be moderately clear, for example, how a definition for Betti groups of LC-sets might be set up on a purely combinatorial basis, using cell-images. For spaces with no local connectedness properties, the first difficulty, apparently, to be overcome is the inability to realize cells. But if one recalls the manner of orientation of a simplex, as in setting up an indicatrix, for example (§6.1), it is apparent that the notion of k-cell as the homeomorph of the set of points $(x_1, x_2, \cdots, x_k)$ in E_k such that $x_1^2 + x_2^2 + \cdots + x_k^2 < 1$ is for the moment of less importance than the set of $k+1$ vertices related thereto; for the orientation of the simplex at least, only the latter are of importance.

Taking this into account, a theory of homology has been developed by Čech for very general spaces based on systems of coverings by open sets [47]. For compact metric spaces, in which we are especially interested below, this theory is equivalent to that based on V-cycles [48] which we now describe.

Let M be a compact metric space and G an abelian group. A specified set E^n of $n+1$ points of M, such that $\delta(E^n) < \epsilon$, we call an ϵ-n-cell of M; the points of E^n we call its "vertices." To E^n corresponds a positively oriented cell σ^n as in §4.1—merely an assignment of a certain ordering (and its even permutations) to the vertices. Each proper subset of $k+1$ points of E^n constitutes the vertices of a cell E^k, which is again oriented, and the boundary function F may be defined as before. An ϵ-n-chain of M over G is simply an n-chain in terms of the oriented ϵ-n-cells and G. A sequence $C^n = \{C_i^n\}$ of ϵ_i-n-chains over G is called a *V-n-chain over G* of M if $\lim_{i \to \infty} \epsilon_i = 0$. If the elements of a V-n-chain γ^n are cycles such that for each i there exists a $\delta_i - (n+1)$-chain C_i^{n+1} of M such that $F(C_i^{n+1}) = C_i^n - C_{i+1}^n$, where $\lim_{i \to \infty} \delta_i = 0$, then we call the sequence γ^n a *V-n-cycle.* Thus, if we define the sum of V-n-chains $C_1^n = \{C_{i1}^n\}, C_2^n = \{C_{i2}^n\}$ as $C_1 + C_2 = \{C_{i1} + C_{i2}^n\}$, we have additive groups of chains and cycles for M. If we call a V-n-cycle

$\gamma^n = \{Z_i^n\}$ *bounding* provided there exists a V-n-chain $\{C_i^n\}$ such that $F(C_i^n) = Z_i^n$ for all i, then we obtain a group of bounding cycles; and hence the Betti group $B^n(M, G)$. These groups are obviously topological invariants, and by showing that for a complex they agree with the groups defined in Chap. IV, the topological invariance of the latter may be established. And using these groups on M, the Pontrjagin duality (§4.5) extends to the case where M is any closed subset of S_n [29].

Many variations of the definitions given in the preceding paragraph have proved useful. For example, if G is a subgroup of a group G', a V-n-cycle γ^n over G is also a V-n-cycle over G', and can be called *bounding over* G' provided there exists a V-n-chain over G', say C^n, such that $F(C^n) = \gamma^n$, obtaining a Betti group $B^n(M, G, G')$. The most common case of this sort is that where G is G_0 and G' is G_r. Or one may, for example, use only ϵ -n cycles over G as elements of a sequence $\{C_i^n\}$, and call the latter a cycle if the differences $C_i^n - C_{i+1}^n$ bound $\delta_i - (n+1)$-chains over G', etc. [49].

In this connection, it is interesting to note a result of Steenrod [50] to the effect that for any compact metric space M (or for a general topological space in case the Čech homology theory is employed), the group R (§4.1) is a universal coefficient group for the homology theory in the sense that if the groups $B^k(M, R)$ are known and G is a given abelian group, then the groups $B^k(M, G)$ are determined.

For a locally compact metric space, one may obtain a homology theory by restricting the V-n-chains used to those which are at the same time V-n-chains of compact subspaces of the given space.

In terms of V-cycles, we may state another extension of the notion of Peano space. We first note that in order that a space C satisfying Axioms $0-3$ of Chapter II should be a Peano space, it is necessary and sufficient that for $x \,\varepsilon\, C$ and $\epsilon > 0$ there exist $\delta > 0$ such that any 0-cycle (mod 2) of $S(x, \delta)$ bound in $S(x, \epsilon)$ (the proof of this is left to the reader). The group G_2 may of course be replaced by other groups, and having selected a coefficient group G, one may call a locally compact metric space *locally i-connected* (l.i-c.) in the sense of V-chains over G if for $x \,\varepsilon\, M$ and $\epsilon > 0$ there exists $\delta > 0$ such that every V-cycle over G of $S(x, \delta)$ bounds in $S(x, \epsilon)$. Similar to the notions LC^p, LC^∞, we have the notions lc^p, lc^∞ defined in terms of the V-cycles.

Regarding the relations of this new type of local connectedness with the types previously described, one can show by simple examples that the properties n-LC and l.n-c. are independent. But it can be shown that LC^n is in general a stronger property than lc^n. The most striking result in this connection, however, is that of Hurewicz [51] to the effect that if one uses chains over G_0 in defining the l.n-c. property, and confines himself to those compact spaces that are 1-LC, then the properties lc^n, LC^n are equivalent. Thus, *in terms of homotopies relating to mapping of S_1 alone*, one is able to determine a class of spaces in which these two important types of local connectedness are equivalent. For a discussion of the implications of the property lc^n, one is referred to [52]. We noted in §6.4 that if a continuum M in S_n is an ANR-set, hence an LC-set, the domains of $S_n - M$ are finite in number and have accessible peanian boundaries. In terms of the lc^n-property, this result may be generalized as follows: If a continuum M in S_n is lc^{n-2}, then the domains D_i, $(i = 1, 2, \cdots)$, of $S_n - M$, if infinite in number, are such that $\lim_{i \to \infty} \delta(D_i) = 0$, their boundaries are all peanian, and are accessible from their respective domains. For $n = 2$ this result (with the exception of the peanian property of the domain boundaries, which was obtained later by M. Torhorst) was established by Schoenflies [11]. If one generalizes the notion of accessibility as has been done by Alexandroff [53], all points of an lc^{n-2} compact set in S_n are i-accessible for $i = 1, 2, \cdots, n - 2$. [54].

6.6. **Spaces** $S_n{}^A$. We are now equipped to discuss more fully the spaces $S_n{}^A$, where A is compact and metric, and their applications. When A is an S_m, we have already described certain known results (§6.2). The suggestions for the more general results which we presently recount are contained in certain results obtained by Alexandroff, Borsuk, Čech, and Hopf. Alexandroff [49] showed that if A is n-dimensional, then A contains a certain type of nonbounding cycle ("power-cycle") if and only if $S_n{}^A$ is not connected, and as a corollary, the latter is a necessary and sufficient condition that, in case $A \subset S_{n+1}$, A separate S_{n+1}; the latter result was also obtained independently by Borsuk [55]. In [56] Hopf found that the number of components in $S_n{}^A$, if A is an n-dimensional complex, is infinite if $p^n(A, G_0) > 0$, otherwise the number is equal to the order of the $(n-1)$th torsion group (the group generated by the generators of finite order of the $(n-1)$th Betti group). Earlier Hopf [40] established that if A is any complex, the condition $p^1(A, G_0) = 0$ is equivalent to the connectedness of $S_1{}^A$; a result which was extended by Borsuk [57] to the case where A is compact metric. The latter results were carried by Bruschlinsky [58] to the determination of the "reduced" 1-dimensional Betti group $B^1(A, G_0, G_r)$, by the device of turning $S_1{}^A$ into a group.

Suppose T is a topological group, and consider $f, g \in T^A$. For any $x \in A$, let $h(x) = f(x) \cdot g(x)$, the operation on the right being that in T. Since T is a topological group, it follows that $h \in T^A$, and we may write $h = fg$, where now the operation on the right is the one induced in T^A, and relative to this operation the elements of T^A form a group whose identity is the mapping of A into the identity. The component determined by the identity in T^A is a normal divisor D of T^A, and the factor group T^A/D has as its elements the components of T^A. Let us call this factor group the *mapping class group of A rel. T*, as distinguished from the mapping group T^A. If we consider the group operation in S_1 to be that of the rotations of the circle, then the mapping class group of A rel. S_1 is isomorphic to the 1-dimensional reduced Betti group of A. In particular, then, the Betti number

$p^1(A, G_0)$ is determined solely from a consideration of the mapping group $S_1{}^A$.

Similarly, by setting up a suitable group operation in S_3, Bruschlinsky showed that if A is 3-dimensional, then $B^3(A, G_0, G_r)$ is isomorphic to the factor group of the mapping class group of A rel. S_3 modulo the subgroup formed of elements of finite order; and if A is in addition a complex, then the "full" Betti group $B^3(A, G_0)$ is isomorphic to this mapping class group of A rel. S_3. The difficulty encountered in extending these results to other dimensions is due to the lack of a group operation in the corresponding S_n's. However, Freudenthal [59] overcomes this obstacle by setting up a "partial" operation in S_n, sufficient to define a group, analogous to the mapping class group, whose elements are the components of $S_n{}^A$. This group he calls the "Hopf group" and shows that for an n-dimensional A, it completely determines the Betti group $B^n(A, G_m)$, $m=0$, or $m>1$.

It will be noted that, with the single exception $n=1$, the results quoted concerning the determination of Betti groups through mappings of A into S_n all hold only for dimension $A=n$. To attack the problem for the general dimension $A>n$, one obviously needs to modify or refine the above procedures in some way, in view of known examples; for instance, as shown by Hopf [40], the space $S_2{}^{S_3}$ is not connected, and yet $p^2(S_3, G)=0$. That this is possible has been shown by Lefschetz and Hopf [60], who, for any complex K, have been able to determine the Betti groups of all dimensions purely from a consideration of certain types of mappings into the various S_n's. We omit further details here, while observing that it is quite apparent, from a consideration of results already obtained, that from mappings into S_n, considerable information concerning the topology of a space, hitherto derivable only by purely combinatorial methods, may be secured. Our citations above do not, as a matter of fact, give a complete picture by any means; for example, Borsuk and Eilenberg [61] have made a special study of $S_1{}^A$ and employed mappings into S_1 in a most effective manner in the investigation of plane topology, establishing with this tool many theorems ordinarily obtained only by combinatorial methods.

6.7. **Spaces** A^{S_n}. We saw in §6.3 how an important type (n-LC) of local connectedness may be introduced by imposition of homotopy conditions on certain elements of A^{S_n}, namely those elements whose related images in A are "small." Without the latter restriction, but with $n=1$, we encounter a notion basic in the definition of the so-called *Poincaré group*, or *fundamental group*. (For more detailed exposition than is possible here, see especially [62].) Poincaré discovered certain 3-dimensional manifolds ("Poincaré spaces") whose Betti groups were the same as those of S_3, but whereas $S_3{}^{S_1}$ is connected, the Poincaré spaces contain images of S_1 not homotopic to a point.

Suppose M is an arcwise connected space and $x \, \varepsilon \, M$. Let $\sigma_1 = P^0P^1$ be any oriented 1-cell (on E_1^* for instance), and consider an $f \, \varepsilon \, M^{\sigma_1}$ such that

$f(P^0) = f(P^1) = x$. Then the image (§1.3) $u = f(\sigma_1)$ is called an *oriented* (closed) *path* of M; the image $f(-\sigma_1)$ is also an oriented path of M, and is denoted by u^{-1}. If $u = f(\sigma_1)$, $v = g(\sigma_2)$ are two oriented paths of M, we may define a path $s = u \cdot v$, *product* of u and v, by considering the "terminal" and "initial" points (and only these) of u and v, respectively, as coincident, and letting s be the image $\phi(\sigma)$ where σ is the geometric sum of σ_1 and σ_2, and identical with f, g on σ_1, σ_2 respectively. The fundamental group of M is a group $\pi_1(M)$ whose elements are sets of oriented paths of M (end points fixed at x), two paths u and v being in the same set if and only if $u \cdot v^{-1}$ is homotopic to x. The identity of $\pi_1(M)$ is the set of paths homotopic to x; the product $S = U \cdot V$ of U, $V \ \varepsilon \ \pi_1(M)$ is that set S which contains $s = u \cdot v$ for any $u \ \varepsilon \ U$, $v \ \varepsilon \ V$; and the inverse U^{-1} of $U \ \varepsilon \ \pi_1(M)$ is the set containing u^{-1} for any $u \ \varepsilon \ U$. In general, $\pi_1(M)$ is not abelian, in contrast to the abelian character of the groups $B^1(M, G)$. (For M a complex or, more generally, a locally contractible space, the factor group of $\pi_1(M)$ modulo its commutator group is isomorphic to $B^1(M, G_0)$.) It is not dependent on the particular choice of x, and its topological invariance is obvious.

It was conjectured by Poincaré that among the closed n-dimensional manifolds M_n, the sphere S_n is characterized by its Betti groups $B^k(S_n, G_0)$ and fundamental group $\pi_1(S_n)$. In particular, is S_3, then, the only orientable closed 3-manifold whose fundamental group "vanishes"? To date, no answer to this question has been published, although it is known [63] that the Betti groups and fundamental group of two 3-manifolds may agree without their being homeomorphic.

The fundamental group has furnished a new invariant making possible the differentiation between spaces which agree in other known invariants, as well as a tool fundamental in investigations such as those concerning knots and "covering manifolds" [64]. Rather than discuss these matters, we pass on to the problem of generalizing the group $\pi_1(M)$ and the rôle of the n-sphere therein.

A generalization of the fundamental group. The most successful generalization of $\pi_1(M)$ is due to Hurewicz [65]. With him, we consider M as not only connected, but as a locally contractible, metric, separable space. If A is a finite dimensional, compact metric space, then M^A is locally contractible, a fortiori 0-LC, and has an at most denumerable set of components; and each of the latter is open and arcwise connected. Hence if $f \ \varepsilon \ M^A$, we may consider the group $\pi_1(C_f)$, where C_f is the component of M^A containing f. Since C_f is locally contractible, oriented paths which approximate closely enough a given path u will be in the same element of $\pi_1(C_f)$ as u. Consequently the order of $\pi_1(C_f)$ will be at most denumerable.

The case which most interests us is that where A is S_{n-1}. We may then simplify the above procedure by choosing constant points $x \ \varepsilon \ S_{n-1}$, $y \ \varepsilon \ M$, and limiting ourselves to that subspace $M_{xy}^{S_{n-1}}$ of $M^{S_{n-1}}$ which consists of all $f \ \varepsilon \ M^{S_{n-1}}$ such that $f(x) = y$. It develops that a group $\pi_1(C_f)$ for the space $M_{xy}^{S_{n-1}}$ is independent, not only of the choice of C_f, but also of x and y, and *consequently depends only on M and n*. This group Hurewicz calls the *nth homotopy group*, $\pi_n(M)$, of M. For $n=1$, it obviously agrees with the fundamental group $\pi_1(M)$. However, whereas the latter is not abelian, the homotopy groups $\pi_n(M)$ for $n>1$ are all abelian. Also, whereas for complexes, the factor group of $\pi_1(M)$ modulo its commutator group agrees with $B^1(M, G_0)$, for $n>1$, $\pi_n(M)$ appears in general to be independent of the Betti group. For example, in the case of closed 2-manifolds with positive Betti numbers, $\pi_2(M)$ reduces to the identity. However, if the first $n-1$ homotopy groups $(n>1)$ of M reduce to the identity, then $B^n(M, G_0)$ and $\pi_n(M)$ are isomorphic; in particular, then, the first n homotopy groups reduce to the identity if and only if the like holds for the first n Betti groups and the group $\pi_1(M)$. Also the reduction of $\pi_n(M)$ to the identity is equivalent to the connectedness of the space M^{S_n}.

An interesting by-product of these investigations [65, II] is the establishing of an equivalence between the Poincaré conjecture cited above and each of the following statements (M_n denoting a closed n-manifold): (1) If every closed proper subset is contractible to a point in M_n, then $M_n = S_n$; (2) if S_n can be mapped on M_n with degree 1 (see below), then $M_n = S_n$.

6.8. **Degree of a mapping; cohomology groups.** Of central importance in the theory of mappings as developed by Brouwer is the *degree* of a mapping (*Abbildungsgrad*). Let M and N be two orientable closed n-manifolds, oriented as in Chap. IV, and consider any $f \, \varepsilon \, N^M$. On the basis of a well known deformation theorem of Alexander and Veblen [66], it may be shown that for some simplicial subdivisions of M and N there will exist $g \, \varepsilon \, N^M$ such that f and g are in the same mapping class and $g(M)$ constitutes a *simplicial mapping*—that is, each cell of M maps onto a cell of N, vertices of M going into vertices of N. If $g(\sigma^n)$ is the image of an oriented cell of M, and $g(\sigma^n)$ covers an oriented cell ξ^n of N, then, since vertices map onto vertices, one defines in an obvious way agreement of orientation of $g(\sigma^n)$ with ξ^n; if the orientation of $g(\sigma^n)$ agrees with that of ξ^n, we say the degree $d_g(\xi^n, \sigma^n)$ of the covering of ξ^n by σ^n is $+1$; otherwise it is -1. If $g(\sigma^n)$ does not cover ξ^n, then by definition $d_g(\xi^n, \sigma^n) = 0$. The number

$$d_g(\xi^n, M) = \sum_{\sigma^n} d_g(\xi^n, \sigma^n)$$

turns out to be the same for all ξ^n, and hence may be denoted by $d_g(N, M)$; it is the degree of the mapping g of M onto N. As shown by Brouwer [67], it is the same for all choices of g, hence by defining $d_f(N, M) = d_g(N, M)$ an invariant of the mapping class is obtained [68].

One naturally asks, if two mappings are of the same degree, do they necessarily belong to the same mapping class? If $N = S_2$ and M is any closed 2-manifold, an affirmative answer was given by Brouwer, a result extended later by Hopf to the case $N = S_n$ and M a closed n-manifold.

Later Hopf went further [56], getting a corresponding result for the case of M any n-complex (a very simple proof is given by Whitney in [69]), by suitably defining the notion of degree modulo m, $(m = 0, 1, 2, 3, \cdots)$, of the mapping of a cycle modulo m into S_n, and classifying the mapping classes of $S_n{}^M$ by the medium of the degrees modulo m. Following this line of thought, Hurewicz [65, III], considering the case where M and N are compact spaces, defined f, $g \ \varepsilon \ N^M$ to be of the same *homology type in dimension* n if for every abelian group G the homomorphisms induced by f, g of $B^n(M, G)$ into $B^n(N, G)$ agree. For the case where M is n-dimensional, and N is a connected LC^n whose groups $\pi_i(N)$, $(i = 1, 2, \cdots, n-1)$, reduce to the identity, he showed that if f, $g \ \varepsilon \ N^M$ are of the same homology type in dimension n, they belong to the same mapping class [70].

It should be emphasized here that most of the work of this type (as well as the treatment of dualities mentioned above) is considerably simplified by the use of R as coefficient group or the employment of the cohomology groups. Regarding the latter, in Chap. IV we introduced a boundary operator such that $F(\sigma_i{}^k) = \sum_h e_i^h \sigma_h{}^{k-1}$, or more generally, $F(\sum_i c \sigma_i{}^k) = \sum_i \sum_h c^i e_i^h \sigma_h{}^{k-1}$. The numbers e_i^h were determined by the incidence of the oriented cells, and the first of these relations may be paralleled by introducing a "coboundary" operator F_c such that $F_c(\sigma_i{}^{k-1}) = \sum_h u_i^h \sigma_h{}^k$, where $e_i^h = u_h^i$, the second relation having the analogue $F_c(\sum_i c^i \sigma_i{}^{k-1}) = \sum_i \sum_h c^i u_i^h \sigma_h{}^k$. If we call any polynomial $\sum_i c^i \sigma_i{}^k$ a *co-chain*, we have the corresponding *co-cycles*, *coboundaries*, and finally the *cohomology groups* $B_c^k(K, G)$. If A, B are character groups of one another, then $B^k(K, A)$ and $B_c^k(K, B)$ are character groups of one another [71]. As formulated by Lefschetz and Whitney [72], the Hopf result on mapping classes may be stated as follows: *The mapping classes of* $S_n{}^M$ *(M an n-complex) are in* $(1-1)$-*correspondence with the elements of the cohomology group* $B_c^n(M, G_0)$. For the Hurewicz generalization, a like formulation holds, except that G_0 is replaced by $\pi_n(N)$.

6.9. **Further remarks concerning** $S_n{}^{S_n}$. In §6.2 we have already reviewed briefly the case $S_n{}^{S_m}$. Here we mention some points regarding the case $m = n$. We remarked above that the components of $S_n{}^{S_n}$ are infinite in number. The early work of Brouwer on this case centered about the presence of *invariant* or *fixed points* of a mapping. If we call $f \ \varepsilon \ S_n{}^{S_n}$ *sense-preserving* in case $d_f(S_n, S_n) > 0$, and *sense-reversing* in case $d_f(S_n, S_n) < 0$, then (regarding the original S_n's as identical) for n even and sense-preserving, there is at least one fixed point; that is, there exists $x \ \varepsilon \ S_n$ such that $f(x) = x$; and similarly for n odd and sense-reversing. This work has been greatly extended by Lefschetz [73]; a corollary of his results, of special interest in regard to the material in §6.3 above, is that if M is a compact metric continuum which is an LC$^\infty$ and whose nth Betti numbers $(n > 0)$ vanish, then any $f \ \varepsilon \ M^M$ has at least one fixed point. (Also see §6.4.)

The restriction to the case of an f which is periodic has also received attention. If f is a homeomorphism of such a type that f^n is the identity mapping (and not for $m < n$), then f is called a mapping of period n. It was shown by Brouwer and also by Kérékjarto that every periodic mapping of an S_2 is equivalent to a rotation, or to the product of a rotation by a reflection. This work has been greatly extended by P. A. Smith [74], who considered periodic mappings of certain general spaces having the same Betti groups as an n-sphere, and has succeeded in showing that for the period prime, the set of invariant points also has the same homology properties as a sphere. More particularly, he has shown [75] that the invariant points of a periodic mapping of an S_3 are either a vacuous set, or an S_i where $i = 0$, 1 or 2; the last case being possible only when the period is two and the mapping is sense-reversing.

6.10. **General remarks.** The contents of the present section were planned as an indication of the tendencies of some of the most recent investigations in topology. The determination of homology groups by mappings into S_n, the introduction of general homotopy groups as generalizations of the Poincaré group and the extension to higher dimensions of the peanian idea by mappings of S_n in the space not only show the fundamental rôle still played by the euclidean n-sphere, but emphasize the complete unification of the abstract set-theoretic and combinatorial methods in topology. It seems hardly necessary to point out the problems still to be settled, as the incompleteness of the various topics outlined above is suggestive of itself. We have not, of course, touched on all the important investigations involving the n-sphere—we have omitted, for instance, the *sphere-spaces* recently introduced and investigated by Whitney and reported on in [76]; also the relations of the S_1 to its complement in S_3, among which are the *knot* properties which have received so much attention [64]. But we hope, despite these limitations, that we have achieved the general purpose of this section and that the reader who desires more complete information will find sufficient sources in the citations.

VII. GENERAL CASE OF S_{n-1} IN S_n; A GENERAL "JORDAN CURVE THEOREM"

The contents of §7.1 below belong properly with the material of Chap. V. It seemed best, however, to defer the discussion until the more advanced notions of Chap. VI were available, particularly those of homotopy and general chain and cycle groups. Whereas the cases $n = 2, 3$ of Chap. V were quite readily handled by the machinery introduced previously, the more powerful tools made available in Chap. VI are indispensable in giving a satisfactory picture of the higher dimensional situations. For detailed proofs of the theorems quoted we must refer to the bibliography. In §7.3 we show how the abstract chains and cycles may be applied to obtain a very general theorem of which the Jordan curve theorem is a special case, and which, moreover, applies to a much wider variety of spaces than the S_n's.

7.1. The S_{n-1} in S_n. In Chap. V we discussed the case of an S_{n-1} in S_n for $n = 2, 3$. The unrestricted case offers as chief difficulty the lack of a topological characterization of S_k, for $k > 2$, comparable to those provided for S_1 and S_2 in Chap. II. However, suppose M is an S_{n-1} in S_n; what can be said regarding the topological character of $S_n - M$? From the duality theorem we know that $S_n - M$ is the sum of two domains A and B of which M is the common boundary (the latter fact being established by an argument like that of Theorem J_3, §3.6); also that the Betti numbers of A and B are all zero.

Regarding the homotopy properties of A and B, we have the well-known example [6] for the case $n = 3$ for which the group $\pi_1(A)$ has an infinite set of generators. So far as we know, the question as to whether $\pi_1(A)$ can have a finite set of generators has not been investigated. At any rate, the example referred to shows that neither A nor B need be an n-cell, if $n > 2$. Here we have one of the essential differences between the cases $n = 2$ and $n > 2$, so common in the case of more general point sets, since for $n = 2$, both A and B are 2-cells [77]. For $n > 2$, the question concerning whether, when $\pi_1(A)$ reduces to the identity, the point set A is an n-cell, has not been answered. From the work of Hurewicz on homotopy groups (§6.7) we know that if $\pi_1(A) = 0$, then $\pi_k(A) = 0$ for all $k > 0$; or, to state the matter in different terms, no matter how great n may be, if every S_1 in A is homotopic to a point in A, then every S_k in A for $k > 0$ is homotopic to a point in A.

As for the "smoothness" of the general S_{n-1} in S_n, we may show that not only are A and B u.l.0-c., but also u.l.i-c. for all $i > 0$: A set A is called *uniformly locally i-connected* (u.l.i-c.) if for arbitrary $\epsilon > 0$ there exists $\delta > 0$ such that every i-cycle of A of diameter $< \delta$ bounds a chain of A of diameter $< \epsilon$. The proof, except for the different dimensions involved, is the same as for the $i = 0$ case in Chap. V.

Since A and B are u.l.0-c., all points of M are accessible from both A and B. Moreover, for any non-negative i, the points of M are i-accessible in the senses of Alexandroff and Čech [53, 54]. These are weaker properties, however, than the u.l.i-c. properties.

What can be said by way of converse theorems? Thus, what is the nature of a common boundary in S_n of two u.l.i-c., $(i = 0, 1, \cdots, n-2)$, domains whose Betti numbers are zero? As a matter of fact, it turns out [78] that *if all we know of M is that it is the boundary of a single u.l.i-c., $(i = 0, 1, \cdots, n-2)$, domain A whose $(n-1)$th Betti number is zero, then we may conclude that in $S_n - M$ there is one and only one other domain B whose boundary is again M and which is u.l.i-c. for $i = 0, 1, \cdots, n-2$; and furthermore that for each i, the ith Betti number of A is equal to the $(n-i-1)$th Betti number of B.* It follows that M satisfies the Poincaré duality theorem.

If the Betti numbers of A are all zero, is M an S_{n-1}? We saw in Chap. V that the answer is affirmative for $n = 2, 3$. For $n > 3$ we encounter the difficulty mentioned at the beginning of this section. In this situation we may do the next best thing, which appears to be to show that M has many of the topological properties of S_{n-1}.

7.2. Generalized manifolds. The condition that the Betti numbers of A be zero is not of much moment in the investigation of such a question, since for any $(n-1)$-manifold in S_n the local properties, internally and externally, are the same as for an S_{n-1} in S_n, and the essential properties in the large are embodied in the dualities mentioned in the preceding paragraph; and that $p^{n-1}(M) = 1$ and $p^{n-1}(F) = 0$ for any closed proper subset F of M are, of course, a result of the common boundary property of M. In short, just as the notion of sphere leads to that of manifold, so are we led in generalizing the notion of sphere to generalizing the manifold notion. This has been accomplished in a variety of ways; in the theory of complexes by replacing "cellular" by "cell-like in homology properties," for instance [30]. In passing to general spaces, a like approach may be made. The so-called *generalized manifolds*, recently introduced by a number of authors [78, 79], not only give natural generalizations of the manifold notion, but furnish directions for attack on such a problem as that proposed above.

So far as the various definitions of generalized manifolds that have been given to date are concerned, it turns out that, whenever a continuum M is the boundary of a u.l.i-c., $(i = 0, 1, \cdots, n-2)$, domain A in S_n, then M is a generalized $(n-1)$-manifold in all these senses—indeed, for M to satisfy the definition of any one of them is to satisfy them all; and conversely, if M is an $(n-1)$-generalized manifold in S_n it is the boundary of such a domain. We do not review here the various definitions of generalized manifold, nor the proof of the statements just made; the reader may refer to the above citations for more detailed information. In passing, however, we note that instead of limiting oneself to the boundary of a *domain A*, one can obtain the following general result [78]: *A necessary and sufficient condition that an open subset D of S_n be u.l.i-c. for $i = 0, 1, \cdots, n-2$ is that* (1) *D consist of a finite number of domains $D_1, D_2, \cdots, D_m$ such that $D_j \cdot D_k = 0$ if $j \neq k$;* (2) *each component of B_k, the boundary of D_k, $(1 \leq k \leq m)$, be either a point or a generalized closed $(n-1)$-manifold, and $B_k = B_{k0} + B_{k1} + \cdots + B_{kh} + B_{k(h+1)} + \cdots$, where B_{k0} is the set of point components of B_k and the manifolds B_{kj}, when $j > h$, satisfy the conditions $p^i(B_{kj}) = 0$ for $1 \leq i \leq n-2$;* (3) *$\lim_{j \to \infty} \delta(B_{kj}) = 0$. Furthermore, the Poincaré duality holds for B, the boundary of D, and the duality $p^i(D) = p^{n-i-1}(S_n - B - D)$. For $n = 3$, the sets B_{kj}, $(j > k)$, are all S_2's.*

A recent attempt to define abstractly a space which may possess most of the topological properties of S_n is of peculiar interest [80]: A space S such that for each $x \in S$ there exists a neighborhood U of x such that $S - U$ is an absolute retract (§6.4). For 1- or 2-dimensional S, such a space is the corresponding S_n, and for higher dimensions has all the homology and homotopy properties of S_n. A more general type of space, defined by the same author, is obtained by requiring in the above definition only that $S - U$ have the homology properties of a closed n-cell—the homotopy properties of S_n no longer hold here, although for the 1- and 2-dimensional cases the S_n is the only space satisfying these conditions.

7.3. **A general "Jordan curve theorem."** Throughout Chaps. II–V the Jordan curve theorem played a basic rôle; it furnished a motive for the first two of these sections as well as for the duality theorem of Chap. IV and the theorems of Chap. V. In Chap. II, we found that among Peano spaces the theorem characterizes S_2. We conclude with a theorem of which the Jordan curve theorem is a very special case [81]. In the case of S_n, note that we deal with a Peano space such that $p^n(S^n) = 1$ and $p^n(F) = 0$ for every closed proper subset F of S_n; and that the set M which decomposes S_n into just two domains of which it is common boundary satisfies a like condition with "n" replaced by "$n-1$." Now consider the S_0 in S_1—the former is the common boundary of two domains in S_1. A more or less plausible reason for this is that S_1 has no cut point (§2.2). Let us generalize the notion of cut point [82] as follows:

DEFINITION: *A point $x \varepsilon M$ is called a k-dimensional cut point of M if there exists a cycle γ^k of $M - x$ which bounds on M, but does not bound on any closed subset of $M - x$.*

Intimately related to the cut point notion, but having reference to a specified cycle is that of a barrier: If γ^k is a cycle of M, let us call a *carrier* of γ^k any closed subset F of M such that γ^k is also a cycle of F. Then, given a γ^k which bounds on M, and a carrier F of γ^k, a point $x \varepsilon M - F$ will be called a *barrier* to γ^k (in M) if γ^k fails to bound on every closed subset of $M - x$.

In terms of these definitions, no point of an S_n is an $(n-1)$-dimensional cut point of S_n and a fortiori none is a barrier to an $(n-1)$-cycle. We state and prove the following theorem, using (as in Chap. III) G_2 as coefficient group and the V-cycles of §6.5. For brevity, let us call a cycle *essential* if it has a carrier on which it fails to bound.

THEOREM J. *Let M be a compact Peano space such that $p^n(F) = 0$ for every closed proper subset F of M; and let J be a closed subset of M such that $p^{n-1}(J) = 1$ and $p^{n-1}(F) = 0$ for every closed proper subset F of J. Denoting by γ^{n-1} the essential $(n-1)$-cycle of J, let γ^{n-1} bound on M and no point of $M - J$ be a barrier to γ^{n-1}. Then the set $M - J$ is the sum of two mutually exclusive domains of which J is the common boundary.*

The proof we give is chiefly an application of Lemmas 2 and 3 below. If a cycle γ bounds on a closed set F but bounds on no proper closed subset of F, then F will be called an *irreducible membrane relative to γ*. If a cycle γ

bounds on a set M, then there exists in M at least one irreducible membrane relative to γ; and every cycle γ has an *irreducible* carrier [83].

LEMMA 1. *In a metric space, let γ^n be an essential n-cycle and let M_1, M_2 be irreducible membranes relative to γ^n such that $M_1 \neq M_2$. Then $M_1 + M_2$ is a carrier of an essential $(n+1)$-cycle.*

Proof. If K_1, K_2 are chains bounded by γ^n on M_1, M_2, respectively, and J is the irreducible carrier of γ^n, then some subsequence of the sequence of $\delta_i - (n+1)$-chains forming $K_1 + K_2$ is a cycle γ^{n+1} whose irreducible carrier is $M_1 + M_2$ with possibly certain points of J deleted [84]. We continue to denote the chains derived from harmonizing [84] K_1, K_2, γ^n with γ^{n+1} by the same symbols, and the new J, M_1, M_2 by the same symbols; we still have $M_1 \neq M_2$. Suppose $x \ \varepsilon \ M_1 - M_2$.

Let $\epsilon > 0$ be such that $M_2 \cdot \overline{S}(x, \epsilon) = 0$. The portion of K_1 in $S(x, \epsilon)$ is a chain $F_1 \to \Gamma^n$, where Γ^n is a cycle of $F(x, \epsilon)$ [85]. The chain $E_1 = K_1 + F_1 \to \gamma^n + \Gamma^n$ is a chain of $M - S(x, \epsilon)$, and the cycle $K_1 + K_2$ is identical with $E_1 + F_1 + K_2$.

Suppose there exists $K_3 \to K_1 + K_2$ on $M_1 + M_2$. The portion of K_3 in $S(x, \epsilon)$ is a chain $K_3' \to F_1 + F_2$, where F_2 is a chain of $F(x, \epsilon)$. Then, since $F_1 \to \Gamma^n$, and $F_1 + F_2 \to 0$, we have $F_2 \to \Gamma^n$. But F_2 is a chain of M_1, and hence we have $E_1 + F_2 \to \gamma^n$ on $M_1 - S(x, \epsilon)$, contradicting the fact that M_1 is an irreducible membrane relative to γ^n. Hence $K_1 + K_2$ must be an essential cycle.

LEMMA 2. *Let M be a compact metric space such that $p^n(M) > 0$ and $p^n(F) = 0$ for every closed proper subset of M, and J a closed subset of M such that $p^{n-1}(J) = k$. Then $M - J$ has at most $k+1$ components* [86].

Proof. Suppose $M - J$ has at least $k+2$ components, so that $M - J$ is the sum of $k+2$ mutually separated subsets M_i. Let γ^n be an essential cycle of M. Then $\gamma^n = \Gamma^n + \sum_i \gamma_i^n$ where Γ^n is a chain of J, γ_i^n a chain of M_i, and $\Gamma^n \to \gamma^{n-1}$, $\gamma_i^n \to \gamma_i^{n-1}$, the boundary cycles being cycles of J.

Since $p^{n-1}(J) = k$, some linear combination of the cycles γ_i^{n-1}, $(1 \leq i \leq k+1)$, bounds on J; say $K^n \to \sum_{i=1}^{k+1} c_i \gamma_i^{n-1} = \gamma^{n-1} + \sum_{i=1}^{k+2} d_i \gamma_i^{n-1}$ where $d_i = c_i + 1$ (mod 2) and in particular $d_{k+2} = 1$. Then $H^n = \Gamma^n + K^n \to \sum_i d_i \gamma_i^{n-1}$, H^n being a chain of J. Also, $\sum_i d_i \gamma_i^n \to \sum_i d_i \gamma_i^{n-1}$, hence $\gamma^n + \sum_i d_i \gamma_i^n \to \sum_i d_i \gamma_i^{n-1}$. The cycle γ^n is the sum (mod 2) of the cycles $\gamma^n + \sum_i d_i \gamma_i^n + H^n$ and $\sum_i d_i \gamma_i^n + H^n$, each of which bounds on M since $p^n(F) = 0$ for every proper closed subset of M. But then γ^n bounds on M, contradicting the hypothesis.

LEMMA 3. *Under the hypothesis of Theorem J* [87], *$p^n(M) > 0$ and the set J separates M.*

Proof. Let M_1 be an irreducible membrane of M relative to γ^{n-1}. Let $x \ \varepsilon \ M_1 - J$. As x is not a barrier to γ^{n-1}, there exists in $M - x$ another irreducible membrane relative to γ^{n-1}, say M_2. By Lemma 1, M_1+M_2 carries an essential n-cycle, and since no proper closed subset of M carries an essential n-cycle, $M=M_1+M_2$. Consequently $p^n(M)>0$.

The set $M-M_1\neq0$, else $M_2\subset M_1-x$ and M_1 would not be an irreducible membrane relative to γ^{n-1}. Let H be a component of $M-M_1$; then $H\subset M_2$. If $\overline{H}-H\subset J$, then J separates M by Theorem 26 (§2.2). If $J\not\supset\overline{H}-H$, then H has a limit point $y\;\varepsilon\;M_1-J$. Now $M-y$ contains an irreducible membrane M_3 relative to γ^{n-1}, and arguing as above, we see that $M=M_1+M_3$. But this is impossible, since if $0<\epsilon<\rho(y, M_3)$, $H\cdot S(y,\;\epsilon)\neq0$ and $H\cdot S(y,\;\epsilon)\cdot(M_1+M_3)=0$. Consequently $\overline{H}-H\subset J$ and J separates M.

Proof of Theorem J. By Lemmas 2 and 3, $M-J$ has just two components A and B. The boundary of each of these is J. For if the boundary of A, say, were a proper subset J' of J, then J' would separate M. But $p^{n-1}(J')=0$ and by Lemma 2, such a set as J' cannot separate M.

An interesting feature of Theorem J is that it imposes no conditions on the dimensions of the point sets involved, at least not explicitly. Whether the conditions given imply, for instance, that the space M must itself be n-dimensional we leave unsettled. It would be interesting to know, for example, if in an lc^n, an n-cycle with an at most n-dimensional carrier bounds on an at most $(n+1)$-dimensional set (for $n=0$, Theorem 24 (§2.2) yields a positive answer).

References and Notes

Due to space limitations, a complete list of citations is out of the question. It is expected, therefore, that references to be found in works cited will be consulted, especially since in the case of a sequence of papers on a special topic we sometimes cite only the last. We do not in general go into such historical matters as the origin of various terms used. For detailed bibliographies the reader is referred to S. Lefschetz, *Topology*, and R. L. Moore, *Foundations of Point Set Theory*, respectively, Volumes 12 and 13 of the Colloquium Publications of the American Mathematical Society; and to Seifert-Threlfall, *Topologie*, Leipzig, 1934. For a chronologically arranged list of books relating to topology, see the comprehensive Alexandroff-Hopf, *Topologie*, Berlin, 1935.

1. E. W. CHITTENDEN. *On general topology and the relation of the properties of the class of all continuous functions to the properties of space.* Transactions of the American Mathematical Society, vol. 31 (1929), pp. 290–321. M. FRÉCHET. *Les Espaces Abstraits.* Paris, 1928.

2. E. W. CHITTENDEN. *On the metrization problem and related problems in the theory of abstract sets.* Bulletin of the American Mathematical Society, vol. 33 (1927), pp. 13–34.

3. S. CLAYTOR. *Peanian continua not imbeddable in a spherical surface.* Annals of Mathematics, (2), vol. 38 (1937), pp. 631–646.

4. K. MENGER. *Dimensionstheorie.* Leipzig and Berlin, 1928. G. NÖBELING. *Die neuesten Ergebnisse der Dimensionstheorie.* Jahresbericht der Deutschen Mathematiker-Vereinigung, vol. 41 (1931), pp. 1–17.

5. E. V. HUNTINGTON. *The Continuum.* 2d edition. Cambridge, Massachusetts, 1917.

6. As for instance in the case of a knotted S_1 in E_3, or the Alexander example of the S_2 in S_3 such that S_3-S_2 contains S_1's that are not deformable to a point in S_3-S_2. J. W. ALEXANDER. *An example of a simply connected surface bounding a region which is not simply connected.* Proceedings of the National Academy of Sciences, vol. 10 (1924), pp. 8–10.

7. In citing a theorem given elsewhere than in the chapter under discussion, we shall state the chapter or section that contains it.

8. F. LEJA. *Sur la notion du groupe abstrait topologique.* Fundamenta Mathematicae, vol. 9 (1927), pp. 37–44. D. VAN DANTZIG. *Zur topologischen Algebra.* Mathematische Annalen, vol. 107 (1932–33), pp. 587–626. D. MONTGOMERY. *Continuity in topological groups.* Bulletin of the American Mathematical Society, vol. 42 (1936), pp. 879–882.

9. C. JORDAN. *Cours d'Analyse.* Paris, 1893. 2d edition, p. 90.

10. For references, see: R. L. MOORE. *Report on continuous curves from the viewpoint of analysis situs.* Bulletin of the American Mathematical Society, vol. 29 (1923), pp. 289–302, second footnote, p. 290.

11. A. SCHOENFLIES. *Die Entwickelung der Lehre von den Punktmannigfaltigkeiten.* Jahresbericht der Deutschen Mathematiker-Vereinigung, supplementary vol. 2. Leipzig, 1908.

12. R. L. MOORE, Cit. [12], second footnote, p. 292. G. T. WHYBURN. *Concerning continuous images of the interval.* American Journal of Mathematics, vol. 53 (1931), pp. 670–674.

13. B. KNASTER and C. KURATOWSKI. *Sur les ensembles connexes.* Fundamenta Mathematicae, vol. 2 (1921), pp. 206–255, §2. G. H. HALLETT, JR. *Concerning the definition of a simple continuous arc.* Bulletin of the American Mathematical Society, vol. 25 (1918–1919), pp. 325–326.

14. R. L. WILDER. *Concerning simple continuous curves and related point sets.* American Journal of Mathematics, vol. 53 (1931), pp. 39–55, §2.

15. R. L. MOORE. *Foundations of Point Set Theory.* Loc. cit., p. 86. See also: G. T. WHYBURN. *On the construction of simple arcs.* American Journal of Mathematics, vol. 54 (1932), pp. 518–524.

16. H. M. GEHMAN. *Concerning end points of continuous curves and other continua.* Transactions of the American Mathematical Society, vol. 30 (1928), pp. 63–84.

17. G. T. WHYBURN. *On the structure of continua.* Bulletin of the American Mathematical Society, vol. 42 (1936), pp. 49–73.

18. See cit. [17], especially §3, as well as references therein, and the latter part of the same paper for extensions of the notion. For proofs of the next few theorems and brief historical comments, see: G. T. WHYBURN. *On the cyclic connectivity theorem.* Bulletin of the American Mathematical Society, vol. 37 (1931), pp. 429–433.

19. E. R. VAN KAMPEN. *On some characterizations of 2-dimensional manifolds.* Duke Mathematical Journal, vol. 1 (1935), pp. 74–93.

20. J. W. ALEXANDER. *A proof and extension of the Jordan-Brouwer separation theorem.* Transactions of the American Mathematical Society, vol. 23 (1922), pp. 333–349.

21. O. VEBLEN. *Theory of plane curves in non-metrical analysis situs.* Transactions of the American Mathematical Society, vol. 6 (1905), pp. 83–98.

22. We recall from §1.4 that to say "S_k imbedded in S_n" means merely that the S_k is a point set in S_n that is homeomorphic with an S_k, and not in general a subcomplex of any subdivision of S_n; for example, an S_1 imbedded in S_2 may have a positive area in terms of the metric of S_2.

23. See citation, p. 333 of [20].

24. O. VEBLEN. *Analysis Situs.* American Mathematical Society Colloquium Publications, vol. V, Part 2. 1922.

25. O. VEBLEN and J. W. ALEXANDER. *Manifolds of N dimensions.* Annals of Mathematics, (2), vol. 14 (1913), pp. 163–178 (note footnote bottom p. 164).

26. J. W. ALEXANDER. *Combinatorial analysis situs.* Transactions of the American Mathematical Society, vol. 28 (1926), pp. 301–329.

27. S. LEFSCHETZ. *Closed point-sets on a manifold.* Annals of Mathematics, (2), vol. 29 (1928), pp. 232–254.

28. L. PONTRJAGIN. *Über den algebraischen Inhalt topologischer Dualitätssätze.* Mathematische Annalen, vol. 105 (1931), pp. 165–205.

29. L. PONTRJAGIN. (a) *The theory of topological commutative groups.* Annals of Mathematics, (2), vol. 35 (1934), pp. 361–390. (b) *The general topological theorem of duality for closed sets.* Ibid., pp. 904–914.

30. S. LEFSCHETZ. *Topology*. American Mathematical Society Colloquium Publications, vol. 12, p. 105. 1930.

31. A. KOLMOGOROFF. *Über die Dualität im Aufbau der kombinatorischen Topologie*. Recueil Mathématique (Moscou), vol. 1 (43) (1936), pp. 97–102.

32. H. WHITNEY. *On products in a complex*. Annals of Mathematics, (2), vol. 39 (1938), pp. 397–432 (contains both historical comments and bibliography).

33. R. L. WILDER. *Point sets in three and higher dimensions and their investigation by means of a unified analysis situs*. Bulletin of the American Mathematical Society, vol. 38 (1932), pp. 649–692.

34. L. E. J. BROUWER. *Über Jordansche Mannigfaltigkeiten*. Mathematische Annalen, vol. 71 (1912), pp. 320–327. *Über freie Umschliessungen im Raume*. Proceedings, Koninklijke Akademie van Wetenschappen te Amsterdam, vol. 34 (1931), pp. 100–101.

35. R. L. WILDER. *On the properties of domains and their boundaries in E_n*. Mathematische Annalen, vol. 109 (1933), pp. 273–306 (note particularly footnotes 6 and 55).

36. Obviously "bounded" is sufficient, where we would call a set M bounded if $\delta(M)$ is finite.

37. These classes are what we might call "arc-components" of M^A.

38. L. E. J. BROUWER. *On the structure of perfect sets of points*. Proceedings, Koninklijke Akademie von Wetenschappen te Amsterdam, vol. 12 (1910), pp. 785–794.

39. R. L. MOORE. *Concerning upper semi-continuous collections of continua*. Transactions of the American Mathematical Society, vol. 27 (1925), pp. 416–428.

40. H. HOPF. *Über die Abbildungen der dreidimensionalen Sphäre auf die Kugelfläche*. Mathematische Annalen, vol. 104 (1931), pp. 637–665. (Note citations therein, particularly to Brouwer.) H. FREUDENTHAL. *Über die Klassen der Sphärenabbildungen*. Compositio Mathematica, vol. 5 (1937), pp. 299–314. L. PONTRJAGIN. *Sur les transformations des sphéres en sphéres*. Comptes Rendus du Congrès International des Mathématiciens, Oslo, 1936, vol. 2, p. 140.

41. G. T. WHYBURN. *A decomposition theorem for closed sets*. Bulletin of the American Mathematical Society, vol. 41 (1935), pp. 95–96. R. L. WILDER. *Decompositions of compact metric spaces*. Ibid., vol. 43 (1937), p. 334, abstract no. 270.

42. For instance, see: G. T. WHYBURN. *Interior transformations on surfaces*. American Journal of Mathematics, vol. 60 (1938), pp. 477–490.

43. S. LEFSCHETZ. *On chains of topological spaces*. Annals of Mathematics, (2), vol. 39 (1938), pp. 383–396. (Note bibliography in footnote 1.)

44. K. BORSUK. *Sur les rétractes*. Fundamenta Mathematicae, vol. 17 (1931), pp. 152–170.

45. K. BORSUK. *Über eine Klasse von lokal zusammenhängenden Räumen*. Fundamenta Mathematicae, vol. 19 (1932), pp. 220–242.

46. K. BORSUK. *Zur kombinatorischen Eigenschaften der Retrakte*. Fundamenta Mathematicae, vol. 21 (1933), pp. 91–98. See also: *Un théorème sur les groupes de Betti des ensembles localement connexes en toutes les dimensions $\leq n$*. Ibid., vol. 24 (1935), pp. 311–316.

47. E. ČECH. *Théorie génerale de l'homologie dans un espace quelconque*. Fundamenta Mathematicae, vol. 19 (1932), pp. 149–183. See also the forthcoming work by the same author to appear in the series Actualités Scientifiques.

48. L. VIETORIS. *Über den höheren Zusammenhang kompakter Räume und eine Klasse von zusammenhangstreuen Abbildungen*. Mathematische Annalen, vol. 97 (1927), pp. 454–472.

49. P. ALEXANDROFF. *Dimensionstheorie*. Mathematische Annalen, vol. 106 (1932), pp. 161–238. ALEXANDROFF-HOPF. *Topologie*. Chap. V.

50. N. E. STEENROD. *Universal homology groups*. American Journal of Mathematics, vol. 58 (1936), pp. 661–701.

51. W. HUREWICZ. *Homotopie, Homologie und lokaler Zusammenhang*. Fundamenta Mathematicae, vol. 25 (1935), pp. 467–485.

52. R. L. WILDER. *On locally connected spaces*. Duke Mathematical Journal, vol. 1 (1935), pp. 543–555. P. ALEXANDROFF. *Zur Homologie-Theorie der Kompakten*. Compositio Mathematica, vol. 4 (1937), pp. 256–270.

53. P. Alexandroff. *On local properties of closed sets.* Annals of Mathematics, (2), vol. 36 (1935), pp. 1–35, §5.

54. R. L. Wilder. *Locally connected subsets of euclidean n-space.* Bulletin of the American Mathematical Society, vol. 42 (1936), p. 496, abstract no. 308. E. Čech. *Accessibility and homology.* Recueil Mathématique (Moscou), vol. 1 (43) (1936), pp. 661–662.

55. K. Borsuk. *Über Schnitte der n-dimensionalen Euklidischen Räume.* Mathematische Annalen, vol. 106 (1932), pp. 239–248.

56. H. Hopf. *Die Klassen der Abbildungen der n-dimensionalen Polyeder auf die n-dimensionale Sphäre.* Commentarii Mathematici Helvetici, vol. 5 (1933), pp. 39–54.

57. K. Borsuk. *Über die Abbildungen der metrischen kompakten Räume auf die Kreislinie.* Fundamenta Mathematicae, vol. 20 (1933), pp. 224–231. E. Čech. *Sur les continus Péaniens unicohérents.* Ibid., pp. 232–243 and citations therein.

58. N. Bruschlinsky. *Stetige Abbildungen und Bettische Gruppen der Dimensionszahlen 1 und 3.* Mathematische Annalen, vol. 109 (1934), pp. 525–537.

59. H. Freudenthal. *Die Hopfsche Gruppe.* Compositio Mathematica, vol. 2 (1935), pp. 134–162.

60. S. Lefschetz. *Sur les transformations des complexes en sphères.* Fundamenta Mathematicae, vol. 27 (1936), pp. 94–115. H. Hopf. *Eine Charakterisierung der Bettischen Gruppen von Polyedern durch stetige Abbildungen.* Compositio Mathematica, vol. 5 (1938), pp. 347–353.

61. K. Borsuk and S. Eilenberg. *Über stetige Abbildungen der Teilmengen euklidischer Räume auf die Kreislinie.* Fundamenta Mathematicae, vol. 26 (1936), pp. 207–223 and citations therein.

62. Seifert-Threlfall. *Topologie.* Chap. 7.

63. J. W. Alexander. *Note on two three-dimensional manifolds with the same group.* Transactions of the American Mathematical Society, vol. 20 (1919), pp. 339–342.

64. K. Reidemeister. *Knotentheorie.* Ergebnisse der Mathematik und ihrer Grenzgebiete, vol. 1. Berlin, 1932. O. Veblen. *Analysis Situs.* Chap. V. Seifert Threlfall. *Topologie.*

65. W. Hurewicz. *Beiträge zur Topologie der Deformationen,* I. Proceedings, Koninklijke Akademie van Wetenschappen te Amsterdam, vol. 38 (1935), pp. 112–119. II, ibid., pp. 521–528. III, ibid., vol. 39 (1936), pp. 117–125. IV, ibid., pp. 215–224. Note references to Čech and Dehn in II, footnote 2.

66. See Lefschetz. *Topology.* Chap. II, §3.

67. L. E. J. Brouwer. *Über Abbildung von Mannigfaltigkeiten.* Mathematische Annalen, vol. 71 (1911), pp. 97–115.

68. Consider such mappings as those defined by $w=e^{i\theta}$, $w=e^{2i\theta}$, $0 \leqq \theta < 2\pi$ of $|z| = 1$ into $|w| = 1$.

69. H. Whitney. *The maps of an n-complex into an n-sphere.* Duke Mathematical Journal, vol. 3 (1937), pp. 51–55.

70. As announced in the third paragraph of [69], conditions that f and g be homotopic have also been found by Whitney for $N = S_2$ and M any 3-complex (Bulletin of the American Mathematical Society, vol. 42 (1936), p. 338, abstract no. 220) and for $N =$ projective n-space, M any n-complex.

71. See, for instance, the paper cited in [31].

72. See the paper of Lefschetz cited in [60]; also Whitney in [69].

73. See Lefschetz, *Topology,* and citations therein to Brouwer.

74. P. A. Smith. *Transformations of finite period.* Annals of Mathematics, (2), vol. 39 (1938), pp. 127–164. The bibliography contains citations to the work of Brouwer and Kérékjarto.

75. Unpublished.

76. H. Whitney. *Sphere-spaces.* Recueil Mathématique (Moscou), vol. 1 (43) (1936), pp. 787–791. *Topological properties of differentiable manifolds.* Bulletin of the American Mathematical Society, vol. 43 (1937), pp. 785–805.

77. J. R. KLINE. *A new proof of a theorem due to Schoenflies.* Proceedings of the National Academy of Sciences, vol. 6 (1920), pp. 529–531.

78. R. L. WILDER. *Generalized closed manifolds in n-space.* Annals of Mathematics, (2), vol. 35 (1934), pp. 876–903.

79. Besides the papers of Čech and Lefschetz mentioned in footnote 5 of [78], see [53]. E. ČECH. *On general manifolds.* Proceedings of the National Academy of Sciences, vol. 22 (1936), pp. 110–111. P. ALEXANDROFF and L. PONTRJAGIN. *Les variêtès à n dimensions généralisées.* Comptes Rendus de l'Académie des Sciences, vol. 202 (1936), pp. 1327–1329.

80. K. BORSUK. *Über sphäroidale und H-sphäroidale Räume.* Recueil Mathématique (Moscou), vol. 1 (43) (1936), pp. 643–660.

81. For some very general decomposition theorems, applying to so-called "pseudomanifolds," see: E. ČECH. *On Pseudomanifolds.* Mimeographed lecture notes, Princeton, 1935.

82. Compare: R. L. WILDER. *Sets which satisfy certain avoidability conditions.* Časopis pro Pěstovani Matematiky a Fysiky, 1938, pp. 185–198.

83. P. ALEXANDROFF. *"Gestalt und Lage."* Annals of Mathematics, (2), vol. 30 (1928–1929), pp. 101–187, especially 168–169.

84. See first paper cited in [52].

85. That is, Γ^n may be shifted to $F(x, \epsilon)$ by infinitesimal alterations in the chain F_1; see for instance Anhang I of [83].

86. See [35], Theorem 3; also E. Čech, [81], and *Sur la décomposition d'une pseudovariété par un sousensemble fermé.* Comptes Rendus de l'Academie des Sciences, vol. 198 (1934), pp. 1342–1345.

87. As a matter of fact the only condition that J need satisfy here is that it carry at least one $(n-1)$-cycle nonbounding on J but bounding on M and to which no point of $M-J$ is a barrier.

UNIVERSITY OF MICHIGAN,
    ANN ARBOR, MICH.

DIRICHLET PROBLEMS

BY

GRIFFITH C. EVANS

Contents

I. Primary concepts

1. **Intrinsic energy.** One can encompass the central Dirichlet problem in a brief and simple exposition by basing the approach on the so-called subharmonic functions, according to the method of Perron [26], T. Radó and F. Riesz [32] and C. Carathéodory [4]. The essential feature which makes these methods possible is the mean-value theorem of harmonic functions, that the value of such a function at the center of a sphere is the mean of its values on the surface; and this notion has been even more directly exploited by Phillips and Wiener [28] and Kellogg [19]. In fact, it can hardly be avoided, whatever the approach may be.

There is some advantage, however, in postponing its use until it is necessary to differentiate between Laplace's equation and Newtonian potential on the one hand and related equations or integral expressions on the other. How long a postponement is possible is illustrated in the treatment given by Frostman, in his thesis [13], where the uniqueness of a minimum energy distribution serves to answer a number of important questions, as well for other laws of attraction as for the Newtonian. In fact, perhaps it may be argued that, from a physical point of view, energy in a field or on a body is a more natural concept than Laplace's equation, and that the problems which are solvable in terms of this concept, such as the distribution of electric mass on a conductor and the induction exerted by one charge on another, are the natural problems. This would of course

185

be too narrow a view for mathematicians, but it happens that the bridge from these particular problems to the more general ones is short. Apparently also when one has crossed the bridge he is in a position to survey problems of a different degree of generality than those which have been the object of direct attack. Here we refer not merely to what is called the generalized Dirichlet problem, in which the harmonic function is uniquely determined by continuous boundary data but cannot itself remain continuous at the boundary, but also to problems in which the boundary data themselves are not continuous but where again the solution is unique within a certain class.

Of course, the energy principle and the Dirichlet integral go back many years, and recent papers like those of Frostman [13], de la Vallée Poussin [36], and the author [11] reaffirm them. There is a good deal of overlapping in them, leaving a number of rather difficult questions of priority, if such matters are regarded as of the highest importance. No attempt will be made to settle them here. It is worthy of remark, however, that the relation of potential to general distributions of mass was considered as early as 1911 by Plemelj [29]. And it is quite evident that no one can disregard the importance of the insight of Lebesgue, in recognizing spines and barriers [21, 22, 23], or of Kellogg in his reorientation of the theory of regular points and barriers [16, 17], or of Wiener in generalizing the notion of capacity [40, 41] and showing its relation to fundamental issues. Attention should be called to the work of Vasilesco, and especially of Bouligand, and Zaremba, contributors over a series of years to the solution of the Dirichlet problem [2, 38, 42]. The discussions of Hilbert and Lebesgue on the minimum of the Dirichlet integral, which have now become classics, are even more important for their relation to the calculus of variations than to the Dirichlet problem. One may speak similarly of the classic integral equation theory of Fredholm, of which the culmination is the memoir of J. Radon [33]. In this paper, however, we follow a somewhat different mode of development. For an exposition of the growth of the theory up to the last decade, the reader is referred to the report and book of O. D. Kellogg [17, 18].

With this remark, we proceed to exploit the common ground referred to above, as much with the purpose of learning things by the way as for the sake of the fundamental problem of determining a solution of Laplace's equation by continuously given boundary values.

We consider, then, the potential and the energy of mass distributions. The potential of a positive mass distribution $\mu(e)$, distributed arbitrarily on a bounded set E, may be written in the form

$$(1) \qquad u(M) = \int (1/MP)d\mu(e_P),$$

in which the integral is defined in the customary manner as

$$\lim_{N\to\infty} \int h_N(M, P)d\mu(e_P),$$

where $\{h_N(M, P)\}$ constitutes an increasing sequence of bounded continuous functions, with

$$\lim_{N\to\infty} h_N(M, P) = 1/MP, \qquad M \neq P,$$
$$= +\infty, \qquad M = P.$$

The $\mu(e)$ may be described technically as a not negative completely additive function of sets (thus of finite total amount), with $\mu(e \cdot CE) = 0$, and the integration may be extended over the whole of space, or merely over E. The mass distribution $\mu(e)$ has a *nucleus* F_1, contained in the closed cover F of E consisting of those points P of F such that an arbitrarily small sphere of center P constitutes a set for which the mass is not zero; this nucleus F_1 is evidently closed. It is convenient to admit for $u(M)$ the value $+\infty$, as for instance in the case where $\mu(e)$ consists in part of a point mass on some point Q, that is, $\mu(e) > 0$ for $e = Q$ and $u(M) = +\infty$ for $M = Q$.

We define the energy, or "intrinsic" energy, of the mass distribution $\mu(e)$ on E by the iterated integral

$$(2) \qquad I = I(\mu) = \int_E d\mu(e_P) \int_E \frac{d\mu(e_Q)}{QP} = \int_E u(P)d\mu(e_P)$$

leaving out the customary factor $1/2$ for convenience. This integral may also have the value $+\infty$ if the mass is somewhere sufficiently concentrated. By means of distributions of mass of minimum energy, we are led to the conductor potential of the infinite domain complementary to F and to the Green's function of that domain.

A completely additive set function $f(e)$, distributed on E, which is not necessarily positive, may be written as the difference of two of positive type: $f(e) = \mu(e) - \nu(e)$. Hence the potential and energy of distributions $f(e)$ may be written as the difference or in terms of sums and differences of integrals with respect to positive set functions, and will be said to converge when these converge separately. There are thus introduced the mutual energies

$$I(\mu, \nu) = I(\nu, \mu) = \int_E d\mu(e_P) \int_E \frac{d\nu(e_Q)}{QP} = \int_E u(Q)d\nu(e_Q) = \int_E v(P)d\mu(e_P),$$

where $u(Q)$, $v(P)$ are the potentials of $\mu(e)$ and $\nu(e)$ respectively, with

$$I(\mu \pm \nu) = I(\mu) + I(\nu) \pm 2I(\mu, \nu)$$

if the respective integrals are convergent.

By comparison with the corresponding Dirichlet integrals extended over all space, it is easily verified [10, I] that

$$I(\mu) = 4\pi \int_W (\text{grad } u)^2 d\tau,$$

$$I(\mu, \nu) = 4\pi \int_W (\text{grad } u) \cdot (\text{grad } v) d\tau,$$

and hence that

$$I(\mu) + I(\nu) \geq 2I(\mu, \nu) \geq 0.$$

It follows that if $I(\mu)$ and $I(\nu)$ converge, the same is true of $I(\mu+\nu)$ and $I(f)=I(\mu-\nu)$, and, further, that $I(f)$ is essentially positive and is equal to zero only in the case that $f(e)\equiv 0$.[†] Moreover if $I(f)$ and $I(g)$ are convergent, we have similarly

(3)
$$I(f + g) = I(f) + I(g) + 2I(f, g),$$
$$| 2I(f, g) | \leq I(f) + I(g).$$

2. **Weak convergence and equicontinuity.** The discussion of the minima of Stieltjes integrals is based upon the notion of weak convergence. A sequence of completely additive set functions $\{f_n(e)\}$ converges weakly on E to $f(e)$ if for every continuous function $\phi(P)$ we have

(4)
$$\lim_{n\to\infty} \int_E \phi(P) df_n(e) = \int_E \phi(P) df(e).$$

It is a fundamental theorem that, given on a closed bounded set F a collection of completely additive set functions whose total variations $\int |df_n(e)|$ are bounded uniformly, there exists an $f(e)$, also completely additive on F, and a subsequence $\{f_n^*(e)\}$ from the $f_n(e)$ which converges to $f(e)$ weakly. In particular, it may be remarked that if E is any subset of F, measurable with respect to $f(e)$ (that is, such that $\int_E |df(e)|$ converges), which is such that $\int_{E'} |df(e)| = 0$ where E' is the frontier of E, then

$$\lim_{n\to\infty} f_n^*(E) = f(E).$$

Consider now such a weakly convergent sequence of not negative set functions $\{\mu^n(e)\}$ and suppose that $u(P)$, not necessarily continuous, is the limit of an increasing sequence of continuous functions $\phi_N(P)$. It is a simple result, known as Fatou's theorem, that

$$\liminf_{n\to\infty} \int_F u(P) d\mu_n(e_P) \geq \int_F u(P) d\mu(e),$$

where $\mu(e)$ is the limit distribution. In fact, given $\epsilon > 0$, an N exists such that

$$\int_F u(P) d\mu(e) < \int_F \phi_N(P) d\mu(e) + \epsilon$$

---

† Frostman proves the corresponding fact for more general laws of attraction by means of an integral identity which enables him to write $I(f)$ as a square [13].

if the left-hand member is convergent; but also

$$\liminf_{n \to \infty} \int_F u(P) d\mu_n(e) \geqq \lim_{n \to \infty} \int_F \phi_N(P) d\mu_n(e) = \int_F \phi_N(P) d\mu(e),$$

and the result is obtained by letting N become infinite. An obvious modification takes care of the case when $\int u du = +\infty$.

The same theorem applies to iterated integrals like (2), and it is an immediate consequence of the theorem that the potential of a positive mass distribution is *lower semicontinuous*, that is

$$\liminf_{N \to \infty} u(M) \geqq u(Q).$$

Another fundamental lemma of analysis is based on the notion of equicontinuity. A family of functions $\{\phi_n(P)\}$ is equicontinuous in a closed bounded region D if for P, P' in D and distance $PP' \leqq \delta$ a function $\omega(\delta)$ exists, independent of n and tending to zero with δ, such that $|\phi_n(P') - \nu_n(P)| \leqq \omega(\delta)$. If then there is a subsequence which converges at a single point of D, there is a subsequence $\{\phi_n^*(P)\}$ which converges uniformly in D to some function $\phi(P)$ which has the same modulus of continuity. The proof is based, as is evident, on the Cantor diagonal process.

3. **Elementary notions about harmonic functions.** For convenience in notation, we denote by $\Gamma(\rho, Q)$ the spherical domain of center Q and radius ρ and by $C(\rho, Q)$, its surface. A function which is harmonic in a domain T has at any point Q the value which is the mean of its values over any $\Gamma(\rho, Q)$ which is contained with its $C(\rho, Q)$ in T, or over the $C(\rho, Q)$ of such a $\Gamma(\rho, Q)$. Conversely, if a function $u(M)$ is summable spatially, and for every Q in an arbitrary closed domain D contained in T is equal to its spatial average over spheres $\Gamma(\rho, Q)$, $(0 < \rho < \delta)$, where δ is a constant (depending on D), then $u(M)$ is harmonic in T; likewise if it is equal to its average over spherical surfaces $C(\rho, Q)$, $0 < \rho < \delta$ for such values of ρ as the integral exists. It is a familiar consequence of these mean-value relations that a function which is harmonic in T cannot take on its upper or lower bounds at a point of T, unless it is identically constant. Equally familiar is the application of this fact to the Dirichlet problem: there cannot be two different functions harmonic in T (tending to zero at ∞ if T is an exterior domain) which take on continuously the same limiting values for the same manner of approach to the boundary—even if more than one limiting value may correspond to a given boundary point.

Let now $u(M)$ be harmonic and $|u(M)| \leqq K$ in T. Let F be a closed set in T and η less than the distance of F from the boundary of T. It is easily seen that if the distance MM' is $\leqq \delta \leqq \eta$, the difference $|u(M) - u(M')|$ $\leqq \omega(\delta)$ where $\omega(\delta) = \delta \cdot 6K/\eta$. In fact,

$$\frac{4\pi\eta^3}{3}\left| u(M') - u(M) \right| = \left| \int_{\Gamma(\eta, M')} u(P)dP - \int_{\Gamma(\eta, M)} u(P)dP \right|$$

$$\leqq \int_{\Sigma} \left| u(P) \right| dP$$

where Σ is the region "between" the two spheres, that is,

$$\Sigma = \Gamma(\eta, M) + \Gamma(\eta, M') - \Gamma(\eta, M)\cdot\Gamma(\eta, M').$$

The region Σ has the volume $4\pi\eta^2(2d)$, d being the distance MM'. Hence finally,

$$\frac{4\pi\eta^3}{3}\left| u(M') - u(M) \right| \leqq K4\pi\eta^2(2\delta),$$

which yields the desired result.

But this result amounts to a statement that all harmonic functions in T with a common bound are equicontinuous. Hence, given an infinity of functions harmonic in T and bounded in their set, it follows from the theorem on equicontinuity that there exists a sub-sequence which converges to a function harmonic in T, and the convergence is uniform on any closed bounded set contained in T.

That the limit function $u(M)$ is harmonic in T is easily established. In fact, in any subregion of T whose boundary is distant by at least η from the boundary t of T, considering the convergent sub-sequence $u(M)$, we have for $\rho < \eta$,

$$u(M) = \lim_{n\to\infty} u_n(M) = \lim_{n\to\infty} \frac{3}{4\pi\rho^3} \int_{\Gamma(\rho, M)} u_n(P)dP = \frac{3}{4\pi\rho^3} \int_{\Gamma(\rho, M)} u(P)dP,$$

so that $u(M)$ is equal to its spherical volume average and is therefore harmonic.

When we consider the sequence solution of the Dirichlet problem we shall need to employ a sequence of domains approximating to the given one. We denote as usual the frontier of T by t, with corresponding notation in general for other domains; the set t will be taken as bounded, and the domain T may be either an interior or an exterior domain. A sequence of domains is known as a *nested sequence approximating to T* if (i) T_{n+1} contains $T_n + t_n$; (ii) each point of T lies in some T_n. A sequence of nested approximating domains S_n can first be constructed out of collections of cubes, since T is an open set, possibly not all of the same size, if S_n is to be connected—a domain being a connected open set. These approximating domains, by means of surfaces defined by the equations

$$K_n = \int_{s_n} \frac{dP}{MP^2}$$

may then be replaced by others with analytic boundaries, and by a proper choice of the K^u, these may be made free of singularities [18, pp. 319, 276].

This construction of analytic approximating domains is not difficult, and in order to save space we shall take it for granted.

4. **Distributions on conductors. The conductor distribution.** We follow the method of Frostman [13] and consider possible distributions $\mu(e)$ of positive mass on a bounded closed set F, such that the total mass $\mu(F)$ is unity. If there is no distribution for which I is finite, we say that F is of *zero capacity*; otherwise F is of positive capacity. In the latter case it is easy to see that I is bounded away from 0, but without regard to this fact let I_0 be the lower bound of I for all possible distributions $\mu(e)$; evidently $I_0 \geq 0$. Let $\{\mu_n(e)\}$ be a sequence of these mass distributions such that the energies $I_n = I(\mu_n)$ tend to this lower bound I_0.

The sequence of mass functions $\mu_n(e)$, being uniformly bounded in total, contains a sub-sequence which converges weakly to a mass function $\mu_0(e)$, of total mass unity; and we may take our original sequence as reduced to this sub-sequence. Then, by Fatou's theorem

$$I_0 = \lim_{n \to \infty} I(\mu_n) \geq I(\mu_0).$$

On the other hand, $\mu_0(e)$ is one of the set functions to be admitted as a possible mass distribution, so that

$$I(\mu_0) \geq \text{l. b. } I(\mu) = I_0.$$

Hence $I_0 = I(\mu_0)$.

We turn now to the possible values of the potential on F_1, the nucleus of $\mu_0(e)$. Let $V(M)$ denote this potential.

Let $\delta\mu(e)$ be a mass distribution on F such that $I(\delta\mu)$ is finite. Then $I(\mu_0 + \delta\mu)$ is also finite, and from (3),

$$\Delta I = 2 \int_F V(P) d\delta_\mu(e_P) + I(\delta\mu).$$

Since $I(\mu_0)$ is a minimum, we must have

$$\Delta I \geq 0 \quad \text{if} \quad \int_F d\delta_\mu(e_Q) = 0 \quad \text{and} \quad \mu_0(e) + \delta\mu(e) \geq 0.$$

It is clear that a $\delta\mu(e)$ of the form

$$\delta\mu(e) = \epsilon \left\{ \phi(e) - \frac{\phi(F)}{\mu_0(F)} \mu_0(e) \right\}, \qquad \epsilon < 0,$$

is admissible for ϵ small enough, provided that $\phi(e)$ is an arbitrary positive distribution for which $I(\phi)$ exists. And since $I(\delta\mu)$ contains ϵ^2 as a factor, it follows that we must have

$$\int_F V(P) d\delta\mu(e_P) \geq 0.$$

This integral may be rewritten in the form

$$\int_F V(P)d\left\{\phi(e_P) - \frac{\phi(F)}{\mu_0(F)}\mu_0(e_P)\right\} = \int_F \{V(P) - I_0\}d\phi(e_P)$$

since $I_0 = \int_F V(P)d\mu_0(e_P)$ and since

$$\int_F V(P)d\phi(e_P) = I(\mu_0, \phi)$$

converges. It follows that $V(P) \geq I_0$ everywhere on F except possibly on a subset of capacity zero.

In particular, if F happens to have interior points, it has positive capacity (since a uniform distribution on a sphere has evidently finite energy); and if P is such an interior point of F, we shall have $V(P) \geq I_0$. For it is deduced immediately that $V(P)$, being a potential of positive mass, is greater than or equal to its spherical average on a small sphere about P, and the latter is greater than or equal to I_0.

On the other hand, if for some point on F_1, the nucleus for $\mu_0(e)$, we have $V(P) > I_0 + \epsilon$, there will be a neighborhood including a sphere of center P where $V(P) \geq I_0 + \epsilon$ which will contain a certain mass μ_1, and we shall have

$$I(\mu_0) \geq (I_0 + \epsilon)\mu_1 + I_0(1 - \mu_1) > I_0$$

which is impossible. Hence $V(P) \leq I_0$ on F_1.

That the distribution $\mu_0(e)$ is unique is easily shown. In fact, if there were another possible distribution $\nu_0(e)$ with the same minimum energy I_0, of total mass unity but with potential $U(P)$, we should have $I(\mu_0 - \nu_0) \geq 0$. But

$$I(\mu_0 - \nu_0) = I(\mu_0) + I(\nu_0) - 2I(\mu_0, \nu_0)$$

$$= I_0 + I_0 - \int_{F_1} U(P)d\mu_0(e) - \int_{G_1} V(P)d\nu_0(e).$$

On F_1, $U(P) \geq I_0$ except on a set of capacity 0, and similarly for $V_0(P)$ on G_1, where G_1 is the nucleus of $\nu_0(e)$. Hence

$$\int_{F_1} U_0 d\mu_0 + \int_{G_1} V_0 d\nu_0 \geq 2I_0$$

and $I(\mu_0 - \nu_0) \leq 0$. From the two inequalities, $I(\mu_0 - \nu_0) = 0$ and therefore $\mu_0(e) - \nu_0(e) \equiv 0$, which would be a contradiction.

In resumé, we have, then,

$$V(P) \geq I_0 \text{ everywhere on } F \text{ except on a subset of zero capacity,}$$

(5) $$V(P) \leq I_0 \text{ on } F_1, \text{ the nucleus of } F,$$

$$V(P) = I_0 \text{ at interior points of } F_1.$$

Remarks on zero capacity. To say that a set E measurable Borel is of capacity zero if the energy of any distribution of mass on it is infinite, is the same as Frostman's definition, that it is of capacity zero if every closed set contained in E is of capacity zero. In fact, if E will sustain no positive mass of finite energy, the same is true of any closed set contained in E. Suppose conversely, that no closed set F in E will sustain such a mass but that E will itself. We know that for any distribution $\mu(e)$ on E,

$$\mu(E) = \text{u.b. } \mu(E), \; F \text{ closed, contained in } E.$$

Hence there will be some of the mass on an F contained in E. But $I(F) = \infty$, and $I(E) \geq I(F)$, so that $I(E) = \infty$. Hence if no F will sustain a positive mass with finite energy, E also will not.

A similar remark applies to de la Vallée Poussin's definition of zero capacity [35, p. 226]. A set E is of zero capacity if it will sustain no distribution of mass with potential bounded. But if there is a distribution with bounded potential the same one has bounded energy less or equal to the upper bound of the potential times the total mass. And if there is a distribution with bounded energy, there is such a one on some closed set F contained in E, and on F there is one of minimum energy. Hence there is a potential $V(P)$ whose upper bound on the nucleus of F is I_0. That this potential remains bounded by I_0 over all space will be seen from later considerations. Hence if E is of positive capacity by either definition, it is by the other.

These definitions of zero capacity make a convenient extension of the concept of capacity as first defined for a closed set by Wiener [40]. They are equivalent to the definition of *improper set* as given and used by Vasilesco [37], and based on the concept of Wiener.

We now continue the study of $V(P)$ by proving two simple propositions.

LEMMA 1. *Let Q be a point of the frontier of F_1, and $V(P)$ be continuous at Q for P in F_1. Then $V(P)$ is continuous at Q for arbitrary approach of P to Q.*

Consider first the portion $F_{1\rho}$ of F_1 within $\Gamma(\rho, Q) + C(\rho, Q)$ and denote the potential of the mass within this portion by $V(\rho, P)$. Let M be an arbitrary point not on F_1 and let Q be the nearest point of $F_{1\rho}$ to M. Then evidently for P in $F_{1\rho}$,

$$Q_1 P \leq MP + MQ_1 \leq 2MP,$$

$$V(\rho, M) \leq 2V(\rho, Q_1).$$

Next, we notice that $V(\rho, Q)$ approaches zero with ρ since $V(Q)$ is finite [35]. For we can choose the function $h_N(Q, P)$ of §1 so that $\int h_N(Q, P) d\mu_0$ is as little less than $V(\rho, Q)$ as we please, independently of ρ. But this integral tends to zero with ρ, since there can be no point mass at Q.

Finally, we notice that since $V(\rho, P)$ is continuous at Q for P on F_1 ($V(P) - V(\rho, P)$ being evidently continuous at Q), we have, given $\epsilon > 0$,

$$V(\rho, Q) < \epsilon, \qquad V(\rho, Q_1) < \epsilon$$

for ρ small enough, and Q_1 chosen close enough to Q.

But as M tends to Q, also Q_1 approaches Q. Hence eventually we shall have $V(\rho, M) < 3\epsilon$. And since again $V(M) - V(\rho, M)$ is continuous at Q, we shall have

$$\limsup_{M \to Q} V(M) \leq V(Q) + 3\epsilon, \qquad \limsup_{M \to Q} V(M) \leq V(Q).$$

But

$$\liminf_{M \to Q} V(M) \geq V(Q),$$

and $V(M)$ is continuous at Q.

The second proposition is a simple generalization of a condition of Poincaré and Zaremba [30, p. 228; 42, p. 204]. It is due to Raynor [34] and is a special case of a theorem about exceptional points of mass distributions [10, I]. Consider the bounded closed set F, and denote by T the infinite domain exterior to it, the boundary t of it being a portion of the frontier of F.

LEMMA 2. *Let $C(\rho, Q, E)$ be the measure of the portion of the spherical surface which consists of points of E, and require that*

(P) $$\limsup_{\rho \to 0} \frac{C(\rho, Q, F)}{C(\rho, Q, T)} > 0. \text{ Then } V(Q) \geq I_0.$$

Suppose the contrary, that $V(Q) = I_0 - h$. A set of points on $C(\rho, Q)$ of positive superficial measure is evidently of positive capacity, since it will support with finite energy a distribution of mass of uniform density. There is then a spherical neighborhood $\Gamma(\rho_1, Q)$ such that, given $\epsilon > 0$, except for sets of measure zero on any $C(\rho, Q)$,

$$V(P) \geq I_0, \quad P \text{ in } F \cdot \Gamma(\rho_1, Q),$$
$$V(P) \geq I_0 - h - \epsilon, \quad P \text{ in } T \cdot \Gamma(\rho_1, Q),$$

the latter inequality coming from the fact that $V(P)$ is lower semicontinuous. And since $V(Q)$ is greater than or equal to its spherical average on a sphere about Q,

$$C(\rho, Q)V(Q) \geq I_0 C(\rho, Q, F) + (I_0 - h - \epsilon)C(\rho, Q, T), \qquad \rho \leq \rho_1.$$

But $V(Q) = I_0 - h$, therefore

$$0 \geq hC(\rho, Q, F) - \epsilon C(\rho, Q, T),$$
$$\frac{\epsilon}{h} \geq \frac{C(\rho, Q, F)}{C(\rho, Q, T)}.$$

Since ϵ is arbitrary, it follows that the limit, as ρ tends to zero, of the right-hand member is zero, which contradicts the hypothesis.

These lemmas enable us to complete the description of $V(P)$ for sets F which are sufficiently regular. Suppose that at every point of F, and therefore at every point of F_1, the conditon (P) is satisfied. Then we shall have

$$V(P) \equiv I_0, \quad P \text{ on } CT,$$

(6)
$$V(P) < I_0, \quad P \text{ in } T,$$

$$F_1 \equiv t.$$

In fact, $V(Q) = I_0$ by Lemma 2, for every Q in F_1, and is continuous at every such Q by Lemma 1. Since $V(P)$ is harmonic elsewhere it is continuous throughout all space and less than or equal to I_0.

Moreover, every portion of t bears some of the mass μ_0, and every point of t belongs to F_1. Suppose, contrariwise, that a point Q of t were distant η from F_1. Then since $V(P)$ is harmonic at Q and not identically equal to I_0 in T it must be less than I_0 at Q. But the value of the energy could be lowered by transferring some of the mass from F_1 to the neighborhood of Q. It follows that $V(P) \equiv I_0$ for P on t, and therefore at points P of F, which are not also points of t; (since at such points $V(P)$ is harmonic) there is no mass $\mu_0(e)$ in the neighborhood of such points, and F_1 is identical with t.

The conductor potential. The quantity $1/I_0$ is called the *capacity* of the closed set F. The *conductor potential* is the function $v(P) = V(P)/I_0$ and has the value unity on the nucleus of F except possibly on a set of zero capacity. The distribution $\mu_0(e)/I_0$ is called the *conductor distribution*.

If E is not a closed set we follow Frostman in defining its capacity $K(E)$ as the upper bound of the capacities of closed sets contained in E.

5. **The Green's function.** The Kelvin transformation is a device for transforming by inversion. If $u(M)$ is harmonic in a domain T, and T' is the domain obtained as the collection of points inverse to T with respect to a certain sphere of center O and radius a, so that the respective distances from O satisfy the relation $rr' = a^2$, the function

$$w(M') = C \frac{r}{a} u(M) = C \frac{a}{r'} u(M), \qquad C \text{ const.},$$

is harmonic in T'. By means of this device we can obtain the Green's function $g(M, P)$ from the conductor potential $v(P')$, and vice versa.

We suppose the boundary t of T to lie in the finite space and take F as the complement of T. We take M in T as the center of inversion, and a so that $\Gamma(a, M)$ lies with its boundary in T, and let F' be the inversion image of F, $V(P')$ the conductor potential of F'. With $r = MP$, $r' = MP'$, the function

(7)
$$g(M, P) = \frac{r'}{a^2} (1 - v(P')) = \frac{1}{r} (1 - v(P'))$$

will be the Green's function for T with pole at M. In fact, $g(M, P) - 1/r$ is harmonic in T and, if T is an unbounded domain, $g(M, P)$ vanishes as $P \rightarrow \infty$. Also $g(M, P) \rightarrow 0$ if P tends to a point of t such that at the corresponding point of t', $v(P') \rightarrow 1$.

In particular, if F satisfies the condition (P), the same will be true of F' and therefore $g(M, P)$ will take on continuously the value zero as P tends to a point of t.

It will be noticed that the Kelvin transformation and the Green's function afford the simplest method of treating domains whose boundaries t reach into the infinite domain. This will be apparent in the sequel, and it will be unnecessary to develop the details.

II. The generalized dirichlet problem

1. **Regularity of a boundary point.** A point Q of t is said to be regular for T with respect to the conductor potential $v(M)$ if, for M in T, $\lim_{M \rightarrow Q} v(M) = 1$; similarly, regularity with respect to the Green's function lies in the relation $\lim_{P \rightarrow Q} g(M, P) = 0$. It will be shown that these notions are the same.

2. **Conductor potential and Green's function as sequence solution.** Given T, an exterior domain without restriction except that its boundary is a bounded set and its complementary set F is of positive capacity, let T_n be a nested sequence of exterior approximating domains whose complementary domains F_n satisfy the condition (P) at every point; in fact, the boundaries t_n may be taken without loss of generality as analytic. We take $\mu_n(e)$ as the corresponding minimal energy distributions of total mass unity, with potentials $V_n(M)$, and I_n as the corresponding energies.

Since T_{n+1} contains T_n, F_n contains F_{n+1} and F; hence the minimal distribution $\mu_0(e)$ on F is a possible distribution on F_{n+1}, and the minimal distribution μ_{n+1} also lies on F_n; hence

$$(1) \qquad I_n \leq I_{n+1} \leq I(\mu_0), \qquad \lim I_n \leq I(\mu_0).$$

A subsequence of the $\mu_n(e)$ converges weakly to some distribution $\mu(e)$ of total mass 1, which lies only on t, since $\mu_n(e)$ lies only on t_n. Since t is a portion of F, we have

$$I(\mu) \geq I(\mu_0) = I_0.$$

But also, from Fatou's theorem, restricting n to this subsequence,

$$\lim_{n \rightarrow \infty} I_n = \lim_{n \rightarrow \infty} I(\mu_n) \geq I(\mu),$$

and combining these inequalities with (1),

$$\lim_{n \rightarrow \infty} I_n = I(\mu) = I(\mu_0).$$

The minimizing distribution is, however, unique. Hence $\mu(e) \equiv \mu_0(e)$.

Moreover, since $1/MP$ remains continuous for a suitably large n if M does not lie on t,

$$\lim_{n\to\infty} V_n(M) = V(M), \quad M \text{ not on } t,$$

and by Fatou's theorem,

$$\liminf_{n\to\infty} V_n(M) \geq V(M), \quad M \text{ on } t.$$

Since $V_n(M) \leq I_n$ throughout all space, it follows that $V(M) \leq I_0$, and if $V(Q) = I_0$, $\lim V_n(Q) = I$. By the same reasoning as used for smooth boundaries, we see now that any sphere $\Gamma(\rho, Q)$ with center at a point of t, which contains a portion of F of positive capacity, will also contain some of the mass $\mu_0(e)$.

Turning to the conductor potentials themselves, $v_n(M) = V_n(M)/I_n$, and the corresponding capacities $K_n = 1/I_n$, we note that the $v_n(M)$, K_n constitute monotonic decreasing sequences and from this we can deduce immediately the facts about conductor potentials.

The case where $K(F) = 0$ needs special mention. In this case there is no distribution of positive mass for which $K(F)$ is finite or its potential bounded; we shall therefore define the conductor potential as identically zero. With this convention we still have

$$\lim_{n\to\infty} v_n(M) = v(M), \quad M \text{ in } T, \quad \text{and } \lim_{n\to\infty} K_n = K.$$

Suppose in fact, that $\lim_{n\to\infty} v_n(M)$ is not identically zero in T. Then the set function obtained by the weak convergence of $\mu_n(e)/I_n$ will not be identically zero, but since its potential remains bounded, it will be less than or equal to 1. This contradicts the assumption that $K(F) = 0$. Consequently, also $\lim_{n\to\infty} I_n = \infty$ and $\lim_{n\to\infty} K_n = 0$.

Throughout all space, $v(M) \leq 1$. For points M not on t, $\lim_{n\to\infty} v_n(M) = v(M)$ and for points on t, $\lim_{n\to\infty} v_n(M) \geq v(M)$. The capacity K of F is equal to the capacity of t and satisfies the relation $K = \lim_{n\to\infty} K_n$. If $v(Q) = 1$, Q is a regular point of t with respect to the conductor potential; for every point of T, $v(P) < 1$.

We now pass to the Green's functions for T_n, T by the Kelvin transformation, utilizing suitably chosen sets T_n', F_n', T', F'. The domain T may be either an interior or an exterior domain. Since the T_n form a nested sequence of approximating domains, the same is true of the T_n', and since the condition (P) holds at every point of t_n', we have, for T,

$$(2) \qquad \lim_{n\to\infty} g_n(M, P) = g(M, P), \quad M \text{ in } T, \ P \text{ in } T,$$

and if (with M fixed) Q' is a point of t' which is regular for $v(P')$, the corresponding point Q of t is regular for $g(M, P)$, and vice versa.

It is an elementary fact, established by means of Green's lemma, that for regions T with smooth boundaries, the Green's function is symmetrical in M and P. From (2) it follows that the same relation $g(M, P) = g(P, M)$ remains valid whatever the domain T.

If Q is a point of t which is regular with respect to $g(M, P)$, it is also regular with respect to $g(M_1, P)$, where M_1 is any point of T.

Let T_1 with boundary t_1 be the first of our nested sequence, chosen so as to contain both M and M_1 in its interior. Let B_1 be the upper bound of $g(M_1, P)$ and b the lower bound of $g(M, P)$, for P on t, so that, since the $g_n(M_1, P)$ form a monotonic increasing sequence, we have

$$g_n(M_1, P) \leqq g(M_1, P) \leqq (B_1/b)g(M, P), \quad P \text{ on } t_1.$$

But on t_n we have also

$$g_n(M_1, P) \leqq (B_1/b)g(M, P),$$

since the left-hand member is zero and the right-hand member positive. Since both members are continuous in the closed region bounded by t_n, t_1 and harmonic between these boundaries, the same inequality persists for that region. Hence, letting n become infinite, we have for all points P in $T - T_1$,

$$g(M_1, P) \leqq (B_1/b)g(M, P).$$

From this inequality the theorem follows immediately.

If T is an exterior domain and Q is a regular point of t for T with respect to the conductor potential, it is so also with respect to the Green's function, and conversely.

In order to prove this theorem it is necessary merely to repeat the reasoning just given, substituting the function $1 - v(P)$ for $g(M, P)$ in the right-hand members. In order to prove the converse, the functions $1 - v(P)$, $1 - v_n(P)$ are used in the left-hand members.

It is useful, however, to have a direct statement of the relation between Green's function and conductor potential, without the use of inversion. To this effect, let Γ denote a sphere of radius R and boundary C on the surface of which is spread uniformly a mass of total amount R, thus of density $\kappa = (4\pi R)^{-1}$. This is the conductor distribution for C and its potential is given by a function which has the value unity for M in Γ:

$$v_\Gamma(M) = \kappa \int_C d\sigma/MP.$$

Consider now the function

$$u_n(M) = v_\Gamma(M) - \kappa \int_C g_n(M, P)d\sigma,$$

where for convenience we define $g_n(M, P)$ as zero in the complement of T_n.

We have

$$u_n(M) = \kappa \int_C [(1/MP) - g_n(M, P)]d\sigma_P,$$

and this function is harmonic for M in T_n. We take Γ large enough so that Γ contains t in its interior, and therefore also t_n, n large enough. But as M approaches a point Q_n of t_n, $g_n(M, P)$ is bounded and tends to zero; hence $\lim_{M \to Q_n} u_n(M) = v_\Gamma(Q) = 1$. Accordingly $u_n(M)$ is identical with $v_n(M)$, the conductor potential for t_n.

Let now n become infinite. The function $v_n(M)$ tends to the conductor potential $v(M)$ for every M in T, and since $g_n(M, P)$ changes monotonically with n as a function of P the integral relation remains valid, and, for M in T,

$$(3) \qquad v(M) = v_\Gamma(M) - \kappa \int_C g(M, P)d\sigma_P, \qquad\qquad \kappa = (4\pi R)^{-1}.$$

The device used in obtaining (3) enables us to state a slightly more general result:

If Q is a regular point of t for T, with respect to $v(M)$, and $\Gamma = \Gamma(\rho, Q)$, $C = C(\rho, Q)$, $\kappa = (4\pi\rho)^{-1}$, the function

$$(4) \qquad b_\rho(M) = 1 - \left\{ v_\Gamma(M) - \kappa \int_{C \cdot T} g(M, P)d\sigma_P \right\}$$

has the following properties for arbitrary ρ:

$b_\rho(M)$ *is harmonic and* $\geqq 0$ *in* T, *vanishing at* ∞;

$$(4') \qquad 1 > b_\rho(M) > 1 - \frac{\rho}{QM} > 0, \quad M \text{ in } T, \quad QM > \rho;$$

$$\lim_{M \to Q} b_\rho(M) = 0, \quad M \text{ in } T.$$

In fact, as in the proof of (3), we have

$$b_\rho(M) = 1 - \kappa \int_{C \cdot T} [(1/MP) - g(M, P)]d\sigma_P - \kappa \int_{C - C \cdot T} (1/MP)d\sigma_P,$$

which is harmonic in T; also for $QM > \rho$,

$$\rho/QM = v_\Gamma(M) > v_\Gamma(M) - \kappa \int_{C \cdot T} g(M, P)d\sigma > 0,$$

which establishes the second relation of (4'). Moreover, for $QM < \rho$, $v_\Gamma(M) = 1$ and (4) reduces to the equation

$$b_\rho(M) = \kappa \int_{C \cdot T} g(M, P)d\sigma.$$

As $M \to Q$, the function $g(M, P)$ is bounded, since P lies on $C(\rho, Q)$. $g(M, P)$ tends to zero. Moreover, since Q is regular with respect to $v(M)$ and therefore with respect to $g(M, P) = g(P, M)$, as a function of M for any P in T. Thus we have the third of the relations (4').

3. **The Dirichlet problem for smooth boundaries.** Given a bounded closed set t and a function $f(P)$ continuous on t, the function may be extended by definition so as to be continuous throughout all space. This is a well known theorem of Lebesgue [20]. The function may be constructed as the limit of a step-by-step choice of values and, in particular, may be defined so as to vanish outside a sphere which contains t in its interior.

Consider a region T, exterior or interior, which is bounded by a finite number of closed surfaces sufficiently smooth so that the condition (P) is satisfied for the complementary regions F at every point of the boundary t. *Given $f(P)$ continuous on t, there is a unique function which is harmonic in T, vanishes at ∞ if T is unbounded, and takes on continuously the boundary values $f(P)$.*

The uniqueness has been established already, and the proof of the existence may be given briefly by constructing a sequence of harmonic functions. To this end, let $f(P)$ be continuously extended over space, and vanish outside a large sphere. We may write $f(P)$ as the uniform limit of a sequence of functions $F_k(P)$, which likewise vanish outside a sufficiently large sphere, independent of k, and have continuous first, second, and third derivatives over all space; for instance, we may choose $F_k(P)$ as the third iterated average over spheres with center P and radius $1/k$ [2'].

To each $F_k(P)$ we apply the operation expressed in the formula

$$(5) \qquad u_k(M) = F_k(M) + \frac{1}{4\pi} \int_W g(M, P) \nabla^2 F_k(P) dP$$

in which $g(M, P) = 0$ for P in the complement F of T. For points M in T we have

$$\nabla^2 \int_W g(M, P) \nabla^2 F_k(P) = \nabla^2 \int_T (1/MP) \nabla^2 F_k(P) dP = -4\pi \nabla^2 F_k(M);$$

hence for such points $\nabla^2 u_k(M) = 0$, and $u_k(M)$ is harmonic in T. It evidently vanishes continuously at ∞ if T contains the infinite region, since $g(M, P) \to 0$ as $M \to \infty$ when P is at a finite distance from the origin. The integral part of the expression (5) tends to zero, however, as M approaches a point of t; for $g(M, P)$ is dominated by the summable function $(MP)^{-1}$, and vanishes continuously as M approaches a point Q of t for every P except $P = Q$. The function $u_k(M)$ is therefore the desired solution corresponding to $F_k(P)$. Since the $F_k(P)$ are bounded independently of k, the same is true of the $u_k(P)$.

Consider now the family of functions $u_k(M)$. The function $u_{k+p}(M)$

$-u_k(M)$, harmonic in T, is continuous in $T+t$ and takes on its upper and lower bounds only on t; hence with M in T, P on t,

$$\left| u_{k+p}(M) - u_k(M) \right| \leq \text{u.b.} \left| F_{k+p}(P) - F_k(P) \right|.$$

Since the $F_k(P)$ converge uniformly, the same is true of the $u_k(M)$, and we have

$$\lim_{k \to \infty} u_k(M) = u(M),$$

where $u(M)$ is continuous on $T+t$, equals $f(M)$ on t, and vanishes at ∞.

Since the harmonic functions $u_k(M)$ are bounded in their set, they possess, by I, §3, a subsequence which converges on any given closed bounded region in T to a harmonic function. Hence $u(M)$ is harmonic in any closed bounded portion of T. It is therefore harmonic in T. It is thus the desired solution of the Dirichlet problem.

4. **The generalized problem.** Let T be any domain with its boundary t in the finite space, and $f(P)$ be given continuously on t. We may regard $f(P)$ extended as described in §3, continuous over the whole space, and vanishing outside a bounded region. Accordingly, it is natural to consider a sequence of functions $u_n(P)$ corresponding to a sequence of nested domains T_n approximating to T, and taking on as boundary values the extended $f(P)$. In the portion of space common to T and any given sphere $\Gamma(R, Q)$, arbitrarily large, these functions are bounded. Hence, by I, §3, a subsequence $u_n^*(P)$ converges within that region to a harmonic function $u(P)$.

Let H be the upper bound of $\left| f(P) \right|$, and consider for a moment the case where T is an exterior domain. On the spherical surface $C(R_0, O)$, R being chosen large enough so that t lies in $\Gamma(R_0, O)$, we have $\left| u_n(P) \right| \leq H$. Since the $u_n(P)$ vanish at ∞, they must all satisfy the relation

$$- H \frac{R}{r} \leq u_n(P) \leq H \frac{R}{r}, \quad \text{for} \quad OP = r \geq R,$$

for otherwise $u_n(P) - H(R/r)$ would have a positive maximum, or $u_n(P) + H(R/r)$ a negative minimum, at a point of T. We take then a sequence of values $R_0 < R_1 < R_2 < \cdots$, tending to ∞. Corresponding to each $\Gamma(R_i, O)$ there is a sub-sequence of the $u_n^*(P)$ which converges to a harmonic function, and since within $T \cdot \Gamma(R, O)$ these functions coincide with $u(P)$, they provide a unique extension of $u(P)$ as a function harmonic throughout T. But also, we have

$$- H \frac{R}{r} \leq u(P) \leq H \frac{R}{r}$$

so that $u(P)$ vanishes at ∞.

It has been shown [40] that the function $u(P)$ is uniquely defined by the values given to $f(P)$ on t alone, independently of the choice of the continuous extension of $f(P)$ in W and of the choice of nested domains T_n.

It is called the *sequence solution* for T, belonging to boundary values $f(P)$. It is unnecessary to consider the uniqueness property at this point, however, since it results incidentally from the other theorems that must be given.

A point Q of t will be said to be *regular* for T if $u(P)$ takes on the boundary value $f(Q)$ as P approaches Q from T, whatever may be the function $f(P)$, continuous on t. It will be proved that if Q is regular for T with respect to the conductor potential $v(P)$ or the Green's function, it is regular in this more general sense. All points of t, however, are not necessarily regular. In particular, Lebesgue has shown that if t consists in part of a conical spine, projecting into an exterior domain T with vertex sufficiently sharp, the conductor potential does not tend to the value unity as P in T approaches the vertex of the spine along its axis. We have seen that the conductor potential is itself a sequence solution, corresponding to boundary values $f(P) = 1$.

5. **Barriers.** We say that a function $b(M, Q)$ is a barrier [21; 17, p. 609] for the domain T at a point Q of t if there is a spherical neighborhood Ω with center Q in which the following conditions hold:

(i) The function $b(M, Q)$ is continuous for M in $T \cdot \Omega$ and approaches zero as M approaches Q.

(ii) The function $b(M, Q)$ is superharmonic† (or harmonic) in $T \cdot \Omega$.

(iii) Outside of any sphere $\Gamma(\rho, Q)$, it has in $T \cdot \Omega$ a positive lower bound. The definition as given here has been slightly modified from the usual one so as to make the existence of a barrier obviously a local property. But this definition is entirely equivalent to the customary one in which T is substituted for $\Omega \cdot T$, for the function which is everywhere the lesser of two superharmonic functions is superharmonic, and the properties of $b(Q, M)$ may be extended to the whole of T merely by defining it within Ω as the lesser of the two functions $b(Q, M)$ and b, where b is the lower bound of $b(Q, M)$ on the boundary of Ω, and as the radius of Ω times b/QM in the rest of T.

The following two theorems are essentially theorems of Vasilesco [37, p. 94] and Bouligand [1], respectively. Historically the first is a corollary of the second.

If T is an exterior domain and the point Q is regular for T with respect to the conductor potential, there exists a barrier $b(Q, M)$.

The proof of this proposition is immediate by means of equations (4), (4'). Let $\rho_1, \rho_2, \cdots$ be a monotonic sequence of positive values of ρ tending to zero, and $r_1, r_2, \cdots$ a second sequence of positive values such that

---

† A continuous function $U(P)$ is superharmonic in a domain T if in every closed region D contained in T we have $U(P) \geq u(P)$, where $u(P)$ is harmonic in the interior of D, continuous in D, and less than or equal to $U(P)$ on the boundary of D.

$r_1+r_2+\cdots$ is convergent. Writing $b_k(M)$ for the function defined in (4) with $\rho=\rho_k$, we have the barrier

$$(6) \qquad\qquad b(Q, M) = \sum_1^\infty r_k b_k(M).$$

In fact, the series in (6) is uniformly convergent, has a value which is greater than $r_k(1-\rho_k/QM)$ for M in T with $QM>\rho_k$, and is continuous and harmonic in T. Also, on account of the uniform convergence, $b(Q, M)\to 0$ as M in T tends to Q.

A function which behaves like the conductor potential at a point Q where it approaches unity may be called a *weak barrier*. In the definition of barrier the requirement (iii), is replaced by the less restrictive condition that the function be positive in T. The gist of the above theorem is that the existence of a weak barrer implies the existence of a barrier in the customary sense.

The following is a corollary of the above statement:

If T is an exterior or interior domain and Q is a regular point for T with respect to the Green's function, there exists a barrier $b(Q, M)$.

In fact, a barrier is transformed into a barrier by the Kelvin transformation, so that if T is an interior domain, the existence of a barrier at the corresponding point of the boundary of the exterior domain T' insures its existence at Q for T. If T is itself an exterior domain, the two kinds of regularity are, as we have seen, the same.

Consider now the function $G(P_0, M)=(1/r)-g(P_0, M)$, with $r=P_0M$, P_0 in T. This is a sequence solution for boundary values $1/r$. We have just proved that if $\lim_{M\to Q} G(P_0, M)=1/P_0Q$, there exists $b(Q, M)$. Consequently if Q is regular for T, there exists a barrier at Q.

We prove next the following theorem:

If there is a barrier $b(Q, M)$, the point Q is regular for T.

The proof is direct. Without loss of generality we may assume $f(Q)=0$. We make an extension of $f(P)$ as before and consider a sequence $u_n(P)$, corresponding to a sequence of nested domains approximating to T. For convenience we define $u_n(P)$ as $f(P)$ outside T_n. Let B be the upper bound of $|f(P)|$, and thus of all the $|u_n(P)|$, and let b be the lower bound of $b(Q, M)$ on the portion of spherical surface $T\cdot C(\rho, Q)$.

Given $\epsilon>0$, take ρ small enough so that $|f(P)|<\epsilon$ for P in $\Gamma(\rho, Q)$ and consider the function

$$h(M) = \epsilon + (B/b)b(Q, M).$$

For M in $T\cdot\Gamma(\rho, Q)$ we have, for all n,

$$- h(M) \leqq u_n(M) \leqq h(M).$$

In fact, $\left| u_n(M) \right| < \epsilon$ in $(T - T_n) \cdot \Gamma(\rho, Q)$ and in particular on $t_n \cdot \Gamma(\rho, Q)$, since for such points $u_n(M) = f(M)$. Also, on $(T_n + t_n) \cdot C(\rho, Q)$ we have $\left| u_n(M) \right| \leqq (B/b) b(Q, M)$. Since the above inequality holds on the boundaries $t_n \cdot \Gamma(\rho, Q)$ and $(T_n + t_n) \cdot C(\rho, Q)$ it holds throughout every domain bounded by them, and therefore throughout $T_n \cdot \Gamma(\rho, Q)$; for $u_n(M)$ and $-u_n(M)$ are in such domains harmonic where $b(Q, M)$ is harmonic or superharmonic. The inequality therefore holds for all M in $T \cdot \Gamma(\rho, Q)$.

We may now let $n \to \infty$, so that a subsequence of the $u_n(M)$ has the limit $u(M)$. Hence also,

$$\left| u(M) \right| \leqq h(M), \quad M \text{ in } T \cdot \Gamma(\rho, Q),$$

$$\limsup_{M \to Q} \left| u(M) \right| \leqq \epsilon,$$

and since ϵ is arbitrary,

$$\lim_{M \to Q} u(M) = 0,$$

which was to be proved.

It is thus proved that *a necessary and sufficient condition that a sequence solution should approach $f(Q)$, as M approaches Q from T, for an arbitrarily given continuous $f(P)$ on t, is that a barrier $b(M, Q)$ exists.*

As a final theorem in this section, we now prove the following statement:

The set of points of t at which a barrier for T fails to exist must be of capacity zero.

Suppose the contrary, that the set E of the theorem is of positive capacity. It will contain a closed subset F of positive capacity, by definition. There will then be a point Q of F such that the subset $F \cdot \{ \Gamma(\rho, Q) + C(\rho, Q) \}$ will be of positive capacity for arbitrary ρ. Otherwise, by the Heine-Borel theorem, the set F could be covered by a finite number of spheres such that the portion of F in each sphere would be of zero capacity. But this is impossible since a portion of the conductor distribution on F must lie in one or more of these spheres. We choose ρ small enough so that a portion of T lies outside $\rho(\rho, Q)$, and denote by T' the domain exterior to the set $F \cdot \{ \Gamma(\rho, Q) + C(\rho, Q) \}$, denoting this set itself by t'. It is evident that T' contains T.

The conductor potential of t' has, however, the value 1 except possibly on a subset of zero capacity, so that a barrier for T' exists except at these points of t. But since T' contains T, these are by definition barriers for T. Our hypothesis that there were no barriers for T at points of E is thus contradicted.

This theorem is essentially Kellogg's lemma, which he made a crucial point of the theory of the Dirichlet problem [16, p. 406; 18, p. 337; 8; 9].

6. **The uniqueness theorem and the solution of the problem.** The central theorem is the theorem of Kellogg [18, p. 335]:

If K is the upper bound of a function $U(M)$ in a bounded domain, in which $U(M)$ is bounded and harmonic, the set E of boundary points at which the superior limit of $U(M)$ is greater than or equal to $K - \epsilon$, for any $\epsilon > 0$, has positive capacity.

The set E clearly is closed. Suppose that for some $\epsilon > 0$ it has zero capacity. Then its exterior domain T' contains T, for if any bounded domain had a boundary lying entirely in E, E would be of positive capacity. Let $\{T_n'\}$ constitute a set of nested domains approximating to T' with boundaries everywhere satisfying condition (P), and denote by $v_n'(M)$ the corresponding conductor potentials, which are defined throughout all space and equal to unity on the complement of T_n'. In the domains constituting $T \cdot T_n'$, we have

$$U(M) \leq K - \epsilon + \epsilon v_n'(M),$$

for this relation holds on the boundary of each such domain. Accordingly, letting n become infinite,

$$U(M) \leq K - \epsilon + \epsilon v'(M), \quad M \text{ in } T,$$

where $v'(M)$ is the conductor potential of E.

But if E is of capacity zero, we have $v'(M) \equiv 0$ by §2, and $U(M) \leq K - \epsilon$ in T. This is impossible since K is the upper bound of $U(M)$ in T. Hence the capacity of E is positive.

If T is an exterior domain and $U(M)$ vanishes at ∞, it is deduced as a corollary that the theorem still applies if K is a positive upper bound of $U(M)$, for we may consider $U(M)$ within $T \cdot \Gamma$ where Γ is a sphere chosen large enough so that $U(M) < K$ on its surface.

From this is deduced immediately the following statement:

If $U(M)$ is bounded and harmonic in T (vanishing at ∞ if T is an exterior domain) and has the limit 0 as M approaches a boundary point Q, except for points Q which constitute a set of capacity zero, then $U(M) \equiv 0$.

For if $U(M) \not\equiv 0$, either $U(M)$ or $-U(M)$ has a positive upper bound in T.

We have, in conclusion, the following summary of results:

The sequence solution $u(M)$, already defined, takes on continuously the given continuously assigned boundary values $f(P)$ at all points of t where there is a barrier for T, and that is at all points except possibly those of a set of capacity zero. There cannot be two different functions, harmonic in T, and bounded (vanishing at ∞ if T is an exterior domain) which take on the same continuously assigned boundary values except on a set of capacity zero. The *sequence solution is independent of the choice of the approximating sequence* $\{T_n\}$ *and of the manner of continuous extension of* $f(P)$.

III. The representation of harmonic functions

1. Harmonic functions discontinuous on the boundary. The function

$$\frac{\partial}{\partial \theta} \frac{1 - r^2}{1 + r^2 - 2r \cos \theta} \equiv \frac{2r(1 - r^2) \sin \theta}{(1 + r^2 - 2r \cos \theta)^2},$$

which is harmonic within the unit circle, nevertheless cannot be written as the difference of two functions which are positive and harmonic within the unit circle; it also has the property that it takes on continuously the boundary value zero along every radial direction. In the sphere, A. J. Maria has given an example of a function which is harmonic and vanishes as it approaches the boundary along any direction not tangent to it [24]. Thus arises the question of the classification of harmonic functions and the specification of appropriate boundary conditions which determine them uniquely.

In this Part III, we discuss the representation of positive harmonic functions in spatial domains. The treatment will be based on memoirs by F. W. Perkins, who considered the Dirichlet problem with continuously assigned values on boundary elements for boundaries where a point needs to be counted multiply [27], by A. J. Maria and R. S. Martin who discuss the representation of positive harmonic functions within domains for which the boundary points count simply and satisfy certain appropriate conditions [25], and by J. W. Green who combines the methods of both papers with the aid of a representation in a more abstract space with a consequent increase in the generality of results [15]. These papers afford a treatment in three dimensions of the problems considered by the author in two dimensions [7] who bases his work on the prime-end theory and conformal mapping of Carathéodory [3] and the treatment of Poisson's integral in terms of Lebesgue theory of integration by Fatou [12]. Fatou and Zaremba [42] may properly be regarded as having initiated the study of discontinuous problems. Wiener [39] and the present author [6] discuss them as functionals of their boundary values. The sweeping out method of Poincaré [30] leads to them naturally.

2. Induction of unit mass. Following Poincaré, but with more general domains, de la Vallée Poussin [35, p. 205] makes the sweeping out of unit mass a resolvent for the Dirichlet problem, thus obtaining a generalization of the mass distribution the density of which for smooth boundaries is the normal derivative of the Green's function. Following Frostman he again analyzes the question as a problem of minimum energy [36, p. 30; 11, p. 497].

We consider first a bounded region T. We fix unit negative mass at a point M of T. In order to avoid the complication of an unbounded set we take F as the complement of T within a large closed sphere $\Gamma+C$, with boundary C. On F let there be distributed a mass $m(e)$ of total value $+1$ in such a way as to make the energy a minimum, disregarding the energy of the point charge itself, which is, of course, infinite. In other words, we minimize the quantity

$$(1) \qquad I_M = \int_F \int_F \frac{dm(e_Q)dm(e_P)}{QP} - 2\int_F \frac{dm(e_P)}{MP}.$$

With the same considerations as those advanced for the conductor potential it becomes clear that there exists a unique distribution on F which makes I_M a minimum; the corresponding potential, which is given by the formula

$$(2) \qquad V(M, P) = -\frac{1}{MP} + \int_F \frac{dm(e_Q, M)}{QP},$$

in which $m(e)$ is denoted by $m(e, M)$, has a constant value C_M on the nucleus F_1 of F except at a possible subset of capacity zero, where it is less than C_M. On the rest of F, except for a possible set of capacity 0 it is greater than or equal to C_M.

Suppose now, as a particular case, that the points of F on t satisfy the condition (P). Then all the points of F satisfy the condition, and $V(M, P)$ as a function of P is continuous on F_1 with respect to F_1. In the same way as for the conductor potential, it is deduced that $V(M, P)$ is continuous in the whole space W and therefore takes on its maximum value C_M on F_1. This value must be zero, for otherwise, since $V(M, P)$ vanishes at ∞, the total algebraic mass within Γ could not be zero. The potential $V(M, P)$ is therefore identically zero outside t, and no portion of t is without mass. We note that we have the relation

$$(2') \qquad g(M, P) = -V(M, P),$$

for the Green's function and $-V(M, P)$ are harmonic in T except for the term $1/MP$, and both vanish continuously on t. We have $I_M < 0$.

As for the mass function $m(e, M)$ itself, we find that it is a harmonic function of M within T, assuming still that t satisfies the condition (P).

In fact, if $-\nu(e)$ is any distribution of negative mass, of total amount -1, on a closed set F' interior to T, and $m(e)$ the induced distribution of positive mass of total value $+1$ on F, we find again that for the corresponding minimizing energy the potential

$$V(P) = -\int_{F'} \frac{1}{PM} d\nu(e_M) + \int_\Gamma \frac{dm(e_Q)}{QP}$$

has the constant value $C=0$ on t and remains 0 outside t. Since this condition is satisfied by writing

$$(3) \qquad m(e) = \int_{F'} m(e, M) d\nu(e_M),$$

and the minimizing distribution is unique, we know that (3) is valid.

Take now F' as $C(\rho, M')$ where M' is an arbitrary point of T and ρ is less than the distance of M' from t, and write

$$\nu(e) = (1/4\pi\rho^2) \int_{C(\rho,M')\cdot e} 1dM.$$

The potential of this distribution at a point P outside $C(\rho, M')$ is $1/M'P$, so that the induced distribution on t is $m(e, M')$, as if the mass $-\nu(e)$ were all concentrated at M'. Hence from (3),

$$m(e, M') = \int_{C(\rho,M')} \frac{m(e, M)}{4\pi\rho^2} dM.$$

But the last equation is a statement that $m(e, M')$ is its own spherical surface average, and $m(e, M)$ is accordingly harmonic in T.

A final result we can obtain by specializing still further the nature of t. Later, by means of the sequence method the result can be made to have more general significance. Let us assume that the boundary of t satisfies a condition which we shall call (P_0).

(P_0) At each point of t a sphere can be drawn which passes through that point and contains in its interior no point of T or on its boundary no other point of t.

The following is a special instance of de la Vallée Poussin's theorem [35, p. 203].

Let T be a bounded domain which satisfies the condition (P_0); let Q be a point of t and t_ρ the portion of t which is contained in $\Gamma(\rho, Q)$. Then, for arbitrary ρ, $m(t_\rho, M) \to 1$ as $M \to Q$ from T.

In order to prove this statement, let P' be the center and r the radius of the sphere of condition (P_0) at Q. Since the potential $V(M, P)$ is identically zero for P not in T, we have

$$\int_{t_\rho} \frac{dm(e_P, M)}{PP'} + \int_{t-t_\rho} \frac{dm(e_P, M)}{PP'} = \frac{1}{MP'}.$$

But since for P on t_ρ, $PP' \geq r$ and on $t-t_\rho$, $PP' \geq r+\delta$, where δ depends on ρ and is positive, we have

$$\frac{m(t_p, M)}{r} + \frac{m(t - t_p, M)}{r + \delta} \geq \frac{1}{MP},$$

and letting M approach Q as a limit

$$\frac{1}{r} \lim_{M \to Q} m(t_p, M) + \frac{1}{r + \delta} \lim_{M \to Q} [1 - m(t_p, M)] \geq \frac{1}{r} \cdot$$

But this is impossible unless $\lim_{M \to Q} m(t_p, M) = 1$.

This theorem provides an immediate representation of the solution of the Dirichlet problem, for the function

(4) $$u(M) = \int_t f(P)dm(e_P, M),$$

with $f(P)$ given as continuous on t, is harmonic in T and takes on continuously the values $f(Q)$ as M approaches Q on t. In fact,

$$u(M) = f(Q)m(t, M) + \int_t [f(P) - f(Q)]dm(e_P, M),$$

and if ρ is chosen small enough so that $|f(P) - f(Q)| < \epsilon$ for P in t_p,

$$\left| \int_{t_p} [f(P) - f(Q)]dm(e_P, M) \right| < \epsilon$$

while the rest of the integral, over $t - t_p$, approaches zero as M approaches Q. Hence

$$\lim_{M \to Q} |u(M) - f(Q)| < \epsilon.$$

By considering a sequence of nested approximating domains $\{T_n\}$ to a general bounded domain T, the domains T_n satisfying the condition (P_0) the following results may be obtained, exactly as in the analysis of II, §2'

The induced distribution of unit mass $m(e, M)$ for a bounded domain T lies entirely on t and is unique. Any sphere $\Gamma(\rho, Q)$ with center at a point of t which contains a portion of F of positive capacity will contain a portion of the mass. The potential $V(M, P)$ of unit negative mass at M and the induced mass is zero on t except on a possible set of capacity 0 where it is negative; it is negative except on t.

Consider any cube w enclosing points of t such that none of the mass $m(e, M)$ lies on any of its faces. By the weak convergence there is a sub-sequence $\{n^*\}$ of the sequence $\{n\}$ such that the corresponding $m_n(w, M)$ converge to $m(w, M)$. Since the harmonic functions $m_n(w, M)$ are bounded, it follows that $m(w, M)$ is harmonic. This fact being true for "almost all" cubes, it follows that $m(E, M)$ is harmonic for any open set, and consequently for any set measurable Borel. But $m(E, M) = m(E \cdot t, M)$ since all the mass lies on t.

Making use of (4) for the boundaries t_n, it follows from the weak convergence, since t_n may be replaced by W, that (4) still applies where $u(M)$ denotes the sequence solution for T. This is de la Vallée Poussin's formula [35, p. 205]. The uniqueness of the function $m(e, M)$ for general boundaries was established however by general considerations on the sweeping out process [10, II].

The set function $m(e, M)$ is harmonic and equation (4) represents the sequence solution of the generalized Dirichlet problem. A necessary and sufficient condition that Q be a regular point of t for T is that

$$\text{(5)} \qquad\qquad \lim_{M \to Q} m(e, M) = 1,$$

where $e = t \cdot \Gamma(\rho, Q)$, for all ρ. The Green's function is still given by $(2')$.

So far, T has been considered as a bounded domain. If T is an exterior domain, its boundary t may be enclosed within a sphere $\Gamma(R, O)$ and R allowed to become infinite so that $T \cdot \Gamma(R, O)$ has T as a limit. The induction problem is solved for the region $T \cdot \Gamma(R, O)$ and the weak convergence, as R tends to infinity, gives the solution for T, the total mass on t being the limiting value of the portion of the mass unity which lies on t for R finite. De la Vallée Poussin [35, p. 208] shows that this amount $m(t, M)$ is less than unity. But otherwise the situation is unchanged and the proofs of equations (4) and (5), with trivial modifications, remain valid.

3. **Boundaries with multiple points. The generalized space.** We shall restrict ourselves for convenience to a bounded domain T. A boundary element γ for T is defined by Perkins to be a sequence of partial domains of T: $T_1, T_2, \cdots$ with boundaries $t_1, t_2, \cdots$ such that the following hold:

(i) T_n contains T_{n+1} and the diameter of T_n tends to 0 with $1/n$.

(ii) Each t_n contains at least one point of t.

(iii) $t_{n+1} - t \cdot t_{n+1}$ is at a positive distance from $t_n - t \cdot t_n$.

The set $t_n - t \cdot t_n$ is the portion of t_n which lies in T and with its limit points constitutes what is called the *auxiliary* boundary of T. The requirement (iii) provides that the auxiliary boundaries have no points in common.

Two boundary elements are said to be identical if each T_n of one contains all the partial domains of the other of index sufficiently great; if the condition holds one way, it holds the other. A partial domain is said to contain γ if it contains some T_n of the sequence. There is one and only one point P of t which is common to all the t_n of a boundary element γ, so that γ may be regarded as lying on P. But evidently, as in the simple case of a domain which is bounded partially by both sides of the same piece of surface, more than one γ may lie on the same P. In fact, even in a plane domain, a boundary point may be composed of a non-denumerable infinity of boundary elements [3, p. 363], and if the point is not accessible from the domain will not correspond to any boundary elements.

In particular, "pseudo-spherical" nested domains may be used for the definition of boundary elements, a pseudo-spherical domain being one of the above type whose auxiliary boundary is a portion of a sphere, the center being at a given point P—a statement which is evident from the definition of identical boundary elements. A sequence of such domains defining γ may be denoted by $\{\mathfrak{S}(\gamma, \rho_i)\}$ where γ lies on the center P.

The method of Green is to set up a new space $\mathfrak{T}$ composed of boundary elements and points of T and thus to obtain briefly and extend the results already obtained. The metric is established by defining distance in the following way.

Let π_1, π_2 be two elements of $\mathfrak{T}$ (that is, points or boundary elements of T). Let ρ_1 be the lower bound of ρ such that $\mathfrak{S}(\pi_1, \rho)$ contains π_2 and ρ_2 the lower bound of ρ such that $\mathfrak{S}(\pi_2, \rho)$ contains π_1. The distance (π_1, π_2) is defined by the formula

$$(\pi_1, \pi_2) = \tfrac{1}{2}(\rho_1 + \rho_2).$$

The distance between two elements of $\mathfrak{T}$ cannot be more than $2d$, where d is the diameter of T. In particular, in the above definition, $\rho_1 \leq 2\rho_2$ and $\rho_2 \leq 2\rho_1$ and (π_1, π_2) vanishes only when π_1, π_2 are the same point or boundary element in the sense defined by Perkins. Moreover if π_1, π_2, π_3 are three elements of $\mathfrak{T}$, the triangular inequality $(\pi_1, \pi_3) \leq (\pi_1, \pi_2) + (\pi_2, \pi_3)$ can be verified. If π_1 is not a boundary element but a point of T, we denote by $\mathfrak{S}(\pi_1, \rho)$ the "pseudo-spherical" or spherical domain whose auxiliary boundary consists only of points of the sphere. If $\mathfrak{S}(\pi_1, \rho')$ contains π_2 and $\mathfrak{S}(\pi_2, \rho'')$ contains π_3, then $\mathfrak{S}(\pi_1, \rho'+\rho'')$ contains $\mathfrak{S}(\pi_2, \rho'')$ and therefore π_3. From this the inequality is easily derived.

The space $\mathfrak{T}$ is complete, that is, if the sequence $\{\pi_n\}$ is convergent there is an element π such that $\lim_{n \to \infty} (\pi, \pi_n) = 0$. If some or all of these π_n are not points of T, we may replace them by sufficiently nearby points of T, and if these latter have a limit element π, the former will have the same limit element on account of the triangular inequality. Hence we may suppose that the π_n are points P_n of T and these have a limit point P in T or on t. It is only if P is on t that there is something to prove.

We form a subsequence of the $\{\pi_n\}$. Given $\rho_1 > 0$ we take n_1 so that $(\pi_{n_1}, \pi_{n_1+p}) < \rho_1/2$ for all p. Then $\mathfrak{S}(\pi_{n_1}, \rho_1)$ contains π_{n_1+p} and has for part of its boundary a portion of t, since $P_{n_1}P_{n_1+p} < \rho_1/2$ and $P_{n_1}P \leq \rho_1/2$. Hence $\mathfrak{S}(\pi_{n_1}, \rho_1)$ may be taken as a domain T_1. We take now $\rho_2 < \rho_1/4$ and choose $n_2 > n_1$ so that $(\pi_{n_2}, \pi_{n_2+p}) < \rho_2/2$. The domain $\mathfrak{S}(\pi_{n_2}, \rho_2)$ may then be taken as T_2, for it is contained in T_1 and the two auxiliary boundaries, being parts of the respective spherical surfaces, have no points in common. Proceeding in this way we obtain a sequence of domains T_i which define a boundary element γ. The corresponding element π of $\mathfrak{T}$ satisfies the relation $(\pi, \pi_{n_i}) \leq \rho_i$. Hence the π_{n_i} converge to π. By the triangular inequality, the π_n therefore converge to π.

The space $\mathfrak{T}$ is thus complete and bounded. It is evidently non-linear, and in general it is not compact—for instance, if there is a point of t which is not accessible from T, an infinite sequence of points of T which have this point only as limit point will not converge in $\mathfrak{T}$. Accordingly, for the sake of obtaining systematic results, $\mathfrak{T}$ will in the main be made compact as a restriction on the character of t. The following condition (A) is a necessary and sufficient condition for compactness [15, §2.2]:

(A) Let P be any point of t, and consider the set $T \cdot \Gamma(\rho, P)$. There exists $\delta > 0$ (depending on P and ρ) such that of the finitely or denumerably infinitely many domains whose sum is $T \cdot \Gamma(\rho, P)$ all but a finite number are at distances greater than or equal to δ from P.

The simplification of the compact spaces lies in the fact that simple covering theorems may be employed. Thus it may be proved in the usual way that a function which is continuous on a closed set contained in $\mathfrak{T}$ is uniformly continuous.

We assume then condition (A). The Riemann-Stieltjes integral

$$\int_{\mathfrak{F}} \phi(\pi) df(e_\pi)$$

extended over a closed set $\mathfrak{F}$ of $\mathfrak{T}$ may be defined in the customary manner, $\phi(\pi)$ being a continuous function of elements, and $f(e)$ being defined and completely additive on a closed family of subsets of $\mathfrak{F}$, that is, one containing sums, products and differences, finite or denumerably infinite, of the members of the family, and containing finite or denumerably infinite collections of non-overlapping sets of the family, of diameter arbitrarily and uniformly small, whose sum is $\mathfrak{F}$.

Types of sets of this last category may for instance be constructed by imposing on the euclidean space containing T a lattice whose cells have diameter less than δ, so that T is divided by the planes of the lattice and its own boundary into at most denumerably many domains. If these domains are numbered in a countable order, all the boundary elements of the first domain may be assigned to the first domain to form the first set, all the boundary elements of the second domain, not previously assigned, may be assigned to the second set, and so on. The diameter in $\mathfrak{T}$ of any of these sets of elements of $\mathfrak{T}$ is not greater than 2δ.

The usual properties of the Stieltjes integral follow immediately from the definition. Moreover, the property of weak convergence of a sequence of set functions may be developed with reference to this integral. Let $\{f_n(e)\}$ represent a sequence of completely additive positive functions of sets of elements e of $\mathfrak{T}$, bounded in their set. There exists a function $f(e)$ of the same character and a sub-sequence $\{f_n^*(e)\}$ such that

$$\lim_{n \to \infty} \int_{\mathfrak{F}} \phi(\pi)df_n^*(e_\pi) = \int_{\mathfrak{F}} \phi(\pi)df(e_\pi)$$

for every function $\phi(\pi)$ continuous on $\mathfrak{F}$; in particular $\mathfrak{F}$ may be identical with $\mathfrak{T}$.

A partial extension of weak convergence may be made to domains $\mathfrak{T}$ which do not satisfy the condition of compactness. Assume that there exists a sequence of sets Ω_1, Ω_2, $\cdots$ of elements of $\mathfrak{T}$, where each set contains the next, and a monotone sequence $\{\epsilon_i\}$ of positive numbers approaching 0, such that (a) $\mathfrak{T} - \Omega_i$ is a complete compact space; (b) $f_n(\Omega_i)$ $< \epsilon_i$ for $n \geq n_0 = n_0(i)$, where the $f_n(e)$ are bounded in the set and ≥ 0. Then there exists a function $f(e)$ such that $f(e) = f(e \cdot [\mathfrak{T} - \prod \Omega_i])$ and such that, for a sub-sequence,

$$(6) \qquad \int_{\mathfrak{T}} \phi(\pi)df(e) = \lim_{n \to \infty} \int_{\mathfrak{T}} \phi(\pi)df_n^*(e)$$

where $\phi(\pi)$ is continuous on $\mathfrak{T}$.

4. **Application to Dirichlet problem.** Given $\mathfrak{T}$ compact and a function $f(\gamma) = f(\pi)$ continuous as a function of elements π on the boundary τ of $\mathfrak{T}$. There cannot be more than one function bounded and harmonic in $\mathfrak{T}$ which takes on continuously (in terms of the $\mathfrak{T}$ metric) the boundary values $f(\pi)$ at elements π of τ, even with the exception of elements which lie on a set of points of t of zero capacity. For Kellogg's uniqueness theorem deals with methods of approach to the boundary.

On the other hand, if a barrier for T exists at a point Q of t, the function $f(\pi)$ being continuously extended throughout T, it is but a repetition of the previous proof to show that the sequence solution $u(M) = u(\pi)$ takes on continuously the value $f(\pi')$ as $\pi \to \pi'$ from T, where π' is any of the boundary elements at Q. A barrier exists however, as we have already seen, except at points of t which form a set of zero capacity. Hence there is a unique solution of this extended Dirichlet problem. This, except for the application of Kellogg's lemma and the use of the space $\mathfrak{T}$, is essentially Perkin's theorem.

The uniquely determined solution is represented by means of the unit mass distribution induced on the elements of τ. In fact, for the domains of a nested sequence T, whose boundary points are not multiple—that is, each one counts as a single boundary element,—the representation already found may be used and transferred to the abstract space $\mathfrak{T}$:

$$u(M) = \int_{t_n} u(P)dm_n(e_P, M) = \int_{\mathfrak{T}} u(\pi)dm_n(e_\pi, \mathfrak{M}) = u(\mathfrak{M}).$$

But now, in terms of the weak convergence in the space $\mathfrak{T}$, letting $n \to \infty$,

$$(7) \qquad\qquad u(M) = \int_{\mathfrak{T}} f(\pi) dm(e_\pi, \mathfrak{M}).$$

If the boundary elements are all regular the procedure is direct. If some of them are irregular, all the boundary elements corresponding to the exceptional set of zero capacity may be omitted from $\mathfrak{T}$, and the extension of the weak convergence method is still applicable. Certain domains, where boundary elements fail to exist on sets of restricted character, due, say, to the presence of inaccessible points, may also be brought under this method and yield again equation (7) [15, §8.2].

5. **Extension to representation of positive harmonic functions.** For functions which do not remain bounded, a representation in terms of an additive set function is still possible provided the function is the difference of two positive harmonic functions in T. If the boundary t of the region consists of a finite number of surfaces, each with uniformly bounded curvatures, the function within T is represented by a potential of a double layer on t. To the representation corresponds also a uniquely solvable extension of the Dirichlet problem: to each function $u(M)$ corresponds a unique completely additive function of point sets $F(e)$ on t which is the limit of the indefinite surface integral of the function over portions of surfaces in T neighboring t, and conversely. Boundary values of $u(M)$, which are given by the Lebesgue derivative of $F(e)$, exist almost everywhere on t for directions of approach that keep away from tangency to the boundary, but $u(M)$ is not determined by them [14]. The representation of the function has the form

$$(8) \qquad\qquad u(M) = \int_t f(M, P) dF(e).$$

In the problem for plane domains, the method of conformal transformation is available, so that when the above representation is expressed in a form which is invariant of conformal transformation, that is, in terms of the integral of the normal derivative of the Green's function, it is possible to extend the representation without much difficulty to domains of a considerable degree of generality, but of finite connectivity.

Maria and Martin extended the representation (8) to a very general class of boundaries in an arbitrary number of dimensions, without reference to the connectivity of the domain, or, of course, to conformal transformation. The function $f(M, P)$, which in (8) is the ratio of normal derivatives of the Green's functions with variable pole M and fixed pole O, becomes the Daniell derivative of one set function with respect to another, corresponding to the fact that in two dimensions it is the ratio $dh(M, P)/dh(O, P)$ where $h(M, P)$ is the function conjugate to

$g(M, P)$. The boundary, however, has no irregular points or multiple points.

A slight extension of the general character of the domain and the elimination of the restriction on irregular or multiple boundary points is made by Green [15, §§9–11]. The conditions may be stated as follows:

(A) The corresponding $\mathfrak{T}$ is compact.

(B) Every boundary element of T satisfies a condition of Picard: If $u(P)$, $v(P)$ are positive harmonic functions in T which are bounded except in $\mathfrak{S}(\gamma, \rho)$ for all $\rho > 0$ and vanish at all regular boundary elements of T except γ, then $u(P)/v(P) = \text{const.}$

(C) There exists a sequence $\{T_i\}$ of nested domains approximating to T, with boundaries $\{t_i\}$, having the following properties:

(Ca) T_i admits the Maria-Martin representation of positive harmonic functions. (This would be the case, for instance, if each T_i had bounded curvatures.)

(Cb) Let $u_i(P)$ be a positive harmonic function in T_i, zero on t_i except at the point B_i. Let $\{u_i(P)\}$ converge in T to the harmonic function $u(P)$ and let $\{B_i\}$ converge to the boundary element γ. Then the $u_i(P)$ are uniformly bounded outside any $\mathfrak{S}(\gamma, \rho)$.

Under these conditions the method of weak convergence can be applied to the Maria-Martin representation of $u(M)$, if $u(M)$ is positive and harmonic in T, and a formula obtained of the form

$$(9) \qquad u(M) = \int_t f(\gamma, M) d\mu(e_\gamma),$$

in which the $\mu(e)$ is a positive distribution of mass on boundary elements of t, and the function $f(\gamma, M)$ is continuous in the elements γ and harmonic in M.

The principal restriction on the domain seems to be the Picard condition (B), and this is worthy of a study on its own account. For example, Bouligand [2, p. 32] shows that when T consists of the domain between two spheres, tangent internally, the Picard condition is not satisfied at the point of tangency. The difficulty in this case is not trivial; the singularity subtends an angle of π around the singular point and is movable.

IV. RELATED PROBLEMS

1. **A problem of mixed boundary values for the sphere.** The mixed boundary value problem in the case of plane domains, in which values of the function are given on part of the boundary and values of the normal derivative on the rest, may be reduced to the Dirichlet problem for the first part of the boundary considered as that of an infinite domain. The reduction is effected by the use of the Green's function for this new domain,

in the case of circular boundaries, and the result extended to more general ones by conformal transformation [11, p. 487]. In space, the corresponding boundary value problem depends on the initial domain considered, varying from one domain to another. If the domain is the upper half space, $z \geq 0$, and the boundary the plane $z = 0$, the problem admits the same statement as in the two-dimensional case. In the case of the sphere, which we treat here, the function $u(M)$ is given on part of the surface of the sphere and the values of $u/2 + r\,du/dr$ on the rest. But in order to take account of the generality of the representation merely the integrals of these data will be given, rather than the data themselves, as in the discussion referred to above.

On the spherical surface C of radius a, bounding a domain Γ, let F be a closed set of positive capacity, as a spatial set. The set $C - F$ is the sum of a denumerable infinity $E = \sum I_k$ of domains I_k. Let C_r denote the concentric spherical surfaces $C(r, O)$, σ a two-dimensional region on C and σ_r the radial projection of σ on C_r. We shall deal with functions $u(M)$ which are harmonic within the sphere, of a class described by the following two properties:

(i) Any $u(M)$ is in Γ the difference of two functions, harmonic and non-negative in Γ.

(ii) If σ is any region contained with its boundary in an I_k, the quantity $\int_{\sigma_r} |du/dr|\,d\sigma_r$ remains bounded as r tends to a.

It may be verified, by an integration over a volume contained between σ_{r_0} and σ_r, that the condition that $\int_{\sigma_r} |du/dr|\,d\sigma_r$ remain bounded implies a similar condition on $\int_{\sigma_r} |u|\,d\sigma_r$ and therefore that the condition (ii) is equivalent to requiring the boundedness of $\int_{\sigma_r} |\lambda u + r(du/dr)|\,d\sigma_r$ for any particular λ.

On the domains $\sum I_k = C - F$, we are given a completely additive set function $h(e)$. We shall show that there is a function $U(M)$ of the class defined by (i), (ii) such that

$$(1) \qquad \lim_{r \to a} \int_{\sigma_r} \left\{ \frac{U}{2} + r\,\frac{dU}{dr} \right\} d\sigma_r = h(\sigma)$$

for regions σ on $C - F$ whose boundaries s contribute no mass themselves to $h(e)$, that is, regions σ that $\int_s |dh(e \cdot s)| = 0$. This function will vanish at every point of F which is at a positive distance from $C - F$. The Dirichlet data on F lead however naturally to a function for which the limit of the expression in the left-hand member of (1) is zero. Hence by subtracting the function $U(M)$ above, the problem is reduced to the representation problem of the preceding chapter for the domain complementary to F These statements will now be made precise.

Let $u(M)$ be harmonic in Γ, belonging to the class (ii). If for every circular region σ' in the domain I on $C - F$ we have

(2)
$$\lim_{r \to a} \int_{\sigma_r'} \left(\frac{u}{2} + r \frac{du}{dr} \right) d\sigma_r = 0,$$

then $u(M)$ may be defined so as to be harmonic at the points of I, and admits a unique harmonic extension across I into the entire exterior of C by means of the formula

(2')
$$u(M') = \frac{r}{a} u(M),$$

where M' is the inverse of M with respect to C. It vanishes at ∞.

We note first that if $v(M)$ is harmonic in Γ and $\int_{\sigma_r} |v(M)| d\sigma_r$ is bounded as r tends to a, and the quantity $\int_{\sigma_r'} v(M) d\sigma_r$ approaches 0 as r tends to a, then $v(M)$ admits a unique extension by the formula

$$v(M') = - (r/a) v(M)$$

being 0 on I.

In fact, we may form the average of $v(M)$ over regions of constant following angular radius τ:

(3)
$$v_\tau(M) = \frac{1}{2\pi(1 - \cos \tau)r^2} \int_{\sigma_r'} v(P) d\sigma$$

where $d\sigma = r^2 d\omega$. This function is seen to be harmonic, for τ fixed, as a function of M; it is bounded, by hypothesis, in any cone in Γ with vertex at the center of the sphere and base a closed region Σ in I, distant from the boundary of I by more than τ. Moreover along all radii to points of Σ, $\lim v_\tau(M) = 0$. An iterated average $v_{\tau,\tau'}(M)$, with τ' suitably small, retains these properties and is continuous on C_r within a region Σ_r' inside Σ_r, uniformly in r. It therefore has the boundary values 0 in Σ' continuously and admits a unique harmonic extension, taking at the inverse point M' the value $-(r/a)v_{\tau\tau'}(M)$ and remaining harmonic at points of Σ'.

We can thus let first τ' and then τ approach 0 so that the same properties are valid for $v(M)$ itself. But any point in I may be included in Σ', so $v(M)$ is harmonic at all the points of I.

Returning to the function $u(M)$ we see by direct calculation that the function $u/2 + r\,du/dr$ is harmonic and can thus be chosen as the $v(M)$ of the preceding paragraphs, and extended by the formula

$$v(M') = - \frac{r}{a} \left(\frac{u(M)}{2} + r \frac{du}{dr} \right),$$

vanishing identically on I. We have, however, the relation

$$\frac{\partial}{\partial r} (r^{1/2} u) = r^{-1/2} \left(\frac{u}{2} + r \frac{\partial u}{\partial r} \right) = r^{-1/2} v,$$

and therefore by integration, $u(M)$ approaches finite continuous limits as $r \to a$. Moreover, if we write $u(M') = (r/a)u(M)$ and calculate the value at M' of $u/2 + r'du/dr'$, we find that it is precisely that given for $v(M')$; also $u(M)$ is made continuous at points in I. Since $u/2 + rdu/dr$ takes on continuously the value 0 as r passes through the value a, it follows that du/dr has the same exterior limit as interior limit, and, by the law of the mean, that this common value is the value of du/dr when $r = a$. That the lateral derivatives are bounded is deduced at once from the formula $r^{1/2}u = \int_0^r r^{1/2}vdr$. The function $u(M)$ will therefore be harmonic on I [18, p. 267]. Since $u(M') = (a/r')u(M)$, it vanishes at ∞.

Conversely, if $u(M)$ is harmonically extensible across I by the formula $u(M') = (r/a)u(M)$, the quantity $u/2 + rdu/dr$ vanishes identically on I.

Consider now the Green's function for the set F, taken as a set in space $g(M, P) = 1/MP + G(M, P)$, where $G(M, P)$ is harmonic in M if M is not on F. If P is on $C - F$, the Green's function, as a function of M, admits the transformation $g(M', P) = (r/a)g(M, P)$, for when M' approaches a point of F, M approaches the same point (at perhaps an opposite boundary element) and $g(M', P)$ takes on the same limiting values as $g(M, P)$. Moreover, $g(M', P)$ becomes infinite like $1/M'P$ when $M' \to P$ on $S - F$, since by similar triangles $1/M'P = (r/a)(1/MP)$.

Let $h_k(e)$ be any completely additive function of sets on the domain I_k for each k, such that $\sum_k \int_{I_k} |dh_k(e)|$ is bounded, and form the function

$$U(M) = \sum_k \frac{1}{2\pi a} \int_{I_k} g(M, P)dh_k(e_P)$$

(4)

$$= \frac{1}{2\pi a} \int_{C-F} g(M, P)dh(e),$$

where $h(e) = \sum_k h_k(e \cdot I_k)$.

If σ, contained with its boundary s in an I_k, is such that the contribution of $h(e)$ to s itself is zero, we have

(5)
$$\lim_{r \to a} \int_{\sigma_r} \left(\frac{U}{2} + r \frac{dU}{dr} \right) d\sigma_r = h(\sigma).$$

The function $U(M)$ satisfies the conditions (i), (ii).

That $U(M)$ satisfies the condition (i) is clear, since $g(M, P) \geqq 0$. That it satisfies (ii) comes without difficulty from the inequality

$$\int_{\sigma_r} \left| \frac{\partial U}{\partial r} \right| d\sigma_r \leqq \frac{1}{2\pi a} \int_{C-F} |dh(e_P)|$$

$$\cdot \int_{\sigma_r} \left\{ \left| \frac{\partial}{\partial r_M} \frac{1}{MP} \right| + \left| \frac{\partial}{\partial r_M} G(M, P) \right| \right\} d\sigma_r,$$

the function $G(M, P)$ being harmonic as a function of M, with bounded derivatives so long as M remains at a positive distance from F.

Let I be any one of the domains I_k, and select σ as in the statement of the theorem. We seek to evaluate the integral

$$J_r = \int_{\sigma_r} \left\{ \frac{U(M)}{2} + r \, \frac{\partial U(M)}{\partial r} \right\} d\sigma_r .$$

We have

$$2\pi a J_r = \int_{C-F} dh(e_P) \int_{\sigma_r} \left\{ \frac{g(M, P)}{2} + r \, \frac{\partial g(M, P)}{\partial r} \right\} d\sigma_r$$

$$= - \left(\frac{r}{r'} \right)^{3/2} \int_{C-F} dh(e_P) \int_{\sigma_{r'}} \left\{ \frac{g(M', P)}{2} + r' \, \frac{\partial g(M', P)}{\partial r'} \right\} d\sigma_{r'}$$

$$4\pi a J_r = \int_{C-F} dh(e_P) \int_{\sigma_r} \frac{1}{2} \left\{ g(M, P) - \frac{r}{a} \, g(M', P) \right\} d\sigma_r$$

$$+ \int_{C-F} dh(e_P) \left\{ \int_{\sigma_r} r \, \frac{\partial g(M, P)}{\partial r} \, d\sigma_r - \int_{\sigma_{r'}} \left(\frac{r}{r'} \right)^{3/2} r' \, \frac{\partial g(M', P)}{\partial r'} d\sigma_{r'} \right\},$$

of which the first integral is zero. Likewise, in the second integral, since M and M' are bounded away from F in distance, if we write $g = 1/MP + G$, the only terms which do not cancel as r approaches a are those which correspond to the derivatives of $1/MP$. Hence

$$\lim_{r \to a} 4\pi a J_r = \lim_{r \to a} \int_{C-F} dh(e_P)$$

$$\cdot \left\{ r \int_{\sigma_r} \frac{\partial}{\partial r} \frac{1}{MP} \, d\sigma_r - r' \left(\frac{r}{r'} \right)^{3/2} \int_{\sigma_{r'}} \frac{\partial}{\partial r'} \left(\frac{1}{M'P} \right) d\sigma_{r'} \right\} .$$

But

$$\int_{\sigma_r} \frac{\partial}{\partial r_M} \left(\frac{1}{MP} \right) d\sigma_r(M) = - \int_{\sigma_r} \frac{1}{PM^2} \cos (PM, r) d\sigma_r = \Theta(P),$$

$$- \int_{\sigma_{r'}} \frac{\partial}{\partial r'_M} \left(\frac{1}{M'P} \right) d\sigma_{r'}(M) = \int_{\sigma_{r'}} \frac{1}{PM'^2} \cos (PM', r') d\sigma_{r'} = \Theta'(P),$$

where $\Theta(P)$, $\Theta'(P)$ are respectively the solid angles subtended by σ_r and $\sigma_{r'}$ from P.

It is evident then, that if σ is such that there is no portion of $h(e)$ on s, that is, $\int_s |dh(e \cdot s)| = 0$, since the sum of $\Theta(P)$ and $\Theta'(P)$ approaches 4π when r approaches a, if P is interior to σ, and 0 if P is exterior to σ, we have

$$\lim_{r \to a} 4\pi a J_r = 4\pi a h(\sigma),$$

as was to be proved.

We shall extend this lemma slightly. If σ is bounded by a simple closed curve s, with continuously turning tangent, the formula (5) must be replaced by the following

$$(5') \qquad\qquad \lim_{r \to a} J_r = h(\sigma) + \tfrac{1}{2}\bar{h}(s),$$

where σ denotes the set of points interior to s, and $\bar{h}(s)$ stands for $h(\bar{\sigma}) - h(\sigma)$, where $\bar{\sigma}$ is the closed cover of σ. If, in addition, s is allowed to have a finite number of vertices P_i, at which σ subtends plane angles θ_i, and $h(P_i)$ denotes $h(e \cdot P_i)$, we have

$$(5'') \qquad \lim_{r \to a} J_r = h(\sigma) + \tfrac{1}{2}\big[\bar{h}(s) - \sum h(P_i)\big] + \sum (\theta_i/2\pi)h(P_i).$$

Accordingly, when stated completely, $\lim_{r \to a} J_r$ is given as an additive function of curves s in the domain I rather than as a function of point sets. In accordance with (5'') the function of curves may be spoken of as having regular discontinuities, and in this case it is determined uniquely if it is known merely for curves s for which $\bar{h}(s) = 0$.

Given then a function $u(M)$ of class (i), (ii) such that

$$\lim_{r \to a} \int_{\sigma_r} (u/2 + rdu/dr)d\sigma_r$$

is given as $h(\sigma)$, in the sense of (5''), where $h(e)$ is a completely additive function of sets on $C - F$, and σ is contained with its boundary in any domain of $C - F$, the function

$$w(M) = u(M) - U(M)$$

will still be of class (i). By harmonic extension across the domains I_k of $C - F$, where $[w/2 + rdw/dr]_{r=a} \equiv 0$, $w(M)$ becomes harmonic and of class (i) in the infinite domain complementary to F. Since $w(M') = (r/a)w(M)$, the function w vanishes at ∞. It is therefore representable by Dirichlet data on F, according to the methods of III, §5, in terms of a completely additive set function on F.

2. **The Pleateau problem.** The connection of the Plateau problem with harmonic functions and the Dirichlet problem has been well known since Weierstrass. In the simplest statement of the problem—which does not correspond with the simplest solution—it is to find a surface $z = f(x, y)$, which satisfies the partial differential equation obtained by setting the mean curvature equal to zero and which, on the boundary of a given region in the x, y-plane takes on given values of z. The vanishing of the mean curvature results from the Euler equation associated with minimizing the area of the surface $z = f(x, y)$ which caps the given boundary curve. In a more general statement of the Plateau problem, it is to find the expression of a surface of zero mean curvature (a minimal surface)

which caps a given space curve, in terms of two curvilinear coordinates, that is, to map it on a plane, but not by direct projection. The most important question is the relation of the minimal surface to the surface of least area.

The problem has been solved and the fundamental questions have been answered by Douglas and Radó, throughout the same recent period of years. For these treatments we refer to a book by Radó [31]. The relation to harmonic functions and Dirichlet's principle has been most clearly brought out in a recent paper by Courant [5]. Accordingly we shall present briefly an introduction to the concepts developed there.

The area of a surface of sufficient smoothness may be written as the integral in terms of curvilinear coordinates u, v:

$$A = \int (EG - F^2)^{1/2} du\, dv,$$

where E, F, G are the customary expressions $E = x_u^2 + y_u^2 + z_u^2$, $F = x_u x_v + y_u y_v + z_u z_v$, $G = x_v^2 + y_v^2 + z_v^2$. But

$$(EG - F^2)^{1/2} \leqq (EG)^{1/2},$$

and, by a familiar property of the geometric and arithmetic means,

$$(EG)^{1/2} \leqq \tfrac{1}{2}(E + G).$$

Accordingly, Courant considers the minimum of $(1/2)\int(E+G)du\, dv$ and finds that under suitable conditions this minimum exists and yields the by-product $F = 0$, $E = G$, with x, y, z harmonic functions of u, v. In considering the minimal sequences equicontinuity takes the place of the weak convergence of mass functions.

We may regard the surface as represented on the plane by means of a vector $\rho(u, v)$, where $\rho(u, v) = \{x(u, v),\ y(u, v),\ z(u, v)\}$, and discuss the integral

$$D(\rho) = \frac{1}{2} \int (E + G) du\, dv = \frac{1}{2} \int (\rho_u \cdot \rho_u + \rho_v \cdot \rho_v) du\, dv.$$

In particular, if the corresponding portion of the u, v-plane is a simply covered simply-connected domain, that domain may be taken as the unit circle, for the differential expressions

$$(x_u^2 + x_v^2)(du\, dv),\ (y_u^2 + y_v^2)(du\, dv),\ (z_u^2 + z_v^2)(du\, dv)$$

are seen by direct calculation to be invariant of conformal transformation of the u, v parameters.

Consider a simple closed space curve γ and suppose that there exists a surface S which it bounds, with the following properties:

The vector $\rho(u, v)$ maps S, bounded by γ, on the unit circle B of the u, v-plane with boundary C, so that $\rho(u, v)$ is continuous for (u, v) in $B+C$, has "piecewise" continuous first derivatives in B, with C mapped continuously and monotonically on γ. Further it is supposed that the Dirichlet integral $D(\rho)$ is finite.

Courant's first problem is to show the existence of a vector $\rho(u, v)$ of this kind for which $D(\rho)$ attains its lowest bound. In particular, since $D(\rho)$ is invariant of a conformal map of the circle into itself, it may be assumed that three prescribed points of C go into three prescribed points of γ.

If there are an infinite number of possible surfaces S, let d be the lower bound of $D(\rho)$, and $\rho_1, \rho_2, \cdots$ a sequence of vectors ρ_n such that $D(\rho_n)$ tends to d. Courant shows that the three point condition just mentioned implies that the sequence of functions ρ_n is equicontinuous on C, and that therefore there exists a suitable subsequence, which we denote again by ρ_n, that converges uniformly on C.

We shall have to omit the development, itself an important chapter in connection with the Dirichlet problem, which deals with the minimum value of the Dirichlet integral over a given domain T for functions which take on assigned boundary values. This excursion into the calculus of variations would carry us too far afield.

3. **Minimum Dirichlet integral.** With the advantage of knowing already under what conditions a solution of the Dirichlet problem exists, it is not difficult, however, to establish the minimum property of the corresponding Dirichlet integral. To this effect we give briefly the proof of the following theorem, the statement and proof being extensible to any number of dimensions:

Given a bounded domain T in the u, v-plane, and a continuous function $f(P)$ on its boundary, which can be continuously extended over T in such a way that within T it has piecewise continuous derivatives and $\int_T (f_u^2 + f_v^2) du\, dv$ exists, let $X(u, v)$ be the corresponding sequence solution of the Dirichlet problem for the given boundary values $f(P)$. Then the quantity $D(X) = \int_T (X_u^2 + X_v^2) du\, dv$ exists, and we have

(D) $$D(X) \leqq D(f).$$

As a first case, we assume that the boundary t is composed of a finite number of closed analytic curves and that $f(P)$ is continuous with continuous first and second derivatives in a region T' which contains $T+t$. Then, even under less restrictive conditions, it has been shown by Kellogg [18'] that the corresponding solution $X(u, v)$ of the Dirichlet problem in T for $f(P)$ on t has bounded first derivatives in $T+t$.

Let $W = f - X$. We have for the Dirichlet integrals the relation

$$D(f) = D(X) + 2D(W, X) + D(W),$$

where

$$D(W, X) = \int_T (W_u X_u + W_v X_v) du\, dv$$

$$= \int_t W \frac{dX}{dn} ds - \int_T W \nabla^2 X\, du\, dv = 0.$$

Since $D(W) \geqq 0$, we have $D(f) \geqq D(X)$.

Return now to the theorem. We may suppose that $f(P)$ is extended continuously outside T. We replace $f(P)$ by its twice iterated average $f_h(P)$ over squares of center P and side $2h$. Within any subdomain none of whose points are as close to t as $2h2^{1/2}$, the function $f_h(P)$ has continuous first and second partial derivatives. Let T_h represent a domain, contained with its boundary in such a subdomain, whose boundary consists of a finite number of closed analytic pieces, and is such that $\lim_{h \to 0} T_h = T$. In fact, by taking h small enough, T_h may be any given T_n of the sequence process. Let X_h be the solution of the Dirichlet problem in T_h for $f_h(P)$ on t_h.

With an obvious extension of the notation, we have from the result established in the first case,

$$D_{T_h}(X_h) \leqq D_{T_h}(f_h).$$

But also, interchange of the order of differentiation and averaging is permissible, that is,

$$(f_u)_h = \left(\frac{\partial f}{\partial u}\right)_h = \frac{\partial f_h}{\partial u} = (f_h)_u,$$

which is one of the advantages of the systematic use of the process $[2']$, and moreover it is an immediate application of Hölder's inequality, as used for instance in the theory of area $[25', \text{p. } 687]$, that

$$\int_{T_h} (f_u)_h^2\, du\, dv \leqq \int_T (f_u)^2 du\, dv.$$

Hence

$$D_{T_h}(f_h) \leqq D_T(f); \qquad D_{T_h}(X_h) \leqq D_T(f).$$

If now we let $h \to 0$, the function X_h converges to the sequence solution $X(u, v)$ of the Dirichlet problem in T for $f(P)$ on t; in fact, $\lim_{h \to 0} f_h(P) = f(P)$ uniformly on $T + t$. But by Fatou's theorem, $D_T(X)$ exists and

$$\lim_{h \to 0} D_{T_h}(X_h) \geqq D_T(X).$$

This inequality, combined with the previous one, yields the inequality (D), which was to be proved.

4. **Minimal sequence of harmonic functions.** Returning to the analysis of Courant we denote by $\rho_n{}^*$ the vectors whose components are harmonic in u, v but take on the same boundary values as those of $\rho_n(u, v)$. They are likewise admissible vectors. But as we have just seen,

$$D(\rho_n{}^*) \leqq D(\rho_n).$$

Hence the vectors $\rho_n{}^*(u, v)$ also constitute a minimal sequence. And since the functions $x_n{}^*$, $y_n{}^*$, $z_n{}^*$ converge uniformly on C they converge uniformly to harmonic functions x, y, z in B.

By the Fatou theorem, since the integrands are positive,

$$d = \lim_{n \to \infty} D(\rho_n{}^*) \geqq D(\rho).$$

But also ρ is an admissible vector, since it is monotonic on C; hence $D(\rho) \geqq d$. It follows that $D(\rho) = d$, and a solution of the minimum problem is obtained.

It remains to find the complete description of the surface generated by $\rho(u, v)$, and for this the reader is referred to the article cited. The surface is shown to be a minimal surface by making use of variations $\delta\rho(u, v)$ of a special kind, following Radó; that is, $E = G$, $F = 0$. The mapping on the boundary C is shown to be strictly monotonic; in other words, an interval on C cannot correspond to a single point on γ. From the fact that $E = G$, $F = 0$, it is evident that $D(\rho)$ is the area of the minimal surface; but the question as to whether $D(\rho)$ is the minimum area is not answered at once. This question requires consideration of approximation theorems in terms, say, of the mapping of polyhedra inscribed in the curve γ. It should be mentioned that surfaces of a prescribed degree of connectivity are also treated simply, through the same minimum problem. For example, the surface caps $\rho_n(u, v)$ may be one-sided surfaces, so that the points of them may be considered as counting doubly.

The Plateau problem, as is now well known, may be handled for curves such that there is no finite area corresponding to them. The solution, of course, depends upon approximation theorems.

A natural extension of the Dirichlet and Plateau problems lies in the consideration of the corresponding boundary value problems and variational problems connected with partial differential equations of elliptic type. It is with regret that the author realizes that limitations on the length of this article preclude the exposition of very recent and most significant work in this direction.

BIBLIOGRAPHY

1. BOULIGAND. *Sur le problème de Dirichlet*. Annales de la Société polonaise de Mathématique, vol. 4 (1925), pp. 59–112.

2. BOULIGAND. *Fonctions Harmoniques. Principes de Picard et de Dirichlet*. Mémorial des Sciences Mathématiques, no. 11, 1926.

2'. BRAY. *Proof of a formula for an area*. Bulletin of the American Mathematical Society, vol. 29 (1923), pp. 264–270.

3. CARATHÉODORY. *Über die gegenseitige Beziehung der Ränder bei der konformen Abbildung des Inneren einer Jordanschen Kurve auf einen Kreis*. Mathematische Annalen, vol. 73 (1913), pp. 305–370.

4. CARATHÉODORY. *On Dirichlet's problem*. American Journal of Mathematics, vol. 59 (1937), pp. 709–730.

5. COURANT. *Plateau's problem and Dirichlet's principle*. Annals of Mathematics, (2), vol. 38 (1937), pp. 679–724.

6. EVANS. *Fundamental points of potential theory*. Rice Institute Pamphlet, vol. 7 (1920), pp. 252–329.

7. EVANS. *The Logarithmic Potential*, American Mathematical Society Colloquium Publications, vol. 6. New York, 1927.

8. EVANS. *Application of Poincaré's sweeping-out process*. Proceedings of the National Academy of Sciences, vol. 19 (1933), pp. 457–461.

9. EVANS. *Short proof of Kellogg's lemma*. Bulletin of the American Mathematical Society, vol. 40 (1934), p. 665. Also given by VASILESCO. *Sur la continuite du potentiel a travers les masses, et la démonstration d'un lemme de Kellogg*. Comptes Rendus Hebdomaires de l'Académie des Sciences de Paris, vol. 200 (1935), pp. 1173–1174.

10. EVANS. *Potentials of positive mass*. I. Transactions of the American Mathematical Society, vol. 37 (1935), pp. 226–253. II. ibid., vol. 38 (1935), pp. 201–236.

11. EVANS. *Modern methods of analysis in potential theory*. Bulletin of the American Mathematical Society, vol. 43, (1937), pp. 481–502.

12. FATOU. *Séries trigonométriques et séries de Taylor*. Acta Mathematica, vol. 30 (1906), pp. 335–400.

13. FROSTMAN. *Potential d'Équilibre et Capacité des Ensembles*. Lund, 1935.

14. GARRETT. *Necessary and sufficient conditions for potentials of single and double layers*. American Journal of Mathematics, vol. 58 (1936), pp. 95–129.

15. GREEN. *Harmonic functions in domains with multiple boundary points*. American Journal of Mathematics, in course of publication.

16. KELLOGG. *On the general solution of the classical Dirichlet problem*. Proceedings of the National Academy of Sciences, vol. 12 (1926), pp. 397–406.

17. KELLOGG. *Recent progress with the Dirichlet problem*. Bulletin of the American Mathematical Society, vol. 32 (1926), pp. 601–625.

18. KELLOGG. *Foundations of Potential Theory*. Berlin, 1929.

18'. KELLOGG. *On the derivatives of harmonic functions on the boundary*. Transactions of the American Mathematical Society, vol. 33 (1931), pp. 486–510.

19. KELLOGG. *Converses of Gauss's theorem on the arithmetic mean*. Transactions of the American Mathematical Society, vol. 36 (1934), pp. 227–242.

20. LEBESGUE. *Sur le problème de Dirichlet*. Rendiconti del Circolo Matematico di Palermo, vol. 24 (1907), pp. 371–402.

21. LEBESGUE. *Sur le problème de Dirichlet*. Comptes Rendus Hebdomaires de l'Académie des Sciences de Paris, vol. 154 (1912), p. 335.

22. LEBESGUE. *Sur des cas d'impossibilité du problème de Dirichlet*. Comptes Rendus des Séances de la Société Mathématique de France, (1913), p. 17.

23. LEBESGUE. *Conditions de regularité, conditions d'irrégularité, conditions d'impossibilité dans le problème de Dirichlet*. Comptes Rendus Hebdomaires de l'Académie des Sciences de Paris, vol. 178 (1924), p. 349.

24. MARIA. *Examples of harmonic functions*. Bulletin of the American Mathematical Society, vol. 38 (1932), pp. 839–843.

25. MARIA and MARTIN. *Representation of positive harmonic functions*. Duke Mathematical Journal, vol. 2 (1936), pp. 517–529.

25'. MORREY. *A class of representation of manifolds*, Part I. American Journal of Mathematics, vol. 55 (1933), pp 683–707.

26. PERRON. *Eine neue Behandlung der ersten Randwertaufgabe für* $\Delta u = 0$. Mathematische Zeitschrift, vol. 18 (1923), pp. 42–54.

27. PERKINS. *The Dirichlet problem for domains with multiple boundary points*. Transactions of the American Mathematical Society, vol. 58 (1925), pp. 106–144.

28. PHILLIPS and WIENER. *Nets and the Dirichlet problem*. Journal of Mathematics and Physics of the Massachusetts Institute of Technology, vol. 2 (1923), pp. 105–124.

29. PLEMELJ. *Potentialtheoretische Untersuchungen*. Leipzig, 1911.

30. POINCARÉ. *Sur les équations aux derivées partielles de la physique mathématique*. American Journal of Mathematics, vol. 12 (1890), pp. 211–294.

31. RADÓ. *On the Problem of Plateau*. Berlin, 1933.

32. RADÓ and F. RIESZ. *Über die erste Randwertaufgabe fur* $\Delta u = 0$. Mathematische Zeitschrift, vol. 22 (1925), pp. 41–44.

33. RADON. *Über die Randwertaufgaben beim logarithmischen Potential*. Wiener Sitzungsberichte, vol. 128 (1919), pp. 1123–1167.

34. RAYNOR. *Dirichlet's problem*. Annals of Mathematics, vol. 23 (1922), pp. 183–198.

35. DE LA VALLÉE POUSSIN. *Extension de la méthode du balayage de Poincaré et problème de Dirichlet*. Annales de l'Institut H. Poincaré, vol. 2 (1932), pp. 169–232.

36. DE LA VALLÉE POUSSIN. *Potential et problème géneralisé de Dirichlet*. Mathematical Gazette, vol. 22 (1938), pp. 17–36.

37. VASILESCO. *Sur les singularités des fonctions harmoniques*. Journal de Mathématiques Pures et Appliquées, vol. 9 (1930), pp. 81–111.

38. VASILESCO. *Le problème généralisé de Dirichlet*. Académie royale de Belgique, Classe des Sciences, Mémoires, vol. 16 (1937), pp. 1–55.

39. WIENER. *Discontinuous boundary conditions and the Dirichlet problem*. Transactions of the American Mathematical Society, vol. 25 (1923), pp. 307–314.

40. WIENER. *Certain notions in potential theory*. Journal of Mathematics and Physics of the Massachusetts Institute of Technology, vol. 3 (1924), pp. 24–51.

41. WIENER. *The Dirichlet problem*. Ibid., vol. 3 (1924), pp. 127–146.

42. ZAREMBA. *Sur le principe du minimum*. Bulletin Internationale de l'Académie Polonaise des Sciences de Cracow, II, (1909), pp. 197–264.

UNIVERSITY OF CALIFORNIA,
BERKELEY, CALIF.

HYDRODYNAMICAL STABILITY

BY

J. L. SYNGE

CONTENTS

INTRODUCTION

The preparation for the Semicentennial of an address on the applications of mathematics has involved a difficult decision. Applied mathematics is so vast a subject that anything in the nature of a general review was quite out of the question. It seemed wiser to take some comparatively small field, already well formulated mathematically but offering problems still unsolved, and present it with some degree of completeness. Furthermore, it seemed best to take a subject belonging definitely to applied mathematics, that is, a subject in which any results we can obtain are of interest not only to the mathematician but also to the physicist and the engineer.

Hydrodynamical stability is such a subject. It is concerned with the initial stage of turbulence—its generation from steady flow—but not with turbulent motion, once established. It presents mathematical problems of no small difficulty: triumphs are few and disappointments many. Had a greater fraction of the mathematical energy of the last half-century been directed to these problems, no doubt our present knowledge of the behavior of fluids would be much greater. It is not too late to recommend these problems to the attention of mathematicians, especially those who

227

derive satisfaction from the thought that their work binds them to a wider brotherhood of scientists.

It is not enough to present these problems in their final reduced form. It is essential that the background should be swiftly surveyed. There are three stages in any theory in applied mathematics: (i) creation of a mathematical model, or, equivalently, the formulation of axioms or laws; (ii) mathematical deduction of the behavior of the model; (iii) comparison of these deductions with observation. It is with the second stage that the mathematician is mainly concerned. But he must never lose sight of the other stages. He must always be ready to offer a modification of the fundamental laws if his deductions fail to fit observation. Hence, we must cast a critical glance over the fundamental equations of hydrodynamics in order to appreciate how far they involve fundamental mechanical laws (not to be lightly tampered with) and how far they involve convenient, but not inevitable, assumptions. The necessity for this survey and the desirability of having at hand the essential formulas in convenient notation will explain why so much space is devoted to these matters before coming to grips with the actual problems of stability.

The formulation of adequate axioms for the motion of a viscous fluid exercised the minds of Newton, D'Alembert, and Euler, but it was not until about a century ago that Navier and Stokes developed a successful mathematical model of a fluid. The reader may refer to an interesting account of the history of hydrodynamics by R. Giacomelli and E. Pistolesi [1, vol. 1, pp. 305–394]. There can never be a last word in regard to the axioms of any physical theory. All we can ask of them is that they lead to conclusions in agreement with observation. Sooner or later more refined observations will find the weak point in any set of physical axioms. Nature is far too complicated to be completely described in a few equations. But we may pertinently ask this question: Do the Navier-Stokes equations lead to deductions in obvious discord with observation? It might seem that this is an easy question to answer: actually it is difficult, and the fault lies with the mathematician rather than with the experimental physicist. Only in a few cases has the mathematician been able to make deductions from the Navier-Stokes equations. On account of the weakness of the methods available, the mathematician has tended to simplify the question of stability unduly, concentrating much attention on problems which do not admit a direct physical check. But on the whole we may say that the equations of Navier and Stokes have stood the test so far, their conspicuous triumph being in the work of G. I. Taylor [2] (see §8 below). On the other hand the work of R. von Mises [3, 4] and L. Hopf [5] (see §11 below) may make us doubtful as to the validity of these equations. Every investigation on hydrodynamical stability has a tang of excitement: the result obtained may confirm or undermine a theory now a century old.

The present address does not cover all the attacks that have been made on the problem of hydrodynamical stability: a more complete bibliography has been given by H. Bateman [6], and reference may also be made to a paper by F. Noether [31]. The aim has been rather to give a general conspectus of the subject with the maximum simplicity of presentation, and to direct attention to the discussion of disturbances more general than those usually treated. The rather weak but general and simple conditions for stability contained in §§6, 9, and 11 are believed to be new, and the essential connection between the methods of Part III and those of Part II does not seem to have been previously pointed out.

PART I. THE PHYSICAL PROBLEM AND ITS MATHEMATICAL FORMULATION

1. The observation of instability. An historical account of experimental work on hydrodynamical stability has been given by L. Schiller [7]. Only some outstanding facts will be cited here. *Couette motion* is a steady motion with circular stream-lines of a fluid occupying the region between two rotating coaxial cylinders; *Poiseuille motion* is a steady motion with straight stream-lines through a fixed straight tube.* In each of these cases the steady motion is easily determined mathematically, and, under certain circumstances, there is good agreement between theory and observation. But under other circumstances the simple motion predicted theoretically is not observed at all or disappears on the slightest disturbance. This we explain by saying that such a motion, although possible, is *unstable*.

The stability of Couette motion has been investigated experimentally by G. I. Taylor [2] and J. W. Lewis [8]. It is found that, corresponding to any given speed of the outer cylinder, there is stability if the speed of the inner cylinder is small enough. When the speed of the inner cylinder is increased to a certain critical value, depending on the radii of the cylinders, the speed of the outer cylinder, the relative senses of rotation of the cylinders, and the kinematical viscosity of the fluid, the simple steady motion is replaced by an arrangement of annular vortices. On further increase of the speed of the inner cylinder, the motion becomes irregularly turbulent. Apparently the appearance of the vortices represents the incidence of instability: it is of some theoretical interest that the first step towards instability is the setting-up of a new steady motion. The critical speeds are shown graphically by Taylor and Lewis, the experimental results being in remarkable agreement with Taylor's mathematical work (see §8 below).

As regards Poiseuille motion, we shall refer here only to flow through a tube of circular section and make the briefest possible statement. Stability is found experimentally to depend on the value of the dimensionless *Reynolds number*†

---

* These definitions are more general than those sometimes employed.

† Care must be taken in examining results to see what definition of R is employed. Other definitions, differing by constant numerical factors, may be used.

$$(1.1) \qquad R = U_m D/\nu,$$

where U_m is the mean velocity, D the diameter of the tube, and ν the kinematical viscosity. It is found [6, p. 336; 1, vol. 3, p. 178] that there is stability if $R < R_c$ and instability if $R > R_c$, where R_c is the *critical* Reynolds number: its value is

$$(1.2) \qquad R_c = 2320.$$

On account of the mathematical difficulties involved in the theoretical treatment of the above problems, much attention has been devoted to the discussion of analogous plane problems (§11). Suitable experiments cannot be performed to test mathematical conclusions in these cases, but the problems are of mathematical interest and may be expected to throw light, by analogy, on the more complicated problems.

2. **Equations of motion of a viscous fluid.** Indicial notation will be used, in which Latin suffixes will have the range 1, 2, 3 and Greek suffixes the range 1, 2, with the usual summation convention for repeated suffixes.

For any continuous medium, let x_i be rectangular cartesian coördinates, t the time, ρ the density, u_i the components of velocity, X_i the components of body-force per unit mass, and E_{ij} the stress-tensor $(E_{ji} = E_{ij})$. According to the eulerian plan, x_i and t are the independent variables and the other quantities functions of them.

Application of Newton's laws of motion gives, as the *equations of motion of any continuous medium,*

$$(2.1) \qquad \rho\left(\frac{\partial u_i}{\partial t} + u_j \frac{\partial u_i}{\partial x_j}\right) = \rho X_i + \frac{\partial E_{ij}}{\partial x_j} ;$$

with these is associated the *equation of continuity*

$$(2.2) \qquad \frac{\partial \rho}{\partial t} + \frac{\partial}{\partial x_j}(\rho u_j) = 0$$

(or equation of conservation of mass).

To complete the system of equations, a connection must be set up between the stress and the motion. To this end the *rate-of-deformation tensor* is defined as

$$(2.3) \qquad e_{ij} = \tfrac{1}{2}(\partial u_j/\partial x_i + \partial u_i/\partial x_j),$$

and the *pressure p* is defined as the invariant

$$(2.4) \qquad p = - E_{kk}/3.$$

In a *perfect* or *inviscid* fluid the stress across any plane is normal, from which it follows that in a perfect fluid

$$(2.5) \qquad E_{ij} + p\delta_{ij} = 0$$

where δ_{ij} is the Kronecker delta,

(2.6) $\delta_{ij} = 1$ if $i = j$; $\delta_{ij} = 0$ if $i \neq j$.

As *stress-deformation hypothesis for a viscous fluid*, we assume that the quantities $E_{ij} + p\delta_{ij}$ are linear homogeneous functions of the quantities e_{ij}, or, formally,

(2.7) $E_{ij} + p\delta_{ij} = \mu_{ijkl}e_{kl},$

where μ_{ijkl} are the components of the *viscosity-tensor*, satisfying the symmetry conditions

(2.8) $\mu_{ijkl} = \mu_{jikl} = \mu_{ijlk}.$

We shall assume that the fluid is *isotropic*: then μ_{ijkl} is an isotropic tensor, and hence [9, p. 70]

(2.9) $\mu_{ijkl} = \lambda\delta_{ij}\delta_{kl} + \mu(\delta_{ik}\delta_{jl} + \delta_{jk}\delta_{il}),$

where λ, μ are invariants. Then (2.7) reads

(2.10) $E_{ij} + p\delta_{ij} = \lambda\theta\delta_{ij} + 2\mu e_{ij},$

where $\theta = e_{kk} = \partial u_k/\partial x_k$, the expansion of the fluid. Contracting (2.10) with $j = i$ and using (2.4), we find $3\lambda + 2\mu = 0$, and we have from (2.10) as *stress-deformation relation in an isotropic fluid* [10, p. 574]

(2.11) $E_{ij} = -p\delta_{ij} - 2\mu\theta\delta_{ij}/3 + 2\mu e_{ij};$

μ is the *coefficient of viscosity*. We shall regard μ as a constant, although actually it depends on temperature.

The daring simplicity of (2.7)—its linear character—should be noticed. In a similar situation in the theory of elasticity, it is admitted that the linear stress-strain relation (generalized Hooke's law) is physically valid only for small deformations.

Substituting from (2.11) in (2.1) and associating (2.2), we have as *equations of motion of an isotropic viscous fluid* [10, p. 577]

(2.12)
$$\frac{\partial u_i}{\partial t} + u_j \frac{\partial u_i}{\partial x_j} = X_i - \frac{1}{\rho}\frac{\partial p}{\partial x_i} + \frac{\nu}{3}\frac{\partial \theta}{\partial x_i} + \nu\Delta u_i,$$
$$\frac{\partial \rho}{\partial t} + \frac{\partial}{\partial x_j}(\rho u_j) = 0,$$

where ν is the *kinematical viscosity* $(\nu = \mu/\rho)$ and Δ is the Laplacian operator $(\Delta = \partial^2/\partial x_j \partial x_j)$.

We have in (2.12) four equations for five unknowns, ρ, u_i, p, the body-force X_i being supposed assigned. Another equation, such as a relation between ρ and p, is necessary to make the problem of the motion of a fluid mathematically definite. We shall assume the fluid *homogeneous* and *incompressible*, so that ρ is a constant. We have then for the four unknowns u_i, p the four *Navier-Stokes equations of motion of an isotropic homogeneous incompressible fluid* [10, p. 577]

$$(2.13) \qquad \frac{\partial u_i}{\partial t} + u_j \frac{\partial u_i}{\partial x_j} = X_i - \frac{1}{\rho} \frac{\partial p}{\partial x_i} + \nu \Delta u_i, \qquad \frac{\partial u_j}{\partial x_j} = 0.$$

These are the basic equations to be employed in the discussion of hydrodynamical stability. They have been derived in the above manner in order to show the various hypotheses underlying them. Each simplifying hypothesis represents a possible source of discrepancy between the model fluid and the physical fluid. Indeed, L. V. King [11] has suggested that compressibility may be of importance in the discussion of stability: in that case we should use (2.12) instead of (2.13). We shall, however, follow the usual course and use (2.13).

The *boundary conditions* to be associated with the equations of motion in any form are as follows. *Across a surface separating two fluids or a fluid and a solid, the three components of velocity* and the three components of stress across the surface of separation are continuous.* In symbols, u_i and $E_{ij}n_j$ are continuous, n_j being the direction cosines of the normal to the surface.

As we shall deal only with a single fluid bounded by rigid walls, in which the stress may be supposed adjusted to satisfy the condition of continuity, we shall be concerned only with continuity of velocity.

The equations (2.13) are given for rectangular cartesian coördinates. To pass systematically to any curvilinear coördinates, we may use the methods of tensor calculus [13, chap. 20]. Thus, if the coördinates are x^i and the line element

$$ds^2 = g_{ij}dx^idx^j,$$

the Navier-Stokes equations (2.13) read

$$(2.14) \qquad \frac{\partial u^i}{\partial t} + u^jD_ju^i = X^i - \frac{1}{\rho}D^ip + \nu D^jD_ju^i, \quad D_ju^j = 0,$$

where $u^i = dx^i/dt$, X^i are the contravariant components of body-force, D_i the operation of covariant differentiation, and $D^i = g^{ij}D_j$.

The only curvilinear coördinates we shall require are the cylindrical coordinates r, ϕ, z, and for them the equations of motion are most easily obtained by the use of complex variables [14, p. 371]. Let u, v, w be the components of velocity in the directions of the parametric lines of r, ϕ, z

---

* Thus we exclude the possibility of a fluid slipping on a solid boundary; cf. Brillouin [12, vol. 1, pp. 42 ff.].

respectively and R, Φ, Z the components of body-force in these directions. Then with

$$x_1 = r \cos \phi, \qquad x_2 = r \sin \phi, \qquad x_3 = z,$$

we have

$$u_1 + iu_2 = e^{\phi i}(u + iv), \qquad\qquad u_3 = w,$$

$$X_1 + iX_2 = e^{\phi i}(R + i\Phi), \qquad\qquad X_3 = Z,$$

(2.15)

$$\frac{\partial}{\partial x_1} + i \frac{\partial}{\partial x_2} = e^{\phi i}\left(\frac{\partial}{\partial r} + \frac{i}{r}\frac{\partial}{\partial \phi}\right), \qquad \frac{\partial}{\partial x_3} = \frac{\partial}{\partial z},$$

and we obtain at once from (2.13) the *Navier-Stokes equations in cylindrical coördinates*

$$e^{-\phi i}D_t\left\{e^{\phi i}(u + iv)\right\} = R + i\Phi - \frac{1}{\rho}\left(\frac{\partial p}{\partial r} + \frac{i}{r}\frac{\partial p}{\partial \phi}\right) + \nu e^{-\phi i}\Delta\left\{e^{\phi i}(u + iv)\right\},$$

(2.16)
$$D_t w = Z - \frac{1}{\rho}\frac{\partial p}{\partial z} + \nu\Delta w,$$

$$\frac{1}{r}\frac{\partial}{\partial r}(ru) + \frac{1}{r}\frac{\partial v}{\partial \phi} + \frac{\partial w}{\partial z} = 0;$$

here $D_t = \partial/\partial t + u_i \partial/\partial x_i$, the operator of differentiation following the fluid, so that

(2.17)
$$D_t = \frac{\partial}{\partial t} + u\frac{\partial}{\partial r} + \frac{v}{r}\frac{\partial}{\partial \phi} + w\frac{\partial}{\partial z},$$

and Δ is the Laplacian operator

(2.18)
$$\Delta = \frac{\partial^2}{\partial r^2} + \frac{1}{r}\frac{\partial}{\partial r} + \frac{1}{r^2}\frac{\partial^2}{\partial \phi^2} + \frac{\partial^2}{\partial z^2}.$$

A motion will be said to possess *rotational symmetry* if the body-forces possess a potential Π independent of ϕ, and if u, v, w, p are independent of ϕ. The last of (2.16) then gives

(2.19)
$$\frac{\partial}{\partial r}(ru) + \frac{\partial}{\partial z}(rw) = 0,$$

so that a function $\psi(r, z, t)$ exists such that

(2.20)
$$u = -\frac{1}{r}\frac{\partial}{\partial z}(r\psi), \qquad w = \frac{1}{r}\frac{\partial}{\partial r}(r\psi).$$

We shall refer to ψ as a *stream-function*. For the body-forces we have

$$R = -\partial\Pi/\partial r, \qquad \Phi = 0, \qquad Z = -\partial\Pi/\partial z,$$

and $\Pi + p/\rho$ may be eliminated from the first two of (2.16)—actually three real equations—to yield the *equations of motion in the case of rotational symmetry*

(2.21)

$$\left(D_t - \frac{u}{r} - \nu\Theta\right)\Theta\psi + \frac{2v}{r}\frac{\partial v}{\partial z} = 0,$$

$$\left(D_t + \frac{u}{r} - \nu\Theta\right)v = 0,$$

where

(2.22)

$$D_t = \frac{\partial}{\partial t} + u\frac{\partial}{\partial r} + w\frac{\partial}{\partial z},$$

$$\Theta = \Delta - \frac{1}{r^2} = \frac{\partial^2}{\partial r^2} + \frac{1}{r}\frac{\partial}{\partial r} + \frac{\partial^2}{\partial z^2} - \frac{1}{r^2}.$$

Axial symmetry is a particular case of rotational symmetry, with the additional condition $v=0$, so that the velocity-vectors intersect the z-axis. In this case we have only one equation,

(2.23) $$(D_t - u/r - \nu\Theta)\Theta\psi = 0.$$

In *plane* or *two-dimensional motion*, in which a plane $x_3 = \text{const.}$ is taken as the plane of motion, the Navier-Stokes equations (2.13) take the form

(2.24)

$$\frac{\partial u_\alpha}{\partial t} + u_\beta\frac{\partial u_\alpha}{\partial x_\beta} = X_\alpha - \frac{1}{\rho}\frac{\partial p}{\partial x_\alpha} + \nu\Delta'u_\alpha,$$

$$\partial u_\beta/\partial x_\beta = 0, \qquad \Delta' = \partial^2/\partial x_\beta\partial x_\beta,$$

where u_α, p, X_α are functions of x_1, x_2, t. (We recall that Greek suffixes have the range 1, 2.) The equation of continuity implies the existence of a stream-function ψ such that

(2.25) $$u_1 = -\partial\psi/\partial x_2, \qquad u_2 = \partial\psi/\partial x_1;$$

the vorticity is

(2.26) $$\xi = \tfrac{1}{2}(\partial u_2/\partial x_1 - \partial u_1/\partial x_2) = \tfrac{1}{2}\Delta'\psi.$$

Assuming the body-forces conservative, we eliminate them and p from (2.24), obtaining as the single *Navier-Stokes equation for plane motion*,

(2.27) $$D_t\Delta'\psi = \nu\Delta'\Delta'\psi,$$

where

(2.28) $$D_t = \frac{\partial}{\partial t} + u_\beta\frac{\partial}{\partial x_\beta} = \frac{\partial}{\partial t} - \frac{\partial\psi}{\partial x_2}\frac{\partial}{\partial x_1} + \frac{\partial\psi}{\partial x_1}\frac{\partial}{\partial x_2},$$

or, equivalently,

(2.29) $D_t \xi = \nu \Delta' \xi.$

3. Some steady motions and their first-order equations of disturbance.

A *steady motion* is one in which velocity and pressure are functions of position only. Thus a steady motion $u_i = U_i(x_j)$, $p = P(x_j)$ must satisfy (2.13) in the form

(3.1) $$U_j \frac{\partial U_i}{\partial x_j} = X_i - \frac{1}{\rho} \frac{\partial P}{\partial x_i} + \nu \Delta U_i, \qquad \frac{\partial U_j}{\partial x_j} = 0,$$

together with the boundary conditions. To study small disturbances of the steady motion, we seek solutions of (2.13) of the form

(3.2) $u_i = U_i + \epsilon u_i' + \epsilon^2 u_i'' + \cdots, \qquad p = P + \epsilon p' + \epsilon^2 p'' + \cdots,$

where ϵ is a constant parameter and u_i', u_i'', $\cdots$, p', p'', $\cdots$ are functions of position and time. We demand that (3.2) shall satisfy (2.13) and the boundary conditions for all values of ϵ in a range $0 < \epsilon < \epsilon_1$. Formal substitution of (3.2) in (2.13) gives a sequence of sets of equations, each set corresponding to a definite power of ϵ and having boundary conditions associated with it. The set corresponding to ϵ^0 is (3.1); the set corresponding to ϵ^1 is

(3.3) $$\frac{\partial u_i'}{\partial t} + U_j \frac{\partial u_i'}{\partial x_j} + u_j' \frac{\partial U_i}{\partial x_j} = -\frac{1}{\rho} \frac{\partial p'}{\partial x_i} + \nu \Delta u_i', \qquad \frac{\partial u_j'}{\partial x_j} = 0,$$

with the boundary conditions $u_i' = 0$ on any rigid wall, fixed or moving in a prescribed manner, which bounds the fluid. The equations (3.3) may be called the *first-order equations of disturbance*.

A complete treatment would require consideration not only of (3.3), but also of the equations corresponding to higher powers of ϵ, together with establishment of the convergence of (3.2) and justification of the term-by-term differentiations. It is customary, however, to confine attention to the first-order equations, which, it is reasonable to suppose, determine the behavior of disturbances initially very small. The discussion of these equations is certainly a necessary preliminary to a more complete discussion.

We shall now discuss some familiar steady motions and their first-order equations of disturbance. Body-forces are assumed absent throughout.

(a) **Couette motion.** Let fluid occupy the region between two coaxial circular cylinders of radii a_1, a_2, $(a_1 < a_2)$, which are rotating with constant angular velocities n_1, n_2 about their common axis. Using cylindrical coordinates r, ϕ, z in which the cylinders are $r = a_1$ and $r = a_2$, we see that (2.16) and the boundary conditions are satisfied by

(3.4) $u = 0, \qquad v = V, \qquad w = 0, \qquad p = P,$

where

$$V = Ar + B/r, \qquad P = \rho \int (V^2/r)\,ar.$$

(3.5)
$$A = \frac{n_2 a_2^2 - n_1 a_1^2}{a_2^2 - a_1^2}, \qquad B = -\frac{a_2^2 a_1^2 (n_2 - n_1)}{a_2^2 - a_1^2}.$$

This is *Couette motion.* We note that the ψ of (2.20) is zero.

For a general disturbance of the Couette motion, we write

(3.6)
$$u = \epsilon u' + \cdots , \qquad v = V + \epsilon v' + \cdots ,$$
$$w = \epsilon w' + \cdots , \qquad p = P + \epsilon p' + \cdots ,$$

and obtain from (2.16) the first-order equations of disturbance. We shall not write them here, as we find it more convenient in §6 to appeal directly to (3.3) when the disturbance is general.

For a disturbance possessing *rotational symmetry* we may use (2.21), substituting

(3.7) $\psi = \epsilon \psi' + \cdots , \quad v = V + \epsilon v' + \cdots , \quad u = -\dfrac{\partial \psi}{\partial z}, \quad w = \dfrac{1}{r}\dfrac{\partial}{\partial r}(r\psi).$

Hence we obtain the first-order equations of disturbance

$$\left(\frac{\partial}{\partial t} - \nu\Theta\right)\Theta\psi' = -2(A + B/r^2)\frac{\partial v'}{\partial z},$$

(3.8)
$$\left(\frac{\partial}{\partial t} - \nu\Theta\right)v' = 2A\frac{\partial \psi'}{\partial z},$$

$$\Theta = \Delta - \frac{1}{r^2} = \frac{\partial^2}{\partial r^2} + \frac{1}{r}\frac{\partial}{\partial r} + \frac{\partial^2}{\partial z^2} - \frac{1}{r^2},$$

with the boundary conditions

(3.9)
$$\frac{\partial \psi'}{\partial z} = \frac{\partial}{\partial r}(r\psi') = v' = 0 \quad \text{for} \quad r = a_1 \quad \text{and for} \quad r = a_2.$$

(b) **Poiseuille motion.** Let fluid fill a fixed cylindrical tube of arbitrary section, the axis of x_3 being parallel to the generators. Let C be the boundary of the normal section. We see that (2.13) and the boundary conditions are satisfied by

(3.10)
$$u_\alpha = 0, \qquad u_3 = U_3, \qquad p = P,$$

where

(3.11)
$$U_3 = \tfrac{1}{2}A\Phi, \qquad P = -\mu A x_3 + B,$$

A and B being any constants, and Φ a function of x_1, x_2 satisfying

(3.12)
$$\Delta'\Phi = -2, \qquad \Delta' = \partial^2/\partial x_\beta \partial x_\beta,$$

with the boundary condition $\Phi = 0$ on C.* This is *Poiseuille motion*.

For a disturbance of the steady motion, we write

(3.13) $\quad u_\alpha = \epsilon u_\alpha' + \cdots, \quad u_3 = U_3 + \epsilon u_3' + \cdots, \quad p = P + \epsilon p' + \cdots,$

and obtain from (3.3) the first-order equations of disturbance

(3.14)
$$\frac{\partial u_i'}{\partial t} + U_3 \frac{\partial u_i'}{\partial x_3} + \delta_{i3} u_\beta' \frac{\partial U_3}{\partial x_\beta} = -\frac{1}{\rho} \frac{\partial p'}{\partial x_i} + \nu \Delta u_i',$$

$$\partial u_j'/\partial x_j = 0, \qquad\qquad \Delta = \partial^2/\partial x_j \partial x_j,$$

with the boundary conditions $u_i' = 0$ on C.

For the more familiar Poiseuille motion, in which C is a circle, it is convenient to use cylindrical coördinates r, ϕ, z, the equation of the cylinder being $r = a$. Then (2.16) and the boundary conditions are satisfied by the steady motion

(3.15) $\qquad u = v = 0, \qquad\qquad w = W, \qquad\qquad p = P,$

where

(3.16) $\qquad W = W_0(1 - r^2/a^2), \qquad P = -4\mu W_0 z/a^2 + \text{const.},$

W_0 being a constant, the velocity at the center of the tube. We note that the stream-function ψ of (2.20) is $\psi = \Psi$ where

(3.17) $\qquad\qquad \Psi = aW_0(\tfrac{1}{2}r/a - \tfrac{1}{4}r^3/a^3).$

On account of the singularity in the coördinate system for $r = 0$, cylindrical coördinates do not seem particularly useful for the discussion of general disturbances. For disturbances with *rotational symmetry* in a tube of circular section, we substitute in (2.21)

(3.18)
$$\psi = \Psi + \epsilon \psi' + \cdots, \qquad v = \epsilon v' + \cdots,$$

$$u = -\partial \psi/\partial z, \qquad\qquad w = (1/r)\partial(r\psi)/\partial r,$$

and obtain the first-order equations of disturbance

(3.19)
$$\left(\frac{\partial}{\partial t} + W\frac{\partial}{\partial z} - \nu\Theta\right)\Theta\psi' = 0,$$

$$\left(\frac{\partial}{\partial t} + W\frac{\partial}{\partial z} - \nu\Theta\right)v' = 0,$$

$$\Theta = \Delta - \frac{1}{r^2} = \frac{\partial^2}{\partial r^2} + \frac{1}{r}\frac{\partial}{\partial r} + \frac{\partial^2}{\partial z^2} - \frac{1}{r^2},$$

---

* The problem of finding Φ is identical with the problem of finding the irrotational motion of a perfect fluid inside a rotating cylinder and with the torsion problem for an elastic cylinder.

with the boundary conditions

(3.20)

$$\frac{\partial \psi'}{\partial z} = \frac{\partial}{\partial r}(r\psi') = v' = 0 \quad \text{for} \quad r = a,$$

$$\frac{\partial \psi'}{\partial z} = \psi' = v' = 0 \qquad \text{for} \quad r = 0.$$

For disturbances with *axial symmetry*, we put $v' = 0$ and obtain the single first-order equation of disturbance

(3.21) $$\left(\frac{\partial}{\partial t} + W \frac{\partial}{\partial z} - \nu\Theta\right)\Theta\psi' = 0,$$

Θ being as in (3.19) and the boundary conditions being as in (3.20).

(c) **Plane Couette motion and plane Poiseuille motion.** Let fluid fill the region between the parallel planes $x_2 = \pm h$.

Let these planes have constant velocities U_0, $-U_0$, respectively, in the direction of the x_1-axis. The equation of motion (2.27) and the boundary conditions are satisfied by the steady motion $\psi = \Psi$ where

(3.22) $$\Psi = -\tfrac{1}{2}U_0 x_2^2/h.$$

This is *plane Couette motion*, or simple shearing motion. We shall refer to it as *P.C.M.*

Now let the planes $x_2 = \pm h$ be fixed. The equation of motion (2.27) and the boundary conditions are satisfied by the steady motion $\psi = \Psi$ where

(3.23) $$\Psi = U_0 h(\tfrac{1}{3}x_2^3/h^3 - x_2/h),$$

where U_0 is a constant, the velocity at the center of the channel. This is *plane Poiseuille motion*, or pressure-flow. We shall refer to it as *P.P.M.*

Confining our attention to disturbances in the plane of the motion ($x_3 = \text{const.}$), we write, for the disturbance of any plane steady motion $\psi = \Psi$,

(3.24) $$\psi = \Psi + \epsilon\psi' + \cdots,$$

and obtain from (2.27) the first-order equation of disturbance

(3.25)
$$\frac{\partial}{\partial t}\Delta'\psi' - \frac{\partial \Psi}{\partial x_2}\frac{\partial}{\partial x_1}\Delta'\psi' + \frac{\partial \Psi}{\partial x_1}\frac{\partial}{\partial x_2}\Delta'\psi'$$
$$- \frac{\partial \psi'}{\partial x_2}\frac{\partial}{\partial x_1}\Delta'\Psi + \frac{\partial \psi'}{\partial x_1}\frac{\partial}{\partial x_2}\Delta'\Psi = \nu\Delta'\Delta'\psi'.$$

We substitute from (3.22) and (3.23) in (3.25), at the same time introducing the dimensionless variables

(3.26) $$x = x_1/h, \qquad y = x_2/h, \qquad \tau = \nu t/h^2,$$

and the Reynolds number, defined as

$$(3.27) \qquad\qquad R = U_0 h / \nu.$$

Thus we obtain the first-order equations of disturbance

$$(3.28) \qquad\qquad \left(\frac{\partial}{\partial \tau} + R y \frac{\partial}{\partial x} \right) \Delta \psi' = \Delta \Delta \psi', \qquad P.C.M.,$$

$$(3.29) \qquad \left(\frac{\partial}{\partial \tau} + R(1 - y^2) \frac{\partial}{\partial x} \right) \Delta \psi' + 2R \frac{\partial \psi'}{\partial x} = \Delta \Delta \psi', \qquad P.P.M.,$$

where

$$(3.30) \qquad\qquad \Delta = \partial^2/\partial x^2 + \partial^2/\partial y^2,$$

and the boundary conditions for both cases are

$$(3.31) \qquad\qquad \partial \psi'/\partial x = \partial \psi'/\partial y = 0 \quad \text{for} \quad y = \pm 1.$$

4. Formulation of the problem of stability. In the case of a dynamical system with a finite number of degrees of freedom, a definition of stability of equilibrium or of steady motion is comparatively easy to give, because the motion is determined by the initial conditions—initial position and velocity. But in the case of a continuous medium, the determination of the motion requires a knowledge not only of the conditions at $t=0$, but also the boundary conditions for $t>0$. Some of these boundary conditions, namely, the velocity on fixed or moving walls, are assigned in the hydrodynamical problem. The rest of the boundary consists, in the physical problem, of those parts of the apparatus which the physicist does his best to render unimportant, namely, the ends of the cylinders in Couette motion and the ends of the tube in Poiseuille motion. In the mathematical problem we can do what the experimentalist cannot do—remove the ends to infinity. But that does not absolve us from considering boundary conditions at infinity; some such conditions must be furnished if the problem of fluid motion is to be definite.

It has been an almost universal custom to circumvent this difficulty of boundary conditions at infinity by limiting the discussion to disturbances which are *spatially periodic in the direction in which the fluid extends to infinity*, thus giving to the problem the required definite character. Strangely enough, this periodicity, introduced as a mathematical convenience, has apparently a physical reality, as shown in the experiments of Taylor [2] and Lewis [8].

The following is offered as a definition of hydrodynamical stability. Let R be a region occupied by a fluid in steady motion, specified by U_i, P, satisfying (3.1). Consider now the equations (3.3) to be satisfied by u_i', p'. With these equations we associate (i) initial conditions I for $t=0$, (ii) boundary conditions B for $t \geq 0$. In B we include the condition of spatial periodicity in the infinite direction, and write the condition $B(\lambda)$, where λ is a parameter specifying the wave-length. (In the case of three-dimensional disturbances of plane Couette and Poiseuille motions, we would have two such parameters.) The conditions I are to be consistent with B for $t=0$ and with (3.3).

If *all* solutions u_i' of (3.3), satisfying I and $B(\lambda)$, are bounded for $t>0$, we say that the steady motion is "stable I, $B(\lambda)$"; but if there exists any solution u_i' of (3.3), satisfying I and $B(\lambda)$ and unbounded for $t>0$, we say that the steady motion is "unstable" (absolutely). If we so far weaken the conditions I that they demand nothing more than consistency with $B(\lambda)$ and (3.3) for $t=0$, and the continuity of the initial values of u_i', p', $\partial u_i'/\partial x_j$, then stability may be discussed with reference to $B(\lambda)$ alone. If all such solutions u_i' of (3.3), satisfying $B(\lambda)$, are bounded for $t>0$, we say that the motion is "stable $B(\lambda)$," and if this holds for arbitrary λ, we say that the motion is "stable" (absolutely).

It is not claimed that the word "stable" is used below with quite as precise a meaning as that given above. Our knowledge is so scanty that there has been a natural tendency to concentrate on what appear to be the most important aspects of the stability problem. Thus for simplicity of expression, we shall in Part II refer to a motion as stable if there is no characteristic value with positive real part, not seeking to generalize or critically examine the expansion theorem of Haupt [15].

In Part III we shall be concerned with "stability in the mean," as there explained.

PART II. THE METHOD OF THE EXPONENTIAL TIME-FACTOR

5. Introductory remarks. The method of the exponential time-factor (also called the method of small oscillations) has long been a classical method for the determination of the periods of vibration of continuous systems. It was applied to the problem of hydrodynamical stability (for inviscid liquids) as long ago as 1880 by Rayleigh [16]. In this method we seek solutions of the first-order equations of disturbance (3.3) of the form

$$(5.1) \qquad u_i' = e^{\sigma t}F_i(x_1, x_2, x_3), \qquad p' = e^{\sigma t}G(x_1, x_2, x_3),$$

the constant σ and the functions F_i, G being in general complex. Real velocity and pressure are found by adding to these expressions their complex conjugates. On introducing the spatial periodicity mentioned in §4, the differential system is homogeneous and inconsistent unless σ takes certain characteristic values. If the real parts of *all* the characteristic values of σ are zero or negative, then there is stability for disturbances for which initially $u_i' = F_i$, $p'=G$, but if there is *any* characteristic value of σ with a positive real part, there is instability. Since F_i are characteristic functions, the initial conditions in question are somewhat special and in order to establish stability for arbitrary initial disturbances, it is necessary to discuss the expansion of arbitrary functions in terms of the characteristic functions and the validity of applying to the expansions the required differential operations. This question will not be discussed. We shall for simplicity refer to a steady motion as "stable" if all the characteristic values of σ have zero or negative real parts. As far as instability is concerned, no such question is involved, and hence the method of the exponential time-factor is ideally suited to the establishment of instability. Unfortunately, as we shall see, the methods available are such as to establish conditions under which the real parts of all characteristic values σ are zero or negative much more readily than conditions under which the real part of at least one σ is positive.

In Part III we shall discuss a different approach to the question of stability by the method of decreasing positive-definite integrals, this latter type of stability being *stability in the mean*. The mathematical connection between the two methods is closer than appears to have been realized. Certain arguments, actually developed by the methods of Part III, may also be presented by the methods of Part II. We shall, for simplicity, treat such arguments in Part II and show in Part III how the two lines of argument coalesce.

The method of Reynolds [17] will not be used. His mean values present certain difficulties, and, while the theory of turbulence demands their use, it would seem that first-order stability can be discussed as adequately and more clearly without them.

6. Couette motion with general disturbance. Taking the axis of x_3 along the axis of the cylinders, the Couette motion (3.4) may be written $u_i = U_i$ where

$$(6.1) \qquad U_\alpha = - \epsilon_{\alpha\beta} x_\beta (A + B/r^2), \qquad U_3 = 0, \qquad r^2 = x_\gamma x_\gamma,$$

where $\epsilon_{\alpha\beta}$ is the permutation symbol ($\epsilon_{11} = \epsilon_{22} = 0$, $\epsilon_{12} = -\epsilon_{21} = 1$) and A, B are constants as in (3.5). Let us seek solutions of (3.3) of the form

$$(6.2) \qquad u_i' = f_i(x_1, x_2) e^{\sigma t + i\lambda x_3}, \qquad p' = g(x_1, x_2) e^{\sigma t + i\lambda x_3},$$

the functions f_i, g and the constant σ being in general complex and the constant λ real, taken positive without loss of generality. Substitution from (6.2) in (3.3) and elimination of f_3 and g lead to the two partial differential equations for f_α,

$$(6.3) \qquad \sigma\left(\frac{\partial\theta}{\partial x_\alpha} - \lambda^2 f_\alpha\right) = \nu(\Delta' - \lambda^2)\left(\frac{\partial\theta}{\partial x_\alpha} - \lambda^2 f_\alpha\right)$$
$$+ \lambda^2\left(U_\beta \frac{\partial f_\alpha}{\partial x_\beta} + f_\beta \frac{\partial U_\alpha}{\partial x_\beta}\right) - \frac{\partial}{\partial x_\alpha}\left(U_\beta \frac{\partial\theta}{\partial x_\beta}\right),$$

where

$$(6.4) \qquad \theta = \partial f_\beta / \partial x_\beta = - i\lambda f_3, \qquad \Delta' = \partial^2 / \partial x_\rho \partial x_\rho.$$

The boundary conditions are

(6.5) $$f_\alpha = \theta = 0 \quad \text{for} \quad r = a_1 \quad \text{and for} \quad r = a_2.$$

The consistency of (6.3) and (6.5) demands the satisfaction of a characteristic equation by σ, λ, ν.

We shall now establish conditions under which the Couette motion is stable for general disturbances, in the sense that all characteristic values of σ have negative real parts. Let us multiply (6.3) by $\bar{f}_\alpha dS$ (the bar denoting a complex conjugate and dS an element of area) and integrate over the part of the plane $x_3 = \text{const.}$ occupied by the fluid. On integration by parts, this gives, by virtue of (6.5),

(6.6)
$$\sigma(I_2^2 + \lambda^2 I_1^2) = - \nu(I_3^2 + \lambda^2 I_2^2 + \lambda^2 J_2^2 + \lambda^4 I_1^2)$$
$$- \lambda^2 \int (U_\beta \partial f_\alpha / \partial x_\beta + f_\beta \partial U_\alpha / \partial x_\beta) \bar{f}_\alpha dS - \int U_\beta (\partial \theta / \partial x_\beta) \bar{\theta} dS,$$

where we have denoted certain positive-definite integrals as follows:

(6.7)
$$I_1^2 = \int f_\alpha \bar{f}_\alpha dS, \qquad\qquad I_2^2 = \int \theta \bar{\theta} dS,$$
$$J_2^2 = \int \frac{\partial f_\alpha}{\partial x_\beta} \frac{\partial \bar{f}_\alpha}{\partial x_\beta} dS, \qquad I_3^2 = \int \frac{\partial \theta}{\partial x_\alpha} \frac{\partial \bar{\theta}}{\partial x_\alpha} dS.$$

Let us write

(6.8) $$\sigma = \sigma_1 + i\sigma_2,$$

and add to (6.6) its complex conjugate. Since $\partial U_\beta / \partial x_\beta = 0$, we have

(6.9)
$$\int U_\beta(\bar{f}_\alpha \partial f_\alpha / \partial x_\beta + f_\alpha \partial \bar{f}_\alpha / \partial x_\beta) dS = - \int (\partial U_\beta / \partial x_\beta) f_\alpha \bar{f}_\alpha dS = 0,$$
$$\int U_\beta(\bar{\theta} \partial \theta / \partial x_\beta + \theta \partial \bar{\theta} / \partial x_\beta) dS = - \int (\partial U_\beta / \partial x_\beta) \theta \bar{\theta} dS = 0,$$

and so we obtain

(6.10)
$$\sigma_1(I_2^2 + \lambda^2 I_1^2)/\nu = - (I_3^2 + \lambda^2 I_2^2 + \lambda^2 J_2^2 + \lambda^4 I_1^2)$$
$$- \tfrac{1}{2}(\lambda^2/\nu) \int (\partial U_\alpha / \partial x_\beta)(\bar{f}_\alpha f_\beta + f_\alpha \bar{f}_\beta) dS.$$

The last term may also be written

(6.11) $$- \tfrac{1}{2}(\lambda^2/\nu) \int U_{\alpha\beta}(\bar{f}_\alpha f_\beta + f_\alpha \bar{f}_\beta) dS, \quad U_{\alpha\beta} = \tfrac{1}{2}(\partial U_\beta / \partial x_\alpha + \partial U_\alpha / \partial x_\beta),$$

$U_{\alpha\beta}$ being in fact the rate-of-deformation tensor for the steady motion.

We may note, in passing, the application of (6.10) to another problem. Consider a cylinder of any section (simply or multiply connected) rotating with constant angular velocity about an axis parallel to the generators. We know that a rigid-body rotation of fluid contained in the cylinder is a possible steady motion: this motion is given by (6.1) with $B=0$. For the disturbance of this steady motion, (6.10) holds. But $U_{\alpha\beta}=0$ in a rigid-body motion: hence $\sigma_1 < 0$ and the motion is stable for all values of ν and λ.

Returning to the case of Couette motion, we shall give certain inequalities satisfied by complex functions f_α, arbitrary save for the boundary conditions (6.5), θ being defined by (6.4). For any real constant χ,

$$(6.12) \qquad \int (U_\alpha \theta + \chi f_\alpha)(U_\alpha \bar{\theta} + \chi \bar{f}_\alpha) dS \geqq 0,$$

and hence

$$(6.13) \qquad \left| \int U_\alpha(f_\alpha \bar{\theta} + \bar{f}_\alpha \theta) dS \right| \leqq 2I_1 \left(\int U_\alpha U_\alpha \theta \bar{\theta} dS \right)^{1/2} < 2\tilde{U} I_1 I_2,$$

where $\tilde{U}$ is the maximum velocity in the steady motion: this maximum occurs on one of the cylinders and hence $\tilde{U}$ is equal to the greater of $|n_1 a_1|$, $|n_2 a_2|$. Also, for any real constant χ,

$$(6.14) \qquad \int (U_\alpha f_\beta + \chi \partial f_\alpha/\partial x_\beta)(U_\alpha \bar{f}_\beta + \chi \partial \bar{f}_\alpha/\partial x_\beta) dS \geqq 0,$$

and hence

$$(6.15) \qquad \left| \int U_\alpha(f_\beta \partial \bar{f}_\alpha/\partial x_\beta + \bar{f}_\beta \partial f_\alpha/\partial x_\beta) dS \right|$$
$$\leqq 2J_2 \left(\int U_\alpha U_\alpha f_\beta \bar{f}_\beta dS \right)^{1/2} < 2\tilde{U} I_1 J_2.$$

Now on integration by parts the final integral in (6.10) is

$$(6.16) \qquad \int (\partial U_\alpha/\partial x_\beta)(\bar{f}_\alpha f_\beta + f_\alpha \bar{f}_\beta) dS = - \int U_\alpha(\bar{f}_\alpha \theta + f_\alpha \bar{\theta}) dS$$
$$- \int U_\alpha(f_\beta \partial \bar{f}_\alpha/\partial x_\beta + \bar{f}_\beta \partial f_\alpha/\partial x_\beta) dS,$$

and hence by virtue of the inequalities (6.13), (6.15) we deduce from (6.10) the inequality

$$(6.17) \qquad \sigma_1(I_2^2 + \lambda^2 I_1^2)/\nu < (\lambda^2 \tilde{U}/\nu) I_1(I_2 + J_2)$$
$$- (I_3^2 + \lambda^2 I_2^2 + \lambda^2 J_2^2 + \lambda^4 I_1^2).$$

Obviously $\sigma_1 < 0$ if $I_2^2 + J_2^2 + \lambda^2 I_1^2 - (\tilde{U}/\nu) I_1(I_2 + J_2)$ is a positive-definite form in the real variables I_1, I_2, J_2; a sufficient condition for this is

$$(6.18) \qquad \tilde{U}/(\nu\lambda) < 2^{1/2}.$$

Hence we see that *Couette motion is stable for a general disturbance of wave-length* $l(=2\pi/\lambda)$ *if*

$$(6.19) \qquad\qquad \tilde{U}l/\nu < 2\pi(2)^{1/2},$$

where $\tilde{U}$ *is the greater of the two linear velocities of the cylinders.* Thus any given Couette motion is stable for disturbances of sufficiently short wavelength.

Returning to (6.10) and writing the last term in the form (6.11), we may develop another attack. Choosing temporary axes we can make $U_{12}=0$ at a specified point in the fluid: then at that point (since $U_{\beta\beta}=0$)

$$(6.20) \qquad \begin{aligned} |U_{\alpha\beta}(\bar{f}_\alpha f_\beta + f_\alpha \bar{f}_\beta)| &= 2|U_{11}f_1\bar{f}_1 + U_{22}f_2\bar{f}_2| \\ &\leq 2|U_{11}|f_\alpha\bar{f}_\alpha = 2|D|^{1/2}f_\alpha\bar{f}_\alpha, \end{aligned}$$

where $D=\mathrm{det.}\,U_{\alpha\beta}$. But the final expression in (6.20) is invariant, and so exceeds or is equal to the left-hand side for the original general axes. It is easily seen from (6.1) that $D=-B^2/r^4$ and so

$$(6.21) \qquad \left|\int U_{\alpha\beta}(\bar{f}_\alpha f_\beta + f_\alpha \bar{f}_\beta)dS\right| \leq 2|B|\int r^{-2}f_\alpha\bar{f}_\alpha dS < 2|B|a_1^{-2}I_1^2.$$

Thus by (6.10)

$$(6.22)\ \sigma_1(I_2^2 + \lambda^2 I_1^2)/\nu < (|B|/\nu)(\lambda/a_1)^2 I_1^2 - (I_3^2 + \lambda^2 I_2^2 + \lambda^2 J_2^2 + \lambda^4 I_1^2),$$

and hence $\sigma_1 < 0$ if

$$(6.23) \qquad\qquad |B|/(a_1^2\nu\lambda^2) < 1.$$

Thus *Couette motion is stable for a general disturbance of wave-length* l *if*

$$(6.24) \qquad \frac{|n_2 - n_1|\, l^2}{\nu} \cdot \frac{a_2^2}{a_2^2 - a_1^2} < 4\pi^2.$$

The conditions (6.19) and (6.24) for stability are weak, but they have appeared worth noting on account of the ease with which they are obtained. Returning to (6.10) we may describe a method which has been used to give a fairly wide range of stability when applied to simpler problems than the general disturbance of Couette motion.

Let us consider the functions f_α arbitrary save for the boundary conditions (6.5), and a normalizing condition $I_1=1$. It is evident that the right-hand side of (6.10) has no finite lower bound, because we have only to choose for f_α rapidly oscillating functions to make the term $-I_3^2$ dominant. But it is evident from (6.22) that the expression in question has a finite upper bound. To find it, we apply the calculus of variations and see that the functions f_α providing this maximum satisfy the partial differential equations

$$(6.25) \qquad (\Delta' - \lambda^2)(\partial\theta/\partial x_\alpha - \lambda^2 f_\alpha) + (\lambda^2/\nu)U_{\alpha\beta}f_\beta + Kf_\alpha = 0,$$

where K is a constant; the maximum value in question is K. The boundary conditions associated with (6.25) are (6.5). We have here a new characteristic-value problem, namely, to find the characteristic values of K such that (6.25) may be consistent with (6.5). If all these characteristic values are negative, then the maximum of the right-hand side of (6.10) is negative, and hence $\sigma_1 < 0$.

Now it follows from the reasoning leading to (6.19) that if the motion of the cylinders and λ are assigned, the right-hand side of (6.10) is negative when ν is large enough. Thus, for large ν, all the characteristics K of (6.25) are negative. If we decrease ν, instability cannot appear until the greatest of the characteristics K passes through the value zero. Hence we may make this statement: *Couette motion is stable for general disturbances of wavelength $2\pi/\lambda$ provided that $\nu > \nu_1(\lambda)$, where $\nu_1(\lambda)$ is the greatest characteristic value of ν making the equations*

$$(6.26) \qquad (\Delta' - \lambda^2)(\partial\theta/\partial x_\alpha - \lambda^2 f_\alpha) + (\lambda^2/\nu)U_{\alpha\beta}f_\beta = 0$$

consistent with the boundary conditions (6.5).

7. **Couette motion with plane disturbance.** By a plane disturbance of Couette motion, we mean a disturbance in which the velocity is parallel to the plane $x_3 = $ const. (in the notation of §6) and independent of x_3. This is not a particular case of that considered in §6, because the condition of periodicity in x_3 is replaced by the condition of independence of x_3.

Limitations of space permit only a brief survey of this problem. The Couette motion (3.4) satisfies (2.27) with $\psi = \Psi$ where

$$(7.1) \qquad \Psi = \tfrac{1}{2}Ar^2 + B \log r.$$

Putting first $\psi = \Psi + \epsilon\psi' + \cdots$ and then (introducing the azimuthal angle ϕ)

$$(7.2) \qquad \psi' = f(r)e^{\sigma t + i\lambda\phi}$$

where λ is an integer (positive without loss of generality), we obtain the characteristic value problem for σ in the form

$$\nu LLf = (\sigma + i\lambda V/r)Lf,$$
$$(7.3) \qquad L = \frac{d^2}{dr^2} + \frac{1}{r}\frac{d}{dr} - \frac{\lambda^2}{r^2},$$

with the boundary conditions

$$(7.4) \qquad f = f' = 0 \quad \text{for} \quad r = a_1 \quad \text{and for} \quad r = a_2.$$

The accent here indicates d/dr and V is given by (3.5). Multiplying (7.3) by $r\bar{f}dr$, integrating from $r = a_1$ to $r = a_2$, and adding the complex conjugate, we get (with $\sigma = \sigma_1 + i\sigma_2$)

$$(7.5) \qquad \sigma_1\left(\int rf'\bar{f}'dr + \lambda^2\int r^{-1}f\bar{f}dr\right)\Big/\nu$$
$$= -\int rLf L\bar{f}dr - \tfrac{1}{2}ik\int r^{-2}(f\bar{f}' - \bar{f}f')dr,$$

where the range of integration is (a_1, a_2) and

(7.6) $$k = 2\lambda B/\nu.$$

Considering, as in §6, the upper bound of the right-hand side of (7.5), for f arbitrary save for (7.4) and a normalizing condition, we are led (as we were led to (6.26)) to the statement that *Couette motion is stable for plane disturbances, characterized with respect to periodicity in ϕ by the positive integer λ, provided that $k < k_1(\lambda)$, where $k_1(\lambda)$ is the smallest characteristic value of k making the equation*

(7.7)
$$(rf'')'' - (2\lambda^2 + 1)(r^{-1}f')' + (\lambda^4 - 4\lambda^2)r^{-3}f$$
$$- \tfrac{1}{2}ik\{(r^{-2}f)' + r^{-2}f'\} = 0$$

consistent with (7.4).

Here, although derived in quite a different way, we have equation (19) of K. Tamaki and W. J. Harrison [18]. Since (7.7) is homogeneous, it is easy to get the general solution, but the subsequent calculations are intricate and the reader must be referred for them to a later paper by Harrison [19], where he found it possible to make use of the same type of argument as that used previously by Orr [20] for plane Couette motion.

8. **Couette motion with disturbance having rotational symmetry.** We proceed to discuss the one case where the method of the exponential time-factor has been used successfully to predict instability. For a disturbance with rotational symmetry, the first-order equations of disturbance of Couette motion are as in (3.8). Let us introduce dimensionless variables and constants as follows:

(8.1)
$$t' = \nu t/a_1^2, \qquad r' = r/a_1, \qquad z' = z/a_1,$$
$$\alpha = a_2/a_1 > 1, \qquad \beta = n_2/n_1, \qquad R = n_1 a_1^2/\nu,$$
$$A' = (\alpha^2\beta - 1)/(\alpha^2 - 1), \qquad B' = -\alpha^2(\beta - 1)/(\alpha^2 - 1);$$

we recall that a_1, a_2 are the radii of the cylinders and n_1, n_2 their angular velocities, the subscript 1 referring to the inner cylinder. The constants α, β, R may be called, respectively, the *geometrical ratio*, the *kinematical ratio* and the *Reynolds number* of the steady motion. Substitution of (8.1) in (3.8) gives

$$\left(\frac{\partial}{\partial t'} - \Theta'\right)\Theta'\psi' = -2R(A' + B'/r'^2)a_1\frac{\partial v'}{\partial z'},$$

(8.2)
$$a_1\left(\frac{\partial}{\partial t'} - \Theta'\right)v' = 2RA'\frac{\partial\psi'}{\partial z'},$$

$$\Theta' = \frac{\partial^2}{\partial r'^2} + \frac{1}{r'}\frac{\partial}{\partial r'} + \frac{\partial^2}{\partial z'^2} - \frac{1}{r'^2}.$$

The range of r' is $1 \leq r' \leq \alpha$ and the boundary conditions (3.9) are

(8.3) $\dfrac{\partial \psi'}{\partial z'} = \dfrac{\partial}{\partial r'}(r'\psi') = v' = 0$ for $r' = 1$ and for $r' = \alpha$.

We seek solutions of (8.2) of the form

(8.4) $\qquad \psi' = a_1 f(r')e^{\sigma t' + i\lambda z'}, \qquad v' = ig(r')e^{\sigma t' + i\lambda z'},$

where the functions f, g and the constant σ may be complex; the constant λ is real, and we may suppose it positive without loss of generality. The actual stream-function and azimuthal velocity are to be found by adding to (8.4) their complex conjugates. Substitution in (8.2) gives the two ordinary differential equations

(8.5)
$$(L - \lambda^2 - \sigma)(L - \lambda^2)f = -2\lambda R(A' + B'/r'^2)g,$$
$$(L - \lambda^2 - \sigma)g = -2\lambda RA'f,$$
$$L = \frac{d^2}{dr'^2} + \frac{1}{r'}\frac{d}{dr'} - \frac{1}{r'^2},$$

with the boundary conditions

(8.6) $\qquad f = df/dr' = g = 0$ for $r' = 1$ and for $r' = \alpha$.

The system (8.5), (8.6) will be consistent only if the constants σ, λ, α, β, R satisfy a characteristic equation; it is natural to regard this as an equation for σ, the other (real) constants being assigned.

We have in (8.5), (8.6) a somewhat simpler form of the characteristic value problem than that given by G. I. Taylor [2]; the formal simplification arises from the use of the stream-function ψ. We proceed to give a modification of Taylor's method of obtaining the characteristic equation.*

The Bessel functions $J_1(\kappa r')$, $Y_1(\kappa r')$ are independent solutions of

(8.7) $\qquad\qquad\qquad (L + \kappa^2)\phi(r') = 0.$

Associating the boundary conditions $\phi(1) = \phi(\alpha) = 0$, we have as the characteristic values κ_n, $(n = 1, 2, \cdots)$, of the parameter κ the roots of

(8.8) $\qquad\qquad J_1(\kappa)Y_1(\kappa\alpha) - Y_1(\kappa)J_1(\kappa\alpha) = 0;$

the corresponding characteristic functions ϕ_n of (8.7) are†

(8.9) $\qquad \phi_n(r') = C_n\{J_1(\kappa_n)Y_1(\kappa_n r') - Y_1(\kappa_n)J_1(\kappa_n r')\}, \qquad n = 1, 2, \cdots,$

C_n being a normalizing factor, chosen to make

(8.10) $\qquad\qquad\qquad \displaystyle\int_1^\alpha r'\phi_m\phi_n dr' = \delta_{mn}.$

The constants κ_n, C_n and the functions ϕ_n are calculable in terms of α.

---

* The analytical validity of the processes employed by Taylor has been discussed by Faxén [21], who also proposed alternative treatments.

† The summation convention does not operate in §8.

We assume the existence of solutions of (8.5), (8.6), expansible in series of the above characteristic functions,

(8.11)
$$f = \sum_{n=1}^{\infty} b_n \phi_n, \qquad b_n = \int_1^{\alpha} r' f \phi_n dr',$$

$$g = \sum_{n=1}^{\infty} c_n \phi_n, \qquad c_n = \int_1^{\alpha} r' g \phi_n dr'.$$

Since

(8.12) $$\int_1^{\alpha} r' \phi_n L g dr' = \int_1^{\alpha} r' g L \phi_n dr' = - \kappa_n^2 \int_1^{\alpha} r' g \phi_n dr' = - \kappa_n^2 c_n,$$

multiplication of the second of (8.5) by $r' \phi_n dr'$ and integration from 1 to α gives

(8.13) $$c_n = 2\lambda R A' (\kappa_n^2 + \lambda^2 + \sigma)^{-1} b_n.$$

We may expand the right-hand side of the first part of (8.5) in the form

(8.14) $$- 2\lambda R(A' + B'/r'^2) g = \sum_{n=1}^{\infty} d_n \phi_n,$$

where

(8.15) $$d_n = - 2\lambda R \left\{ A' c_n + B' \int_1^{\alpha} (g \phi_n / r') dr' \right\};$$

by (8.13) we have

(8.16)
$$d_m = - \sum_{n=1}^{\infty} D_{mn} b_n,$$

$$D_{mn} = 4\lambda^2 R^2 A' \left\{ A' \delta_{mn} + B' \int_1^{\alpha} (\phi_m \phi_n / r') dr' \right\} (\kappa_n^2 + \lambda^2 + \sigma)^{-1}.$$

If we substitute from (8.14) in the first of (8.5), multiply across by $r' \phi_m dr'$ and integrate from 1 to α, we get

(8.17) $$- \left[\frac{d\phi_m}{dr'} r' \frac{d^2 f}{dr'^2} \right]_1^{\alpha} + (\kappa_m^2 + \lambda^2)(\kappa_m^2 + \lambda^2 + \sigma) b_m = - \sum_{n=1}^{\infty} D_{mn} b_n,$$

$$m = 1, 2, \cdots .$$

Let us define

(8.18)
$$e_m = (\kappa_m^2 + \lambda^2 + \sigma) b_m,$$

$$E_{mn} = D_{mn}(\kappa_m^2 + \lambda^2)^{-1}(\kappa_n^2 + \lambda^2 + \sigma)^{-1},$$

$$\Phi_m^{(\alpha)} = (d\phi_m/dr')_{r'=\alpha}, \qquad \Phi_m^{(1)} = (d\phi_m/dr')_{r'=1}.$$

Then (8.17) may be written

(8.19)
$$(\kappa_m^2 + \lambda^2)^{-1} \Phi_m^{(1)} (r' d^2 f/dr'^2)_{r'=1} - (\kappa_m^2 + \lambda^2)^{-1} \Phi_m^{(\alpha)} (r' d^2 f/dr'^2)_{r'=\alpha}$$

$$+ \sum_{n=1}^{\infty} (\delta_{mn} + E_{mn}) e_n = 0, \qquad m = 1, 2, \cdots .$$

On account of the boundary conditions on f, the series for f in (8.11) may be differentiated term-by-term, giving

$$(8.20) \qquad df/dr' = \sum_{n=1}^{\infty} b_n d\phi_n/dr', \qquad\qquad 1 \leq r' \leq \alpha,$$

and the vanishing of df/dr' at the ends of the range gives the two equations

$$(8.21) \quad \sum_{n=1}^{\infty} (\kappa_n^2 + \lambda^2 + \sigma)^{-1}\Phi_n^{(1)} e_n = 0, \quad \sum_{n=1}^{\infty} (\kappa_n^2 + \lambda^2 + \sigma)^{-1}\Phi_n^{(\alpha)} e_n = 0.$$

The infinite set of equations (8.19), (8.21), linear in the quantities

$$(r'd^2f/dr'^2)_{r'=1}, \qquad (r'd^2f/dr'^2)_{r'=\alpha}, \qquad e_1, e_2, \cdots,$$

yields the characteristic equation

$$(8.22) \qquad\qquad F(\sigma, \lambda, \alpha, \beta, R) = 0,$$

where F is the infinite determinant

$$(8.23) \quad \begin{vmatrix} 0 & 0 & (\kappa_1^2 + \lambda^2 + \sigma)^{-1}\Phi_1^{(1)} & (\kappa_2^2 + \lambda^2 + \sigma)^{-1}\Phi_2^{(1)} \cdots \\ 0 & 0 & (\kappa_1^2 + \lambda^2 + \sigma)^{-1}\Phi_1^{(\alpha)} & (\kappa_2^2 + \lambda^2 + \sigma)^{-1}\Phi_2^{(\alpha)} \cdots \\ (\kappa_1^2 + \lambda^2)^{-1}\Phi_1^{(1)} & (\kappa_1^2 + \lambda^2)^{-1}\Phi_1^{(\alpha)} & 1 + E_{11} & E_{12} \qquad \cdots \\ (\kappa_2^2 + \lambda^2)^{-1}\Phi_2^{(1)} & (\kappa_2^2 + \lambda^2)^{-1}\Phi_2^{(\alpha)} & E_{21} & 1 + E_{22} \quad \cdots \\ \vdots & \vdots & \vdots & \vdots \quad \cdots \end{vmatrix}$$

The next step should be the evaluation of the roots σ of (8.22) corresponding to assigned values of λ, α, β, R. This would be almost impossibly laborious, however, and we follow Taylor in adopting a less direct attack. The work of §6 for a general disturbance is applicable in particular for a disturbance with rotational symmetry. Translating (6.23) into present dimensionless notation, we know that the real parts of all roots σ of (8.22) are negative provided that

$$(8.24) \qquad\qquad R < \lambda^2 \frac{\alpha^2 - 1}{\alpha^2 |\beta - 1|}.$$

Let us hold λ, α, β fixed and increase R. If instability appears, it will appear when R has such a value that (8.22) has a purely imaginary root. But this consideration does not effectively reduce the task of computation, so Taylor made the bold assumption that the roots σ of (8.22) are real. Then instability will appear when R passes through such a value that (8.22) has a root $\sigma = 0$. This critical value of R, marking the incidence of instability, will be the smallest positive root R of

$$(8.25) \qquad\qquad F(0, \lambda, \alpha, \beta, R) = 0.$$

Regarding α, β as assigned once for all, this critical value of R is a function of λ, say $R(\lambda)$. The absolute critical value R_c will be the minimum of $R(\lambda)$ for arbitrary λ.

The task of solving (8.25) remains formidable, and Taylor found it necessary to limit his calculations to the case where the difference between the radii of the cylinders is small, that is, $(\alpha-1)$ small.* He was then able to substitute trigonometric expressions for the Bessel functions, the value of κ_n being approximately $n\pi/(\alpha-1)$. Even then the calculations are very complicated. The results for particular values of α are exhibited graphically in Taylor's paper. We may quote here in the present notation his approximate expression for R_c for the case where the cylinders rotate in the same sense $(\beta>0)$:

$$
(8.26) \quad
\begin{aligned}
R_c^2 &= \frac{\pi^4}{2} \frac{\alpha+1}{(\alpha-1)^3(1-\beta\alpha^2)(1-\beta)} (0.0571S + 0.00056S^{-1})^{-1}, \\
S &= \frac{1+\beta}{1-\beta} - 0.652(\alpha-1).
\end{aligned}
$$

The corresponding value of λ (minimizing $R(\lambda)$) is $\pi/(\alpha-1)$, giving a wave-length in the z-direction equal to twice the difference between the radii of the cylinders. The formula (8.26) and the corresponding calculations for $\beta<0$ are in very good agreement with experiment.

9. Poiseuille motion in a tube of general section. A problem as general as that of the stability of Poiseuille motion in a tube of arbitrary section does not appear to have been treated previously. It is, however, quite easy to establish some sufficient conditions for stability.

The steady motion is as in (3.11) and the first-order equations of disturbance as in (3.14). We substitute

$$
(9.1) \qquad u_i' = f_i(x_1, x_2)e^{\sigma t+i\lambda x_3}, \qquad p' = g(x_1, x_2)e^{\sigma t+i\lambda x_3},
$$

the functions f_i, g and the constant σ being in general complex and the constant λ real; we assume it positive without loss of generality. On elimination of g, we obtain the two partial differential equations for f_α

$$
(9.2) \quad
\begin{aligned}
\sigma\left(\frac{\partial\theta}{\partial x_\alpha} - \lambda^2 f_\alpha\right) &= \nu(\Delta' - \lambda^2)\left(\frac{\partial\theta}{\partial x_\alpha} - \lambda^2 f_\alpha\right) \\
&+ i\lambda\left\{\frac{\partial}{\partial x_\alpha}\left(f_\beta \frac{\partial U}{\partial x_\beta}\right) - \theta\frac{\partial U}{\partial x_\alpha} - U\left(\frac{\partial\theta}{\partial x_\alpha} - \lambda^2 f_\alpha\right)\right\},
\end{aligned}
$$

where

$$
(9.3) \qquad \theta = \partial f_\beta/\partial x_\beta = -i\lambda f_3, \qquad \Delta' = \partial^2/\partial x_\beta \partial x_\beta.
$$

---

* Without introducing this restriction, one can prove stability if $n_2 a_2^2 > n_1 a_1^2 > 0$, or, equivalently, $\alpha^2\beta>1$; cf. [40].

We have written U instead of U_3 for simplicity in notation. The boundary conditions are

$$(9.4) \qquad\qquad f_\alpha = \theta = 0 \quad \text{on} \quad C,$$

C being the boundary of the section. The consistency of (9.2) and (9.4) demands the satisfaction of a characteristic equation by σ, λ, ν.

One may observe the similarity of (9.2) to the analogous equation (6.3) for Couette motion. This suggests the application of similar methods. One may, however, note that i does not appear explicitly in (6.3), whereas it does appear in (9.2).

We shall now establish conditions under which the Poiseuille motion is stable, in the sense that all characteristic values of σ have negative real parts. Let us multiply (9.2) by $\bar{f}_\alpha dS$ and integrate over the section. On integration by parts this gives, by virtue of (9.4)

$$\sigma(I_2^2 + \lambda^2 I_1^2) = - \nu(I_3^2 + \lambda^2 I_2^2 + \lambda^2 J_2^2 + \lambda^4 I_1^2)$$

$$(9.5)$$

$$+ i\lambda\left\{ \int (\partial U/\partial x_\alpha) f_\alpha \bar{\theta} dS - \int U\theta\bar{\theta} dS - \lambda^2 \int U f_\alpha \bar{f}_\alpha dS \right\},$$

where we have used for certain positive-definite integrals the notation (6.7). Putting

$$(9.6) \qquad\qquad \sigma = \sigma_1 + i\sigma_2,$$

and adding to (9.5) its complex conjugate, we obtain

$$\sigma_1(I_2^2 + \lambda^2 I_1^2)/\nu = - (I_3^2 + \lambda^2 I_2^2 + \lambda^2 J_2^2 + \lambda^4 I_1^2)$$

$$(9.7)$$

$$+ \tfrac{1}{2}i(\lambda/\nu) \int (\partial U/\partial x_\alpha)(f_\alpha\bar{\theta} - \bar{f}_\alpha\theta)dS,$$

which may be compared with (6.10), the difference between the forms of the last terms being noted.

With a view to establishing conditions under which the right-hand side of (9.7) is negative for f_α arbitrary save for the restriction (9.4), we shall now establish some inequalities. We shall use χ to denote an arbitrary real number.

We have

$$(9.8) \qquad \int (f_\alpha + i\chi\theta\partial U/\partial x_\alpha)(\bar{f}_\alpha - i\chi\bar{\theta}\partial U/\partial x_\alpha)dS \geqq 0,$$

and so

$$(9.9) \qquad \left| \int \frac{\partial U}{\partial x_\alpha}(f_\alpha\bar{\theta} - \bar{f}_\alpha\theta)dS \right| \leqq 2I_1\left(\int \frac{\partial U}{\partial x_\alpha}\frac{\partial U}{\partial x_\alpha}\theta\bar{\theta} dS \right)^{1/2} < 2GI_1I_2,$$

where G is the maximum of the gradient of U,

$$(9.10) \qquad\qquad G = \max\left(\frac{\partial U}{\partial x_\alpha}\frac{\partial U}{\partial x_\alpha}\right)^{1/2}.$$

By virtue of equations (3.11) and (3.12) this maximum is attained on the boundary.

Also

$$(9.11) \qquad \int\left(\frac{\partial f_\alpha}{\partial x_\beta} + \chi\frac{\partial f_\beta}{\partial x_\alpha}\right)\left(\frac{\partial \bar f_\alpha}{\partial x_\beta} + \chi\frac{\partial \bar f_\beta}{\partial x_\alpha}\right)dS \geqq 0,$$

or

$$(9.12) \qquad J_2^2 + \chi\int\left(\frac{\partial f_\alpha}{\partial x_\beta}\frac{\partial \bar f_\beta}{\partial x_\alpha} + \frac{\partial \bar f_\alpha}{\partial x_\beta}\frac{\partial f_\beta}{\partial x_\alpha}\right)dS + \chi^2 J_2^2 \geqq 0.$$

But

$$(9.13) \qquad \int\left(\frac{\partial f_\alpha}{\partial x_\beta}\frac{\partial \bar f_\beta}{\partial x_\alpha} + \frac{\partial \bar f_\alpha}{\partial x_\beta}\frac{\partial f_\beta}{\partial x_\alpha}\right)dS = -\int\left(\bar f_\beta\frac{\partial \theta}{\partial x_\beta} + f_\beta\frac{\partial \bar\theta}{\partial x_\beta}\right)dS$$

$$= 2\int\theta\bar\theta\, dS = 2I_2^2,$$

and hence (9.12) gives

$$(9.14) \qquad\qquad\qquad J_2 \geqq I_2.$$

Also

$$(9.15) \qquad \int\left(\frac{\partial U}{\partial x_\alpha}\theta + \chi\frac{\partial \theta}{\partial x_\alpha}\right)\left(\frac{\partial U}{\partial x_\alpha}\bar\theta + \chi\frac{\partial \bar\theta}{\partial x_\alpha}\right)dS \geqq 0,$$

or

$$(9.16) \qquad \int\frac{\partial U}{\partial x_\alpha}\frac{\partial U}{\partial x_\alpha}\theta\bar\theta\, dS + \chi\int\frac{\partial U}{\partial x_\alpha}\frac{\partial}{\partial x_\alpha}(\theta\bar\theta)dS + \chi^2 I_3^2 \geqq 0.$$

But by (3.11), (3.12)

$$(9.17) \qquad \int\frac{\partial U}{\partial x_\alpha}\frac{\partial}{\partial x_\alpha}(\theta\bar\theta)dS = -\int\Delta'U\cdot\theta\bar\theta\, dS = AI_2^2,$$

A being the constant in (3.11), which we may assume positive without loss of generality. We note that

$$(9.18) \qquad\qquad A = -\mu^{-1}dP/dx_3,$$

where dP/dx_3 is the pressure gradient in the steady motion. From (9.16), (9.17) we have

$$(9.19) \qquad\qquad AI_2^2 < 2GI_2I_3, \qquad I_3 > \tfrac{1}{2}I_2A/G.$$

Substituting from (9.9), (9.14), (9.19) in (9.7), we have

$$(9.20) \quad \sigma_1(I_2^2 + \lambda^2 I_1^2)/\nu < (G\lambda/\nu)I_1I_2 - I_2^2(2\lambda^2 + \tfrac{1}{4}A^2/G^2) - \lambda^4 I_1^2.$$

The expression on the left is negative-definite if

$$(9.21) \qquad G\lambda/\nu < \lambda^2(8\lambda^2 + A^2/G^2)^{1/2}.$$

To agree with (1.1) for a circular section, we may define the Reynolds number R for Poiseuille flow through a general section by

$$(9.22) \qquad R = GS/(2\pi\nu),$$

where S is the area of the section. Then, from (9.20), we may say that *Poiseuille motion in a tube of any section is stable for disturbances of wavelength $l(=2\pi/\lambda)$ if*

$$(9.23) \qquad R < (S/l)(32\pi^2/l^2 + A^2/G^2)^{1/2},$$

where A is related to the pressure-gradient by (9.18) and G is as in (9.10). For a tube of circular section of radius a this condition, R being as in (1.1), is

$$(9.24) \qquad R < (2\pi a/l)(1 + 8\pi^2 a^2/l^2)^{1/2}.$$

To obtain stronger conditions for stability, we may return to (9.7) and pursue the same line of reasoning as that which led us from (6.10) to (6.26). Thus we may say that *Poiseuille motion in a tube of any section is stable for disturbances of wave-length $2\pi/\lambda$ provided that $\nu > \nu_1(\lambda)$, where $\nu_1(\lambda)$ is the greatest characteristic value of ν making the following equations consistent with the boundary conditions* (9.4):

$$(9.25) \quad (\Delta' - \lambda^2)\left(\frac{\partial\theta}{\partial x_\alpha} - \lambda^2 f_\alpha\right) + \tfrac{1}{2}i(\lambda/\nu)\left\{\frac{\partial}{\partial x_\alpha}\left(\frac{\partial U}{\partial x_\beta}f_\beta\right) + \frac{\partial U}{\partial x_\alpha}\theta\right\} = 0.$$

10. Poiseuille motion in a tube of circular section with disturbance having rotational or axial symmetry. We have in (9.24) a sufficient condition for stability for Poiseuille motion through a tube of circular section. Since the right-hand side has zero for minimum with respect to variable l, the condition is a very small step indeed towards the theoretical establishment of the experimental fact (1.2), which remains an outstanding challenge to mathematicians. The condition (9.24) has at least the merit that the disturbance is of a general type.

Taylor's success (§8) in handling the problem of the stability of Couette motion by means of a disturbance with rotational symmetry leads us to try the same plan for Poiseuille motion in a tube of circular section. The results are however disappointing, as we shall now see.

In cylindrical coördinates the first-order equations of disturbance are as in (3.19). We note that the variables ψ', v' are separated. Putting, as usual,

$$(10.1) \qquad v' = g(r)e^{\sigma t + i\lambda z},$$

the second equation of (3.19) gives

$$(L - \lambda^2 - \sigma/\nu - i\lambda W/\nu)g = 0,$$

(10.2)
$$L = \frac{d^2}{dr^2} + \frac{1}{r}\frac{d}{dr} - \frac{1}{r^2},$$

$$W = W_0\left(1 - \frac{r^2}{a^2}\right),$$

with the boundary conditions

(10.3) $g = 0$ for $r = 0$ and for $r = a.$

Multiplying (10.2) by $r\bar{g}dr$, integrating from 0 to a, and adding the complex conjugate equation, we see immediately that the real part of σ is negative; thus there is stability as far as v' is concerned. Instability, if it occurs, must arise from the first of (3.19). But this is the single equation (3.21) for axially symmetric disturbances. *Hence the problem of stability for disturbances with rotational symmetry is identical with the problem of stability for disturbances with axial symmetry.*

The axially symmetric disturbance of Poiseuille motion through a tube of circular section was discussed by Orr [20, p. 135]. His fundamental equation may be obtained from (9.25): since the disturbance is axially symmetric, we have

(10.4)
$$f_\alpha = x_\alpha f(r), \qquad\qquad \theta = rdf/dr + 2f,$$
$$U = W_0(1 - r^2/a^2), \qquad f_\beta \partial U/\partial x_\beta = - 2W_0 r^2 f/a^2,$$

and substitution in (9.25) gives

(10.5)
$$(L - \lambda^2)^2 f - \frac{2i\lambda W_0}{\nu a^2 r}\frac{d}{dr}(r^2 f) = 0,$$

$$L = \frac{d^2}{dr^2} + \frac{3}{r}\frac{d}{dr},$$

an equation immediately identified with Orr's (84) on putting $r^2 f = \psi$. The boundary conditions are $f = df/dr = 0$ for $r = a$ and regularity for $r = 0$. Solving his equation by a power series and hence calculating the largest characteristic $\nu_1(\lambda)$, Orr was led, by application of the type of argument associated with equation (6.26), to the conclusion that *Poiseuille motion in a tube of circular section is stable for axially symmetric disturbances of arbitrary wave-length if*

(10.6) $R \equiv W_0 a/\nu < 180.$

(This definition of R is easily seen to be the same as that given by equation (1.1).) Since this is only a sufficient condition for stability, it does not conflict with (1.2).

The problem of axially symmetric disturbances has also been discussed by Sexl [22, 23]. We shall indicate briefly the nature of his argument, using a slightly different approach. Introducing in (3.21) the dimensionless quantities

(10.7) $t' = \nu t/a^2,$ $r' = r/a,$ $z' = z/a,$ $R = W_0 a/\nu,$

and then putting

(10.8) $\psi' = f(r')e^{\sigma t' + i\lambda z'},$

we obtain for f the differential system

$$\{L - \lambda^2 - \sigma - i\lambda R(1 - r'^2)\}\, F = 0,$$

$$(L - \lambda^2)f = F,$$

(10.9)

$$L = \frac{d^2}{dr'^2} + \frac{1}{r'}\frac{d}{dr'} - \frac{1}{r'^2},$$

with the boundary conditions

(10.10)
$$f = df/dr' = 0 \quad \text{for} \quad r' = 1,$$
$$f = 0 \quad \text{for} \qquad\qquad r' = 0.$$

Here we have a characteristic value problem for σ, λ, R. Rejecting one of the solutions of the first of (10.9) on account of a singularity at $r' = 0$, we have

(10.11) $F = F_1(r', \sigma, \lambda, R),$

a power series in r'. With the usual notation for Bessel functions, let us multiply the second of (10.9) by $r'J_1(i\lambda r')dr'$ and integrate over the range $(0, 1)$. We get

(10.12) $\int_0^1 r'J_1(i\lambda r')F_1(r', \sigma, \lambda, R)dr' = 0,$

equivalent to Sexl's transcendental characteristic equation. It is difficult to make general deductions from this equation, and Sexl confines his attention to the cases where λR is either very small or very large, and in the latter case an asymptotic form for F_1 is used. There is further restriction to the cases where λ is either very small or very large. Sexl found in all cases considered that the real value of σ is negative, and this appears to be generally accepted (cf. Müller [24, p. 320]) as a proof that Poiseuille motion in a tube of circular section is stable for axially symmetric disturbances of any wave-length for any value of the Reynolds number.

11. **Plane Couette and plane Poiseuille motions (P.C.M. and P.P.M.).** As remarked earlier, the mathematical complexity of the three-dimensional problems physically most interesting has led to a concentration of attention on analogous plane problems, namely, the stability of plane Couette

motion $(P.C.M.)$ and plane Poiseuille motion $(P.P.M.)$, described in §3(c). The first-order equations of disturbance (for disturbances in the plane of the motion) are given in (3.28), (3.29). It might appear from the analogy of G. I. Taylor's work (§8) that instability should be sought in a disturbance not confined to the plane of the motion, but H. B. Squire [25] has shown that stability is increased by the introduction of such more general disturbances. We shall here confine ourselves to disturbances in the plane of the motion.

We substitute in (3.28), (3.29)

$$(11.1) \qquad\qquad \psi' = f(y)e^{\sigma\tau+i\lambda x},$$

where the function f and the constant σ are in general complex and the constant λ real and positive without loss of generality. Thus we obtain for f the ordinary differential equation of the fourth order

$$LLf = \sigma Lf + i\lambda RMf,$$
$$(11.2) \qquad\qquad L = d^2/dy^2 - \lambda^2,$$
$$M = yL \text{ for } P.C.M.; \quad M = (1 - y^2)L + 2 \text{ for } P.P.M.$$

By (3.31) the boundary conditions are

$$(11.3) \qquad\qquad f = df/dy = 0 \quad \text{for} \quad y = \pm 1.$$

The system (11.2), (11.3) defines the characteristic value problem: for consistency σ, λ, R must satisfy a characteristic equation. We recall that R is the Reynolds number (3.27). It is natural to regard λ, R as assigned, and σ as the unknown characteristic value. If

$$(11.4) \qquad\qquad \sigma = \sigma_1 + i\sigma_2,$$

then $\sigma_1 \leqq 0$ (for all characteristic values) is a sufficient condition for stability.

Doubts would be set at rest and much arduous labor saved, if a simple proof were forthcoming for the following theorem: *For any positive values of the real constants λ, R, no characteristic value σ of the system (11.2), (11.3) has a positive real part.* Such a theorem would establish the stability of $P.C.M.$ and $P.P.M.$ under all conditions. This result appears contrary to physical intuition (because we believe such motions to be unstable for large R), but it is a result towards which the theory appears to be slowly moving, and proofs have already been offered for the case of $P.C.M.$ Before proceeding to discuss these complicated proofs, let us develop some simple results regarding the characteristic values.

Denoting the complex conjugate as usual by a bar and d/dy by an accent, we obtain, on multiplying (11.2) by $\bar{f}dy$ and integrating for the range $(-1, 1)$,

$$(11.5) \qquad \sigma(I_1^2 + \lambda^2 I_0^2) = -i\lambda RQ - (I_2^2 + 2\lambda^2 I_1^2 + \lambda^4 I_0^2),$$

where

(11.6)
$$I_0{}^2 = \int_{-1}^{1} f\bar{f}dy, \qquad I_1{}^2 = \int_{-1}^{1} f'\bar{f}'dy,$$

$$I_2{}^2 = \int_{-1}^{1} f''\bar{f}''dy, \qquad I_3{}^2 = \int_{-1}^{1} f'''\bar{f}'''dy,$$

and

$$Q = \int_{-1}^{1} y(f'\bar{f}' + \lambda^2 f\bar{f})dy + \int_{-1}^{1} f'\bar{f}dy \quad \text{for} \quad P.C.M.,$$

(11.7)
$$Q = \int_{-1}^{1} [(1 - y^2)f'\bar{f}' + \{\lambda^2(1 - y^2) - 2\}f\bar{f}]dy$$

$$- 2\int_{-1}^{1} yf'\bar{f}dy \quad \text{for} \quad P.P.M.$$

Subtracting its complex conjugate from (11.5), we get

(11.8)
$$\sigma_2(I_1{}^2 + \lambda^2 I_0{}^2) = -\tfrac{1}{2}\lambda R(Q + \bar{Q}).$$

For $P.C.M.$ this gives

(11.9)
$$\int_{-1}^{1} (\sigma_2 + \lambda Ry)(f'\bar{f}' + \lambda^2 f\bar{f})dy = 0,$$

and hence (cf. Orr [20, p. 117], Solberg [26, p. 389]),

(11.10)
$$-\lambda R < \sigma_2 < \lambda R.$$

For $P.P.M.$ (11.8) gives

(11.11)
$$\int_{-1}^{1} \{\sigma_2 + \lambda R(1 - y^2)\}(f'\bar{f}' + \lambda^2 f\bar{f})dy = \lambda R \int_{-1}^{1} f\bar{f}dy;$$

thus the integrand on the left must be positive somewhere in the range, and hence $\sigma_2 > -\lambda R$. We can also write (11.11) in the form

(11.12)
$$\int_{-1}^{1} \{\sigma_2 + \lambda R(1 - y^2)\}f'\bar{f}'dy$$

$$+ \lambda^2 \int_{-1}^{1} \{\sigma_2 + \lambda R(1 - y^2) - R/\lambda\}f\bar{f}dy = 0.$$

If $\sigma_2 > 0$, so that the first integral is positive, the second integrand must be negative somewhere in the range, and hence, with the previous result, we have (cf. Solberg [26, p. 389])

(11.13)
$$-\lambda R < \sigma_2 < R/\lambda.$$

The inequalities (11.10), (11.13) are interesting inasmuch as they limit σ to strips in the complex plane, but they tell us nothing directly about stability, since they concern σ_2, not σ_1.

If we add to (11.5) its complex conjugate, we get

$$(11.14) \qquad \sigma_1(I_1^2 + \lambda^2 I_0^2) = -\tfrac{1}{2}i\lambda R(Q - \overline{Q}) - (I_2^2 + 2\lambda^2 I_1^2 + \lambda^4 I_0^2).$$

It is easily seen that

$$(11.15) \qquad \begin{aligned} |Q - \overline{Q}| &< 2qI_0I_1, \\ q = 1 \text{ for } P.C.M.&; q = 2 \text{ for } P.P.M., \end{aligned}$$

and hence

$$(11.16) \qquad \sigma_1(I_1^2 + \lambda^2 I_0^2) < q\lambda RI_0I_1 - (I_2^2 + 2\lambda^2 I_1^2 + \lambda^4 I_0^2),$$

an inequality of the same general type as (6.17), (6.22), (9.20).

We can deduce from (11.16) some simple conditions for stability, valid both for $P.C.M.$ and $P.P.M.$ For any real constants α, β,

$$(11.17) \qquad \int_{-1}^{1} (f + \alpha yf' + \beta f'')(\bar{f} + \alpha y\bar{f}' + \beta \bar{f}'')dy > 0,$$

from which we deduce

$$(11.18) \qquad \beta^2 I_2^2 > I_1^2(\alpha\beta - \alpha^2 + 2\beta) + I_0^2(\alpha - 1),$$

and hence, from (11.16),

$$(11.19) \qquad \begin{aligned} \sigma_1\beta^2(I_1^2 + \lambda^2 I_0^2) &< \beta^2 q\lambda RI_0I_1 - I_1^2(2\lambda^2\beta^2 + \alpha\beta - \alpha^2 + 2\beta) \\ &\quad - I_0^2(\lambda^4\beta^2 + \alpha - 1). \end{aligned}$$

Therefore $\sigma_1 < 0$ if

$$(11.20) \qquad (\beta^2 q\lambda R)^2 < 4(2\lambda^2\beta^2 + \alpha\beta - \alpha^2 + 2\beta)(\lambda^4\beta^2 + \alpha - 1),$$

where α, β are any real constants satisfying

$$(11.21) \qquad 2\lambda^2\beta^2 + \alpha\beta - \alpha^2 + 2\beta > 0, \qquad \lambda^4\beta^2 + \alpha - 1 > 0.$$

We now make certain choices of α, β, satisfying (11.21).

For $\alpha = \beta = 1$, we have $\sigma_1 < 0$ if

$$(11.22) \qquad (qR)^2 < 8\lambda^2(\lambda^2 + 1).$$

For $P.P.M.$ this reads $R^2 < 2\lambda^2(\lambda^2 + 1)$, and improves a condition given by Pekeris [27, p. 66] and also the conditions (7′), (8′) of Solberg [26].

For $\alpha = \beta = 2$, we have $\sigma_1 < 0$ if

$$(11.23) \qquad (qR)^2 < (2\lambda^2 + 1)(4\lambda^4 + 1)/\lambda^2.$$

We note that, given R, there is stability for very great or very small λ, and that there is stability for arbitrary λ if $(qR)^2$ is less than the minimum of the right-hand side of (11.23).

For $\alpha = \beta = 1/\lambda$, we have $\sigma_1 < 0$ if

(11.24) $$(qR)^2 < 8(1 - \lambda^2 + \lambda^3 + \lambda^4).$$

The above conditions are very weak, but they possess the merit of simplicity. To strengthen the conditions, we return to (11.14) and consider the maximum value of the right-hand side, f being arbitrary save for the boundary conditions (11.3) and a normalizing condition. It is unnecessary to repeat the same type of reasoning as that which led us to (6.26). Applying the calculus of variations to the right-hand side of (11.14) and equating the Lagrange factor to zero, we obtain this result: *P.C.M. or P.P.M.* *is stable for disturbances of wave-length $2\pi/\lambda$ provided that $R < R_1(\lambda)$, where $R_1(\lambda)$ is the smallest characteristic value of R for which the system*

(11.25) $$f'''' - 2\lambda^2 f'' + \lambda^4 f = i\lambda R\Phi, \qquad f = f' = 0 \quad for \quad y = \pm 1,$$

is consistent, the function Φ being

(11.26) $$\Phi = -f' \quad for \quad P.C.M.; \qquad \Phi = 2yf' + f \quad for \quad P.P.M.$$

We observe that we have passed from the original characteristic value problem (11.2), (11.3) to a new characteristic value problem (11.25). But whereas a complete consideration of the former might conceivably give a sufficient condition for instability (some $\sigma_1 > 0$), conclusions drawn from (11.25) can only be sufficient conditions for stability.

Although derived in a different way, (11.25) contains the fundamental equations of Orr [20, pp. 125, 131]. The treatments for *P.C.M.* and *P.P.M.* are very different, because for *P.C.M.* (11.25) is an equation with constant coefficients and the general solution can be obtained in finite form. In the case of *P.P.M.*, Orr had recourse to a development of the solution in power series. Space only permits quotation of Orr's results: *the steady motion is stable for disturbances of arbitrary wave-length if*

(11.27) $$R < 44.3 \quad for \quad P.C.M.; \qquad R < 88 \quad for \quad P.P.M.,$$

R being defined as in (3.27). Orr's result for *P.P.M.* was confirmed by MacCreadie [28] with greater accuracy.

There is however another mode of attack. Instead of multiplying (11.2) by $\bar{f}dy$, as we did to obtain (11.5), let us multiply by $L\bar{f}dy$ and integrate over the range $(-1, 1)$. Adding the complex conjugate equation, we obtain in the notation of (11.6)

(11.28) $$\sigma_1(I_2^2 + 2\lambda^2 I_1^2 + \lambda^4 I_0^2) = \tfrac{1}{2}[f''\bar{f}''' + \bar{f}''f''']_{y=-1}^{y=1}$$
$$- (I_3^2 + 3\lambda^2 I_2^2 + 3\lambda^4 I_1^2 + \lambda^6 I_0^2),$$

the same form for both *P.C.M.* and *P.P.M.* Multiplying (11.2) by $\exp(\epsilon\lambda y)dy$, where $\epsilon = \pm 1$, and integrating we obtain

$$(11.29) \qquad [e^{\epsilon \lambda y}(f''' - \epsilon \lambda f'')]_{y=-1}^{y=1} = i\lambda R \int_{-1}^{1} e^{\epsilon \lambda y} M f dy.$$

Solving these two equations for $f'''(1)$, $f'''(-1)$ and substituting in (11.28), the right-hand side becomes a function ϕ of λ, R, $f''(1)$, $f''(-1)$ and of certain integrals involving f, f', f'', f''' taken over the range $(-1, 1)$, the complex conjugates of these quantities occurring also, since the expression is real. We now seek the maximum of ϕ, when f is arbitrary save for the boundary conditions (11.3) *and for assigned values of $f''(1)$, $f''(-1)$.* The calculus of variations gives for the maximizing f a differential equation of the sixth order

$$(11.30) \qquad f^{(6)} - 3\lambda^2 f^{(4)} + 3\lambda^4 f'' - \lambda^6 f = RF(y, \lambda, f''(1), f''(-1)),$$

with an obvious notation for derivatives, where

$$F = i\lambda^2 \operatorname{cosech} 2\lambda \{f''(1) \cosh \lambda(y + 1) - f''(-1) \cosh \lambda(y - 1)\}$$

$$\text{for} \quad P.C.M.,$$

$$(11.31)$$

$$F = -2i\lambda^2 y \operatorname{cosech} 2\lambda \{f''(1) \cosh \lambda(y + 1) - f''(-1) \cosh \lambda(y - 1)\},$$

$$\text{for} \quad P.P.M.$$

The equation (11.30) is easily solved, and the boundary conditions are such as to make the solution unique; it is a function of y, λ, R, $f''(1)$, $f''(-1)$. Substituting it in ϕ, and referring to (11.28), we find that for *P.P.M.*

$$(11.32) \qquad \sigma_1(I_2^2 + 2\lambda^2 I_1^2 + \lambda^4 I_0^2) \leq (A + BR^2)\{f''(1)\bar{f}''(1) + f''(-1)\bar{f}''(-1)\}$$
$$+ (C + DR^2)\{f''(1)\bar{f}''(-1) + \bar{f}''(1)f''(-1)\},$$

where A, B, C, D are complicated but explicit functions of λ alone and $f''(1)$, $f''(-1)$ are evaluated for that characteristic function to which σ corresponds. Hence it follows at once that $\sigma_1 < 0$ and *there is stability if λ, R satisfy*

$$(11.33) \qquad A + BR^2 < 0, \qquad |A + BR^2| > |C + DR^2|.$$

This method has not been worked out in detail for *P.C.M.*, but the results for *P.P.M.* will be reported at the International Congress for Applied Mechanics, Cambridge, Mass., in 1938. It is found that *P.P.M. is stable for disturbances of arbitrary wave-length if*

$$(11.34) \qquad\qquad R < 155.$$

This improves considerably Orr's result, 88, which was quoted in equation (11.27).

When approached as above, it is natural to attack *P.C.M.* and *P.P.M.* by a single method. But this disregards an important difference between the forms of (11.2) for the two cases. This equation is undoubtedly simpler for $P.C.M.$, for then f occurs only in the form Lf, and the equation may be written

$$(11.35) \qquad \phi'' - \lambda^2\phi = (\sigma + i\lambda Ry)\phi, \qquad f'' - \lambda^2 f = \phi,$$

with the boundary conditions $f=f'=0$ for $y=\pm 1$.

This characteristic value problem has been treated by R. von Mises [3, 4] and L. Hopf [5] in quite different ways. They both reach the same conclusion, namely, that the real part of σ is negative for all real values of λ and R, so that $P.C.M.$ is stable under all conditions, a surprising result from a physical point of view. We shall now describe these methods briefly.

In the method of von Mises, we multiply the second of (11.35) by $\exp(\pm\lambda y)dy$ and integrate, obtaining

$$(11.36) \qquad \int_{-1}^{1} e^{\lambda y}\phi\, dy = 0, \qquad \int_{-1}^{1} e^{-\lambda y}\phi\, dy = 0.$$

Instead of considering the original differential system of the fourth order with four homogeneous boundary conditions, we now consider a system of the second order, namely, the first of (11.35), with (11.36) instead of boundary conditions. We already know that the real part of σ is negative if λ is given and R is small enough. Hence, if instability occurs, it will occur when σ passes through a purely imaginary value, $\sigma=i\sigma_2$. In this critical state we have

$$(11.37) \qquad \phi'' - \lambda^2\phi = i\sigma_2(1 + Ky)\phi,$$

where $K(=\lambda R/\sigma_2)$ is real. Hence *if $P.C.M.$ is to be unstable under any circumstances, the system*

$$\phi'' - \lambda^2\phi = \sigma(1 + Ky)\phi,$$
$$(11.38) \qquad \int_{-1}^{1} e^{\lambda y}\phi\, dy = 0, \qquad \int_{-1}^{1} e^{-\lambda y}\phi\, dy = 0,$$

must possess a purely imaginary characteristic value σ for some choice of the real constants λ, K. The aim of the argument of von Mises is to prove that all the characteristic values σ of (11.38) are real. He regards (11.38) as the limit of a set of difference equations. For details, the reader must refer to the original papers. The essential point is that the characteristic values of the difference system are finite in number, and if we can account for them all (with real values) at any stage, then no imaginary characteristic values can occur in the differential system, since characteristic values for the differential system must be limit points of characteristic values for the difference system. Although the general theory of the method is closely developed, the application to our particular hydrodynamical problem is less full, and it is possible to entertain a doubt as to whether the stability of $P.C.M.$ under all circumstances is fully established.*

The method of Hopf, arising out a paper by A. Sommerfeld [29], is quite different. On putting

(11.39) $$z = (\lambda^2 + \sigma + i\lambda R y)/(\lambda R)^{2/3},$$

we transform the first of (11.35) into

(11.40) $$d^2\phi/dz^2 + z\phi = 0,$$

of which independent solutions are

(11.41) $\phi_1(z) = z^{1/2}H_{1/3}{}^{(1)}(\tfrac{2}{3}z^{3/2}),$ $\phi_2(z) = z^{1/2}H_{1/3}{}^{(2)}(\tfrac{2}{3}z^{3/2}),$

where the H's are Hankel functions. The second equation of (11.35) then reads

(11.42) $$d^2f/dz^2 + \kappa^2 f = A\phi_1 + B\phi_2,$$

where $\kappa^3 = \lambda^2/R$ and A, B are constants; multiplying by $\sin\kappa z\, dz$, $\cos\kappa z\, dz$ and integrating from z_1 to z_2 (the values of z corresponding to $y = -1$, $y = 1$), the left-hand sides vanish, and elimination of A, B from the right-hand sides gives the characteristic equation

(11.43) $$\int_{z_1}^{z_2} \int_{z_1}^{z_2} \sin \kappa(z' - z'')\phi_1(z')\phi_2(z'')dz'dz'' = 0,$$

which involves σ, λ, R in the limits of integration and in κ. Obviously the deduction of general results from (11.43) is well-nigh impossible; Hopf found it necessary to limit himself to cases where the argument of the Hankel functions is either very small or very large. In all cases amenable to calculation, he found the real part of σ negative, and concluded that $P.C.M.$ is stable under all circumstances, confirming the conclusion of von Mises.

In view of the theoretical interest of the problem and the complexity and somewhat incomplete nature of the methods described above, it is to be hoped that mathematicians will not regard the problem of the stability of $P.C.M.$ as closed. A simple general proof of stability is greatly to be desired.

The problem of the stability of $P.P.M.$ has not been so fully treated. We can only mention in passing the work of H. Solberg [26], W. Heisenberg [30], and F. Noether [32]. The methods of the last two are asymptotic for large R. Heisenberg's work indicates instability for a range of λ and R, but Noether's indicates only stability. Recently papers have appeared by S. Goldstein [33] and C. L. Pekeris [27], the latter attempting

---

* Professor von Mises has informed the writer that he does not regard his own proof of the stability of $P.C.M.$ as adequate, nor does he accept the proof of Hopf.

a solution in the form of a power series in R; these papers indicate stability as far as the calculations go.*

PART III. THE METHOD OF DECREASING POSITIVE-DEFINITE INTEGRALS

12. **The method of energy.** The method of energy has been more important historically than might appear from the small space devoted to it here. Some investigations actually conducted under this head lead to the same mathematical problems as have already been discussed in Part II, and it is unnecessary to reconsider them here. We shall show below how the method of energy is included in the methods of Part II.

We accept as basic the first-order equations of disturbance of §3. For disturbed motion given by (3.2), we define the *energy of the disturbance* as $\epsilon^2 T'$ where

$$(12.1) \qquad T' = \tfrac{1}{2}\rho \int u_i' u_i' \, d\tau,$$

where $d\tau$ is an element of volume. As in Part II, we shall consider only disturbances spatially periodic; then the region of integration in (12.1) is the cell of periodicity, a region fixed in space. In plane problems, we replace (12.1) by an integral over an area.

The essential feature of (12.1) is the positive-definite character of the integrand: if $T'=0$, then $u_i' = 0$ everywhere, and the first-order disturbance vanishes. If T' remains bounded for all positive values of the time t, then u_i' remain bounded almost everywhere, and thus we are led to accept the boundedness of T' as a sufficient condition for stability; for distinction we may call this *stability in the mean*.

Some writers demand a more stringent condition for stability, namely, $T' \to 0$ as $t \to \infty$. In the applications the actual condition we shall employ is

$$(12.2) \qquad dT'/dt \leq 0 \quad \text{for} \quad t \geq 0,$$

which certainly implies the boundedness of T', but not necessarily $T' \to 0$ as $t \to \infty$. We shall accept (12.2) as a sufficient condition for stability in the mean.

To apply the method we do not have to integrate the equations of disturbance (3.3). By virtue of these equations we can express dT'/dt in terms of u_i', $\partial u_i'/\partial x_j$, $\partial p'/\partial x_i$, $\Delta u_i'$; if the resulting expression is zero or negative for arbitrary u_i' (satisfying the boundary conditions and the equation of continuity), then (12.2) is satisfied and there is stability in the mean. It is important to note that this method may give a sufficient condition for stability, but never a sufficient condition for instability (that is, unbounded

---

* In a later paper by Pekeris [41] approximate characteristic values are found by replacing the differential equation (11.2) for $P.P.M.$ by a difference equation. All the approximate values so found indicate stability.

T'). We are never able to prove even that $dT'/dt > 0$ for arbitrary u_i', because a sufficiently rapid spatial oscillation in u_i' will reverse this inequality.

We shall now consider the application of the method to Couette motion and to Poiseuille motion, using (with slight modification) the notation of §§6, 9. We shall assume spatial periodicity in the direction of the x_3-axis, with wave-length $2\pi/\lambda$.

By (3.3) we have

$$\rho^{-1} dT'/dt = \int u_i'(\partial u_i'/\partial t) d\tau$$

(12.3)
$$= -\int u_i' U_j(\partial u_i'/\partial x_j) d\tau - \int u_i' u_j'(\partial U_i/\partial x_j) d\tau$$

$$- \rho^{-1} \int u_i'(\partial p'/\partial x_i) d\tau + \nu \int u_i' \Delta u_i' d\tau,$$

U_i being the velocity in steady motion. The integrals extend over the portion of the fluid between the planes $x_3 = 0$, $x_3 = 2\pi/\lambda$. Using Green's theorem, with the condition $u_i' = 0$ on the walls, and also the condition of spatial periodicity, we find that the first and third integrals vanish, and so

(12.4) $\quad \rho^{-1} dT'/dt = -\int u_i' u_j'(\partial U_i/\partial x_j) d\tau - \nu \int (\partial u_i'/\partial x_j)(\partial u_i'/\partial x_j) d\tau.$

Let us put

(12.5) $\qquad u_i' = f_i(x_1, x_2, t)e^{i\lambda x_3} + \bar{f}_i(x_1, x_2, t)e^{-i\lambda x_3},$

the functions f_i being complex and λ real and positive. Defining

(12.6) $\qquad\qquad\qquad \theta = \partial f_\beta/\partial x_\beta,$

we have by the last of (3.3) $f_3 = i\theta/\lambda$, and since $\partial U_i/\partial x_3 = 0$ in both Couette and Poiseuille motions, we obtain from (12.4)

$$CdT'/dt = -\tfrac{1}{2}(\lambda^2/\nu) \int (\partial U_\alpha/\partial x_\beta)(f_\alpha \bar{f}_\beta + \bar{f}_\alpha f_\beta) dS$$

(12.7)
$$+ \tfrac{1}{2} i(\lambda/\nu) \int (\partial U_3/\partial x_\alpha)(f_\alpha \bar{\theta} - \bar{f}_\alpha \theta) dS$$

$$- (I_3^2 + \lambda^2 I_2^2 + \lambda^2 J_2^2 + \lambda^4 I_1^2),$$

where C is a positive constant and I_1, I_2, J_2, I_3 are defined as in (6.7), all integrals being taken over the section $x_3 = \text{const}$. The boundary conditions on the walls are

(12.8) $\qquad\qquad\qquad f_\alpha = \theta = 0.$

In the case of Couette motion, the second integral on the right-hand side of (12.7) vanishes since $U_3 = 0$, and we are left with an expression for

CdT'/dt formally the same as the right-hand side of (6.10). Hence the problem of finding conditions under which dT'/dt is zero or negative for arbitrary f_α, satisfying (12.8), is the same as that of finding conditions under which the σ_1 of (6.10) is zero or negative for arbitrary f_α, satisfying (6.5). Thus for Couette motion nothing new is to be learned from the substitution of the method of energy for that of the exponential time-factor, except of course the fact that under those conditions of §6 which make $\sigma_1 \leqq 0$, we have stability in the mean.

In the case of Poiseuille motion, the first integral on the right-hand side of (12.7) vanishes, since $U_\alpha = 0$, and we are left with an expression formally the same as the right-hand side of (9.7). The remarks made above apply equally here; the method of energy coalesces with the method of the exponential time-factor, insofar as the latter makes use of (9.7).

Actually the method of the exponential time-factor seems to be the more powerful method: first, it is capable of establishing instability, which the method of energy can never do; secondly, it admits deductions other than (6.10) and (9.7), which represent the only products of the method of energy; thirdly, it is conceivable that in (6.10) and (9.7) we might make use of the fact that the f_α are characteristic functions, whereas in (12.7) the f_α are arbitrary functions. The only compensating disadvantage in the method of the exponential time-factor lies in the question of expansions in terms of characteristic functions. The method of energy leads without complication to conditions for stability in the mean.

Through lack of appreciation of the true situation, illegitimate deductions have been made from (12.4) or (12.7) or an equivalent equation. Suppose we take some definite u_i', satisfying the boundary and periodicity conditions and the equation of continuity, and substitute in (12.4). A negative value for dT'/dt so obtained is of no significance whatever as far as stability is concerned. It is only when $dT'/dt \leqq 0$ for arbitrary u_i' (subject to the boundary and periodicity conditions and the equation of continuity) that we can deduce stability in the mean. On this point H. A. Lorentz [34] (for $P.C.M.$) and F. R. Sharpe [35] (for $P.P.M.$ and for Poiseuille motion in a tube of circular section) were not clear, and stated results which cannot be maintained.

We shall now briefly consider the method of energy as applied to plane motions, using the notation of §3(c) and §11. Instead of (12.4) we have

$$(12.9) \quad \rho^{-1}dT'/dt = - \int u_\alpha' u_\beta' (\partial U_\alpha/\partial x_\beta)dS - \nu \int (\partial u_\alpha'/\partial x_\beta)(\partial u_\alpha'/\partial x_\beta)dS,$$

the integrals being taken over a rectangle of periodicity in the plane of the motion. We have for both $P.C.M.$ and $P.P.M.$

$$(12.10) \qquad U_1 = U(x_2), \quad U_2 = 0, \quad u_1' = - \partial \psi'/\partial x_2, \quad u_2' = \partial \psi'/\partial x_1,$$

and so, putting

$$(12.11) \qquad x = x_1/h, \quad y = x_2/h, \quad \psi' = f(y, t)e^{i\lambda x} + \bar{f}(y, t)e^{-i\lambda x},$$

where λ is real and positive, we obtain

$$(12.12) \qquad CdT'/dt = \tfrac{1}{2}i(\lambda h/\nu) \int_{-1}^{1} (dU/dy)(f\bar{f}' - \bar{f}f')dy$$
$$- (I_2^2 + 2\lambda^2 I_1^2 + \lambda^4 I_0^2)$$

in the notation of (11.6), the accents on $f, \bar{f}$ denoting $\partial/\partial y$ and C being a positive constant. Since $U = U_0 y$ for $P.C.M.$ and $U = U_0(1 - y^2)$ for $P.P.M.$, it follows that

$$(12.13) \qquad CdT'/dt = -\tfrac{1}{2}i\lambda R(Q - \bar{Q}) - (I_2^2 + 2\lambda^2 I_1^2 + \lambda^4 I_0^2),$$

where Q is as in (11.7) and R as in (3.27). The right-hand side of (12.13) is the same formally as the right-hand side of (11.14), and hence the method of energy coalesces with the method of the exponential time-factor, insofar as the latter employs (11.14).

13. **The method of vorticity.** The integral of energy (12.1) is not the only positive-definite integral which may be used to give sufficient conditions for stability in the mean. An irrotational disturbance u_i' is necessarily inconsistent with the stringent boundary conditions ($u_i' = 0$). Let us write ξ_i' for the vorticity vector of the disturbance, so that

$$(13.1) \qquad \xi_i' = \tfrac{1}{2}\epsilon_{ijk}\partial u_k'/\partial x_j$$

(ϵ_{ijk} being the permutation symbol); then the conditions $\xi_i' = 0$ imply $u_i' = 0$. Hence it is fitting to consider the *integral of vorticity*

$$(13.2) \qquad V = \int \xi_i' \xi_i' d\tau,$$

integrated over the cell of spatial periodicity, and to assert that a steady motion is stable in the mean if V is bounded, $t > 0$, or more particularly, if

$$(13.3) \qquad dV/dt \leq 0 \quad \text{for} \quad t \geq 0.$$

We shall here confine our attention to the plane disturbances of $P.C.M.$ and $P.P.M.$, so that the vorticity integral is

$$(13.4) \qquad V = \frac{1}{4} \int (\partial u_2'/\partial x_1 - \partial u_1'/\partial x_2)^2 dS,$$

integrated over the rectangle of periodicity.* Introducing the notation of (12.10), (12.11) we obtain

$$(13.5) \qquad 2CV = \int_{-1}^{1} LfL\bar{f}dy, \qquad L = \partial^2/\partial y^2 - \lambda^2,$$

---

* This integral has been used by Southwell and Chitty [36]; it may be remarked that their statement (equation (17), p. 230) that this integral is constant for the disturbance of an inviscid liquid flowing with a general velocity profile is not correct; cf. [37, equation (16)].

where C is a positive constant. If we substitute for ψ' from (12.11) in (3.28), (3.29), we get

$$(13.6) \qquad \partial Lf/\partial \tau = LLf - i\lambda RMf,$$

where M is as in (11.2) and τ as in (3.26). Hence

$$
\begin{aligned}
CdV/d\tau &= \frac{1}{2} \int_{-1}^{1} \left\{ Lf(LL\bar{f} + i\lambda RM\bar{f}) + L\bar{f}(LLf - i\lambda RMf) \right\} dy \\
(13.7)\\
&= \frac{1}{2} \left[f''\bar{f}''' + \bar{f}''f''' \right]_{y=-1}^{y=1} - (I_3^2 + 3\lambda^2 I_2^2 + 3\lambda^4 I_1^2 + \lambda^6 I_0^2),
\end{aligned}
$$

where the accents on $f, \bar{f}$ denote $\partial/\partial y$ and I_0, I_1, I_2, I_3 are as in (11.6). But we have here on the right precisely the right-hand side of (11.28), and so apparently the method of vorticity coalesces with the method of the exponential time-factor. However, to use (11.28) we required (11.29), which followed from the fact that f is a characteristic function. If in (13.7) f is an arbitrary function of y (save for $f=f'=0$ for $y=\pm 1$), then (11.29) is not available. However, (11.29) may be established in connection with (13.7) by considerations based on the regularity of the motion (cf. G. Hamel [38], and also [39]), so that the method of vorticity does coalesce with the method of the exponential time-factor.

Conclusion

In conclusion we may pick out what appear to be the outstanding challenges to mathematicians in the field of hydrodynamical stability:

(i) A simple proof, not involving elaborate computations, that plane Couette motion is stable under all circumstances.

(ii) A similar treatment for plane Poiseuille motion, if in fact it is stable under all circumstances.

(iii) The establishment of some inequality defining a condition under which Poiseuille motion in a tube of circular section is unstable. Any attempt to fix a precise critical value for the Reynolds number must inevitably involve elaborate calculation. But we might hope for a simple method to establish that under certain circumstances at least one of a set of characteristic values has a positive real part.

References

1. W. F. DURAND (editor-in-chief). *Hydrodynamic Theory*. Berlin, 1934.

2. G. I. TAYLOR. *Stability of a viscous liquid contained between two rotating cylinders*. Philosophical Transactions of the Royal Society of London, (A), vol. 223 (1923), pp. 289–343.

3. R. VON MISES. *Kleine Schwingungen und Turbulenz*. Jahresbericht der Deutschen Mathematiker-Vereinigung, vol. 21 (1912), pp. 241–248.

4. R. VON MISES. *Beitrag zum Oszillationsproblem, Festschrift Heinrich Weber*. Leipzig and Berlin, 1912, pp. 252–282.

5. L. HOPF. *Der Verlauf kleiner Schwingungen auf einer Strömung reibender Flüssigkeit*. Annalen der Physik, (4), vol. 44 (1914), pp. 1–60.

6. H. L. DRYDEN, F. D. MURNAGHAN, and H. BATEMAN. *Hydrodynamics*. Bulletin of the National Research Council, no. 84. Washington, 1932.

7. L. SCHILLER. *Das Turbulenzproblem und verwandte Fragen*. Physikalische Zeitschrift, vol. 26 (1925), pp. 566–595, 632.

8. J. W. LEWIS. *An experimental study of the motion of a viscous liquid contained between two coaxial cylinders*. Proceedings of the Royal Society of London, (A), vol. 117 (1928), pp. 388–407.

9. H. JEFFREYS, *Cartesian Tensors*. Cambridge, 1931.

10. H. LAMB. *Hydrodynamics*. Cambridge, 1932.

11. L. V. KING. *Theory and experiments relating to the establishment of turbulent flow in pipes and channels*. Philosophical Magazine, (6), vol. 31 (1916), pp. 322–328.

12. M. BRILLOUIN. *Leçons sur la viscosité des liquides et des gaz*. Paris, 1907.

13. A. J. MCCONNELL. *Applications of the Absolute Differential Calculus*. London and Glasgow, 1931.

14. A. S. RAMSEY. *A Treatise on Hydromechanics*. Part II: *Hydrodynamics*. London, 1935.

15. O. HAUPT. *Über die Entwicklung einer willkürlichen Funktion nach den Eigenfunktionen des Turbulenzproblems*. Sitzungsberichte der mathematisch-physikalischen Klasse der K. B. Akademie der Wissenschaften zu München (1912), pp. 289–301.

16. LORD RAYLEIGH. *On the stability, or instability, of certain fluid motions*. Proceedings of the London Mathematical Society, vol. 11 (1880), pp. 57–70; Scientific Papers, Cambridge, vol. 1 (1899), pp. 474–487.

17. O. REYNOLDS. *On the dynamical theory of incompressible viscous fluids and the determination of the criterion*. Philosophical Transactions of the Royal Society of London, (A), vol. 186 (1895), pp. 123–164; Scientific Papers, vol. 2, Cambridge (1901), pp. 535–577.

18. K. TAMAKI and W. J. HARRISON. *On the stability of the steady motion of viscous liquid contained between two rotating coaxal circular cylinders*. Transactions of the Cambridge Philosophical Society, vol. 22 (1912–1923), pp. 425–437.

19. W. J. HARRISON. *On the stability of the steady motion of viscous liquid contained between rotating coaxal cylinders*. Proceedings of the Cambridge Philosophical Society, vol. 20 (1920–1921), pp. 455–459.

20. W. McF. ORR. *The stability or instability of the steady motions of a liquid*. Part II: *A viscous liquid*. Proceedings of the Royal Irish Academy, (A), vol. 27 (1907), pp. 69–138.

21. H. FAXÉN. *Konvergenzuntersuchungen zu G. I. Taylors Abhandlung über die Stabilität der Bewegung einer zähen Flüssigkeit zwischen zwei rotierenden Zylindern*. Arkiv för matematik, astronomi och fysik, vol. 21A, no. 26 (1929), pp. 1–11.

22. TH. SEXL. *Zur Stabilitätsfrage der Poiseuilleschen und Couetteschen Strömung*. Annalen der Physik, (4), vol. 83 (1927), pp. 835–848.

23. TH. SEXL. *Über dreidimensionale Störungen der Poiseuilleschen Strömung*. Annalen der Physik, (4), vol. 84 (1927), pp. 807–822.

24. W. MÜLLER. *Einführung in die Theorie der zähen Flüssigkeiten*. Leipzig, 1932.

25. H. B. SQUIRE. *On the stability of the three-dimensional disturbances of viscous fluid flow between parallel walls*. Proceedings of the Royal Society of London, (A), vol. 142 (1933), pp. 621–628.

26. H. SOLBERG. *Zum Turbulenzproblem*. Proceedings of the First International Congress for Applied Mechanics. Delft, 1924, pp. 387–394.

27. C. L. PEKERIS. *On the stability problem in hydrodynamics*. Proceedings of the Cambridge Philosophical Society, vol. 32 (1936), pp. 55–66.

28. W. T. MACCREADIE. *On the stability of the motion of a viscous fluid*. Proceedings of the National Academy of Sciences, vol. 17 (1931), pp. 381–388.

29. A. SOMMERFELD. *Ein Beitrag zur hydrodynamischen Erklärung der turbulenten Flüssigkeitsbewegung*. Atti del IV Congresso Internazionale dei Matematici, Roma, vol. 3 (1908), pp. 116–124.

30. W. HEISENBERG. *Über Stabilität und Turbulenz von Flüssigkeitsströmen*. Annalen der Physik, (4), vol. 74 (1924), pp. 577–627.

31. F. NOETHER. *Das Turbulenzproblem*. Zeitschrift für angewandte Mathematik und Mechanik, vol. 1 (1921), pp. 125–138.

32. F. NOETHER. *Zur asymptotischen Behandlung der stationären Lösungen im Turbulenzproblem*. Zeitschrift für angewandte Mathematik und Mechanik, vol. 6 (1926), pp. 232–243, 340, 428.

33. S. GOLDSTEIN. *The stability of viscous fluid flow under pressure*. Proceedings of the Cambridge Philosophical Society, vol. 32 (1936), pp. 40–54.

34. H. A. LORENTZ. *Über die Entstehung turbulenter Flüssigkeitsbewegungen und über den Einfluss dieser Bewegungen bei der Strömung durch Röhren*. Abhandlungen über theoretische Physik. Leipzig and Berlin, 1907, pp. 43–71.

35. F. R. SHARPE. *On the stability of the motion of a viscous liquid*. Transactions of the American Mathematical Society, vol. 6 (1905), pp. 496–503.

36. R. V. SOUTHWELL and L. CHITTY. *On the problem of hydrodynamical stability*. I: *Uniform shearing motion in a viscous liquid*. Philosophical Transactions of the Royal Society of London, (A), vol. 229 (1930), pp. 205–253.

37. J. L. SYNGE. *The stability of quadratic velocity-distributions for an inviscid liquid flowing between parallel planes*. Journal of Mathematics and Physics, vol. 15 (1936), pp. 205–210.

38. G. HAMEL. *Zum Turbulenzproblem*. Nachrichten von der Königlichen Gesellschaft der Wissenschaften zu Göttingen, 1911, pp. 261–270.

39. J. L. SYNGE. *Conditions satisfied by the vorticity and the stream-function in a viscous liquid moving in two dimensions between fixed parallel planes*. Proceedings of the London Mathematical Society, (2), vol. 40 (1935), pp. 23–36.

40. J. L. SYNGE. *On the stability of a viscous liquid between two rotating coaxial cylinders*. Proceedings of the Royal Society of London, (A). In press.

41. C. L. PEKERIS. *On the stability problem in hydrodynamics*, II. Journal of the Aeronautical Sciences, vol. 5 (1938), pp. 237–240.

UNIVERSITY OF TORONTO,
    TORONTO, ONTARIO, CANADA

FIFTY YEARS OF AMERICAN MATHEMATICS

BY

GEORGE D. BIRKHOFF

It is indeed a great honor to participate in this Semicentennial Celebration of the founding of the New York Mathematical Society in 1888,
which became in 1894 the American Mathematical Society. As one of the
speakers I have set myself the challenging task of tracing our mathematical development under the auspices of the Society during the years which
have passed. Obviously in such a *coup d'oeil* only the principal factors
involved can be alluded to, and the point of view adopted must necessarily
be more or less personal.

At the very outset it is well to recall the general mathematical background of our country at the time when the Society came into existence.
In colonial days scientific and mathematical knowledge had a certain
definite standing, largely for its practical value but in part also for its own
sake. George Washington was a scientifically-minded gentleman farmer
for much of his life, and in his youth was a skilled surveyor, familiar with
trigonometry; Benjamin Franklin discovered experimentally the electrical nature of the lightning discharge, theorized concerning electricity as a
fluid, and had enough mathematical interest to devise ingenious magic
squares; Thomas Jefferson regarded geometry and trigonometry as "most
valuable to every man," algebra and logarithms as "often of value," while
he classed "conic sections, curves of the higher orders, perhaps even spherical trigonometry, algebraic operations beyond the 2d dimension, and
fluxions" as a "delicious luxury"; in his later years Jefferson spent much
of his time in mathematical reading, and was ever a true friend of mathematics. The interest in science and mathematics continued to be genteel
and amateurish among American scholars and devotees until towards the
middle of the last century, with few notable exceptions. The best mathematicians of those days looked appreciatively toward Europe without
much thought of high emulation.

Then came a gradual change in the temper of the times which led to
the formation of our Society. Characteristic of this change were the outstanding figures of Benjamin Peirce, of Josiah Willard Gibbs, and of
George William Hill. Peirce died in 1880, Gibbs in 1903, and Hill in 1913,
having been fourth president of the Society in the years 1894 to 1896.
But it was the contagious enthusiasm of a group of young Americans,
returning from mathematical studies in Europe, which proved the immediate cause of the formation of our Society; and in this so important
enterprise Thomas Scott Fiske, seventh president of the Society, and
Frank Nelson Cole, long its devoted secretary, took leading parts. The

year 1888 of our beginning as a professional body devoted to the interests of research, marks with precision our coming to a fitting mathematical position among the nations of the earth.

Of the three figures mentioned it was Benjamin Peirce who was by far the most influential in America as a scientific personage. I remember a talk about Peirce with his last pupil, the late Dr. Leonard Waldo, mathematical meteorologist. Waldo said that the first sight of Peirce seated behind his desk at home rendered him quite speechless. Ex-President A. Lawrence Lowell of Harvard University fell under Peirce's mathematical spell while an undergraduate and wrote a few years ago: "Looking back over the space of fifty years since I entered Harvard College, Benjamin Peirce still impresses me as the most massive intellect with which I have ever come into close contact, and as being the most profoundly inspiring teacher that I ever had. His personal appearance, his powerful frame and his majestic head seemed in harmony with his brain."

Benjamin Peirce's papers on *Linear associative algebra*, announced at the first meeting of the American Association for the Advancement of Science in 1864, give him a just claim to be considered an eminent mathematician. His researches in this field were made at a time when English and American mathematicians looked upon the great invention of quaternions by W. R. Hamilton as a supreme achievement, destined to be of incalculable importance for mathematics and physics. Peirce saw more deeply into the essence of quaternions than his contemporaries, and so was able to take a higher, more abstract point of view, which was algebraic rather than geometric. However, he was much more than an algebraist, for he was well informed about some of the most significant mathematical developments of his day. His volumes *Curves, Functions, and Forces* testify to a real interest in the function-theoretic work of Cauchy, albeit somewhat superficial in character. His large book *Analytical Mechanics* showed that he had read and mastered the works of Hamilton, Jacobi, and others in the extensive field of dynamics. In addition, he was skilled in the theory and methods of computation useful for dynamical astronomy, and spent a considerable amount of time during later years in a somewhat unhappy attempt to show that Leverrier and Adams had no adequate basis for the calculations leading to the celebrated discovery of the planet Neptune; one naturally calls to mind the calculations by the eminent astronomer, the late Percival Lowell (brother of A. Lawrence Lowell), which brought about the discovery of the small planet Pluto in 1930, since these calculations have also been occasionally criticized for similar reasons.

Despite Peirce's remarkable ability to inspire especially capable and advanced students, he was not regarded as a good teacher for the rank and file; a characteristic feature of his lectures was a reaching toward seemingly endless vistas of abstract generalizations.

Josiah Willard Gibbs was a man of modest and not especially impressive personality, who did far more to advance physics and chemistry through his work on statistical mechanics and the equilibria of chemical systems than Peirce ever did for pure mathematics. Gibbs' title to be considered a mathematician rests mainly upon his largely notational contributions to vector analysis, a subject also closely related to Hamilton's quaternions. The late Maxime Bôcher, who with William Fogg Osgood really succeeded Peirce at Harvard, later attached the name of "Gibbs' phenomenon" to a fundamental fact about Fourier's series which was observed by Gibbs; this is related to the peculiar behavior of the successive curves of approximation $y = s_n(x)$ to a discontinuous function near the point of discontinuity. As has happened from time to time here and elsewhere, the fundamental contribution of Gibbs' physical work was first recognized by admirers in other countries, in particular by James Clark Maxwell, so that it was only somewhat tardily, by reflected light as it were, that Gibbs came to be properly appreciated in the United States.

George William Hill was a scientific figure of altogether unconventional type who spent more than three decades of his life as an assistant in the Nautical Almanac office in Washington and then went back to the place of his birth, West Nyack, New York, to continue his researches. Hill, like Gibbs, never married. His life was devoted to what were essentially mathematical studies of the solutions of the three-body problem useful to the lunar theory and in making specific astronomical computations. His work on periodic motions was the worthy forerunner and inspiration of the splendid theoretical advances of Henri Poincaré in celestial mechanics, who thus owed much to Hill's achievements. The free introduction of infinite determinants by Hill in his celebrated papers on the restricted problem of three bodies was especially noteworthy, although it is only recently that this interesting analytic instrument has been perfected.

Of these men, Hill would be claimed for themselves by the theoretical astronomers, along with Nathaniel Bowditch, translator and commentator of Laplace's *Mécanique Céleste*, and Simon Newcomb, great perfecter of lunar and planetary theory; while Gibbs would be justly taken by physicists and chemists for their own. Thus there remains to the mathematicians of America only Benjamin Peirce for their undisputed possession. He appears as a kind of father of pure mathematics in our country. In his deep appreciation of the elegant and abstract we may recognize a continuing characteristic of American mathematics. In his concern with its many applications there resides a virtue which we are finding it more difficult to realize, because of the trend towards professional specialization. Without doubt, however, there is a spiritual necessity upon us today to regain a similar breadth of outlook.

Any account, however brief, of American mathematics before 1888 must chronicle an event of the preceding decade which was of extraordinary importance not only to mathematics, but to the whole field of scholarly endeavor, namely, the foundation of the Johns Hopkins University at Baltimore in 1876. Although the Graduate Schools of Yale University (1847) and of Harvard University (1872) were in existence, nevertheless as has been said by Dr. Abraham Flexner in his book *Universities: American, English, German,* the Johns Hopkins University was the first American institution "consciously devoted to the pursuit of knowledge, the solution of problems, the critical appreciation of achievement, and the training of men at a really high level." Thus there was called to the new mathematical department at Baltimore the great English algebraist, James Joseph Sylvester, who remained there until 1884. Under the direction of the department there began in 1878, the American Journal of Mathematics, our first journal given over to mathematical research, and now completing its sixtieth year of high achievement. Ever since, there has continued to be at Baltimore, despite material limitations, an important center of mathematical activity, of which the staunch and kindly remembered British geometer, Frank Morley, was the titular leader from 1900 to 1928.

In all previous mathematical history perhaps no mathematical development in any country has been so extensive and rapid as that which ensued here upon the founding of the Society. All the great nations of Europe had produced illustrious mathematicians of whom they had the right to be extremely proud. The French and German mathematical traditions were particularly well established and of incomparable brilliancy, represented at that moment by Henri Poincaré, the young David Hilbert, and a number of other figures of very high rank. Italy and the Scandinavian countries were also flourishing vigorously. Yet up to that time there had scarcely arisen any occasion for European mathematicians to note the work of their American colleagues. A solitary exception was the early recognition of Hill's lunar theory by Poincaré, while the algebraic advances of Peirce failed to receive the attention which they deserved.

But now able young mathematicians, fresh from studies abroad, began to carry on vigorous and independent research at home, and their contagious enthusiasm soon aroused a deep interest in the younger men around them. Almost over night as it were, the great University of Chicago sprang into existence in 1892, with a mathematical department made up of Eliakim Hastings Moore, Oskar Bolza and Heinrich Maschke from Germany, and others. Of these men, only Bolza is living today. They formed a notable and inspiring group which will ever be remembered in our mathematical annals. At about the same time Osgood and Bôcher, inspired by their German sojourn and in particular by the great Felix Klein of Göttingen, bent their every effort to strengthen the tradition at Harvard. Under the genial leadership of Moore at Chicago, who had studied with Gibbs at Yale University and for a year in Berlin, there was emphasized the abstract and algebraic side of mathematics, although Moore was remarkably catholic in his outlook. At Harvard attention was turned towards the vast field

of analysis. The center in Cambridge was much strengthened by the trans-
ference of the Massachusetts Institute of Technology from Boston across
the Charles River in 1916. Its mathematical group and that at Harvard
University have been in close and mutually stimulating association since
that date.

A few years later, under the wise and benevolent guidance of Dean
Henry Burchard Fine, who had been strongly influenced by his studies
under Leopold Kronecker, promising young men were called to the mathematical staff at Princeton, in particular L. P. Eisenhart, Oswald Veblen,
and J. H. M. Wedderburn. From that day forth there has always been
an important mathematical group at Princeton. There came a notable
further impetus with the founding there in 1930 of the Institute for
Advanced Study, with Abraham Flexner as Director. At the outset the
new Institute devoted its attention to the fields of mathematics and theoretical physics, calling at first Albert Einstein, Veblen, and Hermann Weyl
to ideal research posts. Up to the present time the mathematical staff of
the Institute has worked side by side with the staff of the University in
Fine Memorial Hall. The others at the Institute have in general already
obtained their doctor's degree and come to enjoy a period of uninterrupted
study and research under favorable conditions. The Institute is fortu-
nately able not only to augment its staff through distinguished temporary
appointments, but also to give partial financial support to many of those
who come to study at the Institute.

By great good fortune I have been intimately associated with the
centers at Chicago, Harvard, and Princeton. I feel deeply indebted to
them all. Indeed there are not many American mathematicians who have
not been profoundly influenced by one or another of these three groups.
It was in the spring of 1902 that I made a first journey across the city of
Chicago to the University, and found my way into the excellent mathematical library in Ryerson Physical Laboratory; before that time I had
only been in contact with the mathematical books of the John Crerar
Library and the small mathematical collection at Lewis Institute. I remember the thrill which the sight of the well-filled shelves gave me. Soon I
met Professor Moore of whom I had already heard, and found him then and
always extraordinarily inspiring, suggestive, and kind. During my first
(Junior) year at the University I profited much from my contact with
Bolza also. At his suggestion I read the work of Gauss on the cyclotomic
equation and the equally celebrated paper of Abel on the impossibility
of solving the general quintic by radicals. Bolza's lectures were marvels of
clarity and finish. But it was Moore above all who seemed to me to have
the true fire of genius within him.

The year following I went to Harvard, with Moore's approval, for two
years of study. There I learned more analysis, particularly from Osgood
and Bôcher. I found Bôcher's lectures the equal of Bolza's in lucidity and

superior in placing important points in high relief. It was only later, however, that I came to realize how much I owed to Bôcher for his suggestions, for his remarkable critical insight, and for his unfailing interest in the often crude mathematical ideas which I presented.

On my return to Chicago in the fall of 1905, I profited greatly by two further years of work with Moore, both in his seminar on analysis and outside the class room. Moore was a deep admirer of Hilbert and was then following closely the rapid developments at Göttingen, attendant upon Fredholm's fundamental work in linear integral equations of 1900. It happened that I saw Moore's program of General Analysis taking shape day by day, as he came to appreciate the full abstract significance of the papers of Hilbert and the beautiful dissertation of Erhard Schmidt.

In 1907 I started teaching at the University of Wisconsin and in my two years there I especially valued my scientific and personal relationship with my senior colleague, Edward Burr Van Vleck, whose distinguished son is now at Harvard as a member of the Departments of Physics and Mathematics.

It was in the fall of 1909 that I became a member of the staff at Princeton. The presence of Veblen, nearly of my own age, with large ideas for American mathematics in general and for the Princeton Department in particular, meant much to me during my three years there. Veblen was then completing his important *Projective Geometry*, volume 1, written in collaboration with J. W. Young, whom many will remember kindly. It was my privilege to read the book in page proof, and to learn of Veblen's geometric program and ideas directly from him in our frequent walks and talks together.

I have recounted these personal circumstances only because I know that in their essence they are not very dissimilar from those of many American mathematicians.

In selecting Chicago, Cambridge, and Princeton for especial reference I have realized fully that American mathematics reaches overwhelmingly beyond what is to be found in any three or even in any ten centers. And yet I think it is a comforting thought for American mathematicians everywhere to know that there are centers like these where scholarly conditions have been uniformly good and where high ideals have been steadily maintained. Such places, by their influence and example, support and stimulate mathematical scholarship and achievement throughout the whole of our country.

Concerning the other mathematical centers suffice it to say that there are now about thirty institutions where the advanced student of mathematics may go with advantage to study for the doctorate, while only fifty years ago he was forced to go to Europe to secure adequate training! Among the privately endowed institutions may be mentioned Brown, Bryn Mawr, California Institute of Technology, Chicago, Cincinnati,

Columbia, Cornell, Duke, Harvard, Institute for Advanced Study, Johns
Hopkins, Leland Stanford, Massachusetts Institute of Technology, Notre
Dame, Princeton, Rice Institute, and Yale; and among our state universities, California (at Berkeley and at Los Angeles), Illinois, Iowa, Michigan, Minnesota, Ohio State, Pennsylvania, Texas, Virginia, and Wisconsin; and in Canada, the University of Toronto. The number of such centers
should increase still further. All that is required in many cases is that
mathematicians in a position of influence take the proper steps. As instances in point, I would cite what was done by Fine at Princeton and by
Harris Hancock at Cincinnati.

The extraordinary contrast between 1888 and 1938 is equally mani-
fested by the fact that fifty years ago there were a mere handful of competent mathematicians in the country, whereas there is now a body of over
two thousand American members of our Society. Among these, between
one and two hundred have gone far beyond a doctoral dissertation to
make important additions to mathematical knowledge, and some forty
or fifty are highly creative with established international reputations.
Later on I shall have occasion to refer to a number of these mathematicians and their specific contributions.

For the moment, however, I should like to direct attention to two interesting and important special groups. The first is made up of mathematicians who have shown the rare quality of leadership, of which Moore
was an outstanding instance. Among the earlier of these I would mention
the late eccentric geometer, George Bruce Halsted, who attracted to
mathematics two notable figures, L. E. Dickson and R. L. Moore, both of
whom in their turn have been able to exert a large personal influence. I
would also mention with high esteem James Pierpont, who for many
years was a source of inspiration at Yale. Among the other and younger
men, besides Dickson, R. L. Moore, and Veblen, the names of G. A. Bliss,
G. C. Evans, Solomon Lefschetz, Marston Morse, J. F. Ritt, M. H. Stone,
and Norbert Wiener come to mind as having shown the same quality to
an exceptional degree.

The second special group to which I wish to refer is made up of mathematicians who have come here from Europe in the last twenty years,
largely on account of various adverse conditions. This influx has recently
been large and we have gained very much by it. Nearly all of the newcomers have been men of high ability, and some of them would have been
justly reckoned as among the greatest mathematicians of Europe. A partial list of such men is indeed impressive: Emil Artin, Solomon Bochner,
Richard Courant, T. H. Gronwall, Einar Hille, E. R. van Kampen,
Solomon Lefschetz, Hans Levy, Karl Menger, John von Neumann, Oystein
Ore, H. A. Rademacher, Tibor Radó, J. A. Shohat, D. J. Struik, Otto
Szász, Gabor Szegö, J. D. Tamarkin, J. V. Uspensky, Hermann Weyl,
A. N. Whitehead, Aurel Wintner, Oscar Zariski.

With this eminent group among us, there inevitably arises a sense of increased duty toward our own promising younger American mathematicians. In fact most of the newcomers hold research positions, sometimes with modest stipend, but nevertheless with ample opportunity for their own investigations, and not burdened with the usual heavy round of teaching duties. In this way the number of similar positions available for young American mathematicians is certain to be lessened, with the attendant probability that some of them will be forced to become "hewers of wood and drawers of water." I believe we have reached a point of saturation, where we must definitely avoid this danger.

It should be added, however, that the very situation just alluded to has accentuated a factor which has been working to the advantage of our general mathematical situation. Far-seeing university and college presidents, desirous of improving the intellectual status of the institutions which they serve, conclude that a highly practical thing to do is to strengthen their mathematical staffs. For, in doing so, no extraordinary laboratory or library expenses are incurred; furthermore the subject of mathematics is in a state of continual creative growth, ever more important to engineer, scientist, and philosopher alike; and excellent mathematicians from here and abroad are within financial reach.

Having thus glanced at our mathematical firmament which shines so brightly today, let us turn to survey briefly the general situation in our country which has made it possible. In the year 1888 there were probably about two hundred thousand students in our high schools and preparatory schools; today there are between two and three millions. This enormous increase is a consequence of the unquestioning belief in higher education which pervades our country. At the same time our colleges, universities, and advanced technical schools have increased correspondingly in numbers and resources. There are today nearly a thousand such institutions scattered throughout our land, serving half a million or more students, with a total physical plant staggering the imagination and representing billions of dollars of endowment. Probably the majority of these institutions struggle along under financial as well as educational difficulties, although rendering distinct service. But when all is said and done, there remain some two hundred fifty of them which meet the exacting requirements of approval by the Association of American Universities.

As far as the mathematical side of this vast American enterprise of higher education is concerned, its magnitude is probably best appreciated by means of a different approach. The American Mathematical Society has a membership of over two thousand persons, the great majority of whom hold positions in our institutions of learning. Our highly esteemed sister organization, the Mathematical Association of America, devoted primarily to the interests of collegiate mathematics, has nearly twenty-five hundred members. The conclusion then is plain. There must be between two and three thousand mathematical teaching positions in our higher institutions, with an average salary which must certainly lie between two to three thousand dollars. We see in this way that there is probably a sum of about six millions of dollars which goes each year to the support of higher mathematics!

Since the Great War salaries have been increased and the teaching burden has been reduced, at least in the better institutions. I remember talking some twenty years ago with the late J. C. Fields of Toronto about the status of professors throughout the world; it will be recalled that Fields did more than anyone else to bring about the important International Mathematical Congress held at Toronto in 1924. He told me that, after making a special study of the facts, he had come to the conclusion that the American professor was the worst treated of all! At that time there was much in his contention, even though there were already in existence a number of American professorial chairs where the salary was good and the teaching duties not excessive. Today there are many such positions. In this connection it may be well to mention the fact that Harvard University has been able to reduce the amount of teaching and tutorial routine of the regular mathematical staff to six hours a week, of which only three hours are devoted to more or less elementary mathematical instruction. Such a schedule gives to all concerned a notable opportunity to carry on mathematical research, and would be socially unjustifiable unless the highest standards of achievement were being maintained. Although such ideal conditions are impracticable at present except in a few fortunate institutions, it should be strongly emphasized that twelve hours of instruction a week (including at least one course of advanced grade) is about all that can be required if the best standards of scholarship are expected. Indeed, wherever possible, the hours of instruction should be reduced to not more than nine, and if there are heavy outside duties there should be a compensating diminution in teaching.

But the situation has very definitely a complementary aspect. On our part there is an unescapable, deep responsibility to the nation which, somewhat unwittingly perhaps, has afforded us such splendid support. It is our duty to take an active and thoughtful part in the elementary mathematical instruction of our colleges, universities, and technical schools, as well as to participate in the higher phases. To these tasks we must bring a broad mathematical point of view and a fine enthusiasm. Insofar as possible we must actively continue as competent scholars and research workers. Only by so doing can we play our proper part.

It is interesting to note that the other material accessories useful for our extensive mathematical edifice have also been provided. With our Bulletin and Transactions, with the American Journal of Mathematics, all under Society auspices, and with the Annals of Mathematics, the Duke Mathematical Journal, the Journal of Mathematics and Physics, and the

American Mathematical Monthly, we possess excellent facilities for the publication of original articles in periodicals. Aside from the Journal of Mathematics and Physics there is as yet no journal directed towards applied mathematics. More extensive publication in book form is afforded by our Colloquium Publications, and a similar new series in contemplation by the Institute for Advanced Study. For the prompt publication of short articles there is available the Proceedings of the National Academy of Sciences. There are in addition certain facilities to be found in the annual publications of learned societies (such as the American Academy of Arts and Sciences), and of higher institutions of learning (such as the Rice Institute Pamphlets), etc. Thus far, however, the commercial publishing houses of the country have not contributed much towards the publication of important advanced mathematical texts. In this respect they suffer by comparison with progressive European publishers, who take pride in the publication of significant mathematical books. The University Presses of the country have partly made up for this lack.

In addition to our regular meetings, the Colloquium Lectures, the annual Gibbs Lecture, and the Visiting Lectures of the Society provide important means for direct scientific interchanges among mathematicians. The coming International Congress of Mathematicians to be held at Cambridge in September, 1940, will present still other opportunities of this kind. In fact the facilities for mathematicians to meet intimately with their colleagues at sister institutions are increasing constantly. The importance of such facilities in speeding up mathematical progress has long been recognized in European mathematical centers.

Then there is always the arduous administrative work of the Society, carried on unselfishly by its officers and especially by its present secretary, Dean R. G. D. Richardson, true successor of Frank Nelson Cole. The way in which this work has been carefully and devotedly done without any paid officer has helped to unite the Society more than anything else.

All in all, then, our American mathematical situation is about as favorable as can be hoped for on this very troubled planet. Our one real danger perhaps concerns the general standard of achievement. It is not enough for those who go into the rank and file of our colleges to devote themselves to a useful academic routine; they have a duty to live up to their highest mathematical potentialities, and to awaken a deep mathematical interest in their students. It is not enough for the exceptional man whose early work has led to professional recognition, to take thenceforth an easy-going attitude; such a man should continue with the devotion of a leader in a great cause. Furthermore, we ought all to provide our share of first-rate elementary teaching, by which we justify our privileged positions in immediate practical terms. If we do these things, mathematics in America will rise to still greater heights and there will appear among us mathematical figures comparable to the greatest in the past.

My main purpose today, however, is to lay before you briefly some of the significant mathematical advances which have been made in America during the last fifty years. It is these which really measure the success of our efforts. But in attempting to summarize what has been done, I can do no more than present a bold outline, imperfect because of the limitations of my own knowledge and point of view, and necessarily stressing the less technical aspects of the subjects referred to. I propose to take up successively the fields roughly characterized as logic, algebra, analysis, geometry, and applied mathematics.

Symbolic logic and axiomatics

It was the remarkable discovery of the English mathematician George Boole, contained in his book, *The Laws of Thought*, (1854), that the classical Aristotelian logic can be given a more adequate formulation as a kind of algebra now called Boolean algebra. He saw too that his algebra of propositions could equally well be regarded as an algebra of classes: for to say that the proposition a implies the proposition b is the same thing as to say that the class of objects for which a holds is a subclass of the class of objects for which b holds. Although Leibniz and others, among them some of Boole's own contemporaries, sought to construct a logical calculus, it was Boole's work more than anything else which stimulated a deeper critical study of logical processes, and thus paved the way for such great contributions as the complete logical symbolism of Giuseppe Peano (1888) and the theory of the hierarchy of logical propositions known as the theory of types, due to Bertrand Russell and A. N. Whitehead (1910). On the other hand the works of F. L. G. Frege (1879) and Georg Cantor (1883) have led to an increased understanding of the ideas of number which permeate and at the same time are partly deducible from purely logical ideas. Opposing schools have arisen from attempts to avoid certain deep seated paradoxes: L. E. J. Brouwer in 1912 proposed to reject the law of the "excluded middle," which asserts that a proposition is either true or false, and instead, to require the explicit construction of all logical entities, thereby abandoning such instruments of thought as the principle of arbitrary choice of Zermelo (1907). Hilbert in 1922 and others have asserted that mathematics is a kind of mechanical game played with marks, among which the special marks of the positive integers 1, 2, 3, $\cdots$, are to be admitted without question, while the rules of the game are essentially those systematized in the *Principia Mathematica* of Whitehead and Russell. Among these rules would then be found a principle of arbitrary choice, carefully formulated.

Although the logician and philosopher, C. S. Peirce, son of Benjamin Peirce, contributed to Boolean algebra, definite mathematical work on this subject may be said to have begun in America with E. V. Huntington's set of postulates of 1904. The independence of these postulates was established on the basis of the Boolean sum $a+b$ (interpreted as a or b) and product $a \times b$ (interpreted as a and b) as fundamental operations; and it was also shown that the relation of inclusion, $a < b$, could replace either of these.

A highly elegant paper by H. M. Sheffer, destined to have an important influence upon general logical development, appeared in 1913. In it Sheffer showed that the single operation of nonconjunction, $a \mid b$ (interpreted as neither a nor b), would serve to replace the two operations of Boolean addition and multiplication. His three essential postulates may be written in very brief compass:

$$(a \mid a) \mid (a \mid a) = a, \qquad a \mid (b \mid (b \mid b)) = a \mid a,$$

$$a \mid ((b \mid c) \mid (b \mid c)) = ((b \mid b) \mid a \mid a) \mid ((c \mid c) \mid a).$$

These postulates may be immediately verified: thus the first postulate asserts merely that not (not a) is a. In this manner Boolean algebra was completely transformed in outward aspect and given a simpler form which inevitably suggested the possibility of further syntactical analysis of logical formulae. The single "stroke" operation, $\mid$, of Sheffer was made basic in the revised edition of the *Principia*. Sheffer's postulates were somewhat abbreviated by B. A. Bernstein shortly afterwards.

Other extremely important contributions to Boolean algebra have been made within a year or two by M. H. Stone. The gist of his idea is very simple: In the broad modern sense a set of objects $a, b, c, \cdots$ is to be regarded as a "ring" of numbers with reference to suitably defined operations of addition $(+)$ and multiplication $(\times)$ if the usual associative and commutative laws for addition and the associative law and distributive laws of multiplication hold, with unique solution x of the equation $a+x=b$, and with a unit u such that $a \times u = a$ for any a. There is then a unique zero z such that $a+z=a$ for any a.

We can associate a unique n-partite number a in this sense with each subclass of a class of n objects, by taking to correspond to each object of the class a symbol 1 or a symbol 0 according as the particular object in question does or does not belong to the subclass. Thus $1\ 1\ 0\ 1\ 0\ 0\ 1 \cdots$ would be a number specifying the subclass containing the first, second, fourth, seventh, $\cdots$ but no others of the given objects. If a and b are two such numbers, $a+b$ may be taken to be the similar number formed by adding corresponding figures according to the rule:

$$1 + 0 = 0 + 1 = 1, \qquad 0 + 0 = 1 + 1 = 0$$

(that is, addition modulo 2), while $a \times b$ is formed by multiplying corresponding figures as follows:

$$0 \times 0 = 0 \times 1 = 1 \times 0 = 0, \qquad 1 \times 1 = 1.$$

We may denote the particular numbers

$$1\ 1\ 1\cdots \quad \text{and} \quad 0\ 0\ 0\cdots$$

by u and z, respectively.

It is then immediately verified that the numbers so defined will form a ring, and in addition will obey the commutative law of multiplication $a \times b = b \times a$, and the special laws $a + a = z$, $a \times a = a$. Furthermore $a + b$ will represent precisely that subclass made up of the objects in a but not in b, and in b but not in a. In other words the Boolean sum is replaced by what Stone terms the symmetric difference. However, the product $a \times b$ coincides with the Boolean product, since it represents the subclass of objects contained in both a and b. Furthermore, the Boolean sum can readily be expressed in terms of the operations $+$ and $\times$ used by Stone, being precisely

$$(a + b) + (a \times b).$$

Thus Boolean algebra at last appears in its true light as identifiable with a special algebra in the ordinary sense, with all its elements idempotent ($a \times a = a$) and so necessarily commutative. Conversely, Stone shows that such an algebra with or without unit may be regarded as an algebra of subclasses. Through this identification Stone is able to employ modern algebraic methods in his study of Boolean algebra. To my mind his thoroughgoing papers constitute the most considerable advance in our understanding of Boolean algebras since Boole's own work.

Let us turn next to the broader aspects of symbolic logic as a whole. Here, too, much has been accomplished by Americans. Indeed a world movement in this field is under way in which the Polish school and our own have been foremost. Among our active figures are C. A. Baylis, A. A. Bennett, B. A. Bernstein, Alonzo Church, H. B. Curry, E. V. Huntington, S. C. Kleene, C. H. Langford, C. I. Lewis, J. B. Rosser, H. M. Sheffer, and W. V. Quine. Recently Rudolf Carnap, widely known for his studies of logical syntax, has taken a post in this country. The creation in 1936 of the Journal of Symbolic Logic is symptomatic of the activity of an increasing group of American specialists.

The significance and importance of this movement are unmistakable. For over two thousand years mathematicians have been exerting their every effort in marching upward towards the high summits of mathematical power. But the vast continual ascent bids fair to overwhelm and confuse. It is time to reconsider and determine the paths which we have followed, so that we may go forward more judiciously. Those who desire to help in this task will occupy themselves either with the study of mathematics as symbolic logic, or with axiomatics which aims at the unification of mathematics by the formation of suitable abstractions. It seems certain that work of this kind will be of the utmost importance in the coördination and simplification of all mathematics.

One of the earliest American papers having importance for logic at large was a short note of E. L. Post in 1921, in which he showed that the ordinary propositional calculus was complete in the sense that every proposition is either true or demonstrably false (by a *reductio ad absurdum*). As he stated, this was not a theorem of the propositional calculus itself, but rather a theorem about the calculus. It afforded an early instance of what is called metamathematics, being related to mathematics in much the same way as the general analysis of chess would be to specific games.

An interesting study of the principle of arbitrary choice was made by Alonzo Church in his dissertation of 1927. This principle is a very important one; as Zermelo established in 1907, it leads to a proof of the well-ordering of the continuum when accepted without restriction. On the other hand it is almost impossible to get along in ordinary mathematical reasoning without the use of this principle in some form or other; and indeed its validity had never been questioned until the explicit formulation by Zermelo. Church showed that it was possible to maintain a consistent position, intermediate between the extremes, in which the principle of choice was allowed for an ordered set belonging to the second number class, and that then certain theorems could be deduced.

In the last few years Church, Curry, Kleene, and Rosser, have been studying metamathematical questions involving questions of explicit logical constructibility and similar open logical problems. These belong to the fascinating metamathematical borderland between mathematics and philosophy, in which one is likely to be led astray at times by dubious subtleties.

As developments of the *Principia* reference may be made first to Lewis' theory of "strict implication" developed in C. I. Lewis' *Survey of Symbolic Logic*, 1917. Roughly speaking, this type of implication differs from the "material implication" of Whitehead and Russell in that for them any false proposition implies every other proposition, while for Lewis this is true only of necessarily false propositions. Lewis' modification flows from the omission of one of the postulates of the *Principia*, namely that two propositions which mutually imply one another are equivalent. His ideas are clarified and extended in a recent article by Huntington. Here Huntington introduces a modification $a \equiv b$ (read a quad b) of the $a \equiv b$ of Whitehead and Russell. An essentially similar concept was introduced by A. A. Bennett and C. A. Baylis in 1935.

Secondly, in his *System of Logistic* of 1934 and subsequently, W. V. Quine has studied very deeply various syntactical matters. His theory of ordination makes especial use of an early remark of Wiener's (1914) to the effect that the ordered couple or dyad (a, b) can be logically defined as the class formed by the elements a and the (unordered) couples a, b, while an ordered n-ad can then be readily defined in terms of a set of dyads. By means of ordination a more satisfactory and explicit understanding of the syntax of the well-formed formula can be obtained. Like Church, Quine has devoted a great deal of attention to the highly difficult task of giving the basic theory of types of Whitehead and Russell a different and more satisfactory form.

Correlated with such investigations of the structure of logic as a whole are those of axiomatics, which aim to unify mathematics by the abstract method. A strong impetus towards axiomatics was given by the work of Hilbert on the foundations of geometry in 1899. Veblen's elegant dissertation of 1905 on the same subject was based on the relation of "betweenness" of B as to points A and C on a line, and served as the approach to geometry adopted in the *Principia*. Likewise in his and Young's *Projective Geometry* a postulational basis was adopted which allowed for finite geometries, with only a finite number of points, as well as for the ordinary n-dimensional projective geometries. Such geometries were immediately at hand when the marks of Galois' fields replaced ordinary numbers as coordinate elements.*

A novel approach to ordinary geometry was developed by A. R. Schweitzer in 1909. He showed, for instance, that one could use the intuitive relation of the sameness of sense of coplanar point-triads ABC and $A'B'C'$ as the basic relation in a set of geometric postulates; more generally, Schweitzer showed how to "generate m-dimensional geometry n-dimensionally $(m \geqq n)$" by the use of a similar relation of dimensionality n. Another new approach to geometry was achieved by Huntington in 1913 who showed that one could take the sphere (point $=$ null sphere) as the undefined element, and inclusion as the single undefined relation.

In this connection let us refer to a mathematically much less significant postulational approach to geometry of the author's (1932), which embodies the intuitive ideas of linear and angular one-dimensional measurement (ruler and protractor), and so lies intermediate between the usual qualitative attack and the other extreme of purely analytic systematization.

E. H. Moore was, of course, the great American protagonist, in his day, of the abstract point of view. In a well known dictum contained in his New Haven Colloquium Lectures of 1906 he said that "The existence of analogies between the central features of various theories implies the existence of a general theory which underlies the particular theories and unifies them with respect to those central features." By temperament he was an abstractionist, and, where most mathematicians pass from the special to the general, he appeared to do the opposite. At any rate, upon being asked once if he too did not really begin with the special case, he replied that he was not conscious of doing so. Unfortunately his efforts to develop a movement toward the abstract were not very successful. This was for two reasons: his addiction to unusual symbolism which, while

---

* This possibility had been pointed out by Veblen and W. H. Bussey in 1906.

masterly in its way, failed to attract most of those around him; and a desire to perfect and generalize indefinitely, without regard to any question of publication. But it must be admitted today that his faith in the abstract point of view is being more and more justified.

Whether or not his most ambitious abstract project, that of General Analysis (1906), will leave any important aftereffects remains to be seen. In this he proposed a study of functions of a general variable on an absolutely general range. The nearest analogous work was that of Fréchet (1905) who, however, used the notion of limit in restricting the independent variable. Ideal instances of General Analysis in Moore's sense are furnished by the direct abstraction of the Fredholm theory of linear integral equations and of Schmidt's dissertation already alluded to. But no great interest in these abstractions has so far arisen among mathematicians inasmuch as the natural and easy way to proceed seems to be to grasp the classic results as originally obtained, and to observe that the specified range of the independent variable plays little or no rôle. In this way generalizations or slight modifications will suggest themselves as needed, as for instance the generalization from 1 to n dimensions.

It remains to refer to one other recent abstract development which perhaps will contribute more to the actual unification of mathematical thought than the General Analysis of Moore. We refer to the work of hierarchies, for which the name of "lattices" has been suggested by Garrett Birkhoff, and "structures" by Ore. Such lattices are of as pervasive occurrence in various branches of mathematics as finite groups. It still remains to be seen, however, whether or not the theory of lattices will lead to a technical development as imposing as that of finite groups.

Although the idea of lattices goes back partially to C. S. Peirce and Ernst Schröder, it was Richard Dedekind who first saw their true nature and importance (1897). The fundamental relation in a lattice is, of course, that of inclusion, a includes b, which we write $a > b$. It is interesting to see how analogous the postulates for lattices and Boolean algebras are. In a lattice with elements a, b the sum $a+b$ may be used to indicate the least element containing a and b, while the product $a \times b$ denotes the greatest element contained in both a and b. It is obvious that the associative and commutative laws of addition and multiplication are obeyed, as well as the special laws

$$a = a + (a \times b) = a \times (a + b).$$

Birkhoff's first paper (1933) served to initiate the recent active development of lattice theory. His work, that of von Neumann, and of Ore have been of especial importance. Some of their results will be sketched.

An important type of lattice is the so-called modular lattice of which an example is furnished by the normal subgroups of a given group. Such lattices satisfy the (self-dual) modular postulate of Dedekind:

$$a + (b \times c) = (a + b) \times c, \qquad\qquad \text{if } a < c,$$

as well as those already mentioned. Birkhoff showed that any complemented* modular lattice may be regarded as a sum of projective geometries, the elements of the lattice being given by the collection of linear subspaces through the origin. The corresponding fundamental theorem for the arithmetization of Boolean algebras (distributive lattices) was announced by Stone somewhat earlier.

Von Neumann (1936) was led in this manner to construct projective geometries in the full sense, but *without points*, by abandoning the requirement that each element has a next greater element. This has led him to his remarkable "continuous geometry" with a dimension function which ranges continuously from 0 to 1.

Ore has established that a considerable part of the theory of the representation of groups by direct products in an essentially unique way, and of the corresponding theories for linear algebras, Lie algebras, and finite rings, can be obtained immediately by means of the lattice theory; this is especially clear in the case of groups. Another very significant result of Ore's is the so-called Kurosch-Ore theorem that the invariance of the number of components in irredundant representations of an ideal follows at once from the fact that such ideals form a modular lattice.

The subject of lattices has also important applications to analysis as von Neumann first pointed out. Birkhoff has more recently shown its significance for the theory of dependent probabilities and the related ergodic theorem, and for the partially ordered function spaces first considered by F. Riesz, Kantorovitch, and Freudenthal in Europe.

A partially ordered set is of course one in which the elements of any pair are in a definite order or else are unordered. Obviously a lattice is a particular set of this kind. Any partially ordered set may be constructively imbedded in a lattice, as has recently been proved by H. M. MacNeille.

Summarizing, the Society can be very proud of the numerous distinguished achievements which have been made in symbolic logic and axiomatics. We may also look confidently to the future, because of the central importance and interest of the field with its many open problems, and because of the fact that a strong group is actively pressing forward. A word of warning may not be amiss, however, to those who contemplate specializing in logic, namely that there is a definite attendant danger of overspecialization and of sterility much like that long recognized to exist in the theory of numbers. This danger can be avoided only by definitely seeking to broaden one's outlook, and by engaging in useful systematic work as well as in attempts to solve what may be well-nigh insoluble problems.

---

* That is with a least element 0, a greatest element 1, and such that for any element a there is a complementary element a' such that $a + a' = 1$, $a \times a' = 0$.

LINEAR ALGEBRA, FINITE GROUPS, AND THE THEORY OF NUMBERS

By algebra, in a broad sense, we shall mean not only the subject of linear associative algebras, but also that of finite groups, which is inevitably introduced by the consideration of algebraic equations, and of the theory of numbers, which arises as soon as the idea of the integer comes into play.

America's contribution to algebra in this sense has been a notable one. There are limitations, it is true, but the record since 1888 is very substantial. In glancing over this record it seems natural to begin by reference to the work of Dickson who has probably been the foremost American algebraist of the period. He has added extensively to all three branches of the subject. His *History of the Theory of Numbers* in three volumes (1919, 1920, and 1923) is an invaluable aid to every student of number theory. Moreover, the influence which he has exerted through his students has been very considerable. In the height of his activity today, Dickson will always remain one of our great figures.

It would be difficult for anyone not an algebraist to give a balanced, brief account of his achievements. But there are certain things which are especially impressive and which we venture to single out from among his numerous contributions.

His definition in 1923 of a set of "integral elements" of any linear associative algebra with a modulus 1, over the field of rational numbers, has turned out to be an important advance. In this way he modified the definition of du Pasquier by replacing the condition that the set have a finite basis by the condition that the rank equation of the set have leading coefficient 1 while all of the other coefficients are integers of the field. This definition, contained in his book, *Algebras and their Arithmetics*, has been generally accepted ever since in the extensive German development of the arithmetics of associative algebras, largely centering upon the development of a unitary theory of ideals, by Emil Artin, Helmuth Hasse, the late Emmy Noether, B. L. van der Waerden, and others.

It should be stated at once that three absolutely fundamental theorems of J. H. M. Wedderburn (1908), somewhat overlooked until Dickson's book called attention to them, marked a veritable turning point in the theory of linear associative algebras. These so-called structure theorems make it clear how the study of a particular algebra can be reduced in large measure to the study of certain associated isomorphic "division algebras" (that is, permitting of division except by 0), and the maximum nilpotent subalgebra (that is, such that some power of every element reduces to 0). A simple illustration of such a decomposition is afforded by the ring

$$a + b\epsilon, \qquad\qquad a, b \text{ real}; \epsilon^2 = 0,$$

in which the division algebra is the ordinary one of real numbers, and the maximum nilpotent subalgebra is that of the subring $b\epsilon$. It should also be said in this connection that the important work of A. A. Albert deals largely with the structure of algebras, so that the algebraic tradition at Chicago, begun by Moore and Maschke, is being continued in full vigor by Dickson and Albert.

This contribution of Dickson's was mentioned first because of its relation to Wedderburn's work and of its importance for the modern unified point of view towards linear associative algebras and their arithmetics.

An early group-theoretic contribution of Dickson's consisted in his theorems concerning the orthogonal modular groups in 3, 4, 5, and 6 variables, analogous to classical theorems for real orthogonal groups which connect these with isomorphic projective groups in fewer variables (see his *Linear Groups* of 1901).

There comes to mind next his varied work on the invariants of modular forms under unimodular substitutions, much of which appeared for the first time in his Madison Colloquium Lectures of 1913. This algebraic work has of course a number-theoretic side. As Dickson says, the theory of modular invariants "should be of an importance commensurate with that of the theory of invariants in modern algebra and analytic projective geometry, and should have the advantage of introducing into the theory of numbers methods uniform with those of algebra and geometry." While these expectations may not have been fully realized, nevertheless the subject as developed by him is decidedly interesting.

One thing emerges clearly concerning modular invariant theory, namely that the modular case is fairly analogous to the familiar algebraic case. Suppose, to take an extremely simple illustration, that we consider a ternary quadratic form (mod 5)

$$q_3 = \sum_{i,j=1}^{3} \beta_{ij} x_i x_j$$

of determinant $D = |\beta_{ij}| \neq 0$. If $\beta_{11} \neq 0$ the substitution of

$$x_1 - \beta_{11}^{-1}(\beta_{12} x_2 + \beta_{13} x_3)$$

for x, reduces q_3 to a more specialized form $\beta_{11} x_1^2 + q_2(x_2, x_3)$ with the same determinant. If, however, $\beta_{ii} = 0$, $(i = 1, 2, 3)$, we may replace x_1 for instance by $x_1 + x_2$ and proceed as before. Thus we immediately reduce q_3 to a sum of squares

$$\alpha_1 x_1^2 + \alpha_2 x_2^2 + \alpha_3 x_3^2$$

by use of unimodular substitutions. But if α_1 is a quadratic residue, the further substitution

$$x_1 = \alpha_1^{-1/2} x_1', \qquad x_2 = x_2', \qquad x_3 = \alpha_1^{1/2} x_3',$$

reduces α to 1. Thus we readily reduce two of the α_i's to 1 whenever two of the α_i's are residues, and so obtain a normal form

$$x_1^2 + x_2^2 + Dx_3^2.$$

In any other case, however, since 2 is a nonresidue we obtain one of the alternative forms

$$x_1^2 + 2x_2^2 + (D/2)x_3^2 \qquad \text{or} \qquad 2x_1^2 + 2x_2^2 + (D/4)x_3^2$$

without difficulty, where we can suppose that D is a residue in the first case and a nonresidue in the second. But in the first case the form may be written

$$D(D^{-1/2}x_1)^2 + (x_2 + \tfrac{1}{2}D^{1/2}x_3)^2 + (x_2 - \tfrac{1}{2}D^{1/2}x_3)^2,$$

which is essentially in the first written normal form. And the second form may be written

$$(x_1 - x_2)^2 + (x_1 + x_2)^2 + D(x_3/2)^2,$$

which is in the same normal form. Thus for such a ternary quadratic form of determinant $D \neq 0$, the normal form is entirely analogous to that for the corresponding algebraic case, with single invariant D.

Turning now to the theory of numbers, we first refer to Dickson's result (1908) that Fermat's celebrated equation

$$x^p + y^p + z^p = 0, \qquad\qquad p \text{ an odd prime,}$$

has no solution in integers prime to p for $p < 7000$. This is obtained by an extension of the well-known elementary method of Sophie Germain beyond the previous limit $p < 257$.

In 1930 Dickson published his book, *Studies in the Theory of Numbers*, which contains varied results largely concerning those "universal" quadratic forms which represent all positive integers n as, for instance, xy for $x = n$, $y = 1$, or $x^2 + y^2 + z^2 + w^2$ since every number is a sum of four or fewer squares. One of his simple results, obtained once more by elementary methods, is that every universal indefinite ternary quadratic form is a "zero form," that is, takes on the value 0 when not all the variables vanish.

These investigations show a direction of interest on Dickson's part akin to that of his work on Waring's problem in more recent years. It has been well known for a long time that every integer is expressible as the sum of not more than four squares; similarly every integer can be expressed as a sum of not more than nine cubes. A more general theorem is embodied in the conjecture of Waring that every integer is the sum of a finite fixed number of nth powers, say $g(n)$, so that $g(2) = 4$, $g(3) = 9$. Waring's theorem was first proved by Hilbert; and the subsequent asymptotic researches of Hardy and Littlewood in England and lately of Vinogradow in Russia have yielded much information as to the least number of powers required,

$G(n)$, for sufficiently large integers n, which is far smaller than $g(n)$ in general. Now it is very reasonable to think that the number of powers required to express the integer $3^n - 1^*$ is probably in most cases the true maximum number $g(n)$ of powers which are actually required. By special methods supplementing the general abstruse researches mentioned above, Dickson has shown that $g(n)$ has this value for $9 \leq n \leq 400$, and so has completed in these cases the proof of Waring's theorem in its most natural form.

In a certain sense Dickson's work in these fields reveals a kinship of spirit with Gauss. It will be recalled that Gauss solved by means of square roots alone the cyclotomic equation $x^{17} - 1 = 0$ (and similar equations), and thus was able to prove that the regular polygon of 17 sides was constructible by ruler and compass; but Gauss, presumably, never speculated on the fascinating question of algebraic solubility *in general*, which Galois answered about 1830.

On the other hand, Dickson's teacher and subsequent colleague, E. H. Moore, was an extraordinarily gifted algebraist of quite the opposite temperament. But at the height of his career he forsook algebraic investigation for his General Analysis already alluded to. Two results of his in group theory are deserving of special note. He established (1893) that the group of unimodular substitutions in a Galois field is simple; and he was the first to observe (1898) that any finite group admits an invariant positive definite Hermitian form—indeed such a form is obtained at once by adding together all of the values of $\Sigma x_i \bar{x}_j$ where $x_1, x_2, \cdots, x_n$ and $\bar{x}_1, \bar{x}_2, \cdots, \bar{x}_n$ are respectively conjugate variables. This fundamental result admits of important application to the theory of orthogonal groups as Maschke soon showed.

Turning now to other algebraists, we shall mention four as having done work of especial importance. H. F. Blichfeldt gave close limits for the orders of primitive unimodular linear groups and for the powers of the prime factors occurring therein (1903); in addition he enumerated completely the finite linear groups in four variables (1904), thereby solving a difficult classical problem. More recently he has been engaged in the problem of refining still further the results of Minkowski concerning the approximate solution of incomplete sets of linear equations in integers.

A. B. Coble has contributed to the theory of algebraic invariants and to the modular groups associated with the abelian θ-functions.

G. A. Miller has written extensively on special questions concerning finite groups and has obtained many interesting results. He is perhaps the outstanding authority on special finite groups.

H. S. Vandiver has similarly taken a leading world position as an expert of Fermat's problem mentioned above and the related theory of cyclotomic ideals. It happened that the author was early interested in the theory of

---

* Namely, the integral part of this integer divided by 2^n, plus the remainder after division.

numbers, and that the two collaborated in an elementary study of the integral divisors of $a^n - b^n$; we proved the theorem that if a and b are without a common divisor and $n > 2$, such a form always admits a "primitive divisor" except in the case $n = 6$, $a = 2$, $b = 1$. A primitive divisor, necessarily of the form 1 modulo n, is one which divides no similar form with smaller exponent n'. In the more than thirty years which have elapsed since our youthful venture, Vandiver has continued in this one direction. He has established that the theorem of Fermat certainly holds for any exponent less than 618, thereby considerably extending his similar previous results. He has also proved the elegant result that if Fermat's equation is soluble in integers, then the following congruences hold:

$$x^p \equiv x, \qquad y^p \equiv y, \qquad z^p \equiv z \qquad (\bmod\ p^3).$$

Furthermore, he has extended the criteria of Wieferich and Mirimanoff for $q = 2$, 3 to $q = 5$, by showing that if there is a solution of Fermat's equation, then the congruence

$$5^{p-1} - 1 \equiv 0 \qquad (\bmod\ p^2)$$

is satisfied; Frobenius subsequently obtained a like condition for $q = 11$, 17.

With these preliminary facts before us some further remarks on each of the fields of linear algebras, finite groups, and number theory, must conclude our brief survey.

As far as ordinary algebraic theory is concerned there should be mentioned, among others who have actively contributed, H. T. Engstrom, O. E. Glenn, Olive Hazlett, M. H. Ingraham, Nathan Jacobson, C. G. Latimer, N. H. McCoy, C. C. MacDuffee, Saunders MacLane, J. F. Ritt, J. B. Shaw, and Henry Taber, of whom Taber is no longer living. A number of these are young men, and everything indicates a continued algebraic development in this country. In particular there is today a strong representation at Princeton, comprising von Neumann, Wedderburn, and Weyl.

On the other hand in the somewhat narrow field of finite groups, in which Americans have long been preëminent, there is less activity. Among the distinguished workers in this field not yet mentioned are H. H. Mitchell, whose dissertation gave a very interesting geometrical treatment of linear modular groups in three variables, and W. A. Manning who has especially studied simply and multiply transitive permutation groups. But very few young men seem to pursue the theory of finite groups, once so popular in this country.

In number theory the stimulating work of E. T. Bell has not yet been mentioned; it has largely been in the study of "arithmetical paraphrases." This really is the general theory of the parity (oddness or evenness) of functions in a general algebraic ring. The functional equations satisfied by the ordinary trigonometric functions, the θ-functions, etc., are made to yield important known as well as new identities. American work in the theory of numbers has been enhanced by the presence of Hans Rademacher who has made important contributions to the theory of partitions.

It is very satisfactory to note that there is at present a very active and able group of younger men who have number-theoretic interests and who are obtaining valuable results, as Leonard Carlitz, Marshall Hall, Ralph Hull, R. D. James, D. H. Lehmer, Gordon Pall, and Morgan Ward. Here again the outlook is very propitious.

Thus we see that there has been a great algebraic advance in the direction of a unified theory of linear associative algebras and their arithmetics, in which we have taken an important part. But while in Europe certain outstanding classical problems have been solved—such as the finiteness of complete systems of algebraic invariants and Waring's problem, both in the affirmative sense by Hilbert—we in America have scarcely reached such exalted heights of algebraic achievement. Notwithstanding this fact, however, we have every right to be very proud of what has been already accomplished among us.

ANALYSIS

The field of pure mathematics called analysis is extraordinarily vast and diversified. In attempting to outline our very considerable advances in this field during the last fifty years, only a few significant achievements can be singled out more or less arbitrarily. This is a difficult task; and we begin by referring briefly to the work of four of the older analysts, in whose contributions there can be discerned the beginnings of most of our principal directions of advance—Moore, Osgood, Bôcher, and Van Vleck.

Although Moore was primarily a logician and algebraist rather than an analyst, nevertheless his analytical work was important, and his influence through his General Analysis already mentioned, was considerable. In this, he introduced, for example, the interesting idea of "relatively uniform convergence" of a sequence, in which the difference between the limit and the nth element becomes and remains less than $\epsilon \sigma_p$ in absolute value, where σ_p is one of the linear class of functions under consideration over the range P. Let this class of functions be designated by $\mathfrak{M}$, and the (linear) class of such uniform limits by $\mathfrak{M}^*$. It follows at once that we have $(\mathfrak{M}^*)^* = \mathfrak{M}^*$, a theorem generalizing a well known result for the class of continuous functions, for instance.

His article *Concerning transcendentally transcendental functions* (1897) is very suggestive. In a phrase which has a distinctly Moorean quality he thus designates those transcendental functions which satisfy no algebraic differential equation. This paper was stimulated by Hölder's recent proof that $\Gamma(x)$ had this property, but was much more penetrating. Moore showed just why $\Gamma(x)$ and other simple functions belong to this class. He also did a considerable amount of work on improper definite (Riemann) integrals—a subject which has for the time being lost much of its flavor to mathematicians because of the systematic use of the Lebesgue integral.

Strongly influenced by Felix Klein of Göttingen, Osgood has devoted his attention mainly to the theory of functions of a single complex variable. His article on this subject in the Encyklopädie der mathematischen Wissenschaften (1901) represents the first careful and systematic presentation of the Riemannian point of view, which is dominant today, as against the earlier Weierstrassian approach, based on the use of power series. Osgood's subsequent Funktionentheorie, has provided a large part of the present mathematical world with its fundamental training in this field, and remains today an invaluable adjunct to other books emphasizing more recent developments.

But Osgood has been more than a very thoughtful and systematic expositor of the subject. With much scholarly insight he has made important contributions. Perhaps the best known of these is his extremely elegant and general theorem on conformal mapping (1900), namely, that any simply connected open region in the z-plane possessing more than one boundary point can be mapped in a (1,1) conformal manner on the interior of a circle of the w-plane—a theorem previously established for regions having a much more restricted type of boundary. Similarly in an important paper by himself and A. E. Taylor (1913) they proved* that in such a mapping each neighborhood of an accessible point of the boundary was mapped on the neighborhood of a single point of the bounding circle. By these two results, Osgood has aided greatly in the understanding of conformal mapping problems. Among other American mathematicians, Wladimir Seidel and J. L. Walsh have done most in this direction.

In 1901 Osgood established a now classical, fundamental theorem of the calculus of variations, known by his name, to the effect that under very general conditions the numerical value I of an integral, along any admissible arc C joining two fixed points P_0, P_1 and contained in a fixed neighborhood of a minimizing arc C_0 joining the same points, will exceed I_0 by at least a quantity $\delta(\epsilon) > 0$ where ϵ denotes the (properly defined) distance between the two curves; for example, if I represents arc length, then C_0 will be the straight line segment P_0P_1 of length $I_0 = 2l$, say; and the theorem asserts that the length of any rectifiable arc P_0P_1 exceeds $2l$ by $\delta(\epsilon)$ at least, where we may now take

$$\delta(\epsilon) = 2((l^2 + \epsilon^2)^{1/2} - l).$$

Finally we may refer in this all too brief account, to Osgood's well known treatment of the gyroscope by intrinsic vectorial methods (1922). As the late O. D. Kellogg showed (1923), this elegant approach gave a direct answer to delicate qualitative questions concerning the behavior of the gyroscope.

---

* Osgood had announced these results in 1903.

In his close association with Bôcher until the latter's all too early death, Osgood has always felt most appreciative of Bôcher's clarification of function theory in many directions. Thus Bôcher's visual interpretation of Poisson's integral as the angular average of the values marked on the circle as seen by an observer to whom light travels along circular arcs orthogonal to the given circle, aids in providing intuitive meaning to this important integral. However, scarcely any of Bôcher's contributions fall directly in the domain of functions of a complex variable.

J. L. Walsh would probably be regarded today both here and abroad as the American who has above others continued the excellent tradition in the theory of functions of a complex variable begun by Osgood. Walsh's dissertation gave very interesting extensions of Bôcher's work on the relation between the zeros of two homogeneous binary forms of degree n, and the zeros of their Jacobian—readily interpreted as results concerning the zeros and poles of a rational function, and the zeros of its derivative. Since that time Walsh has contributed extensively to the theory of the approximation to analytic and harmonic functions by polynomials and by rational functions, and to the theory of interpolation in the complex domain (see his Colloquium Lectures of 1935). He has also defined an orthogonal set of step-functions of much interest.

Bôcher's first work of importance is to be found in his book *Die Reihenentwickelungen der Potentialtheorie*, which was essentially an amplification of a dissertation under Klein in 1891. This was in the main the fulfillment of a general program sketched by Klein, to complete the formal theory of expansions in Lamé's functions, derived from the potential equation in three variables by the introduction of general cyclidic coördinates and the subsequent separation of variables. What has been called "Bôcher's theorem" enumerates the various possible degenerate forms of Lamé's functions; these turn out to include practically all of the special functions most useful in mathematical physics.

Nearly all of Bôcher's later work centered around the potential equation, which is indeed a focal point for a great part of analysis, real or complex. He never pursued, however, the difficult and complicated questions of convergence and representation associated with Lamé series of orthogonal functions. Instead, he turned to simpler related problems, in particular to boundary-value problems in one dimension. Among his various extensions of Sturm's comparison and oscillation theorems, basic for this boundary-value problem, it was an elegant short note of 1905 on the solutions of an ordinary linear differential equation of the second order under periodic conditions which first stimulated the author's interest in this special field.

Bôcher's mathematical perspective and his instinct for what was important were very unusual. He was interested in comparison and oscillation theorems simply because of the information which they give concerning solutions of ordinary linear differential equations as functionals of the coefficients. This particular topic interested him as much as any other. In his Paris lectures near the end of his life he chose it as his general theme which was expanded into the *Leçons sur les méthodes de Sturm.*

His unusual modesty led Bôcher more than once to conceal a new result under the guise of an apparently expository article. This happened for instance in his beautiful exposition of the elementary theory of Fourier series (1906), where the first detailed study of Gibbs' phenomenon was run into the body of the text almost without comment. His passion for elegance and simplicity grew with the years. What he sought more than anything else were those simple illuminating insights which contain the germ of a real advance. For instance, he remarked in a brief note published in the same year that one could define a harmonic function $u(x, y)$ (that is, one satisfying the potential equation in two dimensions) as a function continuous, together with its two partial derivations of the first order, which satisfies Gauss' theorem on every circle C. To anyone familiar with the elements of the theory of inversion and Poisson's integral, Bôcher's proof can be presented in a few lines. In the same year the German mathematician Koebe proved that if $u(x, y)$ is merely continuous and satisfies the average-value theorem on every circle, then $u(x, y)$ will be harmonic. However, Bôcher's starting point is much closer to physical intuition, and his paper has been of at least equal importance in its general influence.

Turning now briefly to Van Vleck, we refer to his well known dissertation on continued fractions (1894) of which a partial account is to be found in his Colloquium Lectures of 1903 on *Divergent Series and Continued Fractions.* Such continued fractions are most easily defined by means of certain recurrence relations which are actually linear difference equations of the second order in n, with coefficients dependent on x, so that the functions considered are basically of the form

$$\lim_{n \to \infty} y_n(x)/z_n(x),$$

where $y_n(x)$ and $z_n(x)$ are linearly independent particular solutions of this difference equation.

Although Van Vleck wrote only one brief paper on linear difference equations (1912), the subject engaged much of his attention for several years. It was his suggestive lectures on difference equations during a stay as instructor at Madison that led the author to an appreciation of the open problems in the field. Of Van Vleck's later work we refer only to his interesting example of a nonmeasurable set in the sense of Legesgue (1908) based, as was inevitable, upon the principle of arbitrary choice, and to his studies (with F. H'Doubler) of the general solution of the functional equations satisfied by the elliptic θ functions.

With these facts in mind, let us attempt an evaluation of some of the main American accomplishments in analysis. For this purpose it is proposed to deal successively with some ten directions of effort which seem particularly worthy of consideration: (1) functional analysis; (2) functions of one or more complex variables; (3) the calculus of variations; (4) potential theory; (5) Fourier series and integrals; (6) boundary-value and expansion problems; (7) linear differential equations; (8) linear difference equations; (9) ordinary differential equations; (10) special analysis. Of these, the American tradition in functional analysis goes back essentially to E. H. Moore; in functions of one or more complex variables, to Osgood; in potential theory, Fourier series, boundary-value and expansion problems, and ordinary linear differential equations, largely to Bôcher; in linear difference equations, to Van Vleck; in the theory of ordinary differential equations, perhaps to the author; and in the important field of special analysis, to Wiener more than to any other American. It is felt that the most serious defect of our achievements in analysis is that we have as yet done very little in partial differential equations and analytic number theory. Hans Lewgaud and C. B. Morrey are beginning to make contributions to the former field.

1. **Functional analysis.** In functional analysis it is necessary first of all to consid r the school of thought which originates more or less directly with E. H. Moore and his General Analysis. Here we find much of the work of L. M. Graves, W. L. Hart, and T. H. Hildebrandt. These analysts have formulated abstract theories under which the expansion of a function of n variables in Taylor's series, and existence theorems both for n ordinary differential equations of the first order, and for a set of n implicit functional equations in n unknowns are extended to the case when n becomes infinite. Unfortunately it seems to be the fact that the really interesting special cases of these theories can often be reached by mild artifices and easy extensions of classical theories. Accordingly this kind of work seems to be serviceable rather than particularly exciting.

A somewhat less general point of view is that initiated by Fréchet in which the notion of limit is introduced in dealing with the independent variable. A classical result here was that of E. W. Chittenden (1917), establishing that Fréchet's *écart* and *voisinage* are at bottom equivalent. Several important contributions to functional analysis in the ordinary sense have been made by T. H. Hildebrandt and A. D. Michal.

The present-day trend of mathematical thought seems to be to restrict attention to a few especially significant types of spaces such as topological spaces, linear metric (Banach) spaces, Hilbert spaces, etc., rather than with Moore to use an entirely implicit space as an *omnium gatherium*. This modification of Moore's program has met with much success.

Thus in a very well known paper of 1932, von Neumann solved a problem formulated by Hilbert, as to whether or not every abstract topological group whose parameter-space is locally euclidean, is equivalent to a Lie group. Von Neumann showed that the answer is in the affirmative sense for compact groups (using Haar measure). Later van Kampen treated the commutative case. Furthermore Walther Mayer and T. Y. Thomas have given a rigorous treatment of Lie group nuclei in the topological case. Carrett Birkhoff has considered the case when the parameter-space is a Banach space, while, in the neighborhood of the identical transformation, vector differences are nearly preserved, and has then arrived at a correlated Lie algebra.

Various kinds of abstract integration have been likewise considered in a similar spirit by Birkhoff, Bochner, Dunford, Graves, and others.

Such abstract developments as these are of decided importance because the underlying assumptions are so simple and inevitable, and the methods so elegant, that the abstract subject matter becomes concrete as soon as understood.

We next indicate a general program of functional analysis concerning existence theorems which was initiated by Kellogg and the author (1922). This has proved itself more effective than the obvious treatment by direct abstraction.

The ordinary implicit equations of analysis can be written in the form $f = T(f)$ where f is the "point" in function space whose existence is to be established and $g = T(f)$ for any f is a transformed point in the same functional space. Thus the desired existence theorem merely affirms that the transformation T of the space into a subspace admits of a fixed point. Kellogg and the author started with the fact that if a convex $2m$-dimensional region in euclidean space is transformed into (a part of) itself by a continuous single-valued transformation, there is always at least one fixed point. This immediately yielded, by a passage to the limit, various known existence theorems and other new ones. It was clear that this method could be given a more abstract form, such as the theory later took under the hands of Leray and Schauder.

Another very important class of transformations is furnished by the linear homogeneous transformations of a Hilbert space* into itself, $x' = T(x)$. These are said to be of bounded type if the distance of the transformed point from the origin $|x|$ does not exceed $K|x|$, where K is independent of x. If, furthermore, we have, for x and y real, $\sum x_i y_i' = \sum y_i x_i'$, the operator T is said to be self-adjoint. The transformation is then analogous to those affine transformations of n-dimensional Euclidean space which multiply distances in the directions of n mutually orthogonal axes by corresponding (limited) constants. Of the same order of difficulty is the so-called Hermitian case. The study of bounded self-adjoint trans-

---

* The real points x of Hilbert space consist of these infinite real sequences $x_1, x_2, \cdots$ for which $\sum x_i^2$ is finite; this is essentially the same as the space of all real functions f such that f^2 is integrable in the sense of Lebesgue.

formations was initiated by Hilbert. Recently the unbounded case has been treated by von Neumann and by Stone. The principal results and important applications can be found in Stone's book of 1932, *Linear Transformations in Hilbert Space*. Among the younger men F. J. Murray is especially to be named in this field.

Although we have here a very general theory embracing in a certain sense that of most of the orthogonal series defined by ordinary linear differential equations, nevertheless, just because of this generality, the theory fails to yield an easy direct approach to the discussion of such series.

A very interesting fact about extensions of known facts in n dimensions to function space, is that a trivial fact for n finite may become of prime significance for the corresponding extension. This situation can be illustrated by a theorem of the author. It is trivial in n-dimensional space that, if we vary a set of mutually orthogonal unit vectors continuously, and if initially they define the complete n-dimensional space (that is, are n in number), then they must continue to do so throughout the variation. Under certain restrictions it was proved that an analogous fact holds for function space which allows us, for example, to infer the completeness of the Sturm-Liouville series from that of the Fourier series. The same idea has been found useful in other connections.

2. **Functions of one or more complex variables.** We have already referred briefly to the work of Osgood and Bôcher in this field. Besides their results may be mentioned advances in the difficult field of algebraic functions of more than one variable by Lefschetz and J. W. Alexander, who first realized the desirability of utilizing the methods of analysis situs in this domain.

From this brief list are excluded those who are occupied with topics which involve special functions, or in which the function-theoretic aspect is present but takes a somewhat subordinate position. If such workers were admitted, the names of Boas, Bochner, Bohnenblust, L. R. Ford, Hille, Levinson, W. T. Martin, Rademacher, Radó, Ritt, Shohat, Tamarkin, Walsh, Weyl, D. V. Widder, and Wiener would have to be added since all of these men have made important contributions to one or the other of the types. This is a goodly list.

3. **The calculus of variations.** Here it is well to make mention of the strong tradition at the University of Chicago in this field. While at Chicago, Bolza became more and more occupied with the subject and published there his *Lectures on the Calculus of Variations* of 1904, later expanded into his very important *Vorlesungen über Variationsrechnung*. Bliss has followed in the footsteps of Bolza and has made substantial contributions to the subject; his students, M. R. Hestenes, and W. T. Reid, have done excellent work in the field. At Chicago there has been a systematic study of the interrelated general problems of Lagrange, Mayer, and Bolza.

Among the other younger men, E. J. McShane has been particularly concerned with existence theorems as derivable from the minimum principle itself.

The special interest of the author in the calculus of variations arose through the study of dynamical systems, since dynamical trajectories may be regarded in many cases as geodesics along which the arc length is an extremum. The problem of geodesics is indeed quite a typical one in the calculus of variations. In a paper written in 1918 he considered admissible curves made up of n short geodesic arcs, and showed that the problem of the extrema thus reduced that of the extrema of an ordinary function of n variables. He discussed not only the case of a minimum but also the case of a "minimax," in which the corresponding normalized quadratic form contains a single negative squared term. This new case was proved to be characterized by the fact that the first conjugate point A' of A along the extremal arc AB under consideration lies between A and B, while the second conjugate point lies beyond B. Furthermore, he established a simple interrelation between the number of minima and the minimaxes.

This work was then generalized powerfully by M. Morse, a central feature being his fundamental relations between the various *types* of the critical points, as characterized by the number of negative squared terms in the attached normalized quadratic form. The publication of Morse's Colloquium Lectures, *The Calculus of Variations in the Large*, in 1934, constitutes a landmark in the history of the subject. Morse's related oscillation and comparison theorems are a large extension of earlier theorems of this kind, and the purely geometric significance of his work is very considerable.

In 1935 Hestenes and the author took up the problem of characterization of all types of extremal arcs by introducing the notion of "natural isoperimetric conditions." A simple example is furnished by the closed geodesics on a convex surface in ordinary three-dimensional space, for any one of which the integral curvature on either side is necessarily 2π. Consequently, as Poincaré had noted, if we seek the simple closed curve of minimum length which divides the surface in two parts, of equal integral curvature, we obtain the desired closed geodesic. The auxiliary condition imposed is a special "natural isoperimetric condition," and the geodesic obtained is not of minimum type but of minimax type. Thus in a certain sense, the general case of an extremum can be reduced always to that of a maximum or minimum. This new approach leads in a simpler way to the results obtained by Morse and can readily be extended to multiple integrals.

From the purely abstract point of view the calculus of variations may be regarded as a critical point problem for a real function defined over a certain kind of function space. Morse has obtained significant results looking in this direction.

A very important special advance in the calculus of variations has been the solution of the famous problem of Plateau, to find the surface of minimum area bounded by one or more given closed curves. Jesse Douglas and Radó almost simultaneously solved the problem by different methods. Douglas used a boldly novel method in order to arrive at a very general result, while Radó employed a method of conformal mapping. The work of both of these men deserves the highest praise. Significant contributions to this problem were made by Courant and McShane also.

4. **Potential theory.** We have already alluded to the work of Bôcher and Kellogg, both ardent devotees of potential theory. It remains chiefly to bring to your attention some recent important advances concerning the celebrated Dirichlet problem of assigning arbitrary (continuous) boundary values to a harmonic function in the plane. If this assignment can be made for every choice of boundary values, the open region T under consideration is said to be "normal." The fact that the finite plane, less a single point, is not a normal region follows at once from Bôcher's result of 1903, that a bounded harmonic function cannot have an isolated singular point.

In dealing with an illuminating example of a normal region T in the plane having a perfect set of Borel measure 0 on a line as boundary, Kellogg in 1923 showed that, for any normal region T, any sequence of nested normal regions T_n approaching T with near-by boundary values defined a sequence u_n of potential functions which approached the solution u belonging to T. It was the especial merit of Wiener to establish in 1924 the fact that the u_n so obtained converges to a unique limiting function u, whether or not T is normal. Thus if T consists of the interior of a unit circle with the exception of its center taken as the origin, the harmonic function $(\log r)/(\log \epsilon)$ takes on the value 0 on the unit circle and the value 1 on the circle of radius ϵ. If ϵ tends to zero, we obtain a limiting potential function $u=0$, taking on the assigned values 0 on the unit circle but not the assigned value 1 at the origin.

In consequence of Wiener's result there is a unique "conductor potential" corresponding to the assignment of the boundary value 1 on any bounded set, from which we obtain Wiener's "capacity" of the set. Wiener showed how the question as to whether a region was normal or not admitted a theoretic answer in terms of the notion of capacity. For the actual answer in any case the method of "barrier functions" of Lebesgue seems to be equally serviceable.

The important question is to determine whether the boundary points are all "regular" or not; the test for regularity is equally as well that of the existence of a barrier function as it is the convergence of the critical series of Wiener, involving an infinite number of unknown capacities. If all the points are regular, and not otherwise, the region T is normal.

Evans has recently obtained the important result that regular points necessarily occur in three or more dimensions, as well as in the known case of two dimensions. In doing so he solved a problem to which Kellogg and other mathematicians here and abroad had given a great deal of attention.

5. **Fourier series and integrals.** In addition to the work of Bôcher on Gibbs' phenomenon previously noted, the Göttingen dissertation of Dunham Jackson (1911) may be mentioned first. This was an elegant contribution to the problem of the best approximation to a given function $f(x)$, $(0 \leq x \leq 2\pi)$, by a trigonometric sum of order n

$$T_n(x) = \tfrac{1}{2}a_0 + \sum_{k=1}^{n} (a_k \cos kx + b_r \sin kx).$$

The first $n+1$ terms of the usual Fourier series minimize

$$\int_{\sigma}^{2\pi} [f(x) - T_n(x)]^2 dx.$$

Jackson showed that a better result (in a certain sense) would be obtained if the exponent 2 were replaced by 4. Later on he discussed the interrelation between the number of derivatives of $f(x)$ and the order of smallness of the coefficients in its Fourier series. His other work has for the most part been connected with problems of best approximation (in various senses) to a given function.

Wiener has obtained within a few years the remarkable result that if the Fourier series of a continuous non-vanishing function converges absolutely, the reciprocal function possesses also an absolutely convergent Fourier series (1934). As his books on Fourier integrals (1933), and on Fourier transforms with the much lamented R. E. A. C. Paley, demonstrate, his work in these directions has been striking in quality and originality. He has also studied modified trigonometric series of the form

$$\sum_{n} (a_n \cos \lambda_n x + b_n \sin \lambda_n x)$$

and the functions which they represent. His work in the general field of harmonic analysis probably is unsurpassed. Mention should be made of the contributions to the general theory of summability of Fourier series by Hille and Tamarkin.

In conclusion it may be remarked that multiple Fourier series have been investigated by C. N. Moore, as well as questions concerning other multiple series and their summability. To one or both of these fields other significant contributions have been made by Adams, Bochner, Gergen, and others.

6. **Boundary-value and expansion problems.** As has been stated previously, it was Bôcher who first occupied himself seriously with boundary-

value problems, although it should be recalled that William Elwood Byerly's extremely useful book *Fourier's Series and Spherical Harmonics* had appeared in lithographed form in 1891. But Bôcher never occupied himself seriously with the deeper questions raised by the related infinite series, nor did any one else in our country. As a consequence when the author treated the one-dimensional boundary-value and expansion problems in his dissertation, he had never heard of Poincaré's celebrated paper of 1894, in which an analogous method of attack was used. Doubtless he ought to have made a more thorough search of the literature. However, the difference in degree of intractability between the problem for the potential equation, studied by Poincaré, and for an ordinary linear differential equation of the nth order with an arbitrary set of n linear boundary conditions, which he treated, was all in his favor. In fact he showed that basic asymptotic formulae could be established in the latter case; whereas in the former this has not been accomplished satisfactorily even today.

Briefly stated, the method was the following: (1) an asymptotic study of the solutions of the given linear differential equation; (2) then, by means of this, the asymptotic solution of the boundary-value problem for large characteristic numbers; and (3) the direct study of the related expansions in orthogonal or biorthogonal functions of $f(x)$ by means of the unfailing sum formula for n terms of the series,

$$\frac{1}{2\pi(-1)^{1/2}} \int_{C_n} \int_a^b G(x, t; \lambda) f(t) dt d\lambda,$$

where G is the explicitly known Green's function, λ is a complex parameter, and C_n is a contour in the λ-plane containing within it the characteristic values $\lambda_1, \cdots, \lambda_n$ for the boundary problem under consideration.

A year or two earlier Hilbert had established certain properties of these series in the very special real self-adjoint case by different methods.

The researches of Tamarkin, Stone, and Langer have added greatly to our knowledge of these interesting series. In particular Langer has shown how their properties may be discussed in the difficult case when the asymptotic form has a branch-point within the interval considered. This is connected with the so-called "Stokes phenomenon" of the physicists. Here the earlier interesting work of Max Mason, which utilized the methods of the calculus of variations, is to be recalled. Langer and the author have also studied the analogous boundary and expansion problems for a linear system of n equations of the first order; while Bliss has treated the same problem in what is essentially the real self-adjoint case, again from a decidedly different point of view.

The work of Tamarkin, and of Stone, has very much deepened our knowledge of these series in the "regular" case. When the conditions for regularity hold, the series are "equivalent" in a very deep sense to certain Fourier series. What can happen in the way of pathological behavior of these series, when the conditions of regularity are not satisfied, has been investigated by Stone, and quite recently by Langer, in the simplest case of the first order.

7. **Linear differential equations.** Bôcher was well acquainted with the field of linear differential equations in both real and complex variables. It was through his lectures that the author became interested in the theory of ordinary linear differential equations in the complex domain. In the two years at Chicago, he came to the conclusion that it was better to study a single matrix differential equation

$$Y'(x) = A(x)Y(x)$$

(that is, n equations of the first order) than a single linear differential equation of the nth order. Perhaps it was the conspicuous analogy between the first and nth order cases in this symbolic form which attracted me to the matrix notation.

The fundamental point of view was group-theoretic. Suppose that the singular point of the differential equation which is under consideration is taken to be at $x = \infty$, so that the elements $a_{ij}(x)$ of the square matrix $A(x)$ are analytic or have poles at $x = \infty$. It was then clear that the group of transformations

$$Y(x) = B(x)\overline{Y}(x), \quad x = \phi(\bar{x}),$$

where $B(x)$ is made up of elements analytic or with poles at $x = \infty$, with $|B| \neq 0$, and where $\phi(x)/x$ is analytic and does not vanish at $x = \infty$, leaves unchanged the *essential* nature of the singularity in question. Hence the initial query of over thirty years ago took the form: Under this group of transformations of dependent and independent variables, what are the invariants? This problem was first attacked in the so-called general case, leaving aside those cases where unusual purely algebraic complications entered. These exceptional cases have recently been treated by W. J. Trjitzinsky by the same method which we jointly had found to be successful in the case of linear difference equations. The author also formulated and solved a generalized inverse Riemann problem, both in the neighborhood of a singular point and in the large.

The essential advance here was in obtaining a theory of the irregular singular point, although an extremely simple treatment of the regular singular point was found; it was this latter problem to which Fuchs had restricted his attention. In the case of only regular singular points, the Riemann problem had been solved by Hilbert and Plemelj by a different method.

8. **Linear difference equations.** Really significant American work on linear difference equations began with the dissertation of R. D. Carmichael at Princeton (1910). This marked an important advance; for under suitable hypotheses he showed the existence of a complete set of analytic

solutions possessing known asymptotic forms in the positive direction of the axis or equally in the negative direction. In the work immediately following, the author took a single matrix difference equation as fundamental,

$$Y(x + 1) = A(x)Y(x),$$

and in general made similar restrictions on the roots of the characteristic equation. In this very suggestive matrix notation two formal solutions arose, namely

$$A^{-1}(x)A^{-1}(x + 1) \cdots \qquad \text{and} \qquad A(x - 1)A(x - 2) \cdots.$$

This situation supplied the author with the cue for deriving two "principal matrix solutions" $Y_+(x)$ and $Y_-(x)$, of simple known asymptotic form in *all* directions. The formal matrix

$$\cdots A(x + 1)A(x)A(x - 1) \cdots$$

with elements of period 1 played an important rôle. Later was formulated and solved an inverse Riemannian problem. Full generality was obtained only recently, by demonstrating the existence of a full quota of asymptotic series and then taking up, in collaboration with Trjitzinsky, the most general case. Meanwhile C. R. Adams had made definite extensions of the first theory.

We have time only to mention the much simpler theory of the analogous q-difference equation

$$Y(qx) = A(x)Y(x),$$

first treated by Carmichael and by the author, and to refer to other important work in the field of linear difference equations by C. R. Adams, Carmichael, W. B. Ford, I. M. Sheffer, and K. P. Williams.

Very recently (1935) Trjitzinsky has obtained a complete theory for representation of solutions by means of factorial series and Laplace integrals. These were central in Nörlund's basic work on linear difference equations which was done a little earlier than the work of Carmichael and the author, although published later.

The program in these fields of linear differential equations and of linear difference equations has been to take as the unitary basis the square matrix of functions $Y(x)$ rather than the single function. The program has been illustrated further by obtaining the decomposition of a matrix of entire functions into an infinite matrix product of factors of simple type. This gave a generalization of the familiar Weierstrassian decomposition of a single entire function into an infinite product.

In the last year or two the author has been engaged in treating the still more general problems arising from one or more compatible equations in $Y(x)$ of the form

$$Y(\phi(x)) = A(x)Y(x),$$

where the elements of $A(x)$ are analytic or have poles at $x = \infty$ and where $\phi(x)$ has a pole of the first order there. It was begun with the extremely interesting case of order 1, that is, with a set of compatible linear functional equations of the type

$$y(\phi(x)) = a(x)y(x).$$

9. Ordinary differential equations. A piece of significant work in this field was the discussion by Osgood, early (1898) in his career, of the equation of the first order $y' = f(x, y)$. He assumed that f was merely continuous, and showed that the usual uniqueness theorem failed to hold, in which case there was an upper and lower solution passing through a point (x_0, y_0).*

An excellent study of existence theorems, in particular for ordinary differential equations, is contained in Bliss' Princeton Colloquium Lectures of 1909. In the Colloquium Lectures at New Haven in 1906, Mason gave an abbreviated general method in the linear case as follows. By suitable direct integration, convert the given differential equation into a functional equation

$$y = g + S(y), \qquad\qquad g \text{ known.}$$

If then the series

$$g + S(g) + S^2(g) \cdots$$

can be proved to converge uniformly, it furnishes the unique solution of the given differential equation. This method extends at once to n linear differential equations in n dependent variables $y_1, \cdots, y_n$. To apply this to the linear equation $y' = f(x, y)$ mentioned above, for example, we would first write it in the equivalent integral form

$$y(x) = y_0 + \int_{x_0}^{x} f(x, y(x))dx.$$

Of course, this convenient method really is nothing other than the classical method of successive approximations in somewhat more abstract form.

The work of Ritt on the polynomial differential equations $P(x; y, y', \cdots, y^{(n)}) = 0$ satisfied by algebraically transcendental functions has been of much importance. He has given a treatment of the totality of these functions in which the necessary algebraic considerations are for the first time given their proper weight. Our knowledge of the special functions so defined is still in a very rudimentary state. This fact is indicated by the two following important unsolved problems: (1) to determine whether or not any single-valued function $y(x)$, analytic throughout the x-plane ex-

---

* The phenomenon involved had been observed earlier by Peano who also gave an existence proof, a fact unknown to Osgood.

cept at k singular points x_i, $(i = 1, \cdots, k)$, and satisfying near each such
point a corresponding equation

$$P_i(x; y, y', \cdots, y^{(n)}) = 0,$$

where $P_i \not\equiv 0$ is polynomial in $y, \cdots, y^{(n)}$ with coefficients analytic in x
at x_i, $(i = 1, 2, \cdots, k)$, is necessarily algebraically transcendental; (2) to
determine criteria in the case $n \geq 2$ for analytic natural boundaries of the
solutions.

As far as the work of the author in this field is concerned, aside from
that on the differential equations of dynamics, we first mention the ideas
which cluster around the "recurrent motions," which were first defined
about twenty-five years ago. Here take the independent variable as the
time t, and consider n real equations of the first order in $x_1, \cdots, x_n$. In any
closed manifold of motions such recurrent motions will always exist. They
have the characteristic property of filling their entire geometric locus in
$x_1, \cdots, x_n$ space within distance ϵ in *any* sufficiently large interval of
time. Every motion is either recurrent, or approaches indefinitely only
to recede from a set of such recurrent motions. More recently the somewhat analogous "central motions" to which all other motions approach
in the sense of time probability were defined.

These two concepts have already led to a number of further researches
here and abroad. There are many open problems to be solved, of which
three will be signalized: (1) In the analytic case, when there are no periodic
motions in an invariant closed manifold, are the differential equations
essentially reducible to

$$\frac{dx_i}{dt} = c_i, \qquad\qquad i = 1, \cdots, n,$$

where $x_1, \cdots, x_n$ are periodic variables of period 1? (2) In the n-dimen-
sional analytic case, can the basic ordinal process by which the central
motions are defined, ever involve more than n terms? (3) In the analytic
case, does the set of central motions always admit of a *natural* invariant
measure?

By use of surfaces of section first employed by Poincaré, it appears
that the continuous transformations defined by a set of ordinary differential equations and the iteration of a particular continuous point transformation are very closely related. P. A. Smith and the author a number
of years ago discussed the $(1, 1)$ transformations of the surface of a sphere
into itself. Hassler Whitney has proved recently that any continuous transformation without invariant points always gives rise to local surfaces of
section. Within a year, Deane Montgomery and Leo Zippin have discussed
certain nearly periodic continuous transformations. It may be safely predicted that the study of transformations of different types will lead to extensive further developments.

10. **Special analysis.** The term is here used merely for convenience to designate that part of analysis in which either simple explicit expressions are investigated or functions are implicitly defined by simple integral equations. In this domain are found Tauberian theorems and the theory of Fourier transforms to which Wiener has extensively contributed, and the theory of the Laplace transforms which Hille, Tamarkin, and especially Widder have studied to great advantage. Such work as that of C. N. Haskins on the moment problem and that of L. L. Silverman on the summability of divergent sequences would also fall under this head.

This extensive domain is more appreciated in Europe than it is in America, where we tend to take our mathematics as serious business rather than as a means of exercising our talent for free invention. In this connection it is well not to forget that many of the most astonishing mathematical developments began as a pure *jeu d'esprit*.

GEOMETRY

In venturing upon a partial survey of American geometrical developments during these last fifty years, I feel embarrassed for two reasons. The first is my own severe limitation in the field. The second is a disturbing secret fear that geometry may ultimately turn out to be no more than the glittering intuitional trappings of analysis. At any rate the geometers are finding it more and more difficult to tell what the distinguishing mark of geometry really is. Thus in the Introduction of his *Treatise on Algebraic Plane Curves* (1931), J. L. Coolidge said that, for him, "geometry is nothing at all, if not a branch of art, and the underlying force which compels him to treat any particular topic, or to handle it in any particular way, is either that he is ignorant of any other, or else that his aesthetic sense dictates the choice: it pleaseth him to do so." In almost the same vein Veblen and J. H. C. Whitehead said a year later, in their Cambridge Tract on the *Foundations of Differential Geometry*, that a "branch of mathematics is called a geometry, because the name seems good on emotional and traditional grounds, to a sufficient number of competent people."

Whatever else such attitudes toward geometry may signify, they indicate the present lack of any program as convincing as was the famous group-theoretic Erlanger Programm of Klein, announced in 1872.

The uncertainty in point of view is largely due to two obvious causes. In the first place, the advent of Einstein's general theory of relativity made natural the surmise that all of physics might be looked at as a kind of extended geometry; this appeared most clearly in the general theory of gravitation for empty space, in which the world-lines of particles were simply the geodesics in a certain four-dimensional Riemannian geometry. Here was a first powerful suggestion that our geometrical ideas needed to be correspondingly enlarged. In the second place the extremely important and basic kind of geometry called analysis situs, in which the underlying group is formed by the general (1, 1) continuous point transformations, began to be properly appreciated. This further lessened the interest in classical geometric ideas.

As a result there have arisen two notable geometric movements. The first has led to a new theory of "generalized spaces"; and the second to an important development in the field of analysis situs. It is not too much to say that, from either a national or an international point of view, the Princeton group has been in the forefront in both of these directions. This was on the whole only to be expected, inasmuch as Eisenhart and Veblen were both at Princeton and among our most progressive geometers—likely to read aright the signs of the times, and to be among the leaders in any significant geometrical advance.

After these remarks, let us consider briefly the directions in which definite progress has been made.

In elementary geometry, Coolidge's well known work *The Geometry of the Circle and the Sphere* (1910) contained a good deal of value from his earlier researches, and has had an important influence in its field. Most of his results are obtained by means of the familiar "correspondence principle" which associates an appropriate system of homogeneous coördinates for a set of geometric objects (for example, circles, spheres, etc.) with the points of a corresponding projective space. The late C. L. E. Moore and also P. F. Smith have been active in the same domain. The *Projective Geometry* of Veblen and Young has been referred to earlier.

The more advanced field of algebraic geometry has been cultivated by A. B. Coble, A. Emch, T. R. Hollcroft, Lefschetz, F. R. Sharpe, C. H. Sisam, Virgil Snyder, and H. S. White. Unfortunately it is impossible here to attempt adequate reference to this field. Their work has been concerned largely with Cremona transformations and with some of the beautiful geometric configurations in which the subject abounds. Coble's algebraic interests have extended over a wide range.

Eisenhart is probably to be regarded as the first American who has achieved world standing in classical differential geometry. His work in the field has taken directions closely parallel to those of two great European masters of the subject, Bianchi and Darboux, and has achieved a definite place in this tradition. J. A. Eiesland, W. C. Graustein, and the late A. Ranum have also contributed valuable results.

It must be admitted, however, that there are few of our younger men who occupy themselves either with algebraic or classical differential geometry, or any other of the geometric questions which seemed most vital fifty years ago.

Closely associated with ordinary metric differential geometry is the projective differential geometry in which the projective group rather than the group of rigid motions plays the basic rôle. This is a subject with obvious claims to our interest, to which perhaps the late E. J. Wilczynski contributed more than anyone else. However, the first systematic study of the subject goes back to the French mathematician Halphen. A fundamental characteristic of Wilczynski's method is the association of an appropriately chosen set of linear differential equations with the geometric object under consideration. The simplest possible illustration, which may have served as a point of departure for Wilczynski, would be afforded by a curve (not a straight line) in the projective plane,

$$y_1 = y_1(x), \qquad y_2 = y_2(x), \qquad y_3 = y_3(x).$$

This may be associated with the differential equation having the three functions y_1, y_2, y_3 as (linearly independent) solutions,

$$y''' + p_1 y'' + p_2 y' + p_3 y = 0$$

which may be termed the "differential equation of the curve." This equation is evidently unaltered by any projective change of coördinates. But the multiplicative transformation $y = \lambda \bar{y}$ does not change the curve, and if we choose λ so that $3\lambda' + p_1 \lambda = 0$, we obtain a like equation with $\bar{p}_1 = 0$, and with

$$\bar{p}_2 = p_2 - p_1^2 - p_1', \qquad \bar{p}_3 = p_3 - 3p_1 p_2 + 2p_1^3 - p_1''.$$

Here $\bar{p}_2$ and $\bar{p}_3$ are the two "semi-invariants" of the curve, that is, the invariants of the parametrized curve. To obtain the single intrinsic invariant of the curve itself we have to combine the above transformation with a suitable change of the parameter x.

In extending this idea to ruled surfaces in three-dimensional space, for example, Wilczynski used two ordinary linear differential equations of the second order in two variables y and z,

$$y'' + p_{11} y' + \cdots + q_{12} z = 0, \qquad z'' + p_{21} y' + \cdots + q_{22} z = 0,$$

as the "differential equations of the ruled surface." Here the four coördinates of the surface have the form $c y_c(x) + d z_c(x)$, and the two parameters of the surface are c/d and x, of which x specifies the particular ruling. Such is the kind of analytical apparatus which he employed in his investigations of various questions in projective differential geometry.

Another American geometer who has shown much originality and has obtained various elegant results is Edward Kasner. He has particularly studied the invariant theory and the associated geometric characterization of families of dynamical trajectories, and the formal aspects of conformal geometry in the plane. For example, the following is a problem of conformal geometry which Kasner has treated to advantage. What are the (formal) invariants of two analytic curves at a point of intersection? The most simple invariant is, of course, $x_1' y_2' - x_2' y_1'$ if (x_1, y_1) and (x_2, y_2) are the coördinates of the two curves expressed in terms of the arc length. This invariant represents the tangent of the angle between the curves.

Kasner obtains the higher invariants as well, and answers (formally) various interesting questions such as that of the conformal bisector of an angle. His desire is above all for elegance and extreme simplicity, combined with essential novelty.

Despite this auspicious entry into these fields of projective differential geometry and the geometry of dynamical trajectories, the two fields have not been very active. G. M. Green, who died very young, did brilliant work in the field of projective differential geometry about twenty years ago. At present E. P. Lane of Chicago is following ably in the tradition begun by Wilczynski. Perhaps the most able student of Kasner's who has concerned himself with the geometry of trajectories was the late Joseph Lipka.

Let us turn now to the development of the theory of generalized spaces, which has its roots in the highly important notion of "parallel displacement" of Tullio Levi-Civita (1917). A year later Weyl proposed to take this new notion of parallel displacement as the basis of an extended geometry of non-Riemannian type. The starting point is afforded by the affine equations of parallel displacement which tell how neighboring, nearly parallel vectors are related to one another. Obviously a fundamental system of curves, taking the place of geodesics in the Riemannian theory, are those along which the tangent line is displaced parallel to itself. In 1921 Weyl pointed out that these curves did not suffice to identify completely the "symmetric affine connection" and thus he was led to a "projective" theory for the new geometry.

Very shortly thereafter (1922) Eisenhart and Veblen wrote a suggestive note in which the paths themselves were taken as fundamental. The differential equations of the paths is taken in the familiar geodesic form

$$\frac{d^2x^i}{ds^2} + \Gamma^i_{\alpha\beta} \frac{dx^\alpha}{ds} \frac{dx^\beta}{ds} = 0$$

where, however, the Christoffel 3-index symbols Γ^i_{jk} are to be looked upon as arbitrary functions. Actually the geometry thus arrived at turns out to be identical with that of Weyl in his projective theory of affine symmetric connection. Other interesting papers appeared soon by Eisenhart, T. Y. Thomas, Veblen, and others at Princeton, in which various significant results were obtained. In particular, Thomas proved in 1925 that generalized projective spaces were naturally associated with a uniquely determined affine connection, and obtained also a similar result in the conformal case which had been signalized by Weyl. As Veblen had pointed out in 1922, a suitable generalization of the normal coördinates of Riemann lends itself very well to the study of the invariants in the new generalized spaces.

Along with these American advances, much was done abroad, particularly by Emile Cartan in France and J. A. Schouten in Holland. The most recent account of the subject is given in Thomas' book *The Differential Invariants of Generalized Spaces*.

What is required, apparently, in order to validate the especial importance of the new generalized spaces, is either to show their usefulness for theoretical physics or to construct some interesting non-Riemannian cases.

Finally, we turn to the field of analysis situs, long a Cinderella in the geometrical family.

It was Veblen's readable and illuminating Cambridge Colloquium Lectures of 1916 on *Analysis Situs*, published in 1921, which served more than anything else to stimulate the remarkable activity that ensued here and abroad. Veblen concerned himself entirely with the combinatorial aspects of the subject, dealing with the manifolds made up of cells of various dimensions which Poincaré had discussed in his celebrated five papers on analysis situs (1895–1904). Thus the point-set-theoretic side of the subject and applications found no place in his book. Veblen diverged from Poincaré in that his incidence relations, etc., were all at first taken modulo 2.

With Veblen's name should be joined that of Alexander, as furnishing a strong support in the movement towards analysis situs. As early as 1911, Veblen and Alexander, then a graduate student, began to be especially interested in the subject. And before the Cambridge Lectures were given, Alexander had published an article establishing that the combinatorial results obtained were independent of the particular mode of cellular subdivision. His well known "duality theorem," his contributions to the theory of knots, and various other results, have made him a particularly important worker in the field. His papers are notable for their elegance and sustained high quality.

In more recent years Lefschetz has also occupied himself with varied questions in the field of combinatorial analysis situs, often in close relation with Alexander. Perhaps his work on fixed point theorems for n-dimensional manifolds is best known. A simple illustrative case of such a theorem is the fact that any $(1, 1)$ sense-preserving transformation of the sphere into itself leaves at least one point fixed. More generally, it is easily proved that on a surface of any genus $p \neq 1$ there is at least one such fixed point if the given 1–1 transformation belongs to the same "class" as the identity in the sense of Brouwer, that is, can be obtained by continuous deformation from the identity. In fact the subdivision into 2-cells shows that there will be a total index of $2 - 2p$ for all the fixed points, so that there will be at least 2 distinct fixed points for $p = 0$ and $2p - 2$ fixed points for $p = 2, 3, \cdots$ provided that the fixed points are simple. To arrive at such a result in Lefschetz's n-dimensional case as well as in the two-dimensional case, it is sufficient (heuristically speaking) to make the count in a single case. Thus for the sphere it suffices to note that a rotation has two fixed points of index 1. It is Lefschetz's merit to have evaluated the index sum in very general cases, and thus to have arrived at his general fixed point theorems.

Of the other men in the very strong group in analysis situs at Princeton and at the Institute for Advanced Study, Morse has been interested in certain questions in space of infinitely many dimensions which arise in connection with the calculus of variations and his critical point relations; and A. W. Tucker has contributed towards a better abstract foundation of the subject.

Among American workers elsewhere, Hassler Whitney has contributed to the theory of graphs and of differentiable manifolds. In his important work on graphs he establishes incidentally the following simple entertaining result: In any possible map on a sphere in which three countries at most meet at any point and no two or three countries form a ring, a traveler may visit all of the countries in succession without entering the same country twice.

But it was R. L. Moore who foresaw the possibilities of the point-set-theoretical side of analysis situs some thirty years ago, and who has added most to it. Single-handed he gathered around him students who have entered the field and have done work which is also of much importance. Among them may be mentioned W. L. Ayres, H. M. Gehman, J. R. Kline, G. T. Whyburn, and R. L. Wilder. There arose subsequently in Poland a second notable mathematical school with similar interests. A striking fact about the advance thus made is the following. As was first seen by Poincaré, theoretical dynamics leads immediately to an extraordinary variety of point-set-theoretic questions of very fascinating type. Somehow or other, guided by aesthetic sensibility alone, these mathematicians have formulated some of the questions of most interest to dynamics. An instance of this sort is R. L. Moore's "upper limiting sets" which have recently been found to be of central importance for the theory of dynamical systems with two degrees of freedom. In fact, there arose in this theory a division of the ordinary plane into simply connected closed sets, no two sets having a point in common. Thus with any point p was associated a corresponding set Σ_p; it is proved that if the points p_1, p_2, $\cdots$ approach a limit point p, then the corresponding sets Σ_{p_1}, Σ_{p_2}, $\cdots$ approach the immediate neighborhood of Σ_p. If now the elements Σ_p are thought of as points in a nonmetrical two-dimensional continuum, there arise the upper limiting sets envisaged by Moore.

As another illustration of the interrelation of analysis situs and dynamics, let us refer to Poincaré's last geometric theorem established in 1912 by the author. This is the following theorem about fixed points: If a (1, 1) direct, area-preserving transformation of a region bounded by two concentric circles into itself, advances points on one circle in the clockwise sense and on the other in the opposite sense, there will be two invariant points. This conjectured theorem led Poincaré to the conclusion that infinitely many periodic motions exist in the restricted problem of three bodies and similar dynamical problems. The author was able later on to give this interesting theorem a nonmetric form, and to show that there are always two geometrically distinct invariant points. No proper analogue of Poincaré's theorem has been found for spaces of higher dimensions.

So far that mysterious curiosity of analysis situs, the four-color problem, has not been mentioned. Philip Franklin, C. N. Reynolds, and the author have studied this most carefully. Franklin has very recently extended his previous results to show that any map on the sphere of at most 31 regions can be colored in four colors.

APPLIED MATHEMATICS

In default of a better term we use the designation of applied mathematics for that large part of mathematics which seems to be closely connected with physics or some other branch of science. Inasmuch as most of the so-called "pure" mathematics of the present day was at one time "applied," the term is a very vague one. Nevertheless, the field of applied mathematics always will remain of the first order of importance inasmuch as it indicates those directions of mathematical effort to which nature herself has given approval.

Unfortunately, American mathematicians have shown in the last fifty years a disregard for this most authentically justified field of all. It was remarked at the outset that the American tradition was at first of quite the opposite character. Nevertheless today we recall only six Americans who are deeply concerned with applied mathematics in the usual sense, of whom four were brought up in the great British tradition. These are Harry Bateman, Ernest W. Brown (recently deceased), F. D. Murnaghan, H. P. Robertson, J. L. Synge, and R. C. Tolman. Among these men it should be remarked that Brown was the world's foremost lunar theorist, while Tolman is to be regarded as primarily a physical chemist. All six men possessed an extremely broad scientific outlook. The names of Bateman and Tolman will always be mentioned among those who were closest in spirit to the special theory of relativity at the time of its discovery. Furthermore, Bateman has added to classical electromagnetic theory, while Tolman has contributed to the relativistic theory of the expanding universe in which he has shown his daring speculative spirit. Robertson has also contributed in the same relativistic direction. Murnaghan and Synge alike have been creatively interested in geometry, dynamics, classical hydrodynamics and elasticity, and relativity.

Much of the work of the author has also been in the direction of applied mathematics of a somewhat different type—the problem of three bodies and its special cases, qualitative dynamics, the foundations of electrodynamics, relativity, and quantum mechanics. It was the well known work of F. R. Moulton on the periodic solutions of the restricted problem of three bodies which first attracted the attention of American mathematicians to the fundamental advances of Poincaré. W. D. MacMillan has made significant advances in this field. It may perhaps be permitted to state one result in the theory of relativity, discovered independently later by Eiesland, namely that any spherically symmetric solution of the Einstein field equations is necessarily static. This result is of importance in the relativisitic theory of the expanding universe. It has been extended by Banesh Hoffmann.

In this connection Veblen's interesting work on five-dimensional generalized projective spaces should be mentioned. Here as elsewhere the fifth dimension affords a convenient bracket with which to provide for the electromagnetic equations as well as those of gravitation. Let us mention also Eisenhart's elegant observation that in the general theory of relativity a particle attracted by a body of finite mass moves as if directly attracted toward it in accordance with the Newtonian Law, with a variable central mass equal to the natural (rest) mass m increased by precisely $3m\omega^2$, where ω is the angular velocity in light seconds.

In concluding this cursory account of applied mathematics, mention must be made of one development which has been of extraordinary value for mathematics and for statistical mechanics, namely the further development of ergodic theory.

The well known recurrence theorem of Poincaré was stated by him in the following form. The *probability* that a closed dynamical system recurs arbitrarily closely to any initial state is 1. This kind of probability is to be interpreted in the sense of Lebesgue measure, as was first remarked by E. B. Van Vleck. The "ergodic theorem" in its final form affirms that (except for cases of probability 0) this recurrence occurs in a *metrically habitual manner*. For example, imagine an idealized billiard ball moving upon a convex billiard table. According to the theorem, there will then be a limiting mean time-interval between collisions, a mean distance between collisions, a mean angular rotation of the successive directions, a mean part of the time in which the ball is on any assigned part of the table, etc., etc. The proof which we gave involves an essentially new algorithm. The theorem itself is one of the most remarkable in dynamics. It justifies the physical intuitions of Maxwell and Boltzmann in their celebrated ergodic hypothesis, and goes far towards supplying a rigorous foundation for statistical mechanics.

What needs still to be done is to establish "metric transitivity" in the general case. G. A. Hedlund has succeeded in doing so under certain special conditions. The problem is an extremely difficult one.

In the sequence of ideas which led to the discovery of this theorem in 1931 several American mathematicians played a vital part. P. A. Smith and the author first defined the basic notion of metric transitivity. B. O. Koopman, who has always had a broad understanding of mathematical-physical ideas, then showed how to restate the basic transformation problems of dynamics as problems concerning unitary linear transformations in Hilbert space. This interpretation stimulated von Neumann, possessed of wide interests in mathematical physics as well as of an outstanding technique in the theory of Hilbert space, to establish a "mean ergodic theorem" which, however, affirmed nothing about any individual motion. At about the same time the great Swedish mathematician Carleman proved the same theorem independently. Finally, it was the stimulus of personal contact with von Neumann and Koopman, together with extensive personal experience in the difficult problem of stability in dynamics, that led the author to the proof of the ergodic theorem itself; for he suddenly saw that the essential defect in some earlier ideas was that he had used continua where he should have used measurable sets. One other name should be mentioned in connection with the ergodic theorem, that of Eberhard Hopf, now in Leipzig but then in Cambridge. Hopf immediately improved the reasoning of von Neumann, and has contributed more than any one else to the extensions of the ergodic theorem which are suggested by the applications. It is interesting to remark that Hopf has added to theoretical astrophysics as well as to other fields of mathematics.

The fact that the ergodic theorem is destined to be a fundamental theorem of Lebesgue measure theory is clear from the applications to analysis which have already been made by Wiener, Wintner, and others in this country, and by a number of mathematicians abroad. Allusions may well be made here to Wiener's researches in random functions, correlated with the phenomena of white light and the Brownian movement in physics, and to his work on the Fourier transforms which has application in questions of electrical filtering. Wintner has established the convergence of the infinite processes used by Hill in his lunar theory, and has done valuable work in analysis, theoretical dynamics, and quantum mechanics.

In connection with the ergodic theory it is natural to mention the related active fields of probability and statistical theory, in which J. L. Doob and A. H. Copeland have been applying the modern methods.

This must conclude my survey of the splendid accomplishments of American mathematics from our beginning as an organized Society in 1888 until the present day. I have felt as a traveler in a beautiful and unexplored country might feel who had taken his companions to some vantage points familiar to him so that they might enjoy the prospects which he happened to know, all the while realizing that on the morrow they would journey together towards more grandiose mountain peaks glittering along the horizon.

HARVARD UNIVERSITY,
   CAMBRIDGE, MASS.